MILITARY TO CIVILIAN

RESUMES AND LETTERS

Third Edition

Carl S. Savino, Major, USAR (Ret.)

Ronald L. Krannich, Ph.D.

IMPACT PUBLICATIONS

Manassas Park, VA

MAR 08

CH

Military-to-Civilian Resumes and Letters

Third Edition

ISBNs: 978-1-57023-267-1 (13-digit), 1-57023-267-9 (10-digit)

Library of Congress: 2007929455

Publisher: For information on Impact Publications, including current and forthcoming publications, authors, press kits, online bookstore, downloadable catalogs, and submission requirements, visit the left navigation bar on the front page of our main company website: www.impactpublications.com.

Publicity/Rights: For information on publicity, author interviews, and subsidiary rights, contact the Media Relations Department: Tel. 703-361-7300, Fax 703-335-9486, or email: query@impactpublications.com.

Sales/Distribution: All bookstore sales are handled through Impact's trade distributor: National Book Network, 15200 NBN Way, Blue Ridge Summit, PA 17214, Tel. 1-800-462-6420. All special sales and distribution inquiries should be directed to the publisher: Sales Department, IMPACT PUBLICATIONS, 9104 Manassas Drive, Suite N, Manassas Park, VA 20111-5211, Tel. 703-361-7300, Fax 703-335-9486, or email: query@impactpublications.com.

Contributors: The authors wish to thank several individuals and organizations for contributing sample resumes. Several resumes appearing in Chapter 6 come from TAMP managers and counselors as well as two noted employment specialists who work with transitioning military: David Henderson and Wendy S. Enelow (wendy@wendyenelow.com). Contributors of the resumes and letters appearing in Chapter 11 are identified on pages 246-248.

Contents

Military-to-Civilian
Resumes and Letters

1

Why Should We Interview and Hire You?

S O YOU'RE LEAVING THE MILITARY. Thanks for your service. Now, why do you want to work for us? Does this resume represent the real you? How much will you cost us? Do you have some red flags – from questionable work behaviors and personality quirks to substance abuse, anger, and mental health issues – that we might inherit to our detriment? Do you have a clear and predictable pattern of work behavior? What are your major accomplishments? Do you have proven leadership talent that will transfer well to our company?

What differentiates you from other equally qualified candidates? Are you an energetic and enthusiastic self-starter or do you just focus on your assigned work and need constant direction and supervision? Do you have the "right stuff" to make a difference to our bottom line? What type of personality and attitude will we inherit? Will you fit in with our other employees, especially our star performers? Can you work well with our clients?

Are you someone who will quickly adapt and prosper in our environment or are you just "testing the waters" – finding your first job out of the military from which you may soon move on? What exactly will we get for our money? How long will you last here – 90 days, six months, two years, or longer? Can you prosper in a corporate or small business culture? Do we really want to interview and hire you?

Anticipate Issues, Target Employers

While hiring managers usually don't directly ask candidates such cautionary questions before the job interview, nonetheless, these issues and concerns often determine both screening and hiring decisions. They are questions you'll want to anticipate as you prepare to communicate your qualifications and personality to employers in writing **before** they screen you by email, telephone, or in job interviews. Whatever you do, make sure you address many of these key issues and concerns of your targeted audience. For in the end, how well you answer such unstated questions in your resume and letters will be more important to getting a job interview than all the do's and don'ts, "principles," and "bells and whistles" associated with writing so-called expert-crafted, model resumes and letters.

Make a Good Impression

You have lots of valuable military experience, which you hope will be readily marketable in today's civilian job world. Your skills and accomplishments, if properly organized and communicated to employers, should attract the attention of many employers who will want to invite you to job interviews. Given your background, you should make a very good impression on employers, who may call you back for several interviews before offering you a job. If you are lucky, you may receive multiple job offers from which you can choose your perfect job for launching a great new career. At least that's the plan – get an exciting new job which fully uses your many talents, includes a substantial increase in income, and leads to career advancement. If all goes well, you'll soon start a new job that may well change your life for the better.

> *How can you best showcase your talents so that employers will want to invite you to a job interview?*

So where do you start and what do you do next? How will you best showcase your talents to grab the attention of potential employers whom you want to contact you for a job interview? Will it be in the form of a standard one- or two-page resume accompanied by a one-page cover letter or will it be some other form of creative and unconventional communication? Let's begin with your audience. Understanding both the needs of your audience and the requirements of an effective job search will help you decide what you should do next.

Show Me Your Resume

Let's assume we're a civilian employer who may be interested in your talents. Since we're trying to screen for the perfect candidate, we want to see your resume – along with a cover letter, salary history, and salary requirements – **before** we see you in person. Yes, if you want to apply for a job with our company, you need to immediately send us this information via email, fax, or mail. We have many candidates, some with military experience, whom we will be interviewing during the next four weeks.

So what are you going to do when you get this standard message from civilian employers? Are you prepared for us and others who want to first see your credentials on paper, or electronically, before inviting you to the critical job interview? Have you crafted a first-class resume or do you need to contact a career professional who can help you put together a dynamite resume that best showcases your talents?

Develop Job Search Smarts

This may be the first time you've looked for job in the civilian world. In fact, when did you last go job hunting? Did you write a resume and craft various types of job search letters? How effective was your writing? Did you get the response you expected? If you used a resume to find a job, did you mail, fax, or email it in response to job postings and vacancy announcements, pass it around as part of your networking activities, or attach it to completed application forms?

> *Does your resume incorporate the right language for civilian employers or is it filled with military jargon?*

Do you know how to put together an outstanding resume that clearly communicates your qualifications to employers in today's job market? Can you succinctly state your career objective and summarize your experience in one to two pages? Are you prepared to write different types of job search letters for different prospective employers? Can you translate your military experience into the language of civilian employers and then present it in a proper resume format?

Know What You Need to Do

Let's not beat around the bush. It's time to speak truth about your future. Your resume writing skills are probably less than stellar. Accordingly, you may be at a disadvantage in today's highly competitive civilian job market, because you may not know how to write outstanding resumes and letters that command the attention of civilian employers.

If you are like many other members of the military, chances are your first real job, and career, was with the military. You've probably never had to look for a job outside the military. If you did conduct a job search, perhaps you only completed applications rather than used a resume and job search letters. And if you once wrote a resume, chances are it is now outdated, doesn't incorporate your most recent experiences, and may be inappropriate for today's new job market, which requires different types of resumes – chronological, combinational, functional, conventional, electronic – and emphasis on accomplishments. Furthermore, you may be unfamiliar with today's most important resume and letter distribution methods that involve interpersonal networking as well as using email and posting resumes on hundreds of Internet employment sites. When was the last time you talked money to power – negotiated salary and benefits?

To most employers, you are a **stranger** who has military experience that may or may not relate to their specific needs. You're also someone in transition – a new military-to-civilian hire who may only stay around for six to 12 months as you try to figure out what to do with the rest of your life in the civilian work world. Not surprisingly, employers want to see your qualifications summarized on a one- or two-page resume or pasted into a "professional profile" appropriate for Internet employment sites **before** inviting you to an interview. Based on their evaluation of your resume, they may or may not want to invite you to an interview. But they first need to see you on paper or on a computer monitor before meeting you in person. For hiring managers, resumes and letters are all about **screening strangers** for what often become multiple *"let's get to know you better"* job interviews. While your resume may eventually play a role in job interviews – primarily as a basis for asking questions about your background – employers do not make hiring decisions based upon receiving resumes and letters from strangers. In the end, it's how well candidates perform during the job interview that determines who gets hired.

Whatever your past experience in navigating the civilian job market, today you're approaching a different job market. It's a very competitive job market where individuals market their skills in exchange for position and money. If you want to be successful in this job market, you must have a well crafted resume accompanied by a compelling cover letter. When an employer asks you to send a resume, what exactly will you deliver? Does your resume incorporate the right language for the civilian work world, or is it filled with lots of military jargon only fellow service members understand? Does it best state your career goals as well as represent your major strengths? Will an employer in 30 seconds or less understand exactly what it is you can do, will do, and want to do for them?

Communicate Military Strengths as Future Capabilities

As you transition from the military to the civilian work world, you face special challenges in communicating your military background to civilian employers. One of the best ways to deal with these challenges is to begin writing a resume and related letters designed for your new civilian job or career. Starting with our data sheets in Chapter 10 and ending with finished products approximating our examples in Chapters 6, 7, 8, and 11, this exercise will help you pull together what it is you have done, can do, and really want to do in the future. It requires taking an inventory of your education, past work experiences, and current interests, skills, and abilities. It focuses your attention on assessing major strengths and formulating a career objective that communicates accomplishments to employers. Overall, it's a major exercise in persuading others to accept your goals.

Done right, this writing exercise will steer you into the civilian work world by relating your military experience and current interests, skills, and abilities to the specific needs of civilian employers. It will help you select the proper language for communicating with civilian employers. Whatever you do in the process of transitioning to the civilian work world, make sure you start out right by compiling a dynamite resume and letters that clearly communicate what you have done, can do, and will do in the future for your next employer. For in the end, employers are only concerned about your past work history and accomplishments as they relate to predicting your future performance for them. They want to hire your **future** rather than your past. Therefore, make sure your resume and letters provide strong evidence of future capabilities for hiring managers.

Motivate Employers to Take Action

At least to strangers who know little or nothing about you and your capabilities, which includes most civilian employers, you essentially are what you write about yourself. Your one- to two-page resume and accompanying cover letter should succinctly say a great deal about your professionalism, competence, and personality. These documents should go beyond just documenting your work history, experience, education, and qualifying credentials. They should be designed to motivate the reader to take a specific action – invite you to a job interview. Indeed, how you present yourself and what you say through specific words, phrases, sentences, and paragraphs will make the difference between being selected or rejected for a job interview. If you have little or no civilian work experience, you must present your military experience in terms that are easily understood in the civilian world. If you want to best present your qualifications to employers, you must translate military terminology and jargon into the language of civilian employers. Above all, your new civilian resume and letter must clearly communicate to an employer who you are as both a person and a professional and what it is you (1) want to do, (2) have done, (3) can do, and (4) will most likely do in the immediate future for this potential employer.

Your resume and cover letter must have sufficient impact to **motivate** employers to contact you, conduct a screening interview over the telephone, and hopefully invite you to a job interview that leads to a job offer and renewed career success. If you fail to properly write, produce, market, and follow up your resume, you will most likely conduct an ineffective job search.

Become More Effective

When did you last write a resume and various types of job search letters? How important was the selection of language in summarizing your experience? How well did you write, produce, distribute, and follow up your resume? Who evaluated it and how? Did it immediately grab the attention of employers who then called you for interviews? Would it also do well in the face of today's scanning technology? How well did your resume and letter stand out from the crowd of other resumes and letters? Did they clearly communicate your qualifications and future performance to potential employers? What did your resume really say about you as both a professional and a person? Did it become your ticket to interviews or did it dash your job search expectations?

Regardless of what resulted from your previous resume and letter writing efforts, let's turn to your future success which should include dynamite resumes and letters for making that critical military-to-civilian transition. In so doing, we'll help you craft powerful resumes and letters that represent your best professional efforts as well as the "real you."

Don't Abuse and Misuse

Resumes are some of the most abused and misused forms of job search communication. Not knowing how to best communicate their qualifications to employers, many job seekers go through the ritual of writing uninspired documents that primarily document their work history rather than provide evidence for predicting their future performance and value to employers. Lacking a clear sense of purpose, they fail to properly connect their resume writing activities to their larger job search tasks. Rather than communicate their past accomplishments in a form that enables employers to predict their future performance and value, they choose to document their past employment history, which may or may not be relevant to employers' immediate and future needs. In this respect individuals transitioning from the military to the civilian world are no different from many other job seekers – they make similar resume writing and communication mistakes.

But writing a resume really isn't that difficult if done properly. Many individuals make it more difficult than it need be because they lack a basic understanding of how the resume should relate to all other job search activities. Indeed, after writing and producing it, many job seekers don't know how to best manage their resume in relation to potential employers. Most just send it by mail, fax, or email to employers as if job interviews and offers are primarily a function of increased direct-mail, faxing, or spamming activities. Preoccupied with the magic of writing right, few job seekers engage in effective resume **distribution and follow-up** activities – the keys for getting your resume read and responded to. Instead, they circulate lots of pretty documents that often go to all the wrong people and the wrong places and with few results!

You can do better than most job seekers if you produce dynamite resumes and letters. Unlike other resumes and letters, these are designed with the larger job search in mind – they grab the attention of potential employers who, in turn, invite you to job interviews. You conduct dynamite interviews because your answers and questions are consistent with your dynamite resume and letter. Dynamite resumes and letters:

- Consistently observe the rules of good resume and letter writing – structure, form, grammar, keyword selection, categories, punctuation, spelling, inclusion/exclusion, length, and graphic design.

- Clearly communicate a sense of purpose, value, professionalism, competence, honesty, enthusiasm, and likability.

- Are targeted resumes – they link your strongest interests, skills, abilities, and experience to the employer's present and future needs rather than become "one size fits all" generic resumes that demonstrate little understanding of specific employer's needs.

- Are produced in a professional manner – from paper stock and ink to attractive graphic elements – to further communicate your professional image.

- Include the right combination of keywords used by search and retrieval software for scanning resumes electronically.

- Get distributed through the proper channels, including important job fairs and hiring conferences, and delivered into the hands of the right people – those who make the hiring decision.

- Are usually followed up with telephone calls, email, and letters.

■ Stand out from the crowd by clearly speaking to employers – *"Let's interview this candidate who has the qualifications we want!"*

Unlike many other resume and letter writing books, which are primarily preoccupied with presenting proper form and content on paper, or presenting numerous examples of resumes and letters, this book focuses on the whole communication process, from producing outstanding written documents (form, content, and production elements) to distributing and following up your resume and letters with maximum impact. We focus on creating resumes and letters that generate concrete **outcomes** – job interviews which then result in job offers.

Manage 30 Critical Seconds

Resume writing is first and foremost a 30-second image management activity. After all, it takes employers no more than 30 seconds to read and respond to your resume. If it is scanned and processed electronically, it takes only seconds for the computer software to match keywords on your resume to determine whether or not your resume should be selected for human consideration. Therefore, you must quickly **motivate** the reader to take action. Your resume and cover letter must communicate your best professional image in writing **before** you can expect to be invited to a job interview. How and what you write, as well as which methods you choose to disseminate and follow up your message, will largely determine how effective you are in moving the employer to take action on your application.

Keep in mind that most employers are busy people who must make quick judgments about you based upon your written message. Within only 30 seconds, your written communication must motivate the reader to either take you into or take you out of consideration for a job interview. Neglect the importance of a 30-second dynamite resume and you will surely neglect one of the most important elements in a successful job search. Your resume and accompanying cover letter will join the graveyard of so many other ineffective resumes and letters.

Follow 10 Steps to Job Search Success

Finding employment in today's job market poses numerous challenges for individuals who seek quality jobs that lead to good salaries, career advancement, and job security. The whole job finding process is chaotic, confusing, and frustrating. It requires a certain level of organization and communication skills aimed at identifying, contacting, and communicating your qualifications to potential employers. If you want to make this process best work for you, you must do more than just mail resumes and letters in response to classified ads and vacancy announcements.

To be most successful in finding employment, you should develop a plan of action that involves these seven distinct yet interrelated job search steps within a larger 10-step process:

- Assess your skills
- Develop a job/career objective
- Conduct research on employers and organizations
- Write resumes and letters
- Network for information, advice, and referrals
- Interview for jobs
- Negotiate salary and terms of employment

> *In the job search, paper is the great equalizer. Most employers want to see you on paper before meeting you in person.*

As illustrated on page 9, each of these steps represents important **communication skills** involving you in contact with others. Assessing your skills (Step 4), for example, requires conducting a systematic assessment of what you do well and enjoy doing – your strengths or motivated abilities and skills (MAS) that become translated into your "qualifications" for employers. Conducting research on individuals, organizations, communities, and jobs (Step 6) requires the use of investigative skills commonly associated with library and online research. Networking and interviewing (Steps 8-9) primarily involve the use of conversational skills – small talk and structured question/answer dialogues – by telephone and in face-to-face encounters.

But it is the critical resume and letter writing step (7) that becomes the major communication challenge for most job seekers. Without strong writing and presentation skills, you are likely to flounder in your job search. Indeed, your ability to write dynamite resumes and job search letters largely determines how quickly you will transform your job search from the investigative stage (research) to employer contact stages (networking, interviewing, salary negotiations). Your writing skills become the key element in moving your job search from the investigative stage to the final job offer stage. Put simply, your writing is an initial indicator of your possible competence.

Pass the Written Test First

In the job search, paper is the great equalizer. Most employers want to first see you on paper, or on a computer screen, before meeting you in person. You, along with many others, must pass the written test **before** you can be considered for the face-to-face oral test – the critical job interview. Whether you like it or not, you must put your professionalism, competence, and personality in writing before you can be taken seriously for a job interview. Thus, your writing activities may well become the most critical **transformation step** in your job search. Your writing skills become your ticket to job interviews that lead to job offers and employment.

For some reason job search writing skills usually receive little attention beyond the perfunctory *"you must write a resume and cover letter"* advisory. They also get dismissed as unimportant in a society that supposedly places its greatest value on telecommunicating

10 Steps to Job Search Success

10 Negotiate Salary and Benefits Like a Pro

9 Develop Winning Job Interview Skills

8 Network for Information, Advice, and Referrals

7 Write Effective Applications, Resumes, and Letters

6 Conduct Research on Jobs, Employers, and Communities

5 Develop a Powerful Objective

4 Assess Your Skills and Identify Your MAS

3 Select Appropriate Job Search Approaches

2 Seek Assistance and Become Proactive

1 Get Motivated With Winning Attitudes

and interpersonal skills. Indeed, during the past two decades many career advisors have emphasized networking as the key to getting a job; they see resume and letter writing as relatively unimportant job search activities. Some even advise job seekers to eliminate the resume altogether and, instead, rely on cold-calling telephone techniques, "showing up" networking strategies, or completing online applications and professional profile forms.

But such advice is misplaced and misses one of the most important points in the job search. Resumes are an **accepted** means of communicating qualifications to employers; they are becoming essential requirements for today's new electronic recruitment operations. Employers expect to receive well-crafted resumes that represent the best professional efforts of candidates. The problem is that hiring managers receive too many poorly written and distributed resumes. Indeed, many candidates might be better off not writing a resume given the weaknesses they demonstrate by producing poorly constructed resumes. Failure to develop a well-crafted resume will disqualify you for many jobs.

While resumes do not substitute for other equally important communication activities, they do play a critical transformational role in your job search. They must be carefully linked to other key job search activities, especially networking and informational interviews, which function as important **methods for disseminating resumes**.

You simply **must** write a resume if you are to be taken seriously in today's job market. And you will be taken most seriously if you write a dynamite resume.

While some individuals do get interviews without writing resumes, you can do much better if you take the time and effort to develop a well-crafted resume and disseminate it properly. It should be designed for both electronic and human consumption. Your resume should focus on the employer's needs and expectations. It should demonstrate your professionalism, competence, and personality as well as provide initial evidence of your predictable pattern of work-related behavior. Without an effective resume, your job search will have limited impact.

Improve Your Effectiveness

Just how effective are you in opening the doors of potential employers? Let's begin by identifying your level of job search information, skills, and strategies as well as those you need to develop and improve. You can do this by completing the following "job search competencies" exercise:

INSTRUCTIONS: Respond to each statement by circling the number on the right that best represents your situation.

SCALE:	1 = strongly agree	4 = disagree
	2 = agree	5 = strongly disagree
	3 = maybe, not certain	

1. I know what motivates me to excel at work.   1   2   3   4   5

2. I can identify my strongest abilities and skills.   1   2   3   4   5

3. I can identify at least seven major achievements that clarify a pattern of interests and abilities that are relevant to my job and career. 1 2 3 4 5

4. I know what I both like and dislike in work. 1 2 3 4 5

5. I know what I want to do during the next 10 years. 1 2 3 4 5

6. I have a well-defined career objective that focuses my job search on particular organizations and employers. 1 2 3 4 5

7. I know what skills I can offer employers in different occupations. 1 2 3 4 5

8. I know what skills employers most want. 1 2 3 4 5

9. I can clearly explain to employers what I do well and enjoy doing. 1 2 3 4 5

10. I can specify why employers should hire me. 1 2 3 4 5

11. I have the support of my family in this career change. 1 2 3 4 5

12. I can find 10 to 20 hours a week to conduct a part-time job search. 1 2 3 4 5

13. I have the financial ability to sustain a three- to six-month job search. 1 2 3 4 5

14. I can conduct library, Internet, and interview research on different occupations, employers, organizations, and communities. 1 2 3 4 5

15. I know how to best use the Internet in conducting an effective job search. 1 2 3 4 5

16. I know which websites are most useful for helping transitioning military personnel find new employment. 1 2 3 4 5

17. I can write different types of effective resumes and job search/thank-you letters. 1 2 3 4 5

18. I can produce and distribute resumes and letters to the right people. 1 2 3 4 5

19. I can list my accomplishments in action terms. 1 2 3 4 5

20. I can identify and target employers with whom I want to interview. 1 2 3 4 5

21. I'm prepared to fully participate in job fairs and hiring conferences for transitioning military personnel.   1   2   3   4   5

22. I can develop a job referral network.   1   2   3   4   5

23. I can persuade others to join in forming a job search support group.   1   2   3   4   5

24. I can prospect for job leads.   1   2   3   4   5

25. I can use the telephone to develop prospects and get referrals and interviews.   1   2   3 . 4   5

26. I can plan and implement an effective direct-mail job search campaign.   1   2   3   4   5

27. I can generate one job interview for every 19 job search contacts I make.   1   2   3   4   5

28. I can follow up on job interviews.   1   2   3   4   5

29. I can negotiate a salary 10-20% above what an employer initially offers.   1   2   3   4   5

30. I can persuade an employer to renegotiate my salary after six months on the job.   1   2   3   4   5

31. I can create a position for myself in a company.   1   2   3   4   5

TOTAL   [   ]

You can calculate your overall job search effectiveness by adding the numbers you circled for a composite score. If your total is more than 80 points, you need to work on developing your job search skills. How you scored each item will indicate to what degree you need to work on improving specific job search skills. If your score is under 50 points and it accurately reflects your situation, you may be well on your way toward job search success. In either case, this book should help you better focus your job search around the critical writing skills necessary for communicating your qualifications to employers. Other resources, which we address in the next section, can assist you with other important aspects of your job search as well as the whole transition process.

Use the Right Transition Resources

This book represents one of many useful resources for managing a military-to-civilian transition. It's written in conjunction with our three military-to-civilian career transition guides, which are distributed free of charge to everyone who participates in their respective service transition program: *From Army Green to Corporate Gray, From Air Force Blue to Corporate Gray*, and *From Navy Blue to Corporate Gray: A Career Transition Guide for Navy, Marine Corps, and Coast Guard Personnel*. Each of these books is a comprehensive A to Z guide for making a career transition from the military to the civilian work world. They include everything from the 10-step job search process outlined on page 9 to starting your own business, relocating to a new community, and working for defense contractors. If you do not have a copy of your respective Corporate Gray series book, you may want to check with your base transition assistance office, family service center, or library to see if you can borrow a copy.

If you are a veteran, or if you do not have access to these free books, you may want to acquire a copy of *Military Transition to Civilian Success* (see description on page 354), which is compatible with this book and the Corporate Gray volumes. This book is available in bookstores or through Impact Publications (see the extensive career resource section and order form on pages 347-353 or visit Impact's online bookstore at www.impactpublications.com).

Taken together, these books provide the necessary information for launching an effective job search. We also offer additional transitional job search assistance (resume database, job postings,

> *The whole purpose of a job search is to get taken seriously by strangers who have the power to hire.*

job search tips) through our Corporate Gray website (www.corporategray.com). We also sponsor several military transition job fairs each year (see www.corporategray.com for an updated listing of job fair dates and locations).

Impact Publications specializes in career-related materials for service members, military spouses, veterans, and others. You'll find hundreds of useful resources at www.impact publications.com. In addition, Impact Publications produces a comprehensive catalog entitled *Military Transition and Life Skills SuperSource*. You can download it from the catalog section of their website or request a paper copy by contacting them as follows:

IMPACT PUBLICATIONS
ATTN: Free Military Catalog
9104-N Manassas Drive
Manassas Park, VA 20111
Tel. 703-361-7300 or Fax 703-335-9486
Email: query@impactpublications.com

Get Taken Seriously By Employers

The whole purpose of a job search is to **get taken seriously by strangers** who have the power to hire. Your goal is to both discover and land a job you really want. You do this by locating potential employers and then persuading them to talk to you by telephone and in person about your qualifications.

Being a stranger to most employers, you initially communicate your interests and qualifications on paper or electronically (primarily email or online applications) in the form of resumes and cover letters. How well you construct these documents will largely determine whether or not you will proceed to the next stage – the job interview.

The major weakness of job seekers is their inability to keep focused on their **purpose**. Engaging in a great deal of wishful thinking, they fail to organize their job search in a purposeful manner. They waste a great deal of time and money on needless activities. They frustrate themselves by going down the same dead-end roads. Worst of all, they turn off employers by demonstrating poor communication skills, both written and oral.

The average job seeker often wanders aimlessly in the job market, as if finding a job were an ancient form of alchemy. Preoccupied with job search **techniques**, they lack an overall **purpose and strategy** that would give meaning and direction to discrete job search activities. They often engage in random and time-consuming activities that have little or no payoff. Participating in a highly ego-involved activity, they quickly lose sight of what's really important to conducting a successful job search – responding to the needs of employers. Not surprisingly, they aren't taken seriously by employers because they don't take themselves and employers seriously enough to organize their activities around key qualifications that persuade employers to invite them to job interviews. You don't want this to happen to you.

The following pages are designed to increase your power to get taken seriously by employers. Individual chapters provide a quick primer on the key principles involved in writing, producing, evaluating, distributing, and following up your own dynamite resume and letters. The book also presents numerous military-related resume and letter examples that illustrate the key principles involved in writing these important job search documents. As you will see in Chapter 11, many of these examples are produced by career profession-als (see pages 246-248) who regularly work with transitioning service members and others with military experience. Most of them are professional certified resume writers.

Since the examples in this book are presented to illustrate important resume and letter writing **principles**, they should not be copied nor edited. As you will discover in the following pages, it is extremely important that you create your own resumes and letters that express the **unique you** rather than send canned resumes and letters to potential employers.

In the end, our goal is to improve your **communication effectiveness** in the job search. On completing this book, you should be able to write dynamite resumes and letters that result in many more invitations to job interviews.

Do What Is Expected and Produces Results

Based on experience, we assume most employers do indeed expect to receive well-crafted resumes and letters. We proceed on the assumption that resumes and letters are key elements in the job search. Moreover, they are becoming more important than ever given the increased use of resume databases and electronic seaching technology for screening candidates.

The old interview adage that *"You never have a second chance to make a good first impression"* is equally valid for resumes and job search letters. For it is usually the resume and letter rather than your telephone voice or appearance that first introduces you to a prospective employer. Your resume and letter tell who you are and why an employer should want to spend valuable time meeting you in person. They invite the reader to focus attention on your key qualifications in relation to the employer's needs. They enable you to set an agenda for further exploring your interests and qualifications with employers.

Once you discover the importance of writing dynamite resumes and letters, you will never again produce other types of resumes and letters. Your written communications will have the power to move you from stranger to interviewee to employee. It will open many more doors to job interviews and offers!

Put Power Into Your Job Search

Whatever you do, make sure you acquire, use, and taste the fruits of job search power. You should go into the job search equipped with the necessary knowledge and skills to be most effective in communicating your qualifications to employers.

As you will quickly discover, the job market is not a place to engage in wishful thinking. It's at times impersonal, frequently ego deflating, and often unforgiving of errors. It requires clear thinking, strong organizational skills, and effective strategies for making the right moves with employers. Above all, it rewards individuals who follow through in implementing each job search step with enthusiasm, dogged persistence, and the ability to handle rejections. May you soon discover this power and incorporate it in your own resumes and job search letters for the civilian work world!

Coming Up

The following chapters take you step-by-step through the process of developing resumes and letters for the civilian job market. Chapter 2, **"Killer Resume Myths and Mistakes,"** examines some of the most important myths and mistakes that prevent job seekers from becoming effective. Chapter 3, **"69 Resume Rules for Maximizing Your Effectiveness,"** outlines major resume principles that cover everything from writing each section to producing, distributing, and following up the resume for maximum impact. Chapter 4, **"Conduct Two Resume Evaluations,"** includes the necessary forms for conducting both an internal and external evaluation of your resume based on the 69 principles outlined in Chapter 3. Chapter 5, **"Translating Military Experience Into Civilian Language,"** examines the important issue of resume language – how to best state your military experience in the language of civilian employers.

The next three chapters build upon the principles of the previous chapters by including numerous examples of resumes for transitioning military personnel. Chapter 6, **"Resume Examples By Occupations,"** includes 59 examples of conventional resumes which are organized by different occupational fields and reflect experience in various services and at different ranks. Chapter 7, **"Electronic Resumes and Job Search Effectiveness,"** shows how to convert conventional resumes into electronic resumes that can be scanned for keywords. This chapter also includes hundreds of useful websites for posting resumes and contacting military-friendly employers. Chapter 8, "**Essential Letters for Job Search Success,**" outlines the four most important types of letters you must write during your job search – cover, approach, thank you, and resume. Chapter 9, "**Effective Letter Writing,**" identifies 16 major letter-writing mistakes job seekers make, 12 rules for writing powerful letters, 11 elements to include or exclude in a letter, and 16 criteria for evaluating the content of each letter. Chapter 10 "**Creating Your Resume Database,**" includes all the forms required for organizing information that needs to go into your resume. Chapter 11, "**Resumes and Letters From Career Professionals,**" includes nearly 100 pages of examples produced by career professionals. Chapter 12, "**When Going Alone Is Not Enough,**" offers advice for anyone in need of professional assistance in completing various stages of the job search, including critical resume and letter writing activities. We make no assumptions that conducting a military to civilian job search is an easy task best done on your own. There is a season for everything. Indeed, many transitioning military personnel can benefit greatly from the assistance of a career professional at critical stages of his or her job search.

Taken together, these 12 chapters provide a balanced and practical mix of principles and examples to get you started in the right direction in producing your own dynamite resumes and letters for today's civilian job market. Upon completing this book, you should be well on your way to clearly communicating your qualifications in the language of civilian employers who seek people with your kind of experience, talent, and enthusiasm!

2

Killer Resume Myths and Mistakes

DESPITE EXPECTATIONS TO THE contrary, it's neither easy nor fun to look for a job. The whole process can be an extremely ego-deflating experience. From high expectations of quickly landing a great job to the reality of numerous rejections, most job seekers experience a roller-coaster of emotions. However, there are certain things you can and should do to minimize rejections and make this process work for you.

Avoid Mistakes and Follow Principles for Success

Time and again we find most problems in finding a job are self-inflicted – they relate to basic mistakes job seekers make. Indeed, Ron and Caryl Krannich's two books, *No One Will Hire Me!* and *Overcoming Barriers to Employment* (Impact Publications), identify dozens of mistakes and show how to best avoid them. Many of these mistakes relate to myths surrounding resume and letter writing, production, distribution, and follow-up. With a little knowledge you should be able to avoid these mistakes in the process of becoming a savvy job seeker.

If you want your job search to be most effective, you must follow several principles of effective resume writing, production, distribution, and follow-up. Equally important, you must regularly evaluate your progress and measure your performance. The principles range from obvious elementary concerns, such as correct spelling, punctuation, and placement of elements, to more complicated questions concerning when and how to best follow up a resume sent to an employer five days ago. Evaluation involves critiquing your progress both internally and externally.

Do First Things First

But before putting the principles and evaluations into practice, we need to examine the very concept of a resume within the larger job search. What exactly are we talking about? What is this thing called a resume and how does it relate to other steps in your job search? How do prospective employers typically respond to resumes? What are some of the major resume writing and distribution mistakes one needs to avoid?

A great deal of mystery and confusion surrounds the purpose and content of resumes. Occupying a time-honored place – almost ritual – in the job finding process, resumes remain the single most important document you will write and distribute throughout your job search. Do it wrong and your job search will suffer accordingly. Do it right and your resume should open many doors that lead to job interviews and offers.

Communicate Your Purpose

What exactly is a resume? Is it a summary of your work history? An autobiography of your major accomplishments? A statement of your key qualifications? A catalog of your interests, skills, and experience? An introduction to your professional and personal style? Your business calling card? A jumble of keywords for scanning?

Let's be perfectly clear what we are talking about. A resume is all of these things and much much more. It is an important **product** – produced in reference to your goals, skills, and experience – that furthers two important **processes** – "job search" for you and "screening/hiring" for employers. While it is a basic requirement when applying for many jobs, your resume plays a central role in directing you and your job search into productive information-gathering and employment channels. It quickly tells a **story** about you to others who know little or nothing about you and your qualifications. It communicates your goals and capabilities to potential employers who must solve personnel problems – hire someone to perform particular functions and jobs. At the very least, a resume represents the "unique you" to others. Best of all, it may represent the potential solution to employers' problems.

> *A resume is an advertisement for an interview. Its purpose is to get job interviews – nothing more, nothing less.*

Better still, let's define a resume in terms of its **purpose** or **outcomes** for you in relation to hiring officials: **A resume is an advertisement for an interview.** In other words, the purpose of writing, producing, distributing, and following up a resume is to get job interviews – nothing more, nothing less. As such, your resume should follow certain principles of good advertising – grab attention, heighten interest, sell the product, and promote action.

Your ultimate purpose in writing a resume is to **get employers to take a series of actions** – contact you, conduct a telephone screening interview, and invite you to the first of what hopefully will become several job interviews that eventually result in job offers and employment. Thus, the purpose of a resume is to generate a specific series of screening and hiring outcomes.

If you define a resume in these terms, then the internal resume structure and specific elements included or excluded – as well as the production, distribution, and follow-up methods you choose – become self-evident. As you target your resume on specific employers, you should only include those elements that are of interest to that employer and are likely to produce desirable outcomes for both you and the employer. You should not try to develop a generic "one size fits all" resume to blast to many employers.

But what do employers want to see on your resume? They simply want to see sound indicators of your **probable future performance** rather than a general summary of your professional and personal history. They want to know if you have a high probability of **adding value** to their operations. Adding value can have several meanings depending on the employment situation – increase market share, improve profitability, solve specific problems, become more competitive, introduce a new system for improving efficiency.

While the logic here is very simple, it nonetheless needs repeating throughout your job search. Since employers will be **hiring your future**, they are more concerned with your future performance – *"What can you do for me?"* – rather than "the facts" about your past – *"Where did you go to school and what were you doing in the service during 2007?"* Therefore, you must present your past in such a manner that it clearly indicates **patterns of performance** that are good predictors of your future value and performance.

Focus on Employers' Needs and Your Value

Without this central guiding purpose in mind, your resume is likely to take on a different form, as well as move in different directions, than outlined in this book. You simply must keep your resume writing, production, distribution, and follow-up activities focused around your purpose – getting interviews. No distractions or wishful thinking should interfere with this.

Your approach, whether implicit or explicit, to resume writing says something about how you view yourself in relation to employers. It tells readers to what degree you are self-centered versus employer-centered. Are you oriented toward adding value to the employer's operations, or are you primarily concerned with acquiring more benefits for yourself? If you merely chronicle your past work history, you are likely to produce a self-centered resume that says little or nothing about your interests, skills, and abilities in relation to the employer's needs. You say nothing about adding value to the employer's operations. Resumes lacking a central focus or purpose are good candidates for mindless direct-mail approaches – broadcasting them to hundreds of employers who by chance might be interested in your history.

On the other hand, if you thoughtfully develop a job objective that is sensitive to the employer's performance needs and then relate your patterns of skills and accomplishments to that objective, you should produce a resume that transcends your history as it clearly communicates your qualifications to employers and suggests that you know how to add more value to the employer's operations. This type of resume is **employer-centered**; it addresses employers' hiring needs. Such a resume is best targeted toward a select few employers who have job opportunities appropriate for your particular mix of interests, skills, and accomplishments. The type of resume you produce tells employers a great deal about you both professionally and personally.

An intensely ego-involved activity, resume writing often goes awry as writers attempt to produce a document that they "feel good" about. Thinking a resume is analogous to an obituary, many writers believe their resume should summarize what's good about them. If the central purpose is to pile on a lot of good information about the individual's past, then a resume becomes an unfocused dumping ground for a great deal of extraneous information employers neither need nor want. Such a resume may include many interesting facts that must be left to the interpretation of the reader who, by definition, is a very busy person; few such readers have the luxury of spending time analyzing and relating someone's chronicle of work history to their specific employment needs. Your resume may end up like most resumes – an uninspired listing of names, dates, and duties that are supposed to enlighten employers about your qualifications. While you may feel good, thinking you have written a good document, don't expect employers to get excited enough to contact you for an interview. Your resume will likely end up in their "circular files."

Every time you make a decision concerning what to include or exclude in your resume and how and when to produce, distribute, and follow up your job search communications, always keep in mind your purpose: **You are advertising yourself for a job interview**. Such a single-minded purpose will serve you well. It will automatically answer many questions you may have about the details of writing, producing, distributing, and following up your resume. It will tell you what is and is not important in the whole resume writing, production, distribution, and follow-up process.

Beware of 12 Resume Myths and Realities

Numerous myths about finding employment and contacting employers lead individuals down the wrong resume-writing paths. Keep these 12 myths and corresponding realities in mind when writing your resume:

MYTH 1:   **The resume is the key to getting a job.**

REALITY: There is nothing magical about resumes. Indeed, there are many keys to getting a job, from being in the right place at the right time and having good connections to conducting an excellent job interview. The resume is only one step, albeit an important one, in the job finding process. A well written application or "T" letter (see Chapter 8) can substitute for a resume. Other steps depend on well-crafted resumes and cover letters. Remember, your resume is an advertisement for a job interview. Employers do not hire individuals because of the content or quality of their resume; the resume only gets them invited to job interviews. The job interview is the real key to getting the job; it is the prerequisite step for a job offer and employment contract. But you must first communicate your qualifications to employers through the medium of a top quality resume in order to get their attention and motivate them to take desired action – invite you to the critical job interview.

MYTH 2: **The resume is not as important to getting a job as other job search activities, such as networking and informational interviews.**

REALITY: A resume still remains one of the most important written documents you will produce during your job search. If you expect to be interviewed for jobs, you simply must produce a well-crafted resume that clearly communicates your qualifications to employers. In fact, within the past decade the resume has become even more important with the rise of Internet employment sites that incorporate resume databases. For these sites, a well-crafted electronic resume becomes the key to connecting with online employers. Whether you like it or not, employers want to see you on paper **before** talking to you over the telephone or seeing you in person. And they want to see a top quality resume – an attractive, error-free document that **represents your best professional effort**. You should pay particular attention to the details and exacting quality required in producing a first-rate resume. Errors, however minor, can quickly eliminate you from consideration. Without such an error-free resume, you seriously limit your chances of getting job interviews. And without job interviews, you won't get job offers.

MYTH 3: **A resume should primarily document your work history for employers.**

REALITY: First and foremost, your resume should communicate to employers how you will **add value** to their operations. You include work history on a resume as evidence that you have a track record of adding value to other

> *A resume should communicate to employers how you will add value to their operations.*

employers' operations. The assumption for the reader is that you will add similar value to his or her operations. Be sure you always describe your work history or experience in such value-added terms.

MYTH 4: **Paper resumes are obsolete in today's new high-tech job market. Employment websites and employers primarily want to receive electronic and emailed resumes.**

REALITY: You need to produce **both** a paper and an electronic resume. You are well advised to start by producing a paper resume and then create an electronic resume. Electronic and emailed resumes are designed by job seekers for high-speed distribution to resume databases and employers' computer screens. They enable employers to quickly store, retrieve, and analyze large numbers of resumes. Paper resumes still play an important role in the job search. In fact, many small businesses prefer working with paper resumes. Job seekers also need paper resumes when networking for information, advice, and referrals; when attending job fairs; and when interviewing for a job. For the latest information on electronic resumes, see Joyce Lain Kennedy's *Resumes for Dummies, 5th Edition* (John Wiley & Sons, 2007) and Alison Doyle's *The About.com Guide to Job Searching* (Adams Media, 2006).

MYTH 5:   **It's best to send your resume to hundreds of employers rather than to just a few. The more resumes you send, the higher the probability of getting a job.**

REALITY: Power in the job search comes from selective targeting – not through random numbers. Success comes by making a few contacts with the right people who have a specific **need** for your particular skills and qualifications. While it may be comforting to think you are making progress with your job search by sending resumes to hundreds of potential employers, in reality you create an illusion of progress that will ultimately disappoint you; few people seriously read an unsolicited resume and thus consider you for employment when they have no need. A resume broadcast, blasting, or "shotgun" approach to finding a job indicates a failure to seriously focus your job search around the **needs** of specific employers. Your time, effort, and money will be better spent in marketing your resume in conjunction with other effective job search activities – networking and informational interviews. These activities force you to concentrate on specific employers who would be most interested in your interests, skills, and qualifications. These individuals have a need that will most likely coincide with both your resume and job search timing. For an extended discussion on the importance of developing targeted versus generic resumes for today's job market, see Joyce Lain Kennedy's *Resumes for Dummies, 5th Edition* (John Wiley & Sons, 2007)

MYTH 6:   **It's not necessary to include an objective on a resume.**

REALITY: Without an objective your resume will lack a central focus from which to relate all other elements in your resume. An objective gives your resume organization and coherence. It tells potential employers something important about you – that you are a **purposeful individual** who has specific job and career goals in mind that are directly related to your past pattern of interests, skills, and experience as documented in the remainder of your resume. If properly written, your objective will become the most powerful and effective statement on your resume. Without an objective, you force the employer to "interpret" your resume. He or she must analyze the discrete elements in each resume category and draw conclusions about your future capabilities which may or may not be valid. You force the person to engage in what may be a difficult analytical task, depending on his or her analytic capabilities. Therefore, it is to your advantage to control the flow and interpretation of your qualifications and capabilities by including a clear employer-oriented objective. While you can state an objective in your cover letter, it is best to put your objective at the very beginning of your resume. After all, letters do get detached from resumes. On the other hand, many people prefer excluding an objective because it tends to lock them into a particular type of job; they want to be flexible. Such people demonstrate a cardinal job search sin – they really don't know what they want to do; they tend to communicate their lack of focus in their resume as well as in other job search activities. They are more concerned with fitting into a job (*"Where are the jobs?"*) than with finding a job fit for them (*"Is this job right for me?"*).

MYTH 7: **The best type of resume outlines work history by job titles, responsibilities, and employment dates.**

REALITY: This type of resume, the traditional chronological or "obituary" resume, may or may not be good for you. It's filled with historical "what" information – what work you did, in what organizations, and over what period of time. Such resumes tell employers little about what it is you can do for them in the future. You should choose a resume format that clearly communicates your major strengths – evidence of your major accomplishments – to employers. Those strengths should be formulated as **patterns of performance** in relation to your goals and skills as well as the employer's needs. Your choice of formats includes variations of the chronological, functional, and combination resumes – each offering different advantages and disadvantages, depending on your goals.

MYTH 8: **Employers appreciate lengthy detailed resumes because such resumes give them more complete information for screening candidates than shorter resumes.**

REALITY: Employers prefer receiving short, succinct one- or two-page resumes. Longer resumes lose their interest and attention. Such resumes usually lack a focus, are filled with extraneous information, need editing, and are oriented toward your past rather than the employer's future. If you know how to write a dynamite resume, you can put all of your capabilities into a one- to two-page format. These resumes include only enough information to persuade employers to contact you for an interview. Like good advertisements, they generate enough interest so the reader will contact you for more information (job interview) before investing in the product (job offer).

MYTH 9:   **It's okay to put salary expectations and references on your resume.**

REALITY: Two of the worst things you can do is to include salary information (history or expectations) and list your references on your resume. Remember, the purpose of your resume is to get an interview. Only during the interview – and preferably toward the end – should you discuss salary and share information on references. And before you discuss salary, you want to demonstrate your **value** to hiring managers as well as learn about the **worth** of the position. Only **after** you make your impression and gather information on the job, can you realistically talk about – and negotiate – salary. You cannot do this if you prematurely mention salary on your resume. A similar principle applies to references. Never put your references on a resume. The closest you should ever get to doing this is a simple but unnecessary statement appearing at the end of your resume:

References available upon request

You want to control your references for the interview. You should take a list of references appropriate for the position you will interview for with you to the interview. If you put references on your resume, the employer might call someone who has no idea you are applying for a particular job. The conversation could be embarrassing. As a simple courtesy, you need to ask your references ahead of time whether you may use their name as a reference. At that point, you want to brief your reference on the position you seek, explaining why you feel you should be selected by focusing on your goals and strengths in relation to the position. Give this person information that will support your candidacy. Surprisingly, though, few employers actually follow through by contacting stated references, and few references are willing to provide employers with candid assessments of a candidate's work! These are perhaps important reasons why employers often make poor hiring decisions. Many employers are surprised to later discover they had hired a problem employee who had given previous employers similar difficulties.

MYTH 10:   **You should not include your hobbies nor any personal statements on your resume.**

REALITY: In general this is true. However, there are exceptions which would challenge this rule as a myth. If you have a hobby or a personal statement that can strengthen your objective in relation to the employer's needs, consider including it on your resume. For example, if a job calls for someone who is outgoing, energetic, and active, you would not want to include a hobby or personal statement that indicates that you are a very private and sedentary person, such as *"enjoy reading and writing"* or *"collect stamps."* But *"enjoy organizing community fund drives"* and *"compete in the Boston Marathon"* might be very appropriate statements for your resume. Such statements further emphasize the "unique you" in relation to your capabilities, the position requirements, and the employer's needs.

> *You should follow up your resume with a phone call within seven days.*

MYTH 11:   **You should try to get as much as possible on each page of your resume.**

REALITY: Each page of your resume should be appealing to the eye. It should make an immediate favorable impression, be inviting and easy to read, and look very professional. You achieve these qualities by using a variety of layout, type style, highlighting, and emphasizing techniques. When formatting each section of your resume, be sure to make generous use of white space. Bullet, underline, or bold items for emphasis. If you try to cram a great deal on each page, your resume will look cluttered and uninviting to the reader. You may make just the opposite impression you thought you were making in an ostensibly well organized resume – you're disorganized!

MYTH 12:   **Once you send a resume to an employer, there's not much you can do except wait for a reply.**

REALITY: Waiting for potential employers to contact you is not a good job search strategy. Sending a resume to a potential employer is only the first step in connecting with a job. You should always **follow up** your resume with a phone call, preferably within seven days, to answer questions, get invited to an job interview, or acquire information, advice, and referrals. Without this follow-up action, your resume is likely to get lost among many other resumes competing for attention.

Taken together, these myths and realities emphasize one overriding motivational principle when writing a resume:

> The key to effective resume writing is to give readers, within the space of one to two pages, just enough interesting information about your past performance and future capabilities so they will get sufficiently excited and motivated to contact you for a job interview. Your resume content should move them to take positive action.

It is during the interview, rather than on your resume, that you will provide detailed answers to the most important questions concerning the job. Those questions are determined by both the interviewer and you during the job interview. Don't prematurely eliminate yourself from consideration by including too much or too little information, or by being too boastful or too negative, on your resume before you get to the interview stage. In this sense, your resume becomes an important "window of opportunity" to get invited to job interviews that hopefully will translate into good job offers.

Avoid Common Writing Errors and Mistakes

A resume must first get written and written well. And it is at the initial writing stage that many deadly errors are made. The most common mistakes occur when writers fail to focus on the purpose of their resume.

Most errors kill a resume even before it gets fully read. At best these errors leave negative impressions that are difficult to overcome at this or any other point in the hiring process. Remember, hiring officials have two major inclusion/exclusion concerns in mind when reading your resume:

- They are looking for reasons or "negatives" to eliminate you from further consideration.

- They are looking for evidence or "positives" to consider you for a job interview – how much value you will add to their operations.

Every time you make an error, you provide support for eliminating you from further consideration. You should concentrate, instead, on providing **supports** for being considered for a job interview.

Make sure your resume is not "dead on arrival." Whether fair or not to you, employers tend to read a lot into resumes in the process of screening candidates. To ensure against being screened out, avoid these most common errors reported by employers who review resumes:

1. **Not related to the reader's interests or needs.** Not another one of these! Why was this sent to me? I don't have a job vacancy, nor do we perform work related to this person's skills. Did they purchase someone's mailing list or pay for another one of those useless resume blasting services? They need to take

their job search seriously by being more informed about employers and organizations before sending out such junk mail and spam. In the meantime, this person has just wasted my time, which is both limited and precious to me. I hope they don't plan to further waste my time by following up their resume and letter with a phone call! I only interview and hire people when I have a vacancy – not in response to unsolicited resumes.

2. **Too long, short, or condensed**. Ugh! What a waste of time and effort. Doesn't this person have a better sense of self-esteem? What is she trying to tell me about her capabilities?

3. **Poorly designed format and an unattractive appearance**. This person probably doesn't look any better in person than on paper. I have a bad feeling about this one. I've met this type before – really boring and lacks initiative.

4. **Misspellings, bad grammar, and wordiness.** When will they learn to write a simple sentence that conveys a basic level of literacy? This person is either careless or incompetent – two problems I don't need to hire. I wonder what other problems this person brings to the job? These errors are insulting and this person looks like risky business. I really don't need to hire this type of trouble.

5. **Poor punctuation.** Ditto. I wonder how much training this person needs to get up to speed? This could be an expensive hire – and fire!

6. **Lengthy phrases, sentences, and paragraphs.** The language we work in here is English. I wonder where they learned to do this? Maybe they talk the same way – on and on and on.

7. **Uses military jargon.** What's he trying to say? Are these qualifications or some secret code words used in a military bureaucracy? Sorry, this is not the military where such terms are acceptable. Who does he think I am? We speak a different language here. I wonder how long it will take him to learn our language and communicate clearly with co-workers and clients?

8. **Too slick, amateurish, or "gimmicky."** I'm really impressed. I bet this person thinks he's the hottest thing since sliced bread. Comes with lots of baggage. Just what I need – a manipulator on the payroll. I don't need gimmicks – only an enthusiastic individual who has a predictable pattern of performance related to what we do here.

9. **Too boastful or dishonest.** I've seen this one before – he's the candidate from hell – and hired the person against my better judgment. This one's too hot to handle. Indeed, I'll regret the day I contacted him for an interview.

10. **Poorly typed and reproduced.** Isn't this nice. I'm really impressed with the quality of this individual. Maybe I'm not important enough to receive a better quality resume. Or perhaps this is his or her best effort!

11. **Irrelevant information.** Do I really need to know height, weight, children, and spouse's name? I wonder what other irrelevancies this person can bring to the interview, and the job.

12. **Critical categories missing.** Where's the objective? Where did she work? What did she do? Any special awards, recognitions, accomplishments? What about education? What years did this include? What are her major strengths and/or examples of accomplishments during the past 10 years? Doesn't she know what to include on a resume?

13. **Hard to understand or requires too much interpretation.** I really don't have time to do a content analysis of this individual's skills and accomplishments. After reading two pages of military "bio facts," I still don't know what this person can do other than many different jobs in a military setting. How does this all relate in terms of skills and accomplishments to the job in question?

14. **Unexplained time gaps.** What did he do between 2001 and 2003? School? Unemployed? Tried to "find" himself in Paris? A health, drug, or criminal problem? Dropped out of life?

15. **Does not convey accomplishments or a pattern of performance from which the reader can predict future performance.** Interesting, but what can the person do for me? I want to be able to predict what she will likely do in my organization. Show me value and performance.

16. **Text does not support objective.** Nicely stated objective, but there's no evidence this person has any experience or skills in line with the objective. Could this be a statement of "wishful thinking" or something that has been "boiler-plated" from someone else's resume or a resume-writing book?

17. **Unclear or vague objective.** What exactly does this person want to do in my organization? Does he have specific goals for the next three to five years? Perhaps this person really doesn't know what he wants to do other than get a good paying job through me.

18. **Lacks credibility and content – includes lots of fluff and canned resume language.** Where do they get all this dreadful stuff? Probably using the same old resume book that emphasizes action verbs and transferable skills but fails to advise them to include real content. Where's the beef? Show me real skills and accomplishments.

This listing of writing errors and possible reader responses emphasizes how important **both** form and content are when writing a purposeful resume. You must select an important form, arrange each element in an attractive manner, and provide the necessary substance to grab the attention of the reader and move him or her to action. And all these elements of good resume writing must be related to the **needs of your audience**. If not, you may quickly kill your resume by committing some of these deadly errors.

Remember, hiring officials are busy people who only devote a few seconds – usually no more than 30 seconds – to reading a resume and thus screening a candidate at this resume reading stage. They are seasoned at identifying errors that will effectively remove you from consideration. Above all, they want to see you error-free on paper so they can concentrate on what they most need to do – evaluate your qualifications.

Beware of Production, Distribution, and Follow-Up Errors

Employers also report encountering several of these production, distribution, and follow-up errors:

1. Poorly typed and reproduced – hard to read.

2. Produced on odd-sized paper.

3. Printed on poor quality paper or on extremely thin or thick paper.

4. Soiled with coffee stains, fingerprints, or ink marks.

5. Sent to the wrong person or department.

6. Mailed, faxed, or emailed to "To Whom It May Concern" or "Dear Sir."

7. Emailed as an attachment which could have a virus if opened.

8. Enclosed in a tiny envelope that requires the resume to be unfolded and flattened several times.

9. Arrived without proper postage – the employer gets to pay the extra!

10. Sent the resume and letter by the slowest postage rate possible.

11. Envelope double-sealed with tape and is indestructible – nearly impossible to open by conventional means!

12. Back of envelope includes a handwritten note stating that something is missing on the resume, such as a telephone number or email address.

13. Resume taped to the inside of the envelope, an old European habit practiced by paranoid letter writers. Need to destroy the envelope and perhaps also the resume to get it out of the envelope.

14. Accompanied by extraneous or inappropriate enclosures, which were not requested, such as copies of self-serving letters or recommendations, transcripts, or samples of work.

15. Arrived too late for consideration.

16. Came without a cover letter.

17. Cover letter repeats what's on the resume – does not command attention or move the reader to action.

18. Sent the same or different versions of the resume to the same person as a seemingly clever follow-up method.

19. Follow-up call made too soon – before the resume and letter arrive!

20. Follow-up call is too aggressive or the candidate appears too "hungry" for the position – appears needy or greedy.

Since the resume is so important to getting a job interview, make sure your resume is error-free. Spend sufficient time crafting a resume that shouts loud and clear that you are someone who should be interviewed for a position.

Incorporate Qualities of Effective Resumes

A well-crafted resume expresses many important professional and personal qualities employers seek in candidates:

- Your sense of **self-esteem and purpose**.

- Your **level of literacy**.

- Your **ability to conceptualize and analyze** your own interests, skills, and abilities in relation to the employer's needs.

- Your **patterns of performance and value-added behavior**.

- Your ability to clearly communicate **who you are** and **what you want to do** rather than who you have been, what you have done, and what you need.

- Your **view of the employer** – how important he or she is in relation to your interests, skills, and abilities. Are you self-centered or employer-centered?

These qualities are expressed through certain resume principles which you can learn and apply to most employment situations. Your resume should:

- Immediately impress the reader.

- Be visually appealing and easy to read.

- Indicate your career aspirations and goals.

- Focus on your value in relation to employers' needs.

- Communicate your job-related abilities and patterns of performance – not your past or present formal job duties and responsibilities.

- Stress your productivity potential to solve employers' problems.

- Communicate that you are a responsible and purposeful person who gets things done.

- Use a language that communicates skills required by the employer – a language that is also sensitive to resume scanning technology.

If you keep these general principles in mind, you should be able to produce a dynamite resume that will grab the attention of employers, who will be moved to action – invite you to a job interview. To do less is to communicate the wrong messages to employers – you lack purpose, literacy, good judgment, and a pattern of performance. Always keep in mind the employers' perspective: Hiring is a risky business. They frequently make hiring mistakes that can be both costly and embarrassing to the organization. Your goal should be to minimize their risks.

Always Focus on Your Audience and Purpose

When deciding what to include in your resume, always remember these important writing guidelines for creating a dynamite resume:

1. View your resume as your personal **advertisement**, one that should follow the principles of good advertising.

2. Focus on the purpose of your resume – to get a **job interview**.

3. Take the offensive by developing a resume that **structures the reader's thinking** around your objective, qualifications, strengths, and projections of future performance.

4. Make your resume **generate positive thinking** rather than raise negative questions or confuse the reader.

5. Create an employer-centered resume that focuses on the **needs of your audience**.

6. Communicate clearly what it is you have done and then stress what you **want to do and can do** for the reader.

7. Always be **honest** without being stupid. Stress your positives; neither volunteer nor confess your negatives.

If you keep these basic purposes and principles in mind, you should produce a dynamite resume as well as conduct a job search that is both purposeful and positive. Your resume should stand out above the crowd as you clearly communicate your qualifications to employers.

In the next two chapters we'll take an in-depth look at these and several other principles relevant to the whole spectrum of resume activities – writing, producing, distributing, following up, and evaluating.

3

69 Resume Rules for Maximizing Your Effectiveness

EFFECTIVE RESUMES FOLLOW certain key principles that are specific to the resume medium and relevant to the job search process. These principles should be incorporated into every stage of the resume writing, production, distribution, and follow-up process. They also should relate to other elements in your job search. If you fail to incorporate these resume principles, your job search will most likely fail to reach its full potential.

Writing

Overall Strategy

1. **Focus on translating your military experience into civilian employment terminology:** Your resume and cover letter should present your qualifications in terminology that is readily understood by civilian employers. Most of your military experience can be easily translated into civilian terms (see Chapter 5 for details on this translation process, including the useful U.S. Department of Labor military occupational translator: http://online.onetcenter.org/crosswalk). Begin by outlining each of your military positions and corresponding accomplishments. List the equivalent civilian terms for each. Use this "civilianized" language in presenting your qualifications to employers. Avoid using military terminology and jargon unless you are applying for a defense-related position that requires previous military experience and you know the employer understands and appreciates this language.

2. **Do first things first in making your resume represent the unique you:**
   Avoid creatively plagiarizing others' resumes and examples, however tempting
   and easy to do. A widely abused approach to resume writing, creative plagiarizing occurs when people decide to take shortcuts by writing their resume
   in reference to so-called "outstanding resume examples"; they basically edit the
   examples by substituting information on themselves for what appears in the
   example. The result is a resume filled with a great deal of canned resume
   language that may be unrelated to the individual's goals, skills, and experience.

   The best resumes are those based on a thorough **self-assessment** (Step 4
   in our 10-step job search process on page 9) of your interests, skills, and
   abilities, which, in turn, is the **foundation** for stating a powerful objective,
   shaping information in each category, and selecting proper resume language.

   > *Do first things first by starting with a self-assessment that will help you build each section of your resume.*

   What, for example, do you want to do
   before you die? Answering this question
   in detail will tell you a great deal about
   your values and goals in relation to your
   career objectives. You may want to
   incorporate this information into your
   resume. Do first things first by starting
   with a self-assessment that will help you
   build each section of your resume. Numerous exercises and instruments are
   available for conducting your own self-directed assessment of your interests,
   skills, and abilities. These are outlined in several career planning and job search
   guides, including our "Corporate Gray Series" books. Other recommended
   books are found in the "Career Resources" section at the very end of this book.
   Professional testing centers and career counselors also administer a variety of
   useful assessment devices. Information on such services is readily available
   through your base transition office (see Chapter 4 in the "Corporate Gray
   Series" and the DoD TransPortal – www.dodtransportal.org), local community
   college, adult education programs, or employment services office. For a review
   of various approaches and recommended self-assessment resources, see Ron
   and Caryl Krannich's *I Want to Do Something Else, But I'm Not Sure
   What It Is* and *Job Hunting Tips for People With Hot and Not-So-
   Hot Backgrounds* (Impact Publications, 2005).

3. **Develop a plan of action relevant to your overall job search:** Make sure
   your resume is part of your larger job search plan. In addition to incorporating
   self-assessment data, it should be developed with specific goals in mind, based
   on research, and related to networking and informational interviewing activities. Begin by asking yourself the broader *"What do I want to do with this
   resume?"* question about the purpose of your resume rather than narrow your
   focus on the traditional *"What should I include on my resume?"* question.

Structure and Organization

4. **Select an appropriate resume format that best communicates your goals, skills, experience, and probable future performance:** Resume format determines how you organize the information categories for communicating your qualifications to employers. It **structures the reader's thinking** about your goals, strengths, and probable future performance. If, for example, your basic organization principle is chronological (dates you worked for different employers), then you want employers to think of your qualifications in historical terms and thus deduce future performance based upon an analysis of perfo rmance **patterns** evidenced in yo ur wo rk histo ry. If yo ur basic organizational principle is skills, then you want employers to think of you in achievement terms.

   If you decide to write a conventional resume, you essentially have three formats from which to choose: chronological, functional, or combination. While a **chronological resume** – often referred to as an "obituary resume" – is the most popular resume format, it is not the best for everyone, especially career changers. Primarily summarizing work history, this resume lists dates and names of employers first and duties and responsibilities second. It often includes a great deal of extraneous information. In its worst form – the traditional chronological resume – it tells employers little or nothing about what you want to do, can do, and will do for them. In its

   > *If you know your resume will be scanned, be sure to write a scannable resume that incorporates keywords describing your experience and skills.*

   best form – the improved chronological resume – it communicates your purpose, past achievements, and probable future performance to employers. It includes an objective which relates to other elements in the resume. The work experience section includes names and addresses of former employers followed by a brief description of accomplishments, skills, and responsibilities rather than formal duties and responsibilities; inclusive employment dates appear at the end. Chronological resumes should be used by individuals who have a progressive record of work experience and who wish to advance within an occupational field. One major advantage of these resumes is that they include the "beef" employers wish to see.

   Functional resumes emphasize patterns of skills and accomplishments rather than job titles, employers, and inclusive employment dates. These resumes should be used by individuals making a significant career change, first entering the workforce, or re-entering the job market after a lengthy absence. Since many employers still look for names, dates, and direct work experience – the so-called "beef" – this type of resume often disappoints employers who are looking for more substantive information relating to "experience" and "qualifications." You should use a functional resume only if your past work experience does not clearly support your objective.

Combination resumes combine the best elements of chronological and functional resumes. They stress patterns of accomplishments and skills as well as include work history. Work history usually appears as a separate section immediately following the presentation of accomplishments and skills in an "Areas of Effectiveness" or "Experience" section. This is the perfect resume for individuals with work experience who wish to change to a job in a related career field. Many career experts consider this to be the best choice of any resume format because it nicely showcases accomplishments and skills.

You also may want to write electronic and scannable resumes in response to today's technology used in posting and screening resumes. Indeed, job seekers are well advised to write conventional, electronic, and scannable resumes for today's job market. Many employers routinely use scanning technology to initially review resumes. If you know your resume will be scanned, you must write a resume that follows the principles of scannable resumes. This involves using keywords or nouns that describe your experience and skills. Individuals with technical backgrounds should especially use such resumes because their resumes are most likely to be scanned by employers in search of individuals with specific keyword skills.

Examples of these different types of conventional and electronic resumes are included in Chapters 6 and 7. Please examine these examples for ideas in developing your own resume.

5. **Include all essential information categories in the proper order.** What you should or should not include in your resume depends on your particular goals as well as your situation and the needs of your audience. When deciding what to include or exclude on your resume, always focus on the **needs** of the employer. What does he or she want or need to know about you? The most important information relates to your **future performance**, which is normally determined by assessing your **past patterns of performance** ("experience" presented as "accomplishments," "achievements," "outcomes," "benefits," or "performance"). At the very least, your resume should include the following five categories of information which help provide answers to five major questions:

Information Category	Relevant Question
Contact information	Who are you and how can you be contacted?
Objective	What do you **want to do**?
Experience	What **can** you do – your patterns of skills and accomplishments?

| Work history | What **have** you done, including major achievements that distinguish your work behavior? |
| Education | What have you **learned** and what might you be capable of learning in the future? |

Taken together, these information categories and questions will generate important data that should clearly answer a sixth unanswered question:

What will you most likely do for me in the future?

Finding answers to this implicit question is the employer's ultimate goal in the hiring process. Employers must deduce the answer from examining what you said in each category of your one- to two-page resume. Employers must make an important **judgment** about your future performance **with them** by carefully considering what you want to do (your objective), what you can do(your experience), and what you have done and learned (your work history and education). A resume incorporating only these five information categories should answer most employers' pre-interview questions.

Other information categories often found on resumes include the following:

- Community involvement
- Professional affiliations
- Special skills
- Interests and activities
- Personal statement

6. **Sequence the categories according to the principle *"What's most important to both you and the employer should always appear first"*:** You want your most important information and your strongest qualifications to always come first. As a transitioning member of the military, you will want to include your most recent military experience first. On the other hand, if you have recently completed a college degree and it appears more relevant to your next job than your most recent work experience, you may want to put your education first. Indeed, recent graduates with little or no relevant work experience should put education first since it's probably their most important "qualification" at this stage of their work life. Your educational experience tells employers what you may have learned and thus provides some evidence of a certain knowledge, skill, and motivational base from which you possess a **capacity** to learn and grow within the employer's organization, i.e., you are functionally trainable. Your education also may include important work experience and achievements that indicate a pattern of future performance. Educa-

tion should also come first in cases where education is an important **qualifying criterion**, especially for individuals with professional degrees and certifications: teachers, doctors, nurses, lawyers, accountants, and counselors. The sequence of elements should be:

- Contact information
- Education
- Experience
- Work history

If you have several years of direct work experience that supports your objective, and if education is not an important qualifying criteria, then your "Experience" section should immediately follow your objective. In this case "Education" moves toward the end of the resume:

- Contact information
- Experience
- Work history
- Education

Any other categories of information should appear either immediately after "Work history" or after "Education."

7. **Avoid including extraneous information that is unrelated to your objective or to the needs of employers:** However ego-involved you become in the resume writing process, always remember your goal and your audience. You are writing to a potential employer who by definition is a critical stranger who has specific needs and problems he hopes to solve through the hiring process. You are not writing to your mother, spouse, friends, or former teachers. The following extraneous information often appears on resumes:

- **The word "Resume" at the top:** The reader already knows this is your resume, assuming you have chosen a standard resume format. It's not necessary to label it as such.

- **Present date:** This goes on your cover letter rather than on your resume.

- **Picture:** Include a picture only if it is essential for a job, such as in modeling or theater. A picture may indeed be worth "a thousand words," but 990 of those words need not distract the reader from the central focus of your resume! Regardless of what you and your family may think about your picture – even those wonderful glamour shots – it's safe to assume that 50 percent of your readers will like and another 50 percent will dislike your picture. You don't need this type of distraction. Concentrate instead on the words and information you can control.

- **Race, religion, or political affiliation:** Include this information only if these are bona fide occupational qualifications, which they probably aren't, given equal employment opportunity laws.

- **Salary history or requirements:** Never include salary history or expectations on your resume. If you are forced to submit this information at the initial screening stage, do so in your cover letter. Salary usually is negotiable. The salary question should only arise at the end of the interview or during the job offer – after you have had a chance to assess the worth of the job as well as demonstrate your value to hiring officials. When you include salary information on your resume, you prematurely give information on your value before you have a chance to demonstrate your value in job interviews.

- **References:** Always make your references "Available upon request," although you need not include this standard reference statement on your resume You want to control the selection of references as well as alert them that you are applying for a specific position and that they may be contacted.

- **Personal information such as height, weight, age, sex, marital status, religion, health:** Few, if any, of these characteristics strengthen or relate to your objective. Many are negatives. Some could be positives, but only if you are a model, karate instructor, or applying for a position for which these are bona fide occupational qualifications.

- **Any negative information:** Employment gaps, medical or mental problems, criminal records, divorces, terminations, conflicting interests. There is absolutely no reason for you to volunteer potential negatives on your resume. This is the quickest way to get eliminated from consideration. Always remember that your resume should represent your very best self. If hiring officials are interested in learning about your negatives, they will ask you and you should be prepared to respond in a positive manner – but only at the interview stage.

Since most of this extraneous information is a real negative in the eyes of employers – and has little to do with supporting your objective as well as answering employers' six critical questions – avoid including this information on your resume.

Contact Information

8. **Put all essential contact information at the very top of your resume as the header:** The very first element a reader should encounter on your resume is an attractive header. This header should at least include your name, address, and phone number. If you have a fax number and email address, be sure to include them:

JAMES LAWSON
8891 S. Hayward Blvd.
Buffalo, NY 14444
Tel. 707-321-9721
LawsonJ@aol.com

JAMES LAWSON		laws@intra.com
8891 S. Hayward Blvd.	Buffalo, NY 14444	Tel. 707-331-9911

JAMES LAWSON

8891 S. Hayward Blvd.	Tel. 707-321-9721
Buffalo, NY 14444	laws@intra.com

JAMES LAWSON
laws@intra.com

8891 S. Hayward Blvd.	Buffalo, NY 14444	Tel. 707-321-9721

JAMES LAWSON
8891 S. Hayward Blvd.

Buffalo, NY 14444	Tel. 707-321-9721	laws@intra.com

We prefer capitalizing the name, although using upper and lower case letters is fine. Any of these headers would be fine because they are very inviting to readers who quickly survey resumes.

9. **Include your complete contact information:** Employers want to know how to contact you immediately should they have any questions or wish to invite you to an interview. Therefore, include only information which enables the employer to make a quick contact. Be sure to include **complete** contact information – name, address, phone (landline and mobile) number, and email address. If you use a pager, also include that number. Avoid using P.O. Box numbers; they communicate the wrong message about your housing situation – unstable or transient. Also, include a daytime telephone number (landline and cell, if you use both) through which you can be reached. If you do not have a telephone, or if your only daytime number is with your present employer, enlist a telephone answering service or use the number of someone else who will be available and willing to screen your calls. They, in turn, can contact you at work and then you can return the call. Better still, get a mobile phone so you can be contacted immediately. Include your first and last name, and perhaps your middle initial, depending on your professional style. The use of a middle initial is a sign of greater formality and is most frequently used by established professionals. However, using your full first, middle, and last name together is too formal: ROBERT DAVID ALLAN. If you prefer using your middle name rath-

> *An email address is expected – it's a sign that you are technically competent in today's job market.*

er than first name, do so either alone or in combination with your first initial: ROBERT ALLAN or J. ROBERT ALLAN. Do not include nicknames (ROBERT "BUDZY" ALLAN) unless you feel it will somehow help your candidacy, which it most likely will not! Include any professional titles, such as M.D., Ph.D., J.D., immediately after your last name: ROBERT ALLAN, J.D. Never begin your name with a formal gender designation: Mr., Mrs., or Ms. Your address should be complete, including a zip code number. It's okay to abbreviate the state (e.g., NY for New York, IL for Illinois, CA for California) as well as certain common locations: N. for North, SW for Southwest, Ave. for Avenue, St. for Street, Blvd. for Boulevard, Apt. for Apartment. However, it's best to spell out Circle, Terrace, or Lane. Be sure to include your telephone number; you may want to preface it with "Tel." or "Tel:". If you have a fax number, you may want to include it immediately following your telephone number:

Tel. 819-666-2197
Fax 819-666-2222

If you have email, include your email address immediately after your fax number. In fact, an email address is expected by employers. It's a sign that you are technically competent in today's job market. If you are applying for a position abroad, try to include both a fax number and an email address. Do not clutter the header with extraneous information such as your age, marital status, sex, height, and weight. Such information is irrelevant – indeed a negative – on a resume. It communicates the wrong messages and indicates you don't know how to properly present yourself to potential employers. These are not qualifying criteria for most jobs. Such information should never be volunteered during your job search. In fact, this is illegal information for employers to elicit from candidates.

Objective

10. **Include a job or career objective relevant to your skills, employers' needs, and the remaining elements of your resume:** While some resume advisors consider an objective to be an optional item – preferring to keep it general or place it in a cover letter – or provide little guidance on how to structure an objective and relate it to other resume elements, we strongly recommend including a powerful objective at the very beginning of your resume. Your objective should be the **central organizing element** from which all other

> *Your resume objective should tell employers what it is you want to do, can do, and will do for them.*

elements in your resume flow. It should tell employers **what it is you want to do, can do**, and **will do** for them.

Put in its most powerful form, your objective should be employer-centered rather than self-centered. It should incorporate both a skill and an outcome in reference to your major strengths and employer's major needs. Rather than being a statement of wishful thinking ("A position in management") or opportunistic and self-centered ("A research position with opportunity for career advancement"), it should focus on your major strengths **in relation to** an employer's needs. Take, for example, the following objective statement:

> A position in data analysis where skills in mathematics, computer programming, and deductive reasoning will contribute to new systems development.

This type of objective follows a basic **job – skill – benefit** format:

> I want a _____ where I will use my
> (position/job)
>
> _____ which will result in _____.
> (skills and abilities)   (outcomes and benefits)

Restated in this basic format, the above objective would appear in this form:

> A data analysis job where I will use my skills in mathematics, computer programming, and deductive reasoning which will result in new systems development.

An objective based on this originating statement follows a very specific form. The first part of this objective statement emphasizes a specific position in relation to your strongest skills or abilities; the second part relates your skills to the employer's needs. Such an objective becomes a **statement of benefits** employers can expect from you. All other elements in your resume (experience, work history, education, awards) should provide **supports** for your objective. Formulated in this manner, your objective becomes the most important organizing element on your resume as well as in your job search; it directs all other elements appearing on your resume, determining what should or should not be included in each section. It also gives your job search direction, focusing your efforts toward particular employers, and helps you formulate pertinent answers to interview questions. While formulating such an objective may be very time consuming – your two- to three-line objective statement may take several days to develop and refine – the end result will be a well-focused resume that communicates your value and benefits to employers.

11. **An objective should be neither too general nor too specific:** Many resume writers prefer developing a very general objective so their resume can be used for many different types of jobs. However, highly generalized objectives often sound canned or are meaningless (*"A position working with people that leads to career advancement"*); they may indicate you don't know what you really want to do. Indeed, if your purpose is to apply for many different types of jobs, you are attempting to fit into jobs rather than find jobs fit for you. You appear to lack a clear focus on what you want to do. On the other hand, a very specific objective may be too narrow for most jobs; you may appear too specialized for many positions. Another alternative is to write a separate or targeted objective, responsive to the requirements of each position, every time you send a resume to a hiring official. This approach should result in targeted resumes that are most responsive to the needs of individual employers. To accomplish this effectively, you should have word processing capabilities that allow you to custom-design each resume. An objective that is not too general nor too specific will serve you well for most resume occasions. It should indicate you know exactly what you want to do without being overly specific. Look at our examples in Chapter 5 for objectives that are neither too general nor too specific.

12. **Relate all other resume elements to your objective, emphasizing skills, outcomes, benefits, and probable future value to the employer:** All other elements appearing on your resume should reinforce your objective. When deciding what to include or exclude on your resume, ask yourself this question: *"Will this information strengthen my objective, which emphasizes my skills in relation to the employer's needs?"* If the answer is "yes," include it. If the answer is "no," exclude it. Remember, the most effective one- to two-page resume clearly and concisely communicates your objectives and strengths to

employers. If you fail to organize your resume in this manner, you are likely to include a great deal of extraneous information that communicates the wrong message to employers – you don't know what you want to do; your interests, skills, and experience are peripheral or unrelated to the reader's needs; you lack a clear focus and thus appear disorganized. These are cardinal sins committed by many resume writers who produce self-centered resumes that fail to respond to the needs of employers. Make sure each section of your resume clearly and consistently communicates what it is you **want to do**, **can do**, and **will do** for employers.

Summary of Qualifications

13. **You may want to include a "Summary of Qualifications" section imme-diately following your "Objective":** Some resume writers prefer including a short one-line objective but immediately following it with a three- or four-line "Summary of Qualifications" statement (see examples in Chapter 11). This statement attempts to crystallize the individual's major strengths that are also relevant to the objective. It is usually a synthesis of the "Experience" section. We consider this an optional item to be used by individuals with a great deal of work experience and who choose a chronological resume format. It is most effective on chronological resumes where the objective is weak and the experience sections are organized by position, organization, and inclusive employment dates. The "Summary of Qualifications" section enables you to synthesize in capsule form your most important skills and accomplishments as patterns of performance. Especially with chronological resumes, this can be a very effective section. It helps elevate your resume by stressing major accom-plishments and thus overcoming the inherent limitations of chronological resumes. An example of such a statement includes the following:

SUMMARY OF QUALIFICATIONS

Twelve years of progressively responsible experience in all phases of retail sales and marketing with major discount stores in culturally diverse metropolitan areas. Annually improved profitability by 15 percent and consistently rated in top 10 percent of workforce.

The remainder of this resume should provide supports for this statement in the "Experience" section.

Work Experience

14. **Elaborate your work experience in detail with particular emphasis on your skills, abilities, and achievements:** Next to your objective, your work experience section will be the most important. Here you need to provide key

details on your past skills and related accomplishments. To best develop this section, complete worksheets which include the following information on each job:

- Name of employer
- Address
- Inclusive employment dates
- Type of organization
- Size of organization/number of employees
- Approximate annual budget
- Position held
- Earnings per month/year
- Responsibilities/duties
- Achievements or significant contributions
- Demonstrated skills and abilities
- Reason(s) for leaving

We include several worksheets for generating this information in Chapter 10. It's best to complete these worksheets **before** starting to write your resume.

15. **Keep each "Experience" section short and to the point:** Information for each job should be condensed into descriptions of five to eight lines. The language should be crisp, succinct, expressive, and direct. Keep editing – eliminate unnecessary words and phrases – until you have short, succinct, and powerful statements that grab the attention of the reader. Lengthy statements tend to lose the reader's attention and distract from your major points. The guiding principle here is to edit, edit, edit, and edit until you get it right!

16. **Work experience should be presented in the language of skills and accomplishments rather than as a listing of formal duties and responsibilities:** Employers are not really interested in learning about duties and responsibilities assigned to your previous jobs, which are essentially a rehash of formal job descriptions rather than statements of what you actually accomplished on and beyond that job description. After all, assigned duties and responsibilities come with the position regardless of who occupies it. Instead, potential employers want to know how well you **performed** your assigned duties and responsibilities as well as any additional initiative you took that produced positive **results**.

What types of results do employers look for? Four big employee-generated outcomes managers look for are very simple and easy to measure and relate to on-the-job survival skills: (1) generate more profits (i.e., help grow the organization), (2) save the company more money (i.e., increase efficiency and effectiveness), (3) save your boss more time (i.e., take initiative and cooperate), and (4) help promote your boss in the eyes of his or her bosses (i.e., give your boss credit which may be undeserved but nonetheless demonstrates your understanding of organizational dynamics, such as loyalty, networking, mentoring, and politics). Other related positive outcomes are often outlined in evaluation criteria on annual performance appraisals.

Since employers are looking for indicators of your performance, it's to your advantage to describe your previous jobs in **performance** terms – what skills you used, what resulted from your work, and how your employer benefited. These are usually termed your "accomplishments" or "achievements." An accomplishment or achievement is anything you did well that resulted in a positive outcome for the employer, the company/organization, or clients. Accomplishments are what define your "patterns of performance." Examine the following statement:

> Responsibilities included conducting research projects assigned to office and coordinating projects with three research and development offices. Duties also involved evaluating new employees and chairing monthly review meetings.

Now, restate this "work experience" in terms of your actual accomplishments or achievements:

> Conducted research on the transportation of hazardous waste from four Texas area bases in conjunction with the Department of Defense's Base Realignment and Closure (BRAC) Program. Developed three different alternatives for destroying this waste. Proposed a technology-driven solution that was implemented in the region and resulted in documented savings of $250,000 over five years. Received special commendation for innovative work, which subsequently became a model program for other bases.

Accomplishment statements set you apart from so many other resumes that primarily restate formal duties and responsibilities assigned to positions as "Experience." Keep focused on employers' needs by stressing your **accomplishments** in each of your experience statements and descriptions.

17. **When writing a conventional resume, incorporate action verbs and use the active voice when describing your experience:** Some of the most powerful language you can use in a resume incorporates action or transitive verbs. It emphasizes taking action or initiative that goes beyond just formal assigned duties and responsibilities. If your grammar rules are a bit rusty, here are some examples of action or transitive verbs:

administered	conducted
analyzed	coordinated
assisted	created
communicated	designed
developed	planned

directed	proposed
established	recommended
evaluated	recruited
expanded	reduced
generated	reorganized
implemented	revised
increased	selected
initiated	streamlined
investigated	supervised
managed	trained
negotiated	trimmed
organized	wrote

When applied to the **active voice,** action or transitive verbs follow a particular grammatical pattern:

Subject	Transitive Verb	Direct Objective
I	increased	profits
I	initiated	studies
I	expanded	production

If written in the passive voice, these examples would appear in the "Experience" section of a resume in the following form – which you should avoid:

"Profits were increased by 32 percent."

"The studies resulted in new legislation."

"Production was expanded by 24 percent."

The passive voice implies the object was subjected to some type of action but the source of the action is unknown. If written in the active voice, these same examples would read as follows:

"Increased profits by 32 percent."

"Initiated studies that resulted in new legislation."

"Expanded production by 24 percent."

When using action verbs and the active voice, the action verb indicates that you, the subject, performed the action. The active voice helps elevate you to a personal performance level that gets de-emphasized, if not lost, when using the passive voice.

18. **Uses keywords appropriate for resume scanning technology:** Since more and more employers scan resumes and use automated applicant tracking systems to initially sort resumes based on keywords, it would be wise to incorporate as many keywords in your resume as possible. Unlike the language of action or transitive verbs (Principle #17), keywords reflect the jargon of particular industries and employers – desired skills, interpersonal traits, duties, responsibilities, positions held, education attained, or equipment used. While many keywords are technical in nature, others can be more generic: "curriculum development," "customer service," "employee relations," "market research," "negotiations," "public speaking," "team building." An employer may select a list of 30 keywords which will be used for sorting resumes. If your resume includes many of the words identified in the employer's keyword profile, the higher the probability your resume will be selected for visual examination. Of course, the more research you perform on the company, the better your chances of using the right keywords. For an excellent collection of keywords, along with resume, cover letter, and interview examples, see Wendy Enelow's *Best KeyWords for Resumes, Cover Letters, and Interviews* (Impact Publications, 2003).

19. **Avoid using the personal pronoun "I":** When using the active voice, the assumption is that you are the one performing the action. As indicated in Principle #17, there is no need to insert "I" when referring to your accomplishments. The use of "I" is awkward and inappropriate on a resume. It makes your resume too self-centered when you should be making it more employer-centered.

20. **Use numbers and percentages whenever possible to demonstrate your performance on previous jobs:** It's always best to state action and performance in some numerical fashion. Numbers command attention and communicate accomplishments. For example, take this "experience" statement:

> "Increased sales each year for five straight years."

The same statement can be stated in more powerful numerical terms that are equally truthful:

> "Increased sales annually by 23% ($147,000) during the past five years."

Which of these statements makes a more powerful impression on employers who are looking for evidence of performance patterns that might be transferred to their organization? To state you "increased" sales without saying by "how much" leaves a great deal to the imagination. Was it 1 percent or 100 percent? $5 or $500,000? If performance differences appear impressive, cite them in numerical terms.

21. **Include quotes relevant to your performance:** Avoid including personal testimonials that are self-serving or are assumed to be solicited; they may appear dishonest to readers. But do include any special professional praise you have received from a company award or from a performance evaluation. Statements such as "Received the Employee of the Year Award for outstanding performance" or "Praised by employer for *exceptional performance* and consistently ranked in the upper 10 percent of the workforce" can be powerful additions to your resume. They **differentiate you behaviorally** from most other candidates who primarily restate formal duties and responsibilities that automatically come with a position.

22. **Eliminate any negative references, including reasons for leaving:** Keep your language focused on describing your accomplishments in positive terms. Never refer to your previous employers in negative terms and never volunteer information on why you left an employer, regardless of the reason. If you were terminated, volunteer this information only if asked to do so. This will usually occur during the job interview – not at the initial resume and letter writing stage. If an employer wants this information, he or she will ask for it during a telephone or face-to-face interview.

> *Never refer to your previous employers in negative terms and never volunteer information on why you left an employer.*

23. **Do not include names of supervisors:** Your experience and work history sections should only include job titles, organizations, inclusive employment dates, responsibilities, and accomplishments. Names of individuals other than yourself should be subjects you address in face-to-face interviews rather than given on resumes.

24. **If you choose a chronological resume, begin with your most recent job and work backwards in reverse chronological order:** In a chronological resume, your present or last job should always be described first and in greater detail than your other jobs. The next job should be the one before that one and so on. However, it is not necessary to include or provide detailed information on all jobs you ever held – only the most recent ones. Keep in mind that hiring managers are looking for patterns of performance. The best evidence of such patterns is found by examining your most recent employment – not what you did 10, 20, or 30 years ago. Include your most recent employment during the past 10 years. If you held several part-time or short-term jobs, or your employment record goes back for many years, you can summarize these jobs under a single heading. For example:

Leadership development positions, 2003-2006.
Served in progressively important leadership development roles during the early
stages of my military career.

Part-time employment, 2000-2002.
Held several part-time positions – waitress, word processor, lab assistant – while
attending college full-time.

25. **Be consistent in how you handle each description or summary:** The rule
    here is parallel construction. Each description or summary should have a
    similar structure and size. Use the same type of language, verb tense, gram-
    matical structure, and punctuation in each section.

26. **For each job or skill, put the most important information first:** Since
    most hiring officials want to know what you can do for them, put that
    information first. If you choose a chronological resume, begin with your job
    title and unit and then stress your accomplishments. Your inclusive dates of
    employment should appear last, at the end of the description, rather than at
    the very beginning where it will tend to be the center of attention. If you
    choose a functional or combination resume format, put your most important
    accomplishments first in relation to your objective.

27. **Be sure to account for major time gaps:** If you use a chronological resume
    in which inclusive employment dates are prominent, check to see that you do
    not have major time gaps between jobs. You need to account for obvious time
    gaps. Were you in school or some type of training? If you were unemployed for
    a short time, you can easily handle this time gap by using years rather than
    exact months of a year when including dates of employment. For example,
    rather than state your last three jobs began and ended on these dates,

    > June 2005 to present
    > July 2002 to April 2005
    > December 1999 to February 2002

    State they began and ended on these dates:

    > 2005 to present
    > 2002 to 2005
    > 2000 to 2002

    If you specify exact months you began and left jobs, you encourage the reader
    to look for obvious time gaps and thus raise negative questions about your
    employment history. If you only use years, you can cover most short-term time
    gaps.

28. **If you are an obvious job hopper, you may want to choose a functional or combination resume rather than a chronological resume:** The job descriptions associated with a chronological resume format will accentuate employment dates and make it easy for the reader to determine a pattern of career progression from one job to another. If you do not have a clear chronological pattern of employment, you are well advised to use the functional or combination resume formats. These formats stress skills and accomplishments rather than employment dates. If you choose the chronological resume, your time gaps will stand out as possible red flags to prospective employers who literally "look between the lines" for clear patterns of career development. They may ask themselves, *"Was this person unemployed, incarcerated, or ill?"* You don't want them raising such questions at this point in your job search!

Other Experience

29. **Include "Other Experience" only if it further strengthens your objective in reference to the employer's needs or it helps account for employment time gaps:** Standard categories include:

   - **Prior civilian work:** Describe any work experiences you may have had prior to joining the military. Make it concise and easily understood by prospective hiring managers. Describe this experience as you would your military jobs – emphasize your skills and accomplishments. Relate this experience to your job objective, if possible.

   - **Civic/Community/Volunteer:** You may have volunteer experience that demonstrates skills and accomplishments supporting your objective. For example, you may be involved in organizing community groups, raising funds, or operating a special youth program. These volunteer experiences demonstrate organization, leadership, and communication skills.

   In each case, be sure to emphasize your accomplishments as they relate to both your objective and employers' needs.

Education and Training

30. **State complete information on your formal education, including any highlights that emphasize your special skills, abilities, and motivation:** Begin with your most recent education and provide the following details:

   - Degree or diploma
   - Graduation date
   - Institution
   - Special highlights, recognition, or achievements (optional)

The completed section might look like this:

B.A. in Sociology, 2005:
Ohio State University, Columbus, OH
Highlights:
Graduated Magna Cum Laude
Member, Phi Beta Kappa Honor Society

B.S. in Criminal Justice, 2003.
Ithaca College, Ithaca, NY
- Major: Law Enforcement Administration
- Minor: Management Information Systems
G.P.A. in concentration 3.6/4.0

If your grade point and other achievements are not exceptional, do not highlight them here. Your educational achievements may appear mediocre to the reader and thus become a negative.

31. **Recent graduates with little relevant work experience should emphasize their educational background more than their work experience:** Follow the principle that one's most important qualifications should be presented first. For recent graduates with little relevant work experience, education tends to be their most important qualification for entering the world of work. In such cases the "Education" category should immediately follow the "Objective." Include any part-time jobs, work-study programs, internships, extracurricular activities, or volunteer work under "Experience" to demonstrate your motivation, initiative, and leadership in lieu of any progressive work experience.

32. **It's not necessary to include all education degrees or diplomas on your resume:** If high school is your highest level of education, include only high school. If you have a degree from both a community college and four-year college, include both under education, but eliminate reference to high school. Individuals with graduate degrees should only include undergraduate and graduate degrees.

33. **Include special training relevant to your objective and skills:** This may include specialized training courses or programs that led to certification or enhanced your knowledge, skills, and abilities. For example,

Additional training, 2002 to present
Completed several three-day workshops on written and oral communication skills: Making Formal Presentations, Briefing Techniques, Writing Memos, Audio-Visual Techniques.

When including additional education and training, include enough descriptive information so the reader will know what skills you acquired. Don't be surprised if your special training is viewed as more important to an employer than your educational degrees.

Professional Affiliations

34. **Include professional affiliations relevant to your objective and skills:** While you may belong to many groups, it is not necessary to include all of them on your resume. Select only those that appear to support your objective and skills and would be of interest to an employer. Include the name, inclusive dates of membership, offices held, projects, certifications, or licenses. Normally the name of the group would be sufficient. However, should your involvement go beyond passive dues-paying membership, briefly elaborate on your contributions. For example,

> **American Society for Training and Development:** Served as President of Tidewater Virginia Chapter, 2003-2006. Developed first corporate training resource directory for Southeast Virginia.

Special Skills

35. **It's okay to include any special skills not covered in other sections of your resume:** These special skills might include an ability to communicate in foreign languages, handle specific computer software programs, operate special equipment, or demonstrate artistic talent. Again, if you have special skills relevant to your job objective and which should appeal to employers, include them in a separate section labeled "Special Skills" or "Other Relevant Skills."

Awards and Special Recognition

36. **Include any awards or special recognition that demonstrate your skills and abilities:** Receiving recognition for special knowledge, skills, or activities communicates positive images to employers: you are respected by your peers; you are a leader; you make contributions above and beyond what is expected as "normal." However, be selective in what you include here by relating awards or special recognition received to your objective and skills. If you are seeking a computer programming position, including an award for "First Prize in Howard County's Annual Chili Cook Off" would distract from the main thrust of your resume! But receiving the "Employee of the Year" award in your last job or "Community Achievement Award" would be impressive; both awards would get the attention of employers who would be curious to learn more about the basis for receiving such awards – a good interview question.

Interests and Activities

37. Consider including a personal statement on your resume: Normally we would not recommend including personal information on a resume. However, there is one exception and you should include such information sparingly. In

> *It's okay to include personal information, but only if it enhances your job objective.*

addition to keeping your resume focused on your objective and skills as well as the employer's needs, you want to make you and your resume appear unique in comparison to other candidates. You may be able to achieve this in a "Personal Statement" or "Special Interests" section. This section might include hobbies or avocations. For example, if you are seeking a position you know requires a high energy level and the employer looks favorably on stable, married, family-oriented employees, you might include some personal information as well as interests and activities that address these considerations. For example, your personal data could include the following:

PERSONAL: 35 . . . excellent health . . . married . . . children . . . enjoy challenges . . . focused on results

Alternatively, you could write a personal statement about yourself so that the reader might remember you in particular. For example,

SPECIAL   Love the challenge of solving problems,
INTERESTS: taking initiative, and achieving results . . .
                  be it in developing new marketing strategies,
                  programming a computer, climbing a mountain,
                  white water rafting, or modifying a motorcycle.

Such statements can give hobbies and special talents and interests new meaning in reference to your objective. But, again, be very careful about including such statements. More often than not, they can be a negative, distracting the reader from the most important information included on your resume. By all means avoid trite statements that may distract from the main thrust of your resume.

Salary History or Expectations

38. Never include salary information on your resume: While hiring officials are interested in your salary history and expectations, there is no good reason for including this information on your resume or even in your cover letter. Salary is something that needs to be **negotiated**, but only after you have had a chance to learn about the value of the position as well as communicate your value to the employer. This occurs at the end of the job interview and should be the very **last** thing you talk about or after receiving an offer of a position. If you include salary information on your resume or in your cover letter, you are likely to prematurely eliminate yourself from consideration – your expectations are either too high or too low.

References

39. **Never include names, addresses, and phone numbers of references on your resume:** You may want to include a final category on your resume:

     REFERENCES: Available upon request

     However, this is an empty category that does nothing to enhance your resume. Our recommendation is to eliminate it altogether or use it as filler to round out a short resume that could use more text for aesthetics. Remember, you want to control your references by providing the information upon request which usually occurs during the interview stage. If you volunteer your references on the resume, your references may be unprepared to talk about you to employers. It's best to list the names, addresses, and phone numbers of your professional references on a separate sheet of paper, but take that list with you to the job interview rather than volunteer the information on your resume. Ask your references for permission to use their names and brief them on your interests in relation to the position. Make sure they have a copy of your resume for reference.

Other Information

40. **You may want to include a few other categories of information on your resume, depending on your experience and the relevance of such information to employers:** You may want to include the following categories of information:

     - Security clearances
     - Certificates
     - Accreditations
     - Licenses
     - Publications
     - Patents
     - Foreign languages

     However, include them only if they strengthen your qualifications in reference to the needs of hiring officials. For example, if foreign languages are important to employers, include them on your resume. If you are in a professional field that requires certificates and licenses, include the appropriate information on your resume.

Language, Style, and Tone

41. **Use an appropriate language to express your productivity and your understanding of the employer's needs:** In addition to using action verbs and the active voice, try to use the language of the employer when describing your skills and experience. Use the jargon of the industry in demonstrating your understanding of the employer. As we note in Principle #18 (page 48) and again in Principle #43 (see below), this type of language will serve you well if your resume is electronically scanned into automated applicant tracking systems. Always stress your value in relation to the employer's needs – you will **add value** to the employer's operations!

42. **Incorporate a crisp, succinct, expressive, and direct language:** Avoid poetic, bureaucratic, vernacular, and academic terms that often tend to turn off readers. For example, instead of stating your objective as:

    > I would like to work with a consulting firm where I can develop new programs and utilize my decision-making and system-engineering experience. I hope to improve your organization's business profits.

    Re-word the objective so it reads like this:

    > An increasingly responsible research and development position, where proven decision-making and system engineering abilities will be used for improving productivity.

    Use the first person, but do not refer to yourself as "I" or "the author." The first person "I" is understood but not stated. The use of action verbs and the active voice implies you are the subject. Always use active verbs and parallel sentence structure. Avoid introductory and wind-up phrases like "My duties included..." or "Position description reads as follows..." Use jargon only if appropriate to the situation or enhances keywords relevant to employers.

43. **Incorporate numerous keywords throughout each section of your resume:** Pay particular attention to the specific language you select for your resume. As noted in Principle #18, the language component is now more important than ever in the history of resume writing. Given recent changes in employer resume screening techniques, there's a high probability your resume will be electronically scanned sometime during your job search. The key to getting your resume "read" in electronic screening systems is the specific language you incorporate in your resume. If you want to increase your probability of being "electronically acceptable" to employers, you must incor-

porate such keywords in your resume writing. The key to getting your resume "read" in electronic screening systems is the specific language you incorporate in your resume. When scanning resumes electronically, employers select certain **keywords** which should appear on your resume. If you want to increase your probability of being "electronically acceptable" to employers, you must incorporate such keywords in your resume writing. For more information on the language requirements for scanned resumes, see Pat Criscito, _e-Resumes_ (Barron's Educational Series, 2005) and Susan Whitcomb and Pat Kendall, _e-Resumes_ (McGraw-Hill, 2001). At the same time, you need to incorporate keywords acceptable to human readers. These keywords are usually associated with the buzz words or jargon of a profession. For information on these types of keywords, see Wendy Enelow's _Best KeyWords for Resumes, Cover Letters, and Interview_ (Impact Publications, 2003).

Appearance and Visual Techniques

44. **Use appropriate highlighting and emphasizing techniques:** The most important information on a one- or two-page resume needs to be highlighted since many readers will only spend a few seconds skimming your resume. The most widely used highlighting and emphasizing techniques involve CAPITAL-IZING, underlining, _italicizing_, and **bolding** headings, words, and phrases or using bullets (•), boxes (■), hyphens (–), or asterisks (*). However, use these techniques sparingly. Overuse of highlighting and emphasizing techniques can distract from your message. A major exception to this general rule relates to electronic resumes: avoid using italics, script, and underlining if your resume is likely to be electronically scanned.

45. **Follow the "less is more" rule when deciding on format and type style:** The fear of not getting all information onto one page leads some writers to create crowded and cramped resumes. Be sure to leave ample margins – at least 1" top to bottom and left to right – and white space. Use a standard type style (Times Roman but not Helvetica) and size (10-11 point). Remember, the first thing a reader sees is layout, white space, and type style and size. Your resume should first be pleasing to the eye.

46. **Do not include special borders, graphics, or photos unless you are applying for a job in graphic arts or desktop publishing:** Keep the design very basic and conservative. Special graphics effects are likely to distract from your central message. However, if you are in the graphic arts or related art field, you may want to dress up your resume with graphics that demonstrate your creativity and style. Your photo does not belong on a resume. The rule of thumb for photos is this: Regardless of how great you or your mother may think you look, at least 50 percent of resume recipients will probably dislike your photo – and you. The photo gives them something to pick apart – your

hairstyle, smile, eyes, or dress – and thus distracts from your bona fide qualifications. Why set yourself up by including a photo that will probably work against you? Your ego is best served with an invitation to an interview based solely on the content of your resume. Focus on your language rather than your photo. This principle is especially important for those who plan to do an online and/or video resume – see Principle #58 – which we do not recommend since such resumes mix critical face-to-face job interview elements with a resume.

Resume Length

47. **Keep sentences and sections short and succinct:** Keep in mind your readers will spend little time reading your resume. The shorter and more succinct you can write each section and

> *The shorter you write, the more powerful will be your message.*

sentence, the more powerful will be your message. Try to limit the length of each job description paragraph to five to eight lines.

48. **Limit your resume to one or two pages:** We agree with most resume advisors that the one- to two-page resume is the most appropriate, although a single page is preferable. There are situations where three or more pages may be appropriate, but these are exceptional situations which may involve developing a curriculum vita (CV) for jobs in education or applying for a job abroad (see Ronald L. Krannich and Wendy S. Enelow, *Best Resumes and CVs for International Jobs*, Impact Publications, 2002). We prefer the one-page resume because it focuses the busy reader's attention on a single field of vision. It's especially reader-friendly if designed with the use of highlighting and emphasizing techniques. The one-page resume is a definite asset considering the fact that many hiring officials must review hundreds of resumes each week. Research clearly demonstrates that retention rates decrease as one's eyes move down the page and nearly vanish on a second or third page! At first the thought of writing a one- or two-page resume may pose problems for you, especially if you think your resume should be a presentation of your life history. However, many executives with 25 years of experience, who make in excess of $100,000 a year, manage to get all their major qualifications onto a one-page resume. If they can do it, so can you. When condensing information on yourself into a one-page format, keep in mind that your resume is an advertisement for a job interview. You only want to include enough information to grab the attention of the reader who hopefully will contact you for a job interview. If you must present your qualifications in two pages rather than one, consider making the second page a "continuation page" that provides additional details on the qualifications outlined on the first page.

Production

Employers also want to see your best professional effort at the production stage of resume writing. For paper resumes, this involves making the right choices on paper color, weight, and texture as well as production methods. Above all, the resume they receive must be error free or they are likely to discard it as an example of incompetence.

49. **Carefully proofread and produce two or three drafts of your resume before producing the final copies:** Be sure to carefully proofread the resume for grammatical, spelling, and punctuation errors before producing the final copy. Any such errors will quickly disqualify you with employers. Read and reread the draft several times to see if you can improve various elements to make it more readable and eye-appealing. Read for both form and content. Have someone else also review your resume and give you feedback on its form and content. Use the evaluation forms in Chapter 4 to conduct both internal and external evaluations.

50. **Choose white, off-white, ivory, or light grey 20 to 50 lb. bond paper with 100% cotton fiber ("rag content"):** Your choice of paper – color, weight, and texture – does make a difference to resume readers. It says something about your professional style. Choose a poor quality paper and inappropriate color and you communicate the wrong messages to employers. There is nothing magical about ivory or off-white paper. As more and more people use these colors, off-white and ivory colors have probably lost their effectiveness. To be different, try a light grey or basic white. Indeed, white paper gives a nice bright look to what has become essentially a dull-colored process. Stay with black ink or use a dark navy ink for the light grey paper, if you have your resume professionally printed. If you are applying for a creative position, you may decide to use more daring colors to better express your creative style and personality. However, stay away from dark-colored papers. Resumes should have a light, bright look to them. The paper should also match your cover letter and envelope.

51. **Produce your resume on 8½" x 11" paper:** This is the standard business size that you should follow. Other sizes are too unconventional and thus communicate the wrong message to readers. Make sure the envelope matches the size of the paper (see "Principle #63).

52. **Print only on one side of the paper:** Do not produce a two-sided resume. If your resume runs two pages, print it on two separate pages. Label the second page as "Page Two" or "Page 2" at either the top or bottom and include your name, similar to this example:

Mary Smith _____ Page 2

53. Use a good quality printer and an appropriate typeface: It's best to produce your camera-ready copy (for reproduction) on a letter quality printer, preferably a laser printer. Never produce your resume on a dot matrix printer. Most such printers produce poor quality type that communicates a "mass production" quality. If you use a desktop publishing program, choose serif typefaces (Times Roman, Palatino, New Century). Avoid sans serif typefaces (Gothic, Helvetica, Avant Garde), which are more difficult to read. Be sure you print dark, crisp type.

Most individuals reproduce their resume on a copy machine. Indeed, given the high quality reproduction achieved on many copy machines available at local print shops, it's not necessary to go to the expense of having your resume professionally printed. However, if you need 2,000 or more copies – which is most unlikely unless you resort to a broadcast or "shot-gun" marketing approach – it may be more cost-effective to have them printed. Just take your camera-ready copy, along with your choice of paper, to a local printer and have them make as many copies as you need. The cost per copy will run anywhere from 3¢ to 15¢, depending on the number of copies run. The larger the run, the cheaper your per unit cost. However, we prefer composing a resume using a standard word processing (Word or WordPerfect) or desktop publishing program (InDesign or QuarkXpress) that enables you to customize each resume for particular employers and then printing it on a laser printer with a dpi of 600. This approach gives you flexibility and top quality at very low cost.

Marketing and Distribution

Your resume is only as good as your marketing and distribution efforts. What, for example, will you do with your resume once you've completed it? How can you best get it into the hands of individuals who can make a difference in your job search? Are you planning to mail, fax, or email it in response to vacancy announcements and want ads? Maybe you plan to broadcast it to hundreds of employers in the hope someone will call you for an interview? Should you post your resume online, which means including it in resume databases of Internet employment sites? Perhaps you only want to send it to a few people who can help you with your job search? Or maybe you really don't have a plan beyond getting it produced in a "correct" form.

54. It's best to target your resume on specific employers rather than broadcast it to hundreds of names and addresses: Broadcasting, shot-gunning, or blasting your resume to hundreds of potential employers will give you a false sense of making progress with your job search since you think you are actually making contact with employers. However, you will be disappointed with the results. For every 100 resumes you send, you will be lucky to get one positive response that leads to a job interview. Indeed, many individuals report no responses after mailing or blasting hundreds of resumes. It's always best to **target** your resume on specific employers through one or two methods:

- **Respond to vacancy announcements or want ads:** Resumes sent in response to job listings also will give you a sense of making progress with your job search. Since competition is likely to be high for advertised positions, your chances of getting a job interview may not be good, although much better than if you broadcasted your resume to hundreds of employers who may not have openings.

- **Target employers with information on your qualifications:** The most effective way of getting job interviews is to network for information, advice, and referrals. You do this by contacting friends, professional associates, acquaintances, and others who might have information on jobs related to your interests and skills. You, in effect, attempt to uncover job vacancies before they become publicized or meet an employment need not yet recognized by employers who may create a position for you in line with your qualifications. The resume plays an important role in this networking process. In some cases, you will be referred to someone who is interested in seeing your resume; when that happens, send it along with a cover letter, and follow up your mailing with a telephone call. In other cases, you will conduct informational interviews with individuals who can give you advice and referrals relevant to your career interests. You should take your resume to the informational interview and, at the very end of your meeting, ask your informant to critique your resume. In the process of examining your resume, your network contact is likely to give you good feedback for further revising your resume as well as refer you and your resume to others. If you regularly repeat this networking and informational interviewing process, within a few weeks you should begin landing job interviews directly related to the qualifications you outlined in your dynamite resume!

> *Broadcasting your resume to hundreds of potential employers will give you a false sense of making progress with your job search.*

55. **The best way to broadcast your resume is to include it in a variety of resume databases:** We view the resume databases operated by various Internet employment sites as a new form of high-tech resume broadcasting. Resumes in these databases, which can be from 500 to over 70 million in number, are usually accessed by employers who search for candidates with a particular mix of keywords on their resume. If you have the right combination of skills and experience and know how to write a keyword resume with language sensitive to the search-and-retrieval software, you should be able to connect with employers through such electronic mediums. At the same time, you may want

to use a more traditional direct-mail approach to broadcasting your resume via email – spend from $19.95 to $49.95 on a service to have your resume sent to thousands of employment specialists (primarily headhunters) and websites with resume databases who wish to receive resumes. Dozens of groups, such as www.resumezapper.com and www.resumeblaster.com, will broadcast your resume for a fee. However, we do not regard these services as effective ways to distribute a resume. Most make exaggerated claims of effectiveness. Indeed, few recruiters and employers welcome, read, or respond to such obvious junk emails. At best, they will give you a false sense of making progress with your job search since you feel you are "doing something" related to finding a job. For an expanded discussion of this subject, see pages 192-194.

56. **Learn to properly send your resume by email**: More and more employers request that resumes be sent to them by email rather than by regular mail or by fax. The principles for producing and distributing (formatting, type style, etiquette, etc.) an emailed resume differ from those relevant for a paper resume sent by mail or faxed. If you communicate a great deal with employers on the Internet, you will need to frequently transmit an email version of your resume. Make sure you know how to write and distribute a first-class emailed resume.

57. **Be prepared to complete online profile forms in lieu of a resume.** Many of today's employers operate their own online career centers rather than advertise positions in newspapers or through employment websites. Indeed, you are well advised to visit employers' websites for details on employment opportunities, including vacancy announcements and online applications. Candidates complete online applications which often include a candidate profile form that substitutes for a resume. Much of the information requested for completing this form can be taken directly from your resume. You can clip and paste sections from your resume to complete this form.

58. **Be careful in creating online and video resumes.** We do not encourage job seekers to create online or video resumes. Online resumes often provide too much information to employers. They also assume busy employers will actually access your website to view your online creation. Video resumes include too many verbal and nonverbal elements that should be reserved for a job interview. Always remember the purpose of a resume – to persuade a hiring manager to invite you to a face-to-face interview. Online and video resumes are much less persuasive than traditional paper and electronic resumes.

59. **Your resume should always be accompanied by a cover letter**: A resume unaccompanied by a cover letter is a naked resume – like going to a job interview barefooted. The cover letter is very important in relation to the resume. After all, if sent through the mail, the letter is the first thing a hiring official reads before getting to the resume. If the letter is interesting enough,

the person proceeds to read the resume. A well-crafted cover letter should complement rather than repeat the content of your resume. It should grab the reader's attention, communicate your purpose, and convince the reader to take action. See Ron and Caryl Krannich's *Nail the Cover Letter, 201 Dynamite Job Search Letters,* and *Haldane's Best Cover Letters for Professionals* books (Impact Publications) for an extensive discussion of the principles of effective cover letter writing, production, distribution, and follow-up. If you neglect the cover letter, you may effectively kill your resume! In many cases, your cover letter may be more important than your resume in landing an interview and getting the job. Your cover letter should command as much attention as your resume.

60. **Never enclose letters of recommendation, transcripts, or other information with your resume unless requested to do so:** Unsolicited letters of recommendation are often negatives – designed to manipulate the employer with self-serving information. Readers know such letters have been specially produced to impress them and thus they may question your integrity. Is this how you will also do your job – with lots of window dressing? Only a foolish employer would take such letters of recommendation seriously. Like personal photos, unsolicited transcripts may communicate negative messages, unless you have perfect grades. Such information merely distracts from your resume and cover letter. It does not contribute to getting a job interview. It indicates you do not know what you are doing by including such information with your resume and letter. On the other hand, once invited to a job interview, you are well advised to put together a portfolio that includes samples of your work and other materials providing evidence of your resume claims of performance.

61. **Address your resume to a specific person:** Always try to get the correct name and position of the person who should receive your resume. Unless you are specifically instructed to do so, addressing your correspondence to "Dear Sir," "Director of Personnel," or "To Whom It May Concern" is likely to result in lost correspondence; the mail room may treat it as junk mail. If you later follow up your correspondence with a phone call, you have no one to communicate with. A couple of phone calls should quickly result in the proper name. Just call the switchboard or a receptionist and ask the following:

> *"I need to send some correspondence to the person in charge of*
> *_____. Whom might that be? And what is the correct address?"*

Keep in mind that the people who have the power to hire are usually not in the Personnel Office; they tend to be the heads of operating units. So target your resume accordingly!

62. Don't limit the distribution of your resume only to vacancy announcements. Your goal should be to get your resume into as many hands as possible. Send it to individuals in your network – your relatives, friends, former colleagues and employers, and anyone else who might be helpful in uncovering job leads. Remember, you want to cast a big net. Let your resume do the fishing by casting it on as many waters as possible

63. Enclose your resume and letter in a matching No. 10 business envelope or in a 9" x 12" envelope: We prefer the 9" x 12" envelope because it keeps your correspondence flat and makes a better presentation than the No. 10 business envelope. Keep all your stationery matching, including the 9" x 12" envelope. If, however, it's difficult to find a matching 9" x 12" envelope, go with a white or buff-colored envelope or use a U.S. Postal Service "Priority Mail" envelope.

64. Type the envelope or mailing label rather than handwrite the address: Handwritten addresses look too personal and amateurish, give off mixed messages, and suggest a subtle form of manipulation on your part. This is a dumb thing to do after having enclosed a professional looking resume. Contrary to what others may tell you, in a job search handwritten addresses – and even handwritten letters or notes – do not gain more attention nor generate more positive responses; they may actually have the opposite effect – label you as being unprofessional or someone who is

> *Avoid handwritten messages in your job search. This is business correspondence requiring your best professional effort.*

trying to manipulate the employer with the old handwritten technique. Typed addresses look more professional; they are consistent with the enclosed resume. After all, this is business correspondence – not a social invitation to invite yourself to an interview. Don't confuse communicating your qualifications to employers with selling real estate, insurance, and automobiles – fields that tell salespeople to routinely handwrite addresses and notes to potential customers. Such a sales analogy is inappropriate for your job search.

65. Send your correspondence by first-class or priority mail or special next-day services, and use stamps: If you want to get the recipient's immediate attention, send your correspondence in one of those colorful next-day air service envelopes provided by the U.S. Postal Service, Federal Express, UPS, or other carriers or couriers. However, first-class or priority mail will usually get your correspondence delivered within two to three days. It's best to affix a nice commemorative stamp rather than use a postage meter. A stamp helps personalize your mailing piece and does not raise questions about whose postage meter you used!

66. **Never fax or email your resume unless asked to do so by your recipient:** It is presumptuous for anyone to fax or email his or her resume to an employer without express permission to do so. Such faxes or emails are treated as junk mail and are thus viewed as unwarranted invasions of privacy. If asked to fax or email your correspondence, be sure to follow up by mailing a copy of the original and indicating you sent materials by fax or email on a specific date as requested. A mailed resume and letter will always look better (assuming you've followed our production advice) than faxed or emailed correspondence. A paper follow-up also reminds the individual of your continuing interest in the position. When you email your resume, do so as part of the body of your email message (cover letter) and as a Word attachment. Don't assume strangers will open your email attachment – most will not. Many employers prefer receiving resumes as part of the email rather than as an attachment that could include a virus.

Follow-Up

Follow-up remains the least understood but most important step in any job search. Whatever you do, make sure you follow up **all** of your job search activities in a timely and intelligent manner. If you fail to follow up, you are likely to get little or no response to your job search initiatives. Follow-up means taking action that gets results.

67. **Follow up your resume within seven days of sending it:** Do not let too much time lapse between when you initially sent your resume and when you contact the resume recipient. Seven days should give the recipient sufficient time to examine your communication and decide on your future status. If a decision has not been made, your follow-up action may help accelerate a decision.

68. **The best follow-up to a resume and letter is a telephone call:** Don't expect your recipient to take the initiative in calling you for an interview. State in your cover letter that you will call the recipient at a particular time to discuss your resume:

    > I will call your office on the morning of March 17 to answer any questions you might have about my qualifications as well as see if we can meet at a mutually convenient time.

    And be sure you indeed follow up with a phone call at the designated time. If you have difficulty contacting the individual, try three times to get through. After the third try, leave a message as well as write a letter as an alternative to the telephone follow-up. In this letter, inquire about the status of your resume, mention your continued interest in the position, and thank the individual for his or her consideration.

69. Follow up your follow-up with a thank-you letter: Regardless of the outcome of your follow-up phone call, send a nice thank-you letter based upon your conversation. You thank the letter recipient for taking the time to speak with you and reiterate your interest in the position. While some career counselors recommend sending a handwritten thank-you note to personalize communication between you and the employer, as we noted in Principle #64, we caution against doing so. Remember, you are engaged in a business transaction rather than in social communications. We feel a handwritten letter is inappropriate for such situations. Such a letter should be produced in a typed form and follow the principles of good business correspondence. You can be warm and friendly in what you say. The business letter format keeps you on stage – you are putting your best business foot forward.

Resume Examples and Professional Assistance

The military-to-civilian resume examples found in the remainder of this book (see the 133 examples showcased in Chapters 6, 7, and 11) are based upon many of our resume writing principles. Examine our examples for ideas on how to develop each resume section of your resume. But be sure **you write your own resume** based upon the above principles rather than on the subsequent examples.

If you decide to hire a career professional to put together your resume (see our examples and recommendations in Chapters 11 and 12), be sure to communicate your needs according to the many principles outlined in this chapter. Above all, be a **smart shopper** for such services by asking the right questions, communicating your goals, and providing important information about your skills and accomplishments. And evaluate the final product according to our criteria outlined in Chapter 4.

For an extended treatment of the whole resume writing, production, distribution, and follow-up process – including how to assess your skills, develop an objective, write each resume section, and network for information, advice, and referrals with your resume – see Ron Krannich's and William Banis's latest edition of *High Impact Resumes and Letters* (Impact Publications).

Senior military personnel expecting to transition to $100,000+ jobs in the private sector are well advised to examine many of our examples in Chapter 11 as well as consult the following resume and letter writing books by Wendy S. Enelow and Louise M. Kursmark, which are published by Impact Publications (see the Career Resources section at the very end of this book, especially pages 349-350):

Best Career Transition Resumes for $100,000+ Jobs
Best Cover Letters for $100,000+ Jobs
Best Resumes for $100,000+ Jobs
Executive Job Search for $100,000 to $1 Million+ Jobs

4

Conduct Two Resume Evaluations

ONCE YOU COMPLETE YOUR resume, be sure to evaluate it according to the principles outlined in Chapter 3. You should do this by conducting two evaluations: internal and external. With an **internal evaluation**, you assess your resume in reference to specific self-evaluation criteria. An **external evaluation** involves having someone else critique your resume for its overall effectiveness. This chapter includes the criteria as well as the forms for quickly conducting both types of evaluations.

Internal Evaluation

The first evaluation should take place immediately upon completing the initial draft of your resume. Examine your resume in reference to the following evaluation criteria. Respond to each statement by circling the appropriate number at the right that most accurately describes your resume:

1 = Strongly Agree	4 = Disagree
2 = Agree	5 = Strongly Disagree
3 = Neutral	

The numbers at the end of each statement correspond to each principle previously outlined in Chapter 3. Refer to these principles for further clarification.

Writing

1. Translated my military experience and skills
   into civilian employment terms that should
   be readily understood by employers with
   little or no military experience (#1).   1   2   3   4   5

2. Wrote the resume myself – no creative
   plagiarizing from resume examples produced
   by other people. (#2)   1   2   3   4   5

3. Conducted a thorough self-assessment
   which became the basis for writing each
   resume section. (#2)   1   2   3   4   5

4. Have a plan of action that relates my resume
   to other job search activities. (#3)   1   2   3   4   5

5. Selected an appropriate resume format that
   best presents my interests, skills, and
   experience. (#4)   1   2   3   4   5

6. Included all essential information categories
   in the proper order. (#5-6)   1   2   3   4   5

7. Eliminated all extraneous information
   unrelated to my objective and employers'
   needs (date, picture, race, religion, age,
   political affiliation, sex, height, weight,
   marital status, health, hobbies) or better
   saved for discussion in the interview
   (salary history and references). (#7)   1   2   3   4   5

8. Put the most important information
   first. (#6)   1   2   3   4   5

9. Resume is oriented to the future rather
   than to the past. (#5)   1   2   3   4   5

10. Contact information is complete – name,
    address, and phone number. No P.O.
    Box numbers or nicknames. (#8-9)   1   2   3   4   5

11. Limited abbreviations to a few commonly
    accepted words. (#9)   1   2   3   4   5

12. Contact information attractively
    formatted to introduce the resume. (#9)   1   2   3   4   5

13. Included a thoughtful employer-oriented objective that incorporates both skills and benefits. (#10)   1   2   3   4   5

14. Objective clearly communicates to employers what I want to do, can do, and will do for them. (#10)   1   2   3   4   5

15. Objective is neither too general nor too specific. (#11)   1   2   3   4   5

16. Objective serves as the central organizing element for all other sections of the resume. (#12)   1   2   3   4   5

17. Considered including a "Summary of Qualifications" section. (#13)   1   2   3   4   5

18. Elaborated work experience in detail, emphasizing my skills, abilities, and achievements. (#14, 16)   1   2   3   4   5

19. Each "Experience" section is short and to the point. (#15)   1   2   3   4   5

20. Consistently used action verbs and the active voice. (#16-17)   1   2   3   4   5

21. Incorporated language appropriate for the keywords of electronic resume scanners. (#18)   1   2   3   4   5

22. Did not refer to myself as "I." (#19)   1   2   3   4   5

23. Used specifics – numbers and percentages – to highlight my performance. (#20)   1   2   3   4   5

24. Included positive quotations about my performance from previous employers. (#21)   1   2   3   4   5

25. Eliminated any negative references, including reasons for leaving. (#22)   1   2   3   4   5

26. Does not include names of supervisors. (#23)   1   2   3   4   5

27. Summarized my most recent job and then included other jobs in reverse chronological order. (#24)   1   2   3   4   5

28. Descriptions of "Experience" are
     consistent. (#25)   1   2   3   4   5

29. Put the most important information about
     my skills first when summarizing my
     "Experience." (#26)   1   2   3   4   5

30. No time gaps nor job hopping apparent
     to reader. (#27-28)   1   2   3   4   5

31. Documented "other experience" that might
     strengthen my objective and decided to
     either include or exclude it on the
     resume. (#29)   1   2   3   4   5

32. Included complete information on my
     educational background, including
     important highlights. (#30)   1   2   3   4   5

33. If a recent graduate with little relevant work
     experience, emphasized educational back-
     ground more than work experience. (#31)   1   2   3   4   5

34. Put education in reverse chronological
     order and eliminated high school if a
     college graduate. (#32)   1   2   3   4   5

35. Included special education and training rele-
     vant to my major interests and skills. (#33)   1   2   3   4   5

36. Included professional affiliations and member-
     ship relevant to my objective and skills;
     highlighted any major contributions. (#34)   1   2   3   4   5

37. Documented any special skills not included
     elsewhere on resume and included those
     those that appear relevant to employers'
     needs. (#35)   1   2   3   4   5

38. Included awards or special recognitions
     that further document my skills and
     achievements. (#36)   1   2   3   4   5

39. Weighed the pros and cons of including
     a personal statement on my resume. (#37)   1   2   3   4   5

40. Did not mention salary history or
     expectations. (#38)   1   2   3   4   5

18.   Paper size and stock   1   2   3   _____

19.   Overall production quality   1   2   3   _____

20.   Potential effectiveness   1   2   3   _____

SUMMARY EVALUATION: _____

_____

_____

_____

After completing these external evaluations and incorporating useful suggestions for further improving the quality of your resume, it's a good idea to send a copy of your revised resume to those individuals who were helpful in giving you advice. Thank them for their time and thoughtful comments. Ask them to keep you in mind should they hear of anyone who might be interested in your experience and skills. In so doing, you will be demonstrating your appreciation and thoughtfulness as well as reminding them to remember you for further information, advice, and referrals.

In the end, **being remembered in reference to your resume** is one of the most important goals you want to repeatedly achieve during your job search. As you will quickly discover, your most effective job search strategy involves networking with your resume. You want to share information, by way of the informational interview, about your interests and qualifications with those who can give advice, know about job vacancies, or can refer you to individuals who have the power to hire. Your resume, and especially this external evaluation, plays a critical role in furthering this process.

5

Translating Military Experience Into Civilian Language

ONE OF THE FIRST HURDLES you'll encounter en route to developing a conventional or electronic resume is how to translate your military experience into civilian terminology. Regardless of the duties you performed in the military, it's your responsibility to clearly communicate your qualifications in a language that prospective employers can easily understand.

Check Your Language

Depending on the nature of the jobs you held, this translation process will be an easy task for some and a more challenging task for others. For example, if you were a pilot in the Air Force, a nurse in the Navy, or a military policeman in the Army and your desire is to be a pilot, nurse, or policeman, respectively, in your civilian work life, the translation should be a relatively straightforward process. If, on the other hand, your jobs were unique to military service, the task is more challenging; it requires closer identification of transferable skills, such as leadership, rather than content-specific skills like computer programming.

Before beginning the translation process, it's important that you have a complete understanding of the work you did in the military as well as civilian equivalent skills and experiences. Can you thoroughly describe the different activities you performed? How did you accomplish the associated tasks? What were the skills or knowledge you used along the way? What did you produce or accomplish?

Let's start by completing the form on page 77. This exercise will help you organize your thoughts in regard to the nature of jobs held and to trigger your thoughts with regard to analogous employment in the private sector. You may find it useful to have your resume

MILITARY JOB # _____

Job Title:

_____   _____

Education / Training Required:

_____

_____

Skills Used:

_____

_____

_____

Activities Performed:

_____

_____

_____

Certification Achieved:

_____

_____

Similar Civilian Jobs:

_____

_____

_____

Required Experience / Training:

_____

_____

_____

_____

as a reference. However, note that this exercise is not intended to duplicate your documented work history. Instead, it should help you crystallize your thoughts regarding past employment and motivate you to seek information on those civilian jobs that may allow you to build on the expertise you developed while in the military. It may be the case that you can't fill in the equivalent civilian jobs just yet. That's fine and certainly not unexpected. In the next step, however, you will research those jobs that appear to match your interests so that you will have the knowledge required.

Researching the Marketplace

To become well versed in the language of your target industry, you must thoroughly research the civilian marketplace. Where should you begin? You may be surprised with how many resources are available to assist you with all phases of your job search. First, you should visit your local ACAP (Army), Family Service Center (Navy), or Airman and Family Readiness Center (Air Force) office and read the job openings in those occupations for which you have an interest. Career counselors at these sites will be glad to help you access the Operation Transition website (www.dmdc.osd.mil/ot) and the DoD Job Search on America's Job Bank (http://dod.jobsearch.org). When reviewing the job openings on the DoD Job Search website, pay special attention to the requirements for each job listed. As you read through these listings, think about the jobs you've held in the military and the potential connection in terms of skills employed, activities performed, work accomplished, etc. For those readers leaving the Army, there is an interactive, computer-based training program called **ACAP XXI**. Make sure you see your local career counselor to take full advantage of its extensive capabilities.

A second source of job information can be found in the reference section of your local base/fort/post or public library. Make sure you look at reference books such as the Department of Labor's *Occupational Outlook Handbook* and *The O*NET Dictionary of Occupational Titles*. These books will give you useful information about many different types of jobs. They will provide you with excellent insight into the educational, training, or work experience required for thousands of civilian jobs. You can access these handbooks and other related information through these U.S. Department of Labor URLs:

- *Occupational Outlook Handbook*   www.bls.gov/oco.
- *O*NET OnLine*   http://online.onetcenter.org

You also can order the print versions of these books directly from Impact Publications by completing the order form at the end of this book (see page 349) or visiting their online bookstore: www.impactpublications.com.

A third source of job information is right at your fingertips – the employment section of your local Sunday newspaper. Read the employment ads for the types of jobs that interest you. Look specifically at the skills or experience required. You might also consider calling the company or employment agency to see if they could provide you with additional details concerning the requirements for the job.

A fourth method of obtaining information on the requirements for current job openings is to engage in informational interviews. As discussed more fully in Chapter 10, "Network Your Way to Career Success," of your "Corporate Gray Series" book, the purpose of the informational interview is to solicit useful information, advice, and referrals about jobs, the job market, and your career interests. Call or write those friends, colleagues, acquaintances, and others who are currently employed in a civilian occupation in which you are interested. See if they will spend some time talking with you about the nature of their responsibilities. Remember, one of your goals should be to learn what it takes to be successful at the type of job they hold. You will find that most people, especially those with former military experience, will be helpful and offer you a wealth of information. During these networking sessions, we recommend following the "2/3, 1/3" rule. Approximately two-thirds of the time you should be in "listen mode," soaking up as much information as possible while the other person talks about his or her job, company, or industry. In the remaining one-third you should ask insightful, intelligent questions that trigger a more in-depth response in those areas of greatest interest to you. Naturally, the more research you do prior to any given networking session, the more likely you will be in a position to ask intelligent questions and, more importantly, have useful information revealed to you.

Fifth, you can go online and traverse cyberspace where a wealth of career opportunities can be found. We recommend accessing the Internet's World Wide Web and visiting such sites, Monster.com, CareerBuilder.com, JobCentral.com, NationJob.com, HotJobs.com (http://hotjobs.yahoo.com), Employment911.com, and CareerJournal.com, which daily post thousands of job opportunities for hundreds of companies across the U.S. (and even overseas!).

In addition to the numerous online job databases, you can also access other Internet services such as America Online and Microsoft Internet Explorer; you can visit chat rooms and forums focused on your civilian career interests. We also recommend surfing the Web prior to any networking opportunity. By using a search engine, such as Google (www. google.com), Yahoo (www.yahoo.com), MSN (www.msn.com), or Ask (www.ask.com), you should find a great deal of information about various companies in your targeted industry.

Your goal in sifting through the volumes of information available through the World Wide Web is to build a strong repository of knowledge that you can tap whenever and wherever needed. The broader and deeper your basis of knowledge, the more impressive you will be when engaged in networking or interviews.

For additional information on these and other useful online resources and services, see the latest editions of Ron and Caryl Krannich's *America's Top Internet Job Sites*, Richard Nelson Bolles's *Job-Hunting on the Internet*, and Margaret Riley Dikel's *Guide to Internet Job Searching*, as well as review the following gateway employment sites:

- **AIRS Directory**   www.airsdirectory.com/mc/forms_jobboard.guid
- **Riley Guide**   www.rileyguide.com
- **Quintessential Careers**   www.quintcareers.com
- **JobHuntersBible**   www.jobhuntersbible.com

Finally, we suggest visiting and/or joining an association in your desired employmen field. Often these associations will have newsletters or websites that contain job listings. Again, we recommend contacting these companies to better understand the skills and experience they are seeking for their respective positions. As you may be aware, there are several associations that often bridge the gap between military and civilian employment in a particular career field. An example of such an association is the Society of Logistics Engineers, or SOLE. If your work in the military involved logistics and you are interested in pursuing a logistics career in the civilian work world, then you should consider contacting SOLE and becoming a member. One of the most important benefits of joining an association like SOLE is the opportunity to talk with other career professionals, many of whom have worked in that particular career field in both the public and private sectors. Other examples of this type of association include the Society of Military Engineers, the Society of Military Comptrollers, and the American Society of Industrial Security. In addition to these industry-specific associations, we also recommend contacting more general associations such as The Military Officers Association of America (MOAA), the Non Commissioned Officers Association (NCOA), the Naval Enlisted Association (NEA), the Air Force Association (AFA), and the Veterans of Foreign Wars (VFW), among others. Many of these associations sponsor events or have programs that help you network with other members.

Associations can also take a more purely civilian flavor as well. There are literally thousands of civilian associations. For more information on associations, see the latest editions of *The Encyclopedia of Associations* and *Associations USA,* which you can find in many base or public libraries. Also check out these online directories to professional associations:

- **Associations on the Net**   www.ipl.org/div/aon
- **American Society of Association Executives**   www.asaenet.org

Using these comprehensive sources for locating associations, you will readily find one or more associations in your desired civilian career field. Give those that appeal to you a call. Ask about their membership requirements and annual dues. You might also ask if you could attend a local meeting. Most of these associations are relatively inexpensive, charging anywhere from $20 to $100 per year for membership. We recommend joining the one or two that appear to be right for you. By participating in selected association events, we're confident you'll quickly make new acquaintances who will likely be willing to spend time talking with you about their job or industry. Remember your goal in these sessions is to practice the 5Rs of informational interviews. You want them to:

1. **Read** your resume
2. **Revise** your resume
3. **Reveal** useful information to you
4. **Refer** you to others
5. **Remember** you for future job opportunities

At the same time, you should be making a mental note of the phrases and expressions they use to describe their job, company, and industry.

Closely related to professional associations are nonprofit organizations. Many of these groups offer excellent job and career opportunities for transitioning military personnel. For quick online access to thousands of nonprofit organizations, visit these two gateway nonprofit websites:

- **GuideStar**　　　　　　　www.guidestar.org
- **Action Without Borders**　www.idealist.org

We stress the importance of networking because it's central to your job search, both in terms of "learning the lingo" and learning about various civilian employment opportunities. Never forget that it is your responsibility to effectively communicate your qualifications in language that civilian hiring managers will understand and appreciate.

Military Assistance

Whether you are transitioning from the Army, Navy, Air Force, Marine Corps, or Coast Guard, your military service understands the challenge you face in translating your military work experience into civilian terms and offers tangible assistance to facilitate your efforts. Here we discuss some of the most important.

First, every separating service member is provided with DD Form 2586, "Verification of Military Experience and Training," at least 120 days prior to separation. If you did not receive the DD Form 2586, we recommend contacting your local ACAP, TAMP, CRMC, or TAP office and asking for assistance in obtaining this form.

We recommend using this document as a starting point for considering how your military experience and training translate into equivalent civilian occupations. From this list identify those items that relate to the types of civilian work you are interested in pursuing. Then document your experience – both within and outside the military – that relate to this item. If you feel you need some assistance, contact your local ACAP, TAMP, CRMC, or TAP office and ask to meet with a career counselor. He or she will be pleased to critique your document and provide helpful suggestions.

There are also various government-sponsored publications that you should find helpful. One of these is entitled *Military Careers*. Developed under the auspices of the U.S. Department of Defense, this book serves as an excellent guide to understanding nearly 200 military occupations within the Army, Navy, Air Force, Marine Corps, and Coast Guard and their relevance to the civilian work world. Each occupation is described according to a template consisting of the following sections: Work Environment, Physical Demands, Helpful Attributes, Training Provided, Opportunities, and Civilian Counterparts. The Civilian Counterparts section should be especially helpful in that it describes those civilian occupations that require similar duties and training for the military occupation under consideration. In addition, you will learn about the types of civilian companies and organizations associated with each occupation. At the end of *Military*

Careers you will find "A Dictionary of Occupational Titles (DOT) Code Index." Use this index to identify the corresponding civilian occupations specific to your background. Where can you find *Military Careers*? Since it is primarily a book for describing military career opportunities to prospective new recruits, we recommend visiting a local military recruiting office. If you want to purchase the book, call the Government Printing Office directly at 202-512-1800. To contact the organization that developed *Military Careers*, write to HQ USMEPCOM/ MEPCP-E, 2564 Green Bay Road, North Chicago, IL 60064.

Six-Step Translation Process

Now it's time to take your general knowledge of the translation process and apply it to your particular situation. To assist you in this process, follow this six-step approach:

STEP 1   On a clean sheet of paper, write down your military assignments in reverse chronological order as if you were doing a chronological resume. Under each of those assignments, describe **what** you did in detail. Across from each skill, describe how you applied the skill to accomplish a given task or project. Where possible, accentuate the content-specific (as opposed to transferable) skills or knowledge you applied in the performance of your military duties. Don't worry at this point about using military-specific terms or acronyms. We'll take care of them in a later step.

STEP 2   Based on the job-seeking research you have performed to date, make a list of the required skills or experience in which prospective employers in your chosen civilian career field have interest. Here is where your informational interviewing and other networking activities pay dividends. Because you have thoroughly researched those civilian occupations, you will know the types of skills, knowledge, and experience that hiring managers seek. If such is not the case, you might consider doing some additional research, perhaps by contacting an association in the desired industry, to better understand the language and skills relevant to individuals working in your chosen career field.

STEP 3   On another page, list your military skills in the left column and the needed civilian skills in the right. Now compare the items on these two lists. Can you connect any of the items on the first list to those on the second? If not, is it a problem of semantics (different words but similar meanings) or is it the case that you simply do not currently have the skills required? If the latter, you might consider obtaining additional training or schooling either on a part or full time basis. (Don't forget to explore your military service connected education benefits!)

STEP 4   Once you have matched items in the left and right columns, return to the detailed experience chronology you created in Step 1. For those military skills that relate to the civilian occupations in which you are interested, carefully revise your documented skills and experience by incorporating appropriate civilian expressions that relate to what you did in the military. Your objective is to accurately and honestly restate your military experience using language that civilian hiring managers will understand. Wherever you used military acronyms or unique expressions in Step 1, consider how you can restate the information in a more industry-relevant way without losing the meaning or impact of your experience.

STEP 5   Show this revised write-up to civilian friends and colleagues who are currently working in your employment field(s) of interest. Ask them to objectively critique your write-up and evaluate whether it conveys your qualifications in terms relevant to their industry. When they are done, don't forget to send them a thank-you note expressing your appreciation for the time and effort expended on your behalf. Such thoughtfulness will keep you remembered in a positive way.

STEP 6   Continually refine this document by incorporating the comments received in the previous step. The finished document should clearly and accurately portray your qualifications in terms appropriate to your targeted industry. Keep this document – it is the WORK HISTORY section of your resume.

If you follow these six steps, we're confident that you will have succeeded in translating your military experience into civilian terms. Remember that perseverance is key. You must discipline yourself to seek better ways of expressing your qualifications in words that match the needs of civilian employers.

Job Titles

As you go through this six-step process, another issue you are bound to wrestle with is the translation of your military job titles into equivalent civilian titles. Because of the large number of military job titles, we can provide only limited translation guidance. In general, we suggest using your enhanced knowledge of the civilian marketplace to help you convey the title in terms that a civilian hiring manager in your desired line of work would understand. For example, if you were an Air Force Technical Sergeant who managed electrical maintenance activities for a particular type of aircraft, we suggest using a functional title that has civilian relevance, such as Electronics Supervisor rather than a more military-specific title. Similarly, if you were a Navy officer responsible for managing the distribution of supplies and materiel across a class of ships, we suggest highlighting your functional title, Logistics Manager, rather than a military title.

For each job you held in the military, you should carefully think through the level of responsibility you had in the military and, based on your research of the civilian market-place, choose words that correspond to your level of responsibility in the civilian workplace. Honesty and common sense will serve you well. If you have doubts, ask a professional career counselor on base for an opinion.

At times, you may want to use your military title in lieu of a functional job title. The following table should prove to be a useful starting point.

Equivalent Titles

Military Title	Civilian Title
General Officer / Admiral (O-7 to O-10)	Senior Director Managing Director
Field Grade Officer (O-4 to O-6)	Program Director Program Manager
Company Grade Officer (O-1 to O-3)	Manager Project Officer
Warrant Officer (WO1 to CWO)	Technical Manager Technical Specialist
Senior NCO / Senior Chief (E-7 to E-9)	Operations Manager Senior Advisor
Platoon Sergeant (E6-E7)	Supervisor Foreman
Squad Leader (E5-E6)	First Line Supervisor
Asst. Squad Leader (E-3 to E-4)	Section Leader Task Leader
Crew Member (E-1 to E-2)	Team Member

Military Schools

Another important resume issue is the translation of military schools and training into civilian terms. Whether the training in question is "boot camp" or an advanced officer leadership school, your attendance and completion demonstrate to potential employers your perseverance and ability to learn. And assuming that this training was in an area roughly analogous to a private sector position, you can be assured that the civilian organization in which you are interested will value the investment the government has made in you. The reason is simple. Mainly, the company will not have to make nearly the same investment in training you as they would someone walking in off the street. Hence, they save time and money – two commodities that private sector firms cherish. You should not construe, however, that this would preclude you from receiving additional training in your new place of employment. More likely, it will enhance your chances for receiving more advanced training depending upon the nature of your responsibilities and the needs of the company.

As we know, many military schools focus on developing management and leadership skills and instilling basic military values. Other schools are more specific in focus and teach skills applicable to a given skill area. Regardless of the training you received, your task is to relate it to your job objective and target employment opportunities.

The table below offers some suggested translations. Some schools and courses are peculiar to a given military service. For those schools/colleges whose training program or course duration exceeds three months, we also recommend listing the course length on the resume.

School Translations

Military School	Civilian Translation
War College	Executive Military Leadership School
Command and Staff College	Senior Military Leadership School
Combined Arms Staff College	Officer Leadership School
Officer Advanced Course	Advanced Officer Leadership School
Basic Officers Course	Entry Level Officer Leadership Course
Advanced Non Commissioned Officers Course (ANOC)	Advanced Leadership and Management Development Course
Basic Non Commissioned Officers Course (BNOC)	Leadership and Management Development Course
Primary Leadership Development Course (PLDC)	Introductory Leader Development Course
Advanced Individual Training (AIT)	Advanced Skill Training
Basic Training	Introductory Military Training

When you complete this process, you have the necessary information to complete the Education and Training section of your resume. In this regard, we recommend starting with any college degrees you may have (in reverse chronological order, i.e., put a master's degree before a bachelor's degree), and then enter the training courses, also in reverse chronological order. You should not include all training you have ever received. Instead, include only those training programs that relate to your job objective. If you have not yet completed a college degree, we recommend that you include your high school diploma. If you are taking courses toward a college degree, it is appropriate to state that you are in the process of completing a degree.

Online Translators

While we prefer conducting the above paper-and-pencil exercise for identifying your civilian-related military skills, several military-to-civilian career transition websites also include online military skills translators related to your Military Occupational Code (MOC). Just enter your MOC code and these automated translators will generate descriptions of equivalent civilian jobs. Our own www.corporategray.com site includes this link to the U.S. Department of Labor's popular military occupational translator:

http://online.onetcenter.org/crosswalk

Other sites with useful military skills and occupations translators include:

www.taonline.com/mosdot
www.military.com
http://www.acinet.org/MOC/

Implementation

As in other aspects of the career transition process, success depends on implementation. Successful translation of your military experience is hard work and takes time if done right. As you go through the six-step translation process, remember what we said. This is NOT a one-time exercise. You must repeatedly refine this translation as you go through the job search process. As you learn more about the civilian workplace, you must re-examine your resume with the benefit of this enhanced knowledge and carefully consider how you can better state a given skill or accomplishment so that it better relates to those employment opportunities of interest to you.

Remember that we live and work in a skills-based society. Prospective employers want to know if you are qualified for the job and whether you'll fit in with the rest of their workforce. By telling them about similar work you've done (whether in or outside your military service) in terms they will understand, you will have reassured them that you have what it takes to do the job well.

In the next chapter as well as in Chapters 7 and 11, we will use the knowledge gained in translating your military experience to develop a resume that gets results!

6

Resume Examples by Occupations

W E ASSUME THAT PRIOR TO reading this chapter, you have conducted a thorough self-assessment of your skills, abilities, and interests and have a clear understanding of what you do well, what you enjoy doing, and what you want to do in the future. If not, you may want to consult our companion self-assessment guide entitled *I Want to Do Something Else, But I'm Not Sure What It Is* (Impact Publications) as well as complete the assessment sections found in Chapters 5-7 of your appropriate service "Corporate Gray" career transition guide (see reference on pages 12-13). In addition, we assume that you have researched the civilian marketplace in your field(s) of interest and have a solid understanding of the language used. Based on this knowledge and using the sample worksheets in Chapter 11, you must now develop a one- or two-page resume that effectively conveys your qualifications to prospective employers. If you are like many job seekers, you will have more than one job or career interest. Therefore, you should develop a resume for each.

Examples

To facilitate your resume writing endeavors, we have assembled a wide array of examples for different occupational fields. The 59 resume examples presented in this chapter represent a broad cross-section of the types of jobs that most transitioning military service members would likely seek. These resumes represent a rich collection of military experience that should appeal to many civilian employers. While most resumes do not directly relate to your background, they do convey a sense of structure and style that you should try to incorporate in your own resume writing activities.

You might best benefit from these examples by locating those resumes that most closely match your job or career interest. Examine the structure, layout, language, and other key elements we discussed in Chapters 3 and 4. You will find most of these examples are anchored with an Objective. As you will see in Chapter 11, which includes resume examples produced by career professionals who regularly work with transitioning military personnel, most of these resumes begin with a skills-oriented qualifications summary or profile in lieu of an objective.

As you examine our examples, put yourself in the shoes of a prospective employer and ask yourself this question: Would you be sufficiently motivated to invite this person to an interview? Remember, each person and his/her resume is unique. Your goal in writing your resume is to accurately present your qualifications in the best possible light so that the hiring managers will want to call you in for a face-to-face interview. That is the true test of an effective resume!

Whether you served in the Army, Navy, Air Force, Marine Corps, Coast Guard, or National Guard you offer prospective employers a unique set of experiences, skills, and knowledge. It's your job to convey those qualifications in terms civilian hiring managers will understand. In the final analysis, you are attempting to match your skills and knowledge with the requirements of an open position. The more insight you have into the position's requirements, the better you'll be able to map your skills and qualifications to the job.

In some cases, your background may not be a good fit for the job in which you're interested. Don't despair – there are several options. One is to seek additional training or education, either on a full- or part-time basis. Another option is to seek temporary employment in a related field for which you do qualify. For example, let's assume that you want to become a licensed electrician. If you're not quite ready to make this job leap, you might work initially as an electrician's helper to obtain some hands-on experience and take electrical courses in the evening to develop a solid underpinning for the theory side, i.e., understanding how electricity works. By steadily enhancing your skills, work experience, and job knowledge, you will soon be a strong candidate for the position you desire.

For the time being, however, we will assume that you already have the requisite background for the types of jobs that you seek. Now it's time to get down to business. The resumes that follow are categorized by the types of positions you will find in the civilian workforce.

Account Executive

Available: September 20XX

ANTHONY BROWN
123 Americana Lane
Aiken, SC 12345
H: (222) 111-8888 / W: (222) 123-4567
BrownA@aol.com

OBJECTIVE: An account executive position where sales ability and knowledge of the aviation industry will result in increased revenue for a firm specializing in aviation-related equipment.

QUALIFICATIONS SUMMARY: Extensive experience in purchasing and managing aviation materiel for large and diverse organizations. Excellent phone and sales presentation skills. Results-driven, detail-oriented professional who understands the importance of fulfilling customer demands in a timely manner. Know how to "close the deal."

EXPERIENCE: **Aviation Logistics Operations Director**, Oceana Naval Air Station, Virginia Beach, VA, 2005-present.
- Managed a 145-person aviation supply depot with $105 million in assets. Saved $360,000 annually by streamlining maintenance procedures.
- Surpassed aircraft readiness goals by 15% in the management of over 34,000 line items, from aircraft engines to flight clothing.

Repairable Materiel Acquisition and Control Manager, Pearl Harbor, HI, 2001-2004
- Led 30-person team in aviation logistics operations. Exceeded supply effectiveness goals by 7%.
- Managed all facets of a $20 million repairable aviation materiel account with 1,700 line items. Improved purchasing, storage, and issuance procedures. Streamlined maintenance repair activities.

Squadron Supply Officer, Twentynine Palms, CA, 1997-2000
- Supervised 9-person team in squadron supply activities. Exceeded inventory accuracy goals for a $225,000 inventory by 18%.
- Surpassed timeliness standards for requisition processing in support of all equipment in air traffic control squadron.

Human Resources Manager, Camp Lejune, NC, 1994-1996
- Developed integrated training, retention, and promotion plans for 165,000 people in 330 occupational specialties.
- Used computer planning models to identify and eliminate logistics acquisition inefficiencies, resulting in a savings of $12 million.

EDUCATION: **MBA**, University of Hawaii, Honolulu, HI, 2002
B.S., Business Administration, University of South Carolina, 1994

Administrative Assistant   *Available: January 20XX*

SEAN T. JEROME
1821 Pine Street
Los Angeles, CA
(213) 123-4567 (W) / (213) 345-6789 (H)
JeromeS@erols.com

OBJECTIVE:

Administrative assistant position for a professional services company seeking to benefit from proven administrative skills and experience.

SUMMARY OF QUALIFICATIONS:

- Highly organized; accomplish assigned tasks in an efficient manner.
- Goal oriented professional with excellent interpersonal and communication skills.
- Self-starter; able to work well with minimal directions.
- Computer literate with expertise in Microsoft Office.
- Five years of administrative experience.

WORK EXPERIENCE:

Administrative Assistant, Office of the Deputy Chief of Staff for Personnel, 2005-Present
Organize and direct a team of four support personnel who provide administrative services to senior military officials. Keep the calendars of these senior executives, ensuring 100% attendance at planned meetings. Process administrative actions in a timely and efficient manner. Handle confidential material with tact and discretion. Received Army Commendation medal in recognition of outstanding work.

Administrative Clerk, 82nd Airborne Division, Fort Bragg, NC, 2002-2004
Process range of administrative actions in support of a 500-person battalion. Type correspondence, answer telephone calls, and maintain extensive filing system on a daily basis. Achieved rating of outstanding in both announced and unannounced audits of administrative operations.

EDUCATION AND TRAINING:

MacArthur High School, Jacksonville, FL, 2001
Advanced Individual Training, Inventory and Supply, 2002

COMPUTER SKILLS:

Microsoft XP, Microsoft Access, Internet Explorer

Aircraft Maintenance *Available: May 20XX*

DANA TIMMONS
6431 Saint Thomas Lane
Alamogordo, NM 88531
W: 505-321-0189 / H: 505-432-4138
TimmonsD@Earthlink.net

OBJECTIVE   Position in aircraft maintenance for a commercial airline where technical know-how and supervisory skills will improve readiness and safety rates.

QUALIFICATIONS SUMMARY

MANAGEMENT
- Supervised, managed, and trained personnel on the maintenance of assorted military aircraft, including the F-15, F-16, F-117A, and T-38A.
- Effectively supervised the inspection and maintenance activities of 20 Air Force and contractor personnel involved in the overhaul of jet aircraft.
- Managed 15-person team supporting the daily operation and maintenance of 22 F-16 aircraft. Supervised troubleshooting activities affecting major aircraft subsystems, including the hydraulics, fuel, and electrical systems.

AIRCRAFT
MAINTENANCE
- Over 20 years experience in all aspects of aircraft operation/maintenance.
- Supervised maintenance inspections of the F-117A aircraft. Ensured repair and rigging of major airframe components were done correctly, reducing error rates by 14% within one year.
- As an aircraft maintenance specialist, performed troubleshooting of flight controls, hydraulics, engine components, and fueling subsystems.
- FAA-certified Airframe and Powerplant mechanic.

QUALITY
CONTROL
- Hand-picked by senior management to ensure contracted repair work was performed in accordance with manufacturer-directed requirements.
- Coordinated inspection maintenance plans with scheduling managers, production superintendents, and 1st level managers. Inspection team was rated in the top 5%.
- As a Project Control specialist, proposed several operational improvements that enhanced the safety of the F-15, F-117A, and T-38A aircraft. Adoption of ejection seat redesign resulted in 40% decrease in probability of injury.

EMPLOYMENT HISTORY

Maintenance Supervisor, Holloman Air Force Base, NM, 2005-Present
Aircraft Inspector, Langley Air Force Base, VA, 2001-2004
Quality Assurance Manager, McGuire Air Force Base, NJ, 1998-2000
Line Supervisor, Randolph Air Force Base, TX, 1994-1997
Aircraft Maintenance Specialist, Lackland Air Force Base, TX, 1989-1993

EDUCATION & TRAINING

A.A. Aircraft Technology, College of the Air Force, 2004
Eisenhower High School, Dallas, TX, 1988

Airline Pilot   *Available: April 20XX*

CHARLES SCHUSTER
9851 Kennedy Lane, Apt. #123
Travis Air Force Base, CA 32542
W: 904-232-1832 / H: 904-763-1321
SchusterC@aol.com

OBJECTIVE

Position as a pilot for a well-established commercial airline where extensive flight experience will positively impact the carrier's safety and on-time performance record.

SUMMARY OF QUALIFICATIONS

Air Force pilot with 20 years of single- and multi-engine aircraft experience in domestic and international environments. Technically proficient leader with over 6,000 flight hours in a variety of high-performance jet aircraft, including the C-130 and B-1. Polished communicator who inspires and motivates subordinates to excel in all assigned tasks. Consistently accomplished difficult missions while minimizing the associated risks to assigned crews. Caring leader who sets and enforces high standards of personal and professional conduct. Active DoD Secret clearance.

EDUCATION

M.S. Aeronautical Engineering, Air Force Institute of Technology, 1998
B.S. Aeronautical Engineering, U.S. Air Force Academy, 1988

PROFESSIONAL EXPERIENCE

Squadron Commander, Eglin Air Force Base, FL, 2005-Present
    Responsible for successful performance of a B-2 squadron supporting operations in Haiti. Plan, organize, and lead the activities of 25 pilots. Maintain combat readiness through efficient execution of training sorties. As the senior safety officer, ensure pilots and their crews adhere to flight procedures and policies. Strictly enforce rules of engagement for assigned aircraft. Effectively guide and advise pilots in all aspects of flight operations.

Operations Officer, Eglin Air Force Base, FL, 2002-2004
    As second in command of a B-1 bomber squadron, ensured the combat readiness of all pilots assigned to the squadron. Performed numerous flight evaluations of B-1 pilots to verify their flying skills. Performed safety checks of squadron pilots, assessing crew's knowledge of safety procedures, and ensured combat readiness of aircraft. High quality program resulted in perfect safety record.

Staff Officer, Operations and Plans, Office of the Air Force Deputy Chief of Staff, Operations, Pentagon, Washington DC, 1998-2001
    Served as a principal advisor to the Deputy Chief of Staff for Operations and Plans. Developed plans and policies affecting the worldwide operation of Air Force aircraft. Wrote decision papers and prepared briefings for senior management. Interfaced effectively with members of the House and Senate Armed Services Committees on national security issues.

Instructor Pilot, C-130, Kelly Air Force Base, TX, 1994-1997
    Instructed over 60 student pilots through C-130 jet training in all phases of flight, including aerobatics, formation, instrument, and navigation. Enhanced the existing training program by integrating new, innovative training techniques that reduced the training period by a week,

thereby saving the government $50,000 per student. Maximized the use of simulator training. Trained new instructors on the use of simulators. Voted top instructor by 3 consecutive classes.

Aircraft Commander, Travis Air Force Base, CA, 1992-1993
Supervised 4-member crew in all phases of C-130 flight operations. As the lead pilot, flew 2200 hours both domestically and internationally under all weather conditions. Managed, supervised, and evaluated the performance of aircrew personnel. Instructed crew members on all aspects of flight operations, aircraft maintenance, and safety procedures. Developed a strong team atmosphere to accomplish assigned missions.

Pilot, U.S. Air Force, 1988-1991
Gained extensive flying experience in both day and night environments, both domestically and internationally. Overseas flight experience in South and Central America, Europe, Canada, Southeast Asia, and the Pacific Rim. Consistently rated as one of the best pilots in the squadron.

TRAINING

Air Command and Staff College, 2000
Instructor Pilot Training, Air Training Command (Distinguished Graduate), 1995
Instrument Flight Course, Strategic Air Command, 1988
Squadron Officer School, 1985

Attorney   *Available: August 20XX*

STEVEN MARSH

2001 West James Ct.   Home: 501/789-4321
Seattle, WA 98322   Work: 501/789-5539

OBJECTIVE

A position in aviation law where proven management, organization, and supervisory skills and an exceptional record of success in investigating, adjudicating, settling, defending, and prosecuting cases will be used in settling cases to the benefit of employer and clients.

EXPERIENCE

Chief Circuit Defense Counsel, Davis Air Force Base, Ogden, UT, 2001-Present
Personally defended all Flying Evaluation Boards, winning every one. Successfully defended felony trials covering offenses of drug use, distribution, assault, DUI, and perjury. Supervised, trained, and directed 22 attorneys and 17 paralegals responsible for total defense services across 16 Air Force installations located in 12 states. Included oversight of over 500 trials with every offense up to and including premeditated murder.

Chief, Aviation Settlement Branch, U.S. Air Force, Washington, DC, 1999-2000
Directed the investigation, adjudication, and either settlement or litigation of all aviation, environmental, medical malpractice, and other tort claims filed against the Air Force. In 1993, this topped a $40 billion dollar exposure with the percentage of payout to claimed amount the lowest in over a decade. Supervised staff of 13 attorneys and 5 paralegals. Re-formulated U.S. Air Force policy on tort claim and litigation matters in conjunction with the Department of Justice, leading to a better concept and application of paying the losers and spending time and resources to win the winners.

Chief, Tort Section, U.S. Air Force, Washington, DC, 1996-1998
Supervised the investigation and recommended adjudication or litigation of all aviation tort claims against the Air Force, including the last of the Agent Orange cases and the KAL 007 Korean airliner shoot-down by the Soviet Union. Supervised staff of 3 attorneys and 1 paralegal. Recommended U.S. Air Force policy change on aviation tort claims that directly resulted in greater Agency latitude for meritorious claims independent of the previously required GAO Office requirements.

Staff Judge Advocate, Stevens Air Force Base, Miami, FL, 1994-1995
Advised top management of all legal issues to include the convening of Aircraft Accident Boards and Flying Evaluation Boards. Directed tort, labor, environmental, procurement, and criminal law procedures. During this period, defended two state environmental Notice of Violations successfully, and over 40 criminal cases were prosecuted without a single acquittal. Served as management's Chief Labor Resolution Negotiator securing settlements at 60 percent of the previously approved maximums. Supervised staff of 4 attorneys and 5 paralegals.

Assistant Staff Judge Advocate, Lowry Air Force Base, CO, 1990-1993
Served as government prosecutor for over 35 trials with no acquittals. Served as government representative in over 20 administrative hearings with no losses. Counseled clients on rights/duties under state and federal law.

Area Defense Counsel, Marshall Air Force Base, Austin, TX, 1986-1989
Defended over 300 clients in criminal trials, administrative hearings, or minor disciplinary concerns.

EDUCATION

J.D., Boston University College of Law, Boston, MA, 1980
B.A. (Political Science), University of North Carolina, Chapel Hill, NC, 1977

TRAINING

Air War College, USAF, Seminar Program, 1998
Armed Forces Staff College, Joint Service Program, Residence, 1995
Air Command and Staff College, USAF, Seminar Program, 1994

AWARDS

Stuart Reichart Award, Senior Attorney, HQ USAF, 1997
Ramirez Award, Outstanding Attorney Tactical Air Command, 1993
Outstanding Attorney, U.S. Air Forces Colorado, 1990

OTHER EXPERIENCE

U.S. Parole Board Hearing Member, USAF, 1995
Joint Services Consolidation Committee, 1993-1994

BAR MEMBERSHIPS

U.S. Supreme Court, 1997
U.S. Court of Appeals, 4th Circuit, 1993
U.S. Court of Military Appeals, 1990
Supreme Court of Texas, 1986

Aviation Maintenance Supervisor   *Available: August 20XX*

SAMUEL ADAMS
2913 West Broad St.
Fairfax, VA 22313
(703) 888-3333
AdamsS@erols.com

OBJECTIVE   Supervisory position where aviation maintenance experience can
be used to improve the effectiveness and quality of an airline's
maintenance operations.

QUALIFICATIONS SUMMARY

MAINTENANCE
- Extensive maintenance experience in a variety of jet aircraft, including the B-1, C-117, and C-130.
- Innovative problem solver who developed efficient methods for ensuring aircraft were maintained at peak levels. Recommended cost-cutting measures that saved the Air Force $1.5 million over a 3-year period.
- Developed maintenance checklists and enforced compliance, resulting in a perfect safety record for all assigned aircraft.

MANAGEMENT
- Evaluated performance of 15 maintenance technicians on a daily basis.
- Developed customized maintenance training program, which resulted in a 98% pass rate for staff under my supervision.
- Executed action-oriented plans, ensuring assigned missions were accomplished on time and within budget.

COMMUNICATION
- Effectively communicated aircraft maintenance tasks to fellow teammates.
- Briefed senior leaders on the readiness status of aircraft. Developed innovative plans for repairing defective components.
- Taught aviation maintenance courses to newly assigned staff.

EMPLOYMENT HISTORY

Assistant Director, Maintenance, 79th Tactical Air Wing, Hanscom AFB, 2003-Present
Manager, Aircraft Maintenance, 339th Fighter Squadron, Nellis AFB, NV, 2000-2002
Staff Non Commissioned Officer, Andrews AFB, MD, 1997-2000
Aviation-related leader development positions, 1988-1997

EDUCATION & TRAINING

A.S. Aircraft Maintenance, Community College of the Air Force, 2003
Aircraft Maintenance Training, Nellis AFB, NV, 2001
Basic Training, Randolph AFB, TX, 1988

Commercial Helicopter Pilot *Available: July 20XX*

DAVID P. JONES
322 Gregor Street
Fort Rucker, AL 22311
W: (999) 222-3333 / H: (999) 222-4444

OBJECTIVE

Position as a helicopter pilot where military aviation experience and skills can be used by a commercial firm located in a major metropolitan area.

SUMMARY OF QUALIFICATIONS

Exceptionally skilled aviator with over 20 years experience flying various types of Army helicopters. Logged over 18,000 hours of flight time under all weather conditions. Hand-picked for several critical missions affecting U.S. national security. Experienced flight trainer with an unblemished safety record. Recognized by senior Defense Department officials as one of the best Army aviators.

PROFESSIONAL EXPERIENCE

Safety Evaluator, Fort Rucker, AL, 2005-Present
Inspect U.S. Army aviation sites to ensure 100% compliance with the Defense Department's aviation safety policies. Evaluate Army aviators' knowledge of safety procedures and practices in all phases of flight operations. Inspect aviation accident sites worldwide to identify common shortfalls in training or procedures. Recommended changes in pre-flight inspections that reduced the number of accidents annually by 27%.

Instructor Pilot, Fort Rucker, AL, 2002-2004
Instructed Army aviators on all phases of flight operations involving the Blackhawk helicopter. Incorporated state-of-the-art flight simulator equipment into all aspects of training, shortening course by 1 week for a savings of $75,000 per student aviator. Evaluated students' flight performance. Rated 1st out of 9 instructors.

Pilot, 101st Airmobile Division, Saudi Arabia, 2000-2001
Logged 55 air combat missions during Operations Desert Shield/Desert Storm while flying the Army's Blackhawk helicopter. Supported troop and logistics transport to Army combat units. Flew day and night missions under severe environmental conditions. Received Bronze Star.

Pilot, 1st Infantry Division, Fort Riley, KS, 1997-1999
Logged over 2000 hours of flying time in the Blackhawk helicopter. Flew numerous missions under all weather conditions. Trained and evaluated supporting flight crew, raising readiness level by 18%.

Pilot, 1988-1996
Piloted the Huey helicopter in assignments spanning North America, Europe, and Southeast Asia. Excelled in all phases of flight operations. Received many awards for outstanding performance.

EDUCATION & TRAINING

B.S., Aeronautics, University of Alabama, 1993
Black Hawk Training, Fort Rucker, AL, 2002
Flight Training, Fort Rucker, AL, 1993

Construction Supervisor   *Available: June 20XX*

MICHAEL RAMIREZ
313 Bradley Drive
Bremerton, WA 90972
W: (206) 222-3333 / H: (206) 888-3321
RamirezM@aol.com

OBJECTIVE   A foreman position where skills and experience as a construction supervisor will benefit a firm seeking to expand its scope of operations.

QUALIFICATIONS SUMMARY

MANAGEMENT
- Supervised construction crew of 25 personnel involved in building new homes and offices.
- Trained numerous junior operators on the proper use and maintenance of construction equipment.
- Attained a 100% safety record through strict adherence to standard operating procedures.

CONSTRUCTION
OPERATIONS
- Operated bulldozers, roadgraders, and other heavy equipment in building over 25 miles of runway in record time, under combat conditions.
- Used scrapers and other heavy machinery to remove ice and snow from runways.
- Operated winches, cranes, and hoists in constructing over 200 new homes.

INTERNATIONAL
- Fluent in Spanish.

WORK HISTORY

Construction Supervisor, 23rd Engineer Battalion, McChord AFB, WA, 2005-Present
Construction Equipment Operator, 110th Construction Battalion, Keesler AFB, MO, 2001-2004

EDUCATION & TRAINING

A.A., Construction, Washington Community College, Seattle, WA, 2005
Air Force certified apprenticeship program in Heavy Construction, 2001
Diploma, Homer High School, Homer, NY, 2001

Contracts Manager   *Available: September 20XX*

DANA T. EDWARDS
1187 MacArthur Blvd.
Springfield, VA 22121
H: (703) 888-3333 / W: (703) 111-2345
EdwardsD@aol.com

OBJECTIVE   Senior contracts manager for a management consulting firm interested in reducing costs and improving acquisition efficiencies.

QUALIFICATIONS SUMMARY

CONTRACT MANAGEMENT

- Initiated and administered invitations for bid and requests for proposals. Awarded over 250 contracts valued in excess of $900,000.
- Negotiated/contracted for commodities, facilities, maintenance, and services.
- Prepared formal contracts and ensured all Government terms, specifications, legal requirements, and restrictions were incorporated and satisfied.
- Expert knowledge of federal acquisition guidance (FAR, DFARS, & FIRMR).

PROJECT MANAGEMENT

- Directed 37 system engineers responsible for acquiring the equipment necessary to support 5 Government research & development laboratories.
- Led the Tactical Exploitation of National Capabilities Program, directing the acquisition activities of 89 staff. Responsible for administering $8 million annual budget.
- Effectively managed two major weapon system projects valued in excess of $250 million. Increased accuracy of system deliveries ten-fold through stringent enforcement of technical specifications.

CERTIFICATIONS

- Warranted U.S. Government contracting officer
- Certified GSA Trail Boss

EMPLOYMENT HISTORY

Chief, Advanced TENCAP Plans & Programs, Space Applications Project Office, 2003-Present
Deputy Director, Key Technologies, Air Force Ballistic Missile Defense Program, 2000-2002
Reconnaissance Liaison Officer, Combined Field Army, Air Liaison Office, Seoul, Korea, 1998-99
Chief, Reconnaissance/Intelligence Plans & Programs, HQ Air Force Systems Command, 1993-97
Flight Instructor, Academic Instructor, Flight Test RF-4C, 1985-1992

EDUCATION & TRAINING

M.S., Systems Management, U.S.C., 2001
B.S., Contract Administration, University of Maryland, 1985
Air Command and Staff College, Maxwell AFB, Alabama, 1997

ASSOCIATIONS

Treasurer, National Contract Management Association
Vice President, National Association of Purchasing Managers

Corporate Communications   *Available: May 20XX*

KAREN BENTON
200 West Brookfield Place
Palm Springs, CA 92200
(619) 321-0987
BentonK@aol.com

OBJECTIVE

Corporate Communications position for a large, international defense firm where proven communication skills will enhance internal coordination and strengthen the firm's public image.

Training & Development. Strong qualifications in the design, development and instruction of field and classroom training programs for professional, management and support personnel. Created training manuals and handbooks. Trained other trainers.

Administrative Operations. Detail-oriented with strong organizational and project management skills. Evaluated existing operations, standardized operating procedures to streamline core operating functions, and introduced quality, efficiency and productivity initiatives. Excellent qualifications in office management, policy/procedure development, employee performance measurement and cross-functional team leadership.

General Management. Cross-functional experience in business development, sales, personnel recruitment training, customer relationship management, accounting, financial reporting and administration. Strong decision-making, problem solving and crisis management skills.

Graphic Arts & Communications. Creative and artistic with the ability to translate concepts and images into strong visual presentations. Designed business marketing and promotional materials.

PC Skills. Proficient in Microsoft Word, Excel, and PowerPoint.

PROFESSIONAL EXPERIENCE

U.S. AIR FORCE   1980-2000

Fast-track promotion through a series of increasingly responsible technical and supervisory positions. Held multi-functional responsibility for the receipt, processing and control of sensitive electronic information, developed operating plans and procedures, and coordinated the deployment of assigned personnel and equipment during crisis situations. Top security clearance. Career highlights include:

Command & Control Supervisor, Utah & Germany
Command & Control Technician, California & Germany
Avionics Communications Specialist, Arizona

Had management oversight for a team of six responsible for technical assessment, maintenance and troubleshooting of high-tech information systems. Maintained computer systems and automated data processing equipment for worldwide military command. Assumed additional management role for monitoring all aircraft traveling throughout Europe, Africa and the Middle East to facilitate rapid deployment in the event of a crisis.

Wrote complete training instruction procedures for command computer systems. Led training, development and certification programs for new personnel. Evaluated and documented performance of systems team. Led monthly readiness training sessions to enhance the unit's response capability. Conducted on-site inspections of numerous command centers to audit reporting procedures, identify deficiencies in quality control, and ensure compliance with all military and federal regulations. Presented findings to headquarters for evaluation.

Communications Technician

One-year position between tours of duty with the U.S. Air Force. Directed building control, alarm and security systems for the university's Plant Services Division. Designed and implemented procedures to dispatch law enforcement, medical and rescue personnel in response to emergency and crisis situations including power loss, fire, vandalism and burglary.

EDUCATION & TRAINING

Eisenhower High School, Biloxi, MI, 1985

Completed numerous programs sponsored by the Air Force and regional community colleges. Course highlights included:

- Staff Development Training
- Computer Data Handling
- Human Resource Management
- Management Communications

Electrician   *Available: June 20XX*

FRANCIS X. SEABEE
456 Bay Bridge Lane
San Diego, CA 92111
H: (619) 555-9999/ W: (619) 123-4567
SeabeeF@aol.com

OBJECTIVE   Position as an electrician for a company that seeks an experienced, skilled technician.

QUALIFICATIONS

- 8 years experience as an Industrial Electrician
- Rated superior in technical repair activities
- Demonstrated ability to maintain, operate, repair, and install a wide variety of commercial and industrial electronic equipment

SKILLS SUMMARY

Experienced in preventative and corrective maintenance on the following equipment:
- 3 phase and single phase AC/DC plant equipment
- Power and lighting circuits, switches, and fuse boxes
- Amp meters, volt meters, ohm meters, and other test equipment
- Motors, controllers, and related power generation equipment
- Alarm systems and other power monitoring equipment

Knowledgeable at using the following tools and equipment to troubleshoot and repair equipment malfunctions:
- Logic test equipment
- Automatic-testing
- Spot welding machine
- Trickle and impregnation machine
- Power presses
- Undercutting machines
- Coil winding machine
- Soldering tools

Experienced in reading blueprints/drawings and using the following tools to install or repair cables, conduit, and circuits:
- Conduit benders
- Pipe threaders
- Wire and cable cutters
- Hand and power tools
- Cable pullers

Supervised the operation of turbine generators and emergency diesel generators. Trained junior personnel.

EMPLOYMENT

2004-Present, U.S. Navy, Naval Surface Force Pacific
2001-2003, U.S. Navy, U.S.S. Lightning (FF-1000)
1999-2002, U.S. Navy, U.S.S. Ranger
1997-1998, U.S. Navy, Navy Yard, Washington, D.C.
1994-1996, U.S. Navy, San Diego, CA

EDUCATION

Electrician 400 Hz Motor-Generator Maintenance, 1999
Electrician "C" School, 1991
Electrician "A" School, 1990
Graduated Lompoc High School, Lompoc, CA, 1989

Electronic Maintenance Supervisor   *Available: June 20XX*

THOMAS JONES
2121 Main Street
Norfolk, VA 22211
H: (757) 333-4444 / W: (757) 112-2345
E-mail: ThomasJ@aol.com

OBJECTIVE

Electronics Maintenance Supervisor position where electronics expertise and management know-how can be used by an aerospace firm to significantly improve its maintenance operations.

SUMMARY OF QUALIFICATIONS

- Results-oriented professional with significant management and hands-on electronic and mechanical maintenance experience.
- Skilled technician with expertise in an array of electro-mechanical disciplines.
- Articulate communicator who conveys technical concepts in clear terms.
- Adept problem solver who easily transfers knowledge to teammates.

PROFESSIONAL EXPERIENCE

MANAGEMENT

- Supervised over 45 electronics technicians in 5 shops performing a wide range of electrical and mechanical repair on over 20 aircraft.
- Coordinated and implemented technical training and reassignment of technicians in a manner that mitigated the impact of manpower shortages.
- Maintained 100% accountability of over 2,000 component parts, electronic test equipment, and materials with inventory values in excess of $3 million.
- Ensured strict adherence to quality control in repair cycle by conducting receiving, in-process, and final inspections of electronic systems and associated components.

ELECTRONIC REPAIR

- Repaired 10 different, high-tech electrical and electronic aircraft systems and components using industry-standard equipment, such as oscilloscopes, signal generators, voltmeters, ammeters, and time domain reflectometers.
- Employed standard troubleshooting methods using technical manuals, wiring schematics, block diagrams, and drawings to rapidly isolate malfunctions in system wiring, sub assemblies, and other components.
- Skilled at wire, cable bundle, coaxial, and connector repair.

TRAINING & EDUCATION

Total Quality Management Training, 2003
Advanced Electrical/Electronic Technical Training, 2001
Miniature Electronics Repair QA/Supervisor Course, 1999
Diploma, Martin Luther King High School, Biloxi, MI, 1998

Electronics Repair   *Available: December 20XX*

DONALD J. BUOY
834 Market Lane
Groton, CT 98031
W: (206) 918-7623/ H: (206) 231-8710
BuoyD@aol.com

OBJECTIVE

Electronics System Repair position where technical training and skills can benefit a large aerospace firm that also manufactures major weapon systems.

QUALIFICATIONS SUMMARY

- Electronic weapon systems repairer with over 10 years hands-on and supervisory experience.
- Recognized expert in the maintenance of multiple weapon systems electronics. Troubleshoot and solve difficult electrical faults.
- Extensive experience adjusting weapon systems' firing guidance and launch sub-systems using electronic test equipment, calibrators, and other fine precision instruments.
- Knowledgeable in the repair and maintenance of missile mounts, platforms, and launch mechanisms.
- Demonstrated ability to use schematics and underlying knowledge of electronic principles and techniques to diagnose electrical system failures.
- Certified electronic weapons system repairer.

WORK HISTORY

Shop Supervisor, San Diego Coast Guard Station, San Diego CA, 2004-Present
Responsible for ensuring all electrical repairs are done on time and to standards. Schedule work and training assignments for 25 personnel. Provide technical guidance and advice to shop personnel on a daily basis. Inspect and approve all electronic weapons system repair work performed in the shop.

Senior Electronic Weapon System Repairer, Coast Guard Station, Melbourne, FL, 1999-2003
Set up and ran electronic test equipment used to repair Coast Guard weapon systems. Installed and calibrated guidance, telemetry, and electronic fire control subsystems to ensure accurate firing of weapons systems. Used wiring system knowledge and troubleshooting techniques to detect faulty electronic parts and identify causes for system breakdowns. Provided on-the-job training to new technicians; assisted them with difficult electrical repairs.

Electronic Weapon System Repairer, Coast Guard Station, San Diego, CA, 1997-1998
Troubleshot electronic components of various weapon systems by analyzing associated maintenance and wiring diagrams. Repaired or replaced faulty electrical components. Used electronic equipment and test probes to check missile fire control guidance systems.

EDUCATION & TRAINING

Diploma, Miami Central High School, Miami, FL, 1996
Advanced Supply School, 7th District, FL, 1998
Coast Guard Basic Training, 1997

Electronics Technician   *Available: February 20XX*

DALE PARKER
200 Main St, #2
Middlesex, NJ 08820
(908) 543-2111
ParkerD@aol.com

OBJECTIVE: Electronics technician for an international Defense firm where experience, leadership, and communication skills will strengthen a small-to-medium sized staff.

HIGHLIGHT OF QUALIFICATIONS

- Eight years experience as a RF Telecommunications specialist.
- Two years experience as a supervisor/manager.
- Implemented successful inventory control management system to include a database.
- Trained in basic AC/DC principles, solid state and digital devices, control systems and communication theory.
- Experienced in development and implementation of training requirements.
- Held Top Secret security clearance. Recent Special Background Investigation.

PROFESSIONAL EXPERIENCE

UNITED STATES NAVY, Electronics Technician, 1990-Present

Technical Knowledge:

- System diagnosis and quality assurance of Submarine Communications Equipment to component level using schematics, blueprints and technical manuals.
- Operate and coordinate Communication Systems including automated networks, satellite data links, and a full spectrum of voice, teletype and data circuits.
- Identified a difficult Antenna problem resulting in a cost savings repair to the Navy of over $28,000.
- Repaired or replaced electrical/electronic cables and cable connectors.
- Knowledge of basic test equipment.
- Operation of signal converters, modems, associated peripheral communication equipment.
- Trained in Hydraulic and Pneumatic systems and compliance with a variety of extensive procedures.

Administration:

- Extensive office skills to include filing, copying, maintaining multiple files and logs, typing messages and reports and administrative control over various collateral duties.
- Organized and corrected Hazardous Material/Waste System; familiar with E.P.A. requirements.
- Two years experience managing the security access of a U.S. Navy submarine.

EDUCATION/TRAINING

Basic Enlisted Submarine School
Submarine Electronic Technical Training School
Submarine Radioman A (Basic) School
Submarine Radioman C (Advanced) Receivers Combined Maintenance School
Submarine Radioman C (Advanced) Special Communications School
Submarine Radioman C (Advanced) Tactical Communications School

Electronics Technician   *Available: June 20XX*

SANDY FISHER
101 Arlington Blvd.
San Diego, CA 92100
(619) 512-3456
FisherS@aol.com

Objective

Position as an Electronics Technician for a West Coast firm seeking to strengthen its engineering staff with a dedicated, experienced, and highly motivated professional.

Qualifications Summary

- Expert in testing, troubleshooting and repairing complex navigation, fire control, and display systems.
- Proficient in the operation, calibration, and maintenance of multimeters, oscilloscopes, signal analyzers, and numerous types of test equipment.
- Utilized total quality management to develop valuable time/stress management skills.
- Exceptional interpersonal, client service, and liaison skills.
- U.S. Navy Electronics Instructor
- Expertise in WordPerfect, MS Windows 2000, and the Internet.
- Quality Assurance inspector.

Work History

- *Electronics Technician*, U.S. Navy - USS Coronado (AGF-11), 2003-Present
- *Electronics Instructor*, U.S. Navy - Service School Command, Naval Training Center, San Diego, CA, 1998-2002

Education and Training

- Associate of Science Degree, San Diego State University, 2002
- Total Quality Management Training
- Instructor Training School
- Various U.S. Navy Electronics Schools

Emergency Medical Technician   *Available: October 20XX*

KATHLEEN SMITH
8841 Greensboro Drive
Boston, MA 01755
W: 617-632-1343 / H: 617-232-3212

OBJECTIVE

Position as an Emergency Medical Technician where my military-refined health care skills and experience will benefit a private health care facility seeking to improve its patient care quality.

SUMMARY OF QUALIFICATIONS

- Over 10 years experience in the health care profession as a Navy corpsman.
- Trained to provide emergency medical care in response to accidents, fire, natural disasters, etc.
- Proficient in a variety of first-line tasks, including: recording of vital signs, reading and updating of patients' medical records, and taking of blood for laboratory analysis.
- Communicated effectively with patients and administrators.
- Demonstrated ability to work well under stressful conditions.

WORK HISTORY

Emergency Medical Technician, **U.S.S. Mercy, 2005-Present**

Provide first-line emergency medical care to sailors and Marines onboard ship. Take patients' vital signs, including temperature, pulse, and blood pressure. Prepare patients for follow-up treatment by registered nurses or medical doctors. Update patients' medical records.

Medical Service Technician, **Bethesda Naval Hospital, MD, 2001-2004**

Responsible for ensuring 500 patients' records were properly filed. Responded to record requests by nurses and doctors. Performed quality assurance checks of medical records. Identified missing documents and persevered until records were properly completed. Recommended an innovative color-coding scheme that reduced confusion and saved health care professionals' time.

Medical Service Technician, **Tripler Army Hospital, Honolulu, HI, 1998-2000**

Drew patients' blood for analysis by laboratory technicians. Resuscitated those patients who fainted during the procedure. Explained the importance of wellness programs that emphasize proper diet and exercise.

EDUCATION AND TRAINING

Emergency Medical Training, Bethesda Naval Hospital, MD, 2001
St. Elizabeth Seton High School, Rockville, MD, 1997

Engineering Manager   *Available: May 20XX*

LEE CHAPPEL
50 Winding Road
Darien, CT 06000
(203) 444-7890
Chappel@aol.com

OBJECTIVE

Position as an Engineering Manager for a Fortune 500 manufacturing firm where extensive experience, broad technical knowledge, and proven management skills will further strengthen a quality organization.

EDUCATION

M.S., Mechanical Engineering, Rensselaer Polytechnic Institute, 2004
B.S., Mechanical Engineering, University of New Haven, 2001, Summa Cum Laude,
   3.97/4.0 GPA

PROFILE

- Proven performer in development and implementation of quick turnaround solutions to interdisciplinary engineering problems in a fast-paced environment.
- Team player with extensive engineering background developed over 25 years of experience in Naval Engineering and Naval Nuclear Propulsion.
- Extensive knowledge of industry standards, military standards, and military specifications.
- Trained and proficient in Total Quality Management (TQM) methods.

PROFESSIONAL EXPERIENCE

PLANNING OFFICER, Naval Submarine Support Facility New London, 2005-Present

- Coordinated efforts of 40 planner/estimators in preparation of detailed, step-by-step, user-friendly technical work procedures in support of 1,000-man production work force.
- Organized interdisciplinary teams eliminating craft barriers. Resulted in 20% reduction in planning lead time; elimination of revisions and associated work stoppage caused by inaccurate job scope of inadequate procedures.
- Trained craftsman in skills required of effective planners: ship checks; technical research; technical writing; quality assurance; make/buy decisions; long lead-time material identification/resolution; identification of problem causes vs. symptoms; assessment of shop capabilities; development of critical path timelines.
- Specified, procured, installed, and trained personnel in use of a Local Area Network (LAN). Streamlined procedure preparation, improved accuracy, enabled repetitive use procedures.
- Essential member of department Quality Management Board and command Automatic Data Processing/Management Information Systems Steering Committee.

ASSISTANT ENGINEER, Commander, Submarine Squadron Two, 2002-2004

- Actively managed efforts of multiple industrial activities in execution of extensive shipyard maintenance periods. (Average of 120,000 man-days/$50 million per year.)
- Provided liaison between shipyard, squadron, customer, and Naval Sea Systems Command management to resolve schedule conflicts, arrange shipchecks, review work packages, and train ship's company. Ensured best product, least cost, shortest time.

- Evaluated Propulsion Plant watchstanding/administration. Resulted in significant improvements in the proficiency and performance of new construction crews in meeting crew certification milestones, and in the performance of operating crews on Operations Reactor Safeguards Exams.
- Monitored Radiological Controls, Nuclear Work Practices, and Quality Assurance Procedures. Assisted in identification and correction of deficient work practices, material deficiencies, and documentation problems before they impacted production.
- Coordinated the efforts of four major industrial activities in intensive maintenance period including first dry-docked battery replacement and major repairs/replacement of unique propulsion shafting. *Commended for direct role in early completion.*

NUCLEAR REPAIR OFFICER, USS Fulton (AS-11), 1999-2001

- Directed all phases of Nuclear Repairs to submarine Nuclear Propulsion Plants including planning, qualification, and continuing training, production, production management, and quality assurance.
- Project Officer for major inspection of steam generating equipment: selected, trained, and qualified personnel; researched, ordered, staged material and special equipment; developed computerized logistic support database; implemented stringent cost controls resulting in savings of $350,000; directly supervised procedure preparation; actively managed production and testing phases. *Personally commended for cost savings, incident free inspection, and early completion.*
- Supervised restoration of Ship Service and Main Propulsion Generators and Main Propulsion Motors following major fire in FULTON's aft engine room: arranged outside technical support; organized assets; trained technicians. Restored to full capability, in place, in one-half time, saving $500,000.

PROJECT OFFICER, Supervisor of Shipbuilding, Conversion & Repair, San Francisco, 1996-1998

- Led project team of 50 contract administrators/surveyors, engineers, contract specialists in management of multiple intensive Nuclear Aircraft Carrier industrial maintenance periods (1000 man-days/day). Average total contract value of $100 million/period. Funds administrator.
- Worked directly with structural engineers, loftsmen, and production to design, loft, fabricate, and install stabilizing fin to reduce shaft vibration and propeller cavitation. Completed in half the time at one-third of the estimated cost due to innovative pre-fabrication of major subassemblies.

ADDITIONAL EXPERIENCE

- Nuclear Propulsion Plant Engineering Watch Supervisor/Mechanical Division Superintendent.
- Mechanical Systems Instructor, Naval Nuclear Power Training Unit, Idaho Falls, Idaho.
- Highest security clearance held: Top Secret.

AFFILIATIONS

American Society of Mechanical Engineers, Vice President of local chapter.
American Nuclear Society, active member.

Executive Assistant   *Available: July 20XX*

PATRICK SMITH
20 Elm Street
Norwich, CT 06300
(860) 890-1234
SmithP@erols.com

OBJECTIVE: Executive Assistant for a Defense contractor where experience, motivation, and knowledge of the military will increase the number of contracts awarded annually.

SUMMARY OF QUALIFICATIONS

- 20 years experience as an administrative assistant and supervisor. Processed correspondence, transmitted messages, and operated sophisticated communications equipment.
- Computer proficient—expertise in MS Word, Excel, Access, and PowerPoint.
- Polished communicator with excellent interpersonal skills.
- Supervised 25 staff members.
- Hold a Top Secret clearance with current SBI.

PROFESSIONAL EXPERIENCE

United States Navy. Senior Communications Specialist. 1998-Present

OFFICE AND ADMINISTRATIVE MANAGEMENT

- Responsible for the operations of a 20-person staff, comprised of culturally diverse members who implemented beautification program for a submarine base.
- Possess strong clerical skills; able to type 50 wpm. Experience with Xerox, fax machines, and multi-line telephones.
- Safeguard classified material as the Confidential Material Control Clerk. Collect, distribute, file all documents and computer disks. Maintain accurate log of all material transferred.

SUPERVISION/TRAINING

- Taught Recruit Training to over 400 students maintaining the highest class average for a female group in Orlando, FL. Instructed a company of 80 on all facets of Basic training
- Supervised up to 10 staff members training on routing Naval messages, use of Message Distribution Terminal system, and Digital Encryption equipment.
- Trained and supervised 25 staff members to prepare facilities for top level civilian and military executives at the annual national Security Industrial Association (NSIA) Conference. *"...successfully planned and flawlessly executed countless details which went into making every facet of the seminar a resounding success."* (CAPT A.B. Jones, 2004)

EDUCATION & TRAINING

Bachelor of Science degree (Candidate, 2004), Eastern Connecticut State, CT
Associate degree, St. Petersburg Junior College, FL, 2002
Relevant training:
    Navy Leadership and Development Program for Supervisors
    Instructor Basic Course/Fundamentals of TQL (Total Quality Leadership)
    Basic and Advanced Communications

Financial Management   *Available: June 20XX*

JEFFREY SIMMONS
2913 West Broad St.
Fairfax, VA 22313
(703) 888-3333
SimmonsJ@erols.com

OBJECTIVE   Financial management position where extensive finance and accounting background can be used to improve a startup company's financial operations.

QUALIFICATIONS SUMMARY

ACCOUNTING AND FINANCE
- Experience in general ledger, financial analysis, budgets, projections, cash management, and supervision of accounting staff.
- Project manager for conversion to new computerized accounting system, which saved $1 million annually through reductions in personnel expenses.
- Senior accountant for a $10 million organization involved in national defense.

PLANNING
- Accurately forecasted organizations' expenditures over a 5-year period.
- Projected shortfalls and modified plans to mitigate the impact.
- Developed financial plans for organizations ranging in size from 300 to 10,000.

MANAGEMENT
- Supervised groups of 5-37 personnel involved in all facets of finance and accounting operations.
- Trained and mentored staff in both individual and team-based settings.
- Evaluated employee performance and provided suggestions for improvement.

EMPLOYMENT HISTORY

Senior Finance Director, Defense Information Systems Agency, Arlington, VA, 2005-Present
Finance Manager, Fort Hood, TX, 2000-2002
Staff Finance Officer, Fort Carson, CO, 1997-1999

EDUCATION & TRAINING

M.B.A., Finance, American University, 2004
B.S., Accounting, University of Colorado, 1997
Planning, Programming, and Budgeting Course, Fort Harrison, IN, 1999

Financial Services   *Available: August 20XX*

MARK BRANSCOM
2913 West Broad St.
Philadelphia, PA 19199
555-222-2121 (H) / 555-222-1212 (W)
MBranscom@aol.com

OBJECTIVE: A financial services position for a brokerage house where strong
communication and analytical skills will result in increased sales.

ACCOMPLISHMENTS:

Financial Management   Assisted in developing a $12 million annual budget for a department of 180 employees. Introduced new cost-cutting measures that resulted in saving $500,000 per year.

Leadership   Excelled in progressively responsible leadership positions as an officer in the U.S. Army. Natural leader who received numerous awards for excellence. Motivated and inspired organizations ranging in size from 30 to 300 personnel. Set and enforced high standards of personal and professional conduct.

Communication   Designed and developed an innovative aviation training program for the Third Armored Division. Incorporated state-of-the-art flight simulators, saving over $45,000 per month in fuel costs. Aviation training was rated the best in Europe.

Training   Raised training ratings from the worst to the best for six helicopter attack companies on two evaluations. Received a Zero Aircraft Accident Safety Award, and raised aircraft readiness rate to 85%—15% above the standard.

WORK HISTORY   **Assistant Athletic Director, Administration**, U.S. Military Academy, 2004-Present

Division Aviation Staff Officer, Third Armored Division, GE, 2000-2002

Aviation Company Commander, 11th Helicopter Company, Fort Rucker, AL, 1998-1999

Infantry Officer, U.S. Army, 1986-1997

EDUCATION: **University of Michigan, Ann Arbor, MI**
M.S. in Business Administration, Fuqua School, Duke University, 1994

United States Military Academy, West Point, NY
B.S. in General Engineering, 1986

Food Service   *Available: June 20XX*

William Lane
301 Westmoreland Street
Philadelphia, PA 19199
555-222-2121 (H) / 555-222-1212 (W)
WLane@aol.com

OBJECTIVE: Restaurant Manager for a national food service chain.

EDUCATION/TRAINING:

Associate Degree, Food Management, Central Texas College, 2001
Certified Food Manager, International Food Service Executive Association, 2003
Food Service Specialist Advanced Individual Training – 8 weeks, 1996
Basic Food Service Course – 16 weeks, 1994

EMPLOYMENT HISTORY: United States Army, 1995-Present

2nd Infantry Division, Camp Casey, Korea, 2004-Present
Senior Food Operations Manager
Supervise and assist three Food Operations Managers in the feeding of over 3,200 soldiers daily. Key accomplishments include:

- Established effective food service training programs.
- Worked with Food Operations Managers in the planning and delivery of food service.
- Conducted periodic unannounced inspections to ensure quality of food service remained consistently high.

82nd Airborne Division, Fort Bragg, NC, 2001-2003
Senior Food Operations Manager
Responsible for daily food service operations that supported 4,500 soldiers. Key accomplishments include:

- Instituted an innovative culinary specialist competition that resulted in enhancing the overall quality of dining services.
- Provided training and professional development for 65 food service personnel, including four dining facility managers.
- Ensured high quality food handling and sanitation standards through frequent checks and inspections.
- Received Commanding General's Award for best dining facility.

Various Army Bases 1991-1996
Soldier
Learned basic soldiering skills. Served in a variety of positions as a soldier in the U.S. Army. Developed sense of commitment, integrity, loyalty, and honesty.

Healthcare Administration   *Available: September 20XX*

TRACY LAKELAND
2913 West Broad St.
Fairfax, VA 22313
H: (703) 888-3333
LakelandT@earthlink.com

OBJECTIVE   Healthcare administrator position where extensive financial management experience can be used to improve the profitability of a multi-specialty ambulatory care clinic.

QUALIFICATIONS SUMMARY

HEALTHCARE ADMINISTRATION
- Ten years experience in Healthcare Administration in positions of increasing responsibility within the U.S. Navy.
- Managed health service activities, including plans and operations, human resources, logistics, patient administration, and finance.
- Directed the hospital accreditation program, which was successfully completed two months ahead of schedule.

FINANCIAL MANAGEMENT
- Managed departments from 25-600 personnel, responsible for direct supervision of up to 10 second line supervisors.
- Established and administered a $15 million budget.
- Increased third party collections by 45% while reducing expenditures by $3 million through aggressive follow-up communication.
- Developed automated financial plan, which was adopted and implemented, saving the hospital approximately $39,000 annually.

CERTIFICATION
- Certified Healthcare Executive
- Member, ACHE's Regents Advisory Council for the Army Regent

EMPLOYMENT HISTORY

Director, Healthcare Services, Walter Reed Army Medical Hospital, 2005-Present
Senior Healthcare Service Administrator, Walter Reed Army Medical Hospital, 2000-2004
Healthcare Service Administrator, Eisenhower Army Medical Center, Fort Gordon, GA, 1996-1999
Developmental Medical Service Corps positions, U.S. Army, 1987-1995

EDUCATION & TRAINING

MBA, Finance, University of Maryland, 2006
B.S.N., Penn State University, 1987

Heavy Manufacturing   *Available: October 20XX*

THOMAS F. JONES
3212 Cravens Drive
Quantico, VA 29036
W: (703) 123-4567 / H: (703) 321-9999

OBJECTIVE

A supervisory position with a large manufacturing company seeking an experienced machine operator with demonstrated management skills to improve its operations.

HIGHLIGHT OF QUALIFICATIONS

- Dedicated professional with over 15 years experience in heavy machinery.
- Expert knowledge of the operation and maintenance of a wide variety of equipment.
- Possess both hands-on and supervisory experience in heavy machinery.
- Adept, skillful communicator who interacts well with all levels of staff and management.

AREAS OF EXPERTISE

Management

Effectively supervised a staff of 30 personnel who operated and maintained heavy armor equipment. Raised the organization's equipment maintenance status 35% by instituting an innovative quality control program that stressed attention to detail in all facets of maintenance operations. Set and enforced high standards.

Heavy Equipment Maintenance

Demonstrated expertise in troubleshooting inoperable equipment using computer-based diagnostic equipment. Applied ingenuity to quickly restore equipment to operable condition. Received recognition for successfully maintaining assigned equipment at a high state of readiness throughout Operation Desert Storm.

Training

Provided expert training to monthly classes of up to 25 personnel in the operation and care of heavy armor equipment. Made course interesting while ensuring full understanding of key concepts. Received highest possible instructor rating over a three-year period.

EMPLOYMENT HISTORY

Platoon Sergeant, 18th Marine Regiment, Quantico, VA, 2005-Present
Operations Sergeant, 2nd Marine Expeditionary Unit, Camp Lejeune, NC, 2002-2004
Tank Commander, 3rd Marine Expeditionary Unit, Twentynine Palms, CA, 1999-2001
Developmental leadership positions, 1987-1998

EDUCATION & TRAINING

Cortland High School, Cortland, NY, 1987
Material Maintenance Course, Camp Lejeune, NC, 1991

Helicopter Maintenance   *Available: May 1, 20XX*

AURELIO RODRIGUEZ
432 Sailors Pointe
San Diego, CA 99212
619-231-3223 / RodriguezA@yahoo.com

OBJECTIVE: Helicopter Maintenance Supervisor position for a company that provides the U.S. Navy with aviation equipment and support.

MILITARY EXPERIENCE

Maintenance Instructor, Naval Base San Diego, 2004 - 2007
Instructed and graduated 465 students amassing 2200 podium hours in 48 classes in Quality Assurance, Work Center Supervisor and Maintenance Action Form/Subsystem Capability Impact Reporting Organizational Level. Course Curriculum Model Manager of a Chief of Naval Operations approved course in Work Center Supervisor.

Achievements:
- Qualified 4 new instructors in Aviation Maintenance Administration Management
- Successfully piloted 2 new courses – one in organizational maintenance, another in quality assurance
- Twice nominated for instructor of the Quarter

Maintenance Supervisor, Helicopter Anti-Submarine Squadron 2, San Diego, 2001-2003
Supervised 5 personnel in performing scheduled and unscheduled maintenance on the SH-60 F/H helicopter. Performed a wide range of maintenance activities affecting the power plants and transmission systems.

Achievements:
- Received the highest rating possible from higher headquarters following detailed inspection of assigned helicopters
- Received promotion based on superior performance ratings

Earlier assignments were helicopter maintenance-related and of increasing scope and responsibility during the years 1988 - 2000.

EDUCATION

B.S. Aeronautical Engineering, San Diego State University, 2004
3.5 GPA; Dean's List every semester

AWARDS

Navy Achievement Medal
Navy Commendation Medal

Homeland Security Manager

Available: March 1, 20XX

DAVID BROWN
3211 Guadalcanal Way
San Diego, CA 92111
(619) 222-3333 / BrownD@hotmail.com

OBJECTIVE: A senior-level management position where my skills and experience can be used to enhance the nation's security.

SUMMARY OF QUALIFICATIONS:

As a senior-level Marine Corps officer, responsible for a wide range of security and anti-terrorism related activities. Designed and implemented a comprehensive protection scheme that to ensure key Government leaders can continue to perform their responsibilities, even under the highest threat levels. Demonstrated ability to complete complex and dangerous missions while remaining sensitive to the morale and well being of those under my charge. Possess a current Top Secret clearance with full life-style polygraph.

CORE COMPETENCIES:

- Management
- Team Building
- Leadership
- Problem Solving
- Strategic Planning
- Financial Management

ACCOMPLISHMENTS:

Management/Leadership:

Over 20 years of experience training, managing, supervising, and leading diverse organizations to meet warfighting and readiness requirements. Established and led the Fleet-Antiterrorism Security Team Company, the first Marine Corps anti-terrorism unit on the West Coast. *Results*: High-level awards for the organization's outstanding performance.

Team Building/Problem Solving:

Developed and orchestrated the reorganization of a 5,000-person organization to more effectively accomplish its mission. *Results*: Reorganization was completed 90 days in advance of timeline with minimum personnel turbulence and frustration.

Commanded Marine Corps infantry units at every level up to Brigade. Gained combat experience as a team leader and squad leader in Vietnam. *Results*: Awarded Navy Achievement Medal with Combat "V" for valor.

Financial Management:

Developed and supervised the programming, budgeting, and execution of a $150 million operational budget, while achieving cost avoidance of over $10 million in the Marine Corps Recruiting Command. Over 20 years of fiscal management in key leadership billets. Budgets have ranged from $3 million to $150 million.

Strategic Planning:

Developed, reviewed, and assessed major operational plans for Bosnia and Kosovo while serving on the Joint Staff.

As Chief of Staff for the Marine Corps Recruiting Command, developed and orchestrated a strategic plan that resulted in major fiscal and personnel efficiencies, including an annual savings of over $67,000.

WORK HISTORY

Chief of Staff, Marine Corps Recruiting Command, Quantico, VA, 2005-Present

Orchestrate the development of all aspects of policy, marketing, advertising, sales, facilities, fiscal and personnel management, safety and training of a 5000-person, civilian and military, organization. *Results*: Annually recruited 41,000 high quality new men and women, nation-wide, with the most successful year in history in FY06. Annual operating budget is $150 million.

Commanding Officer, 3d Marine Regiment, 3d Marine Division, Hawaii, 2002-2004

Led a 4000-person crisis force focused on assessing requirements and developing anti-terrorism programs for the Asia-Pacific Region. Maintained a 6-hour crisis response element 365 days per year. Developed major operational plans for strategic events with other countries in the Region. Served as the Marine Corp's Regional Force Commander, overseeing complex planning and execution of maritime forces prepared to respond to security threats throughout the world.

Head, Bosnia Desk, Central Eastern European Division, Joint Staff, 1997-2001

Developed strategy, policy and plans for Bosnia security, anti-terrorism operations incident to interactions with senior executive members of the White House, State Department, CIA, NATO, Office of Secretary of Defense, and key European, Russian, and Japanese representatives.

Commanding Officer, 1st Battalion, 3d Marines, Hawaii, 1994-1996

Led a 1000-person crisis force focused on security, anti-terrorism requirements in the Asia-Pacific Region. Developed anti-terrorism programs. Established training, unit cohesiveness, sound fiscal and personnel management of a short notice reaction force.

AWARDS AND RECOGNITIONS

Joint Staff Badge -1992
Defense Superior Service Medal - 2003
Legion of Merit (2 awards) - 2006/2007
Meritorious Service Medal (2 awards) - 1998 and 2000

Human Resources

Available: August 20XX

JOHN C. DILLON
342 Lincoln Lane
Fayetteville, NC 91901
H: (919) 111-2222 / W: (919) 123-4567
DillonJ@aol.com

OBJECTIVE   Human Resources manager for a dynamic manufacturing firm rapidly expanding its operations and seeking to build a quality work force.

QUALIFICATIONS SUMMARY

PERSONNEL
PLANNING
- Assisted senior Army leaders in developing personnel plans and policies that improved leadership opportunities for 80,000 Army officers.
- Developed and presented briefings to senior officials on the implementation of new programs designed to reduce costs and improve quality of life.
- Recommended effective strategies for producing a smaller yet equally effective force through the use of simulation and modeling techniques.

MANAGEMENT
- As the senior officer in charge of a 500-member organization, led and executed national security-related operations.
- Effectively managed a $75 million budget.
- Instituted innovative training program that raised the overall proficiency of unit by 20%, as measured by independent Defense Department evaluators.
- Supervised and directed a staff of 30 personnel on a daily basis.

MULTICULTURAL
- Supervised 21 local national staff while stationed in Germany
- Fluent in Spanish, conversant in German

EMPLOYMENT HISTORY

Executive Officer, DCSPER, Pentagon, 2004-Present
Battalion Commander, 23rd Infantry Battalion, Germany, 2001-2003
Professor of Military Science, Bucknell University, 1997-1998
Developmental Leadership Positions, 1986-1996

EDUCATION & TRAINING

M.S., Business Administration, Wharton School, University of Pennsylvania, 2001
B.S., General Engineering, U.S. Military Academy, West Point, NY, 1987

Industrial Engineer   *Available: December 20XX*

TERRY HARPER
139 Georgia Avenue
Denver, CO 80808
499-217-3219 (H) / 499-217-9123 (W)
HarperT@earthlink.net

OBJECTIVE: **Industrial Engineering** position with a broad-based manufacturing firm in the Northeast where leadership experience and technical skills will enhance operations.

EXPERIENCE: <u>Operations Research Analyst</u>, U.S. Total Army Personnel Command, Alexandria, VA, 2004 to present
Direct a four-person analytical team developing, evaluating, and recommending personnel reduction policies mandated by Congress.

- Applied SAS programming expertise to develop computer models that optimized employees' opportunities to advance based on performance and organizational needs.
- Created and implemented a system acceptance testing plan for a $3 million out-sourced optimization model. Resulted in four critical design enhancements and an 8.2% reporting accuracy increase.

<u>Personnel Officer</u>. US Army, 3rd Support Command, Germany, 2001-2003
Managed human resource matters for a 750-employee organization including finance, education, legal support, performance appraisals, reassignments, and personnel strength.

- Standardized office on the Microsoft suite, reducing administrative processing time by 35%.
- Achieved marked improvements in personnel action processing time through enhanced training and motivational techniques.

<u>General Manager</u>. US Army, 32d Air Defense Command, Germany, 1998-2002
Supervised 180 employees with 34 different specialty skills performing maintenance and supply operations. Managed a 24-hour repair and warehouse facility servicing 13 retail customers' vehicles, missile, and communications equipment valued at $2.1 million.

- Reduced annual operating expenses from $1.5 million to $1.3 million in first year of operation while increasing customer support levels by 7.2%.
- Decreased maintenance backlog by 62.4% in three months through Production control policy changes.
- Relocated $20.3 million supply stockage increasing on-hand inventory accountability by 7.8%.

EDUCATION: **Louisiana State University**, Baton Rouge, LA.
B.S. in Industrial Engineering, 1996, Dean's List; 3.6 GPA in major

Industrial Painter   *Available: December 20XX*

TONI BLAKE
4212 Banters Lane
San Diego, CA 99812
W: 991-221-3232 / H: 991-332-4545

OBJECTIVE

Industrial Painter for a manufacturing firm in the Southeast that values high quality work and attention to detail.

SUMMARY OF QUALIFICATIONS

- Four years experience as a Navy aircraft painter.
- Painted over 150 aircraft and associated equipment.
- Hands-on experience as a Quality Control Representative.
- Adept ability to operate and maintain hand and power tools.
- Excellent team leader and motivator, easily adapt to situations.

PROFESSIONAL EXPERIENCE

Professional painter with extensive experience in the proper use and maintenance of paint guns and other power tools. Consistent performer who ensures assigned paint tasks are thoroughly planned and executed. Expert in the repair of paint guns. Resourceful and innovative—will get the job done even under conditions of high stress. Recognized expert in the paint field.

Painting Experience

- Sandblasted and sprayed ship hulls with airless operated paint units.
- Prepared surfaces to be painted; sanded walls, ceilings and woodwork.

Troubleshooting Equipment/Tools

- Keen ability to rapidly identify potential problems and take proactive steps to avert trouble.
- Excellent troubleshooter who uses technical knowledge of paint guns and other power tools to minimize time required to fix equipment.

Quality Control

- Ensure proper use of prescribed safety equipment, such as safety glasses, helmets, goggles, respirators and protective clothing. Certified to inspect completed paint work.

FORMAL TRAINING

Paint Finish and Insignia School	125 hrs
Aircraft Corrosion Control School	55 hrs

ON-THE-JOB TRAINING

Personnel and Equipment Safety Training	50 hrs
Quality Assurance Certification	75 hrs
Tool Control Training	30 hrs

Information Systems   *Available: December 20XX*

STEPHEN AKROYD
321 Memory Lane
Bethesda, MD 32112
AkroydS@aol.com
Home: 301-666-7787 / Work: 202-331-1234

CAREER OBJECTIVE

Information Systems position in a high technology firm where management and technical skills can be leveraged to the benefit of the company.

KEY SUCCESS FACTORS

Leadership: Outstanding ability to influence others to cooperate by use of common sense, personal example, persuasion and encouragement. Comfortable with authority and decision makers in crisis situations.

Management: Uses all resources to achieve goals and objectives—on time and on budget. Constantly evaluating management effectiveness, eliminating systems that are of little value.

Methodology: Reducing a problem to its basic components; determining where we are, where we want to be, and how to get there. Familiar with various philosophies including "Catalyst."

Planning: Envision "end-state"; identify requirements, research and choose alternatives, develop a blueprint for success, and develop an exit plan.

Organization: Staying logically oriented with respect to time, space, resources, information schedules and events using state of the art information and computer systems management tools.

PROFESSIONAL ACHIEVEMENTS

Information Systems   2005-Present

Considerably improved military email systems connectivity between 29 aviation sites and Washington, DC headquarters. Accomplished in both PC and Macintosh system hardware and software. Oversaw usage of a sophisticated computer tracking system for analyzing manpower flow and demographic data. Developed a web-based system capable of downloading data from several mainframe systems for demographic cost analysis and sourcing skill levels. Extensive computer network and information technology support for annual briefing requirements.

Strategic Planning Officer   2002-2004

A senior manager in procurement, strategic planning and acquisition in a fast-paced diverse environment with multilevel demands. Directed progress development and tracking of multi-million dollar major aeronautical and facility end-items. Coordinated detailed acquisition schedules and prioritized plans of actions and milestones. Personally introduced the largest free-world heavy lift helicopter into the Reserve program. This first time capability in reserves required extensive liaison with Congressional, Industry and DoD leadership.

STEPHEN AKROYD   Page 2

Systems/Training Manager (Operations Officer)   1999-2001

Directed office and field personnel conducting logistical and information coordination for updates to thousands of personnel reporting to 47 separate sites. Successful in mobilizing individual reservists for Desert Storm in the first major call-up since the Korean War.

Team Director (Base Realignment Team Leader)   1996-1998

Successfully lead BRAC 95 process action teams (PAT) of diverse ethnic, gender and cultural personnel in a crisis situation with extreme time pressured deadlines. Eliminated and reduced wasteful expenditures saving $150 million dollars. BRAC teams utilized computers, equipment and subject matter experts to successfully influence the national evaluation of facilities and space. Received Meritorious Service Medal Award for these efforts. Automated and archived approximately 100K pages of BRAC process data enabling smooth and easy retrieval. Commercial/Instrument ratings with 2500 Helicopter and multi-engine aircraft hours.

Corporate Planning Director (Reserve Aviation Plans Officer)   1993-1995

Developed plans for modernization of aviation assets through the year 2005. Wrote concept papers and briefed senior level executives on budget, joint military issues and congressional plans. Established a legacy formulating the squadron designation of new revolutionary tilt-rotor aircraft. Prepared PowerPoint briefs for executive level review.

Variety of increasingly responsible Army leadership positions,1987-1992

EDUCATION

MBA in Business Administration, National University, 1997
BA in Business Administration, Campbell University, 1987

Intelligence Analyst *Available: February 20XX*

CHRIS SIMPSON

2312 Columbus Ave
Fort Meade, MD 99902

W: (222) 231-1232
H: (222) 231-5423

OBJECTIVE Intelligence Analyst position where imagery interpretation and data analysis skills will benefit a Government contractor seeking to expand its intelligence support operations.

QUALIFICATIONS SUMMARY

IMAGERY
INTERPRETATION

- Over 10 years of specialized imagery experience with the U.S. Army.
- Keen ability to translate and interpret imagery data.
- Applied imagery interpretation skills to identify equipment location, troop movement, and other intelligence information.

SUPERVISION

- As a manager, applied technical imagery interpretation knowledge and skills to expertly guide and advise staff in all facets of imagery interpretation.
- Briefed senior management on imagery interpretation findings.
- Maintained detailed files on imagery interpretation data and findings.

PROJECT
MANAGEMENT

- As the project leader for a new imagery system, provided technical guidance and direction that ensured the system met all requirements.
- Participated in all phases of system development. Evaluated operational effectiveness of imagery interpretation equipment. Suggested cost reduction measures that, when implemented, saved $1.5 million.

TRAINING

- Trained classes of 35 students on imagery activities, including imagery interpretation methods, computer renditions, and pattern recognition.
- Developed innovative curriculum that blended classroom training with hands-on field exercises requiring demonstrated proficiency. Evaluated student understanding of imagery interpretation theory through oral and written exams.
- Ensured students mastered the use of sophisticated imagery equipment.

EMPLOYMENT HISTORY

Intelligence Project Specialist, Fort Meade, MD, 2005-Present
Intelligence Manager, 23rd Military Intelligence Detachment, Fort Drum, NY, 2001-2004
Intelligence Specialist, 22nd Military Intelligence Battalion, Baumholder, Germany, 1998-2000
Intelligence Specialist, 12th Military Intelligence Battalion, Fort Polk, LA, 1995-1997

EDUCATION & TRAINING

B.S., Geology, University of Maryland, College Park, MD, 2006
Military Intelligence Warrant Officer Technical Certification Course, 1999
Army Basic and Individualized Training, 1995

SECURITY CLEARANCE

Top Secret security clearance with current Special Background Investigation.

Law Enforcement   *Available: February 20XX*

JOSEPH A. MARTINEZ
95 Colgate Drive, Apt. 131
Killeen, TX 45886
H: (333) 222-1256 / W: (333) 111-5667

OBJECTIVE

Law enforcement position where leadership skills and military police experience will benefit a large metropolitan police force seeking dedicated, community-sensitive law enforcement professionals.

SUMMARY OF QUALIFICATIONS

- Over 10 years experience as a military policeman.
- Extensive training in traditional law enforcement operations.
- Hand-picked for clandestine counter-drug operations.
- Developed innovative and highly effective approaches to crime solving.
- Qualified expert in 9 mm hand gun.

PROFESSIONAL EXPERIENCE

Counter-Drug Specialist, 109th Military Intelligence Company, Fort Bliss, TX, 2004-Present

Infiltrate drug operations in an effort to curtail the import of illegal drugs. Employ specialized police training techniques to identify and eradicate illegal substances in foreign countries. Train foreign security forces in counter-drug techniques.

Operations Manager, 35th Military Intelligence Detachment, Fort Polk, LA, 2000-2002

Assigned tasks daily to 15 military police professionals responsible for maintaining law and order in a community of 25,000. Interacted with colleagues on a daily basis to ensure complete understanding of assigned tasks. Assisted in the training and evaluation of 9 junior military police specialists. Counseled and mentored assigned staff.

Supervisor, 12th Military Police Company, Fort Lewis, WA, 1997-1999

Supervised activities of 8 military personnel responsible for maintaining law and order. Trained and led personnel in all facets of daily police operations. Motivated staff to attain high levels of weapons proficiency. Ensured team members acted professionally and courteously at all times.

Military Policeman, 53rd Military Police Company, Fort Bragg, NC, 1994-1996

Served with distinction as a member of the 82nd Airborne Division's Military Police company. Skillfully applied military police training. Handled infractions with minimal confrontation. Received Commendation Medal for excellent police work.

EDUCATION

High School diploma, Martin Luther King High School, Atlanta, GA, 1994

Logistics Manager   *Available: February 20XX*

MICHAEL FISHER
7829 Newbury Drive
Los Angeles, CA 92101

H: 619-123-5678   E-Mail: fisherm@pacbell.net   W: 619-222-3333

OBJECTIVE:

Management level position for an aerospace firm where extensive logistics management expertise can be used to help achieve significant cost reductions and improved operating efficiencies.

QUALIFICATIONS SUMMARY:

- Over 20 years of professional experience in logistics and materials management
- Exceptional knowledge of inventory, stockage control, security, and distribution.
- Keen trouble shooter with impressive analytical, verbal, and listening skills.
- Customer-oriented professional with strong interpersonal and communication skills

PROFESSIONAL EXPERIENCE:

Chief, Management and Systems Division, McChord AFB, 2005-Present

- Analyzed trends and set procedural guidelines to correct deficiencies in a $748 million account.
- Established and enforced quality performance measurements and implemented quantifiable improvements in stockage procedures, resulting in 99% inventory accuracy.
- Initiated a study of an aging document imaging system. Revised replacement approach resulted in $35,000 savings over a contractor's estimated replacement cost.

Chief, Materiel Management Division, Homestead AFB, 2002-2004

- Achieved stockage effectiveness rate of 87% for over 100,000 line items of property in support of 120 aircraft of 32 different makes, models, designs, and series.
- Coordinated materiel management activities with over 45 organizations to ensure most critical assets were available during a period of tight budgetary constraints.
- Managed the design and installation of a $3 million automated warehouse system, resulting in a 40% increase in warehouse space and a 20% reduction in processing time.

Superintendent, Operations Support Division, Scott AFB, 1999-2001

- Developed training program for research and order placement of priority requirements. Average order time was reduced from four hours to one.
- Addressed Air Force level problems with method of transportation used to deliver parts. Recommendations resulted in 25% pipeline delivery for priority requirements.

Supply Manager, MacDill AFB, FL, 1996-1998

- Led team of 80 logistics technicians in inventorying, accounting, and securing $75 million in critical jet aircraft components in 30 days.
- Achieved established production goals in reconstituting 250 depleted part kits to 100% completion in record time.
- Eliminated duplication of services at two sites, saving 1,000 staff hours monthly, doubling warehouse capacity, and improving customer service.
- Analyzed and solved significant transportation problem affecting multiple sites. Solution resulted in reworked transportation network that resulted in documented savings of $50,000 annually.

Developmental Leadership Positions, 1987-1995

Served in progressively more responsible leader development positions in the logistics field. Consistently recognized as a superlative performer. Received numerous leadership awards.

CAREER HIGHLIGHTS:

Demonstrated leadership abilities resulted in rapid advancement to Chief Master Sergeant, the highest enlisted grade in the U.S. Air Force (top 1% of the enlisted corps). Recognized as Superintendent of the Year twice at the local level (1st out of 40 peers) and once at the Headquarters level (1st out of 200 peers).

EDUCATION:

B.S., Business Management, University of Miami, 1998
A.A., Logistics Management, Community College of the Air Force, 1996
Over 100 hours of executive Total Quality Management training.

Logistics Supervisor   *Available: June 20XX*

EDWARD DANIELS
2813 Lincoln Lane
Tacoma, WA 98031
W: (206) 918-7623 / H: (206) 231-8710

OBJECTIVE   Logistics Supervisor position for an international distribution company
                       where leadership skills and supervisory ability will enhance operational
                       effectiveness and increase profitability.

QUALIFICATIONS SUMMARY

LOGISTICS
- Assisted in directing logistics support operations of 9 Federal Aviation Administration sites and 4 Air National Guard units.
- Executed the redistribution of 2,500 supply items from deactivating sites.
- Optimized maintenance cycles, thereby decreasing time on aircraft repairable from 72 to 12 hours and costs by 28%.
- Provided subject matter expertise to the development of the Air National Guard's Mission Critical Logistics Reporting System, which enhanced the effectiveness of air operations management.

DISTRIBUTION
- Directed the requisitioning and control of aircraft parts to support a fleet of 54 aircraft and 680 vehicles. Cited by senior leaders as a major contributor to improved efficiency of warehouse operations.
- Developed the first Air National Guard inspection checklist for warehouse operations, thereby reducing customer complaints by 55% in the first year.

SUPERVISORY
- Led and guided four inspectors in performing quality control evaluations of 24 line personnel. Achieved 23% increase in proficiency without deviating from standards.
- Coordinated technical training for approximately 300 personnel over 24-month period.
- Prevented the loss of $109,000 in equipment assets by developing and enforcing strict accounting and control procedures.

INTERNATIONAL
- Extensive experience in Europe.
- Fluent in Italian.

EMPLOYMENT HISTORY: U.S. Army, 1987-Present

> *Warehouse Supervisor*, McChord Air Force Base, WA, 2004-Present
> *Distribution Manager*, Travis Air Force Base, CA, 2000-2003
> *Quality Assurance Manager*, Aviano AB, Italy, 1997-1999
> *Training Supervisor*, Andrews Air Force Base, MD, 1994-1996
> Developmental Logistics Assignments, U.S. Air Force, 1987-1993

EDUCATION & TRAINING

A.A., Business Administration, San Francisco State University, San Francisco, CA, 1998
Relevant Training: Total Quality Management Course (1988); NCO Academy (1991), Airman
    Leadership Course (1987)

Maintenance Supervisor *Available: February 20XX*

TERRY GRAHAM
5 High Street
Groton, CT 06300
H: (860) 456-7890 / W: (860) 123-4567
GrahamT@liberty.com

OBJECTIVE

Maintenance supervisor for a company in the Midwest where expertise in electro-mechanical equipment will enhance the company's maintenance operations.

PROFESSIONAL EXPERIENCE

UNITED STATES NAVY, 1993-Present

Senior Electrician

- Operate, repair and maintain components associated with electric and nuclear reactor plants; specifically, turbine and diesel generators.
- Expert knowledge of AC/DC motors and controllers, 60 Hz motor generators, circuit breakers, and voltage regulators.
- Troubleshoot complex electrical equipment minimizing critical equipment downtime
- Perform preventive and corrective maintenance and document repair procedures.
- Involved in complicated testing of steam and reactor plants
- Assess equipment during normal operation to anticipate problems.
- Read and interpret blueprints, schematics and technical manual associated with maintenance procedures.
- Solely responsible for daily operation of electric power generation

Supervisor/Project Management

- Engineering Watch Supervisor. Manage 6-10 team members in daily operation of engineering propulsion and power generation plant.
- Network administrator for 2-server Novell Local Area Networks.
- Inspect completed maintenance items to ensure all regulations and specifications are adhered to.
- Assess and prioritize job orders and assign appropriate personnel to promote timely completion.
- Liaison with Navy and civilian contractors for installation of Local Area Networks.
- Evaluate performance, document progress, counsel and motivate staff to continually improve operations.

Instructor

- Taught formal classes and on-the-job training on operation, maintenance and theory of electrical equipment.
- Reviewed and updated course curriculum, lesson plans, and tests.
- Effectively counseled students with academic and personal problems.

EDUCATION/TRAINING

Electrician's "A" School (640 hours)
Reactor Principles (80 hours)
Naval Nuclear Power School (1040 hours)
Naval Nuclear Power Training Unit (1040 hours)
Equipment Control and Distribution (80 hours)
Quality Assurance Inspector (40 hours)
Digital and Microprocessor Basics (96 hours)

Basic Novell Administration (40 hours)
Basic UNIX (40 hours)
Computer hardware/Novell installation (80 hours)
Instructor Training School (40 hours)
Sexual Harassment Prevention
Equal Opportunity Employment and Affirmative
   Action
Safety Training

PERSONAL

Currently hold Secret Security Clearance

Management Consultant   *Available: January 20XX*

ALEX SMITH
200 Meadow Crossing Way
Sterling, VA 20100
(703) 910-1234 / SmithA@aol.com

OBJECTIVE

A management consultant position where international operations experience, strategic planning, and project management expertise in the former Soviet Union will translate into new business.

HIGHLIGHT OF QUALIFICATIONS

- Successful, performance-oriented manager/leader. Strong interpersonal skills, excellent organizer, analyst/strategist. Outstanding writing and speaking skills.
- Proven success in strategic planning, coordinating requirements, and leading teams to project completion.
- Demonstrated ability to solve complex problems.
- Extensive experience in multi-cultural environments.
- Fluent in Russian, conversational in German and Ukrainian.
- Computer literate and competent with IBM-compatible programs.
- Top Secret security clearance with Special Background Investigation/polygraph.

EDUCATION

M.A., Soviet and Eastern European Studies, University of Kansas, Lawrence, KS, 2001
B.S., General Engineering, United States Military Academy, West Point, NY, 1988

PROFESSIONAL ACHIEVEMENTS

INTERNATIONAL OPERATIONS MANAGEMENT

As Site Commander, managed the operations of a $30 million nuclear missile production monitoring site established under the Intermediate-Range Nuclear Forces (INF) Treaty at Votkinsk, Russia. More recently managed a similar $5 million monitoring site at Pavlograd, Ukraine and consistently exercised all U.S. treaty rights under the Strategic Arms Reduction Treaty (START). At both facilities, supervised the daily operations and inspection activities of 30 U.S. officers and technicians. Interfaced daily with Russian/Ukrainian officials to improve the harsh living conditions and morale of U.S. treaty monitors.

HIGH-LEVEL INTERNATIONAL NEGOTIATIONS

Served as the principal On-Site Inspection Agency representative to the U.S. Ambassador, advising him on current and projected arms control treaties. Interfaced daily with officials from the Ukrainian Ministries of Defense and Foreign Affairs to resolve and implement treaty issues.

PROJECT AND ANALYTICAL MANAGEMENT

Supervised 10 highly trained civilian and military imagery interpretation specialists. Consistently managed limited personnel resources and improved production of intelligence in response to critical intelligence requirements from the National Security Council, Department of State, and other national agencies.

LOGISTICS AND TRANSPORTATION MANAGEMENT

Hands-on experience in supervising the palletization, uploading, air-transport, downloading, and joint inventory with Ukrainian Customs officials of 100 tons of monitoring equipment and supplies for the establishment of the START monitoring facility at Pavlograd, Ukraine.

SECURITY AND TRAINING MANAGEMENT

Actively managed all intelligence and security matters for a 4,100-man armored cavalry regiment. Improved the Opposing Forces training and physical security of the regiment. Supervised the Special Armor Program during the unit's initial acquisition of new M1A1 Abrams tanks.

COMMUNICATIONS/TECHNICAL EQUIPMENT MAINTENANCE MANAGEMENT

Achieved outstanding ratings during NATO tactical evaluations for managing a 30-person imagery interpretation, photo reproduction, and tactical communications unit.

ADMINISTRATIVE AND PERSONNEL MANAGEMENT

Increased assignments of critical intelligence specialists and improved the personnel management of a 700-person organization dispersed in eight locations in Germany and the United Kingdom.

EMPLOYMENT CHRONOLOGY

Commander, On-Site Inspection Agency (OSIA), Washington DC	2004-Present
Principal Advisor, Arms Control Implementation Unit, OSIA, Kiev, Ukraine	2001-2003
Branch Chief, Defense Intelligence Agency, Washington, DC	1996-1999
Staff Officer, 3rd Armored Cavalry Regiment, Fort Bliss, Texas	1993-1995
Commander, 582nd Military Intelligence Detachment, Alconbury, UK	1991-1993
Personnel Officer, 2nd Military Intelligence Battalion, Pirmasens, Germany	1990-1991
Operations Officer, 2nd Military Intelligence Battalion, Zweibrucken, Germany	1988-1990

ADVANCED TRAINING

Certificate, Russian Foreign Area Officer, U.S. Army Russian Institute, Garmisch, Germany, 2002
Graduate, Army Command and Staff College, Fort Leavenworth, Kansas, 2000
Certificate, Defense Sensor Interpretation and Application Training Program, Offutt, NE, 1996

Manufacturing   *Available: June 20XX*

JOHN T. BARNES
3212 Hunter Lane
Fayetteville, NC 92012
(919) 322-8828
BarnesJ@earthlink.net

OBJECTIVE: Production supervisor position where applied leadership, discipline, and esprit is needed to improve the efficiency and profitability of manufacturing operations.

QUALIFICATIONS SUMMARY

MANAGEMENT
- Successfully led teams ranging in size from 10 to 150 personnel in challenging national security-related missions. Applied leadership skills and motivational techniques to ensure success.
- Demonstrated the ability to quickly decompose complex tasks into smaller components, assign responsibilities, and direct operations.
- Effectively translated guidance between different management levels. Ensured team members were well informed and focused on accomplishing assigned tasks with minimum expenditure of resources.

PLANNING AND ORGANIZATION
- Planned and led various teams in physically demanding operations requiring close coordination with the other military services.
- Organized and directed the actions of 30 team members involved in various activities, ranging from scuba diving to mountain climbing.
- Devised and executed a strategy that resulted in the recovery of over $350,000 in government supplies.

COMPUTER SKILLS
- Experienced in several computer software packages, including Microsoft Word, Excel, and Access.

INTERNATIONAL
- Lived and worked in several countries.
- Fluent in Spanish, conversant in German.

EMPLOYMENT HISTORY

First Sergeant (Senior Personnel Advisor), 7th Special Forces Gp, Fort Devens, MA, 2002-Present
Operations Manager, 7th Special Forces Group, Fort Devens, MA, 1999-2001
Operations Team Leader, 10th Special Forces Unit, Fort Bragg, NC, 1995-1998
Member, Special Forces team, Fort Bragg, NC, 1994-1995
Squad Leader, Fort Benning, GA, 1993
Infantry Trainee, 1991-1992

EDUCATION & TRAINING

B.S. (Candidate, 2008), Industrial Engineering, University of Maryland
Special Forces Course (U.S. Army leadership course), 1996
Advanced NonCommissioned Officers Course, 1995
Basic NonCommissioned Officers Course, 1994
Army Basic Training, 1990

Network Specialist   *Available: December 20XX*

DAVID P. JONES
2311 Park Avenue
Langley AFB, VA 22312
Work: 540-123-4567 / Home: 540-123-1234
JonesD@aol.com

OBJECTIVE

Position as a Network Specialist for a small-to-medium size telecommunications firm where proven communication skills and self-motivation will help the organization obtain increased market share.

SUMMARY OF QUALIFICATIONS

Technically adept technician with over seven years experience providing telecommunications support to executives at the highest levels of the U.S. Government. Significant experience installing and maintaining cellular, VHF, UHF satellite, wireline, and line of sight voice and data systems. Articulate, motivated professional with strong desire to excel. Possess a Top Secret security clearance with SCI and Presidential Access Clearance.

PROFESSIONAL EXPERIENCE

Senior Radio Technician, White House Communications Agency, 2002-Present
Supervised five to eight person teams deployed worldwide to provide uninterrupted communications support for Presidential-level officials. Managed $80 million worth of communications equipment with no loss or damage. Received Army medal for outstanding communications support provided to the President and his staff.

Mobile Communication System Technician, White House Communications Agency, 1998-2001
Designed and implemented a mobile communications system that provided secure/non-secure voice, data, and facsimile service via cellular, VHF, UHF satellite, and HF mediums. Ensured high level government officials had uninterrupted communications service regardless of their itinerary. Maintained 98% readiness rate on fleet of 25 mobile communication vehicles.

Radio Operator, 101st Airmobile Division, Fort Cambell, KY, 1995-1997
Operated radio communication systems in support of unit operations. Set up and tuned radio equipment to pre-established frequencies. Transmitted, received, and logged radio messages according to military procedures. Maintained equipment in operational condition.

EDUCATION AND TRAINING

A.S., Computer Technology, Northern Virginia Community College, 2001
Tactical Satellite/Microwave Communications, Fort Gordon, GA, 1995

Outside Sales Representative

Available: June 20XX

LOIS MADISON
345 Ashford St.
Arlington, VA 22000
(703) 456-7890 / MadisonL@aol.com

OBJECTIVE

A position in Outside Sales for a small, entrepreneurial firm where demonstrated ability to bring in new accounts will be instrumental in building the firm's business base.

EXPERIENCE SUMMARY

Over twenty years of success in demanding positions in administrative management, with focus on special projects, program management, and customer and employee relations. Excellent interpersonal skills. Extensive success in recruiting with the uncanny ability to find new market pools. Primary strengths include a creative self-starter with excellent oral communication abilities coupled with many years of public speaking. High degree of personal and professional dedication to loyalty and integrity. Computer literate with knowledge of several software applications (Microsoft Suite, Lotus Notes, Windows, and Netscape). SECRET NATO clearance.

PROFESSIONAL ACHIEVEMENTS

Quality Control and Reengineering
Fort Myer, VA   **2002-2003**

Served as Project Manager on Army Performance Improvement Criteria team. Utilized the Malcolm Baldrige National Quality Award criteria to interview employees, directors, and assess historical data. Collated data and recommendations to existing processes to improve service and support for customers throughout the Washington Metro area. Received commendations from U.S. Army and Department of Defense senior leadership for producing outstanding results. Actions resulted in the reengineering of several processes.

Human Resource Management
Fort Myer, VA   **1999-2001**

Served as First Sergeant for the single largest unit in the United States Army. Serviced over 55 Federal Government agencies employing personnel in 40 states and 28 countries. Upgraded personnel qualifications systems to better ensure the maintenance of employee training, administrative and organizational requirements. Oversaw the administration and enforcement of company personnel programs and policies. Received meritorious recognition from senior executive leadership for efforts and results.

LOIS MADISON   Page 2

Recruiting
Denver Recruiting Region, Denver, CO   **1996-1998**

Served as a recruiter and regional recruiting office manager. Managed recruiting offices in rural and metropolitan areas consisting of up to seven recruiters. Developed new or improved existing recruiting markets extending up to 80,000 square miles of territory. Results included several awards as Top Producing Office, both regionally and nationwide (continuously 150-220% above production requirements), and Recruiter of the Year, worldwide.

Marketing and Sales Research and Analysis
Denver Recruiting Region, Denver, CO   **1994-1995**

Developed a Market Analysis for a District Recruiting Headquarters representing a four-state region. Collected and collated statistical data from local, county, state, and federal agencies. Efforts resulted in a market analysis, which reflected growth patterns from the past ten-year period with projected figures for the next decade that allowed for the realignment of resources. Completed project in 25% less time than any other region nationwide, with fewer resources. Commended by senior leaders for superior results.

Administrative Management
U.S. Army (various locations worldwide)   **1984-1993**

Supervised staffs over a 20-year period ranging from 3 to 25 personnel. Improved administrative management support for employees ranging from 400 to 6,000. Updated several organizational strategic and routine plans on a variety of personnel models. Managed troubleshooting of projects involving personnel and facilities. Planned, generated, executed organization-wide support for a $2 million upgrade to facilities housing over 500 personnel. Oversaw the overall property management and security of three installations housing over 1,000 soldiers and their families. Coordinated an office-automated system to improve information flow to over 55 government agencies and 2,500 personnel. Handled a myriad of daily and long-term care issues ranging from family domestic, alcohol and drug abuse cases, to assisting in major criminal investigations. Received numerous awards for improvements in morale, facilities maintenance and upkeep, and security support areas.

EDUCATION & TRAINING

B.S., Management Studies, University of Maryland, 2002
A.A. in General Studies, University of Maryland, 1998

Relevant training:

Certificate, Advanced Staff Management, Sergeant Major Academy, U.S. Army, Fort Bliss, TX
Certificate, Total Quality Management, Defense Management College, Fort Belvoir, VA
Certificate, Personnel Management, U.S. Army, Fort Bragg, NC

Personnel Management *Available: January 20XX*

LOUIS ARMSTRONG
4221 Apple Lane Court
Fort Hood, TX 77777
(678) 123-4567
larmstrong@ix.netcom.com

OBJECTIVE:

Personnel manager for a mid-to-large sized manufacturing company where proven leadership skills and a disciplined approach to problem solving will result in improved operating efficiency and increased team morale.

SUMMARY OF QUALIFICATIONS:

- Fifteen years experience in office supervision and personnel management.
- Reliable and highly motivated self-starter with an aptitude for quickly learning new tasks.
- Improved efficiency of operations through skilled application of computer technology.
- Proficient in a variety of Microsoft Office software

EMPLOYMENT EXPERIENCE:

Personnel Manager, Dyess Air Force Base, TX, 2004-Present
Provide accurate responses to over 14 inquiries daily using PC SAS and ATLAS, two commercial software packages. Provide instruction in the use of these packages to approximately 30 personnel per month. Recognized as a top instructor through both supervisor and student ratings.

Personnel Supervisor, Andrews Air Force Base, MD, 2001-2003
Managed the Air Force's largest personnel database with a staff of eight. System administrator for eight AT&T 3b2s in a network supporting over 400 users. Achieved 99% reliability rate over a two-year period. Developed and met goals aligned with management's vision.

Personnel Systems Technician, Travis AFB, CA, 1997-2000
Assisted users in preparing decision briefs for senior Air Force managers. Coordinated actions and followed up on assigned taskings to ensure successful completion of projects.

EDUCATION

B.S., Business Administration, University of Maryland, 2003.

PROFESSIONAL ACHIEVEMENTS

Navy Achievement Medal for superior performance in leadership and technical abilities. Three Letters of Commendation for superior performance and leadership.

Project Management   *Available: August 20XX*

LYNN JONES
1229 East York Ave.
New Livery, CT 09558
(Home) 913-558-9877 / (Work) 913-487-8993

OBJECTIVE: A product management position in a fast growing cellular communi-
                     cation company where organization, leadership, and communication
                     experience will be used for improving product quality and innovation.

EDUCATION   ■ B.S., Electrical Engineering, Brigham Young University, Salt Lake
& TRAINING: City, UT, 1994
                     ■ Information Management Course, Fort Gordon, GA, 1999
                     ■ U.S. Army Signal Officer Advanced Course, Fort Gordon, GA, 1997
                     ■ U.S. Army Signal Officer Basic Course, Fort Gordon, GA, 1994

EXPERIENCE: 1992-Present, U.S. Army, Captain, Signal Corps

Organization   Designed and coordinated communications for Pacific Command Joint
                     Training Exercises. Organized and chaired engineering conferences.
                     Presented decision briefings and prepared staff action papers for a
                     variety of communication-related issues of considerable importance to
                     the command. Served as Watch Officer during field exercises.

Leadership   Installed, operated, and maintained satellite, switching, cable, and
                     message communications in support of numerous U.S. Army units
                     distributed throughout central Germany. Led 110 soldiers in performing
                     all assigned communications missions. Total responsibility for the
                     soldiers under my command.

Communication   Planned and supervised installation of telecommunication systems of
                     V Corps exercises. Maintained and accounted for vehicle and com-
                     munications equipment valued at approximately $1.5 million. Planned
                     and conducted individual and collective training in technical skills and
                     general military subjects. Supervised, trained, and led 23 personnel.

WORK   *Communication Staff Officer,* 12th Signal Brigade, Fort Lewis,
HISTORY: Washington, 2004-Present

                     Communications Company Commander, C Company, 430th Signal
                     Battalion, Mainz, Germany, 2001-2003

                     Platoon Leader, B Company, 17th Signal Battalion, Hoechst, Germa-
                     ny, 1998-2000

Project Manager

Available: March 20XX

PETER R. SMITH
2913 West Broad St.
Fairfax, VA 22313
H: (703) 888-3333 / W: (202) 132-7654
SmithP@aol.com

OBJECTIVE   Project Management position where organizational and technical skills will assist an international telecommunications firm implement systems on time and within budget.

EDUCATION & TRAINING

M.S., Computer Science, Cornell University, Ithaca, NY, 1994
B.S., General Engineering, U.S. Military Academy, West Point, NY, 1985
Relevant training: Courses and seminars on Project Management, Systems Engineering, Budgeting

QUALIFICATIONS SUMMARY

PLANNING & ORGANIZATION
- Created and implemented world-wide ISDN installation plan, which was completed on schedule and 15% below budget.
- Developed PERT charts to manage 18-month project to upgrade a telecommunications network, reducing system downtime by 20%.
- Coordinated multi-service exercises with other military services and NATO countries. Validated interoperability of communications systems.

MANAGEMENT
- Managed a 150-person mobile communications unit that was consistently rated best in the organization (1st of 4).
- Re-engineered a personnel management process, resulting in a 20% improvement in staff efficiencies.
- Integrated innovative training techniques that reduced the program course length by one week, saving the government $500,000 per year.
- Planned, programmed, budgeted, and executed an X.400-based electronic mail program for 5,000 users; reduced dependency on proprietary system

TECHNICAL
- Registered Professional Engineer.
- Over 20 years experience in systems engineering, telecommunications, and management information systems.
- Led technically complex acquisition project involving the development and fielding of an all-digital, fiber optic communications network.
- Designed and developed AI-based quality control system that reduced processing errors by 50%.

EMPLOYMENT HISTORY

Communications Director, Fort Hood, TX, 1998-Present
Project Officer, Defense Information Systems Agency, Arlington, VA, 1995-1997
Communications Operations Staff Officer, Frankfurt, Germany, 1992-1994
Communications Manager, Fort Gordon, GA, 1989-1991
Systems Analyst, Pentagon, Washington, DC, 1985-1987
Various Engineering and Junior Management Positions with the U.S. Army, 1981-1984

Public Relations   *Available: June 20XX*

THOMAS HART
3212 Eisenhower Lane
Waldorf, MD 20717

Home: (301) 111-2222   Work: (202) 765-4321   E-mail: HartT@aol.com

---

PUBLIC RELATIONS / MEDIA RELATIONS / COMMUNICATIONS / SPECIAL EVENTS
Talented public relations strategist and campaign director with 20+ years professional experience. Expertise in community/public outreach, multimedia communications, publications management, and crisis management. Accomplished in managing relationships with major print and broadcasting media nationwide. Skilled in large-scale event coordination and management. Consistently effective in meeting budget and schedule requirements.

PROFESSIONAL EXPERIENCE: U.S. Navy, 1987-Present

> *Fast-track promotion through a series of increasingly responsible public relations/public affairs positions nationwide as one of only 200 designated spokespersons in the U.S. Navy. Won several distinguished commendations for outstanding performance in the management of sensitive public relations programs and initiatives.*

Public Relations / Public Affairs, *2003-Present*

- Rebuilt and revitalized inactive public relations function aboard the USS Kitty Hawk.
- Developed course content and taught public relations at seminars.
- Publicized the Navy's assistance to victims of earthquakes and other natural disasters, winning positive media coverage and strengthening the Navy's image.
- Wrote public relations guidelines for Congressional visits emphasizing the management of high profile events and strategies to leverage media exposure.
- Trained and supervised teams of up to 24 PR specialists in printing, graphic arts, photography, media relations, community outreach, and administrative support.

Media / Press Relations, 1999-2002

- Represented the U.S. Navy in front of major print and broadcast media nationwide, including network affiliates, national and local correspondents, National Public Radio, and several major publications, including the *Washington Post, New York Times, Los Angeles Times, Wall Street Journal, Time,* and *Newsweek.*
- Managed liaison affairs with local, national, and international press, White House Press Office, Arlington National Cemetery, and National Cathedral for national coverage of memorial services for national dignitaries.
- Coordinated media events for the first U.S. port visit by Russian warships in 20 years. Managed affairs for 300+ media over a five-day period.

EDUCATION:
B.A., English Literature, Norfolk State University, 1997

SECURITY CLEARANCE:
Top Secret / SCI

Registered Nurse   *Available: January 20XX*

MARY BARKELY
2913 West Broad St.
Fairfax, VA 22313
(703) 888-3333 / BarkelyM@erols.com

OBJECTIVE   Full-time Nurse Practitioner in a Family Practice or Primary Care facility that seeks the services of an experienced and dedicated registered nurse.

QUALIFICATIONS SUMMARY

NURSE PRACTITIONER
- Provided direct nursing care for a variety of acutely/chronically ill adult and pediatric patients in both an in-patient and out-patient care setting.
- Experienced in Pediatrics and Neonatal Intensive Care Units.

MANAGEMENT
- Developed management policies and operating instructions that resulted in more timely and higher quality health care.
- Defined scope of patient care based on doctor prognosis.
- Implemented quality improvement initiatives that generated positive patient feedback on received health care.

NURSING ADMINISTRATION
- Oversaw daily clinical/administrative operations for a 500-bed hospital.
- Supervised, trained, and evaluated 105 nurses, paraprofessionals, and administrative support personnel.
- Planned and directed nursing care activities in Intensive Care Unit.

CERTIFICATIONS
- Certified in Medical Surgical Nursing by the American Nurses Credentialing Center.
- National Certification Corporation for the Obstetric, Gynecologic, and Neonatal Nurse Specialties.
- Advanced Cardiac Life Support Certification.

EMPLOYMENT HISTORY

Department Head, Eisenhower Army Medical Center, Fort Gordon, GA, 2003-Present
Nurse Practitioner, Walter Reed Army Medical Hospital, 1997-2002
Registered Nurse, Surgical Room, Tripler Army Medical Hospital, Honolulu, HI, 1991-1996
Registered Nurse, Emergency Room, Tripler Army Medical Hospital, Honolulu, HI, 1985-1990

EDUCATION & TRAINING

M.S., Nursing, Central Michigan, 1995
B.S., Nursing, University of North Dakota, 1985

Sales Trainer   *Available: June 20XX*

JAMES L. PARK
2829 Creekview Court
Quantico, VA 22312
W: (703) 290-1212 / H: (703) 291-9999
ParkJ@aol.com

OBJECTIVE   Sales training position for a consumer products company seeking
                     highly motivated individual with outstanding salesmanship skills.

QUALIFICATIONS SUMMARY

RECRUITING   ▪ Interacted with candidates and their parents on a daily basis.
                  Highlighted the benefits of military service.
                ▪ Surpassed recruitment goals by 15% annually.
                ▪ Visited over 100 local high schools and community colleges
                  to attract top-notch Marine candidates.

TRAINING   ▪ Indoctrinated 150 new recruits into the traditions and practices
                  of the Marine Corps.
                ▪ Physically and mentally challenged new recruits, preparing them
                  for a wide range of national security related assignments.
                ▪ Trained new recruits on the use of various weapon systems.
                  Achieved unit proficiency rating of 95%.

MANAGEMENT   ▪ Led and directed the activities of a 10-member team; improved both
                  their individual and team skills.
                ▪ Counseled and mentored subordinates; evaluated their performance
                  and provided development advice.

EMPLOYMENT HISTORY

Recruiter, US Marine Corps, Atlanta, GA, 2004-Present
Drill Instructor, US Marine Corps, Parris Island, SC, 2000-2003
Squad Leader, US Marine Corps, Okinawa, Japan, 1997-1999
Member of Squad, US Marine Corps, Okinawa, Japan, 1994-1996

EDUCATION & TRAINING

A.S., Business Administration, Albany Community College, GA, 2005
Marine Corps Recruiter's School, 2004
Advanced Leadership Training, 1997
Marine Corps Basic Training, 1994

Security   *Available: January 20XX*

FRANCIS MITCHELL
1100 Main Street
Dugway, UT 84000
Home: (801) 890-1234 / Work: (801) 123-4567
MitchellF@earthlink.net

PROFESSIONAL PROFILE

Over 15 years experience in Security and Intelligence Operations worldwide. Combines strong planning, analysis, organizational and communications skills with excellent qualifications in the development of security operations. Skilled personnel manager and budget administrator. Expertise includes:

- Scientific & Technical Intelligence
- Tactical Assessment/Planning
- Document Security/Control
- Security Training & Team Leadership

- Operations & Personnel Security
- Counter-Terrorism
- Counter-Espionage
- Reporting/Analysis

Excellent knowledge of the Freedom of Information Act and security policies of U.S. and foreign governments. Familiar with general security practices followed by major industries and corporations nationwide. Held highest level U.S. Government security clearance and positions of trust.

PROFESSIONAL EXPERIENCE

Intelligence & Security Officer, U.S. Army   1992 to Present
Logistics Officer, U.S. Army   1984-1991

Fast-track promotion throughout career. Advanced through a series of increasingly responsible security and intelligence positions with organizations operating worldwide. Won numerous honors and commendations for capabilities in threat analysis, intelligence collection/analysis, security operations planning and personnel training. Career highlights include:

Security Operations Planning & Management

- Authored several major documents impacting security and intelligence operations worldwide. Provided the strategy, organizational structure and processes for security operations development, management and expansion in response to changing demands of worldwide operations.

- Hosted two intelligence planning committees of multi-disciplinary intelligence and operating management personnel challenged to enhance security and operations planning worldwide.

- Provided high-level security and intelligence support to technologically advanced systems and engineering projects.

Intelligence Collection & Analysis

- Directed large-scale intelligence research, collection, analysis and dissemination operations to provide top management with critical information regarding potential threats, breeches to security and technical intelligence.

FRANCIS MITCHELL   Page 2

- Initiated processes to overcome shortcomings in intelligence collection and analysis vital for the success of major projects.

- Authored reports, led executive-level presentations and coordinated information flow between various public and private organizations.

Personnel Training, Supervision & Development

- Designed and led training programs in security and intelligence for operative personnel, management and executives worldwide. Created customized presentations to meet specific operating requirements of each organization.

- Trained, scheduled, supervised and evaluated work performance of up to 85 personnel.

Budgeting & Financial Management

- Participated in the long-term administration of a $7 million annual budget. Provided timely and accurate input to high-level reports and discussions addressing operations planning and budget requirements.

Achievements & Project Highlights

- Developed processes to maintain control of more than 70,000 sensitive security documents.

- Managed systems development and implementation project to computerize a large technical scientific library and integrate advanced optical data technology for long-term document retention.

- Built cooperative working relationships with government agencies worldwide to facilitate the timely exchange of information critical to intelligence and security operations.

- Extensive technical knowledge of chemical, biological, and radiological security threats, electronic surveillance technology, electronic counter-measures and munitions technologies.

EDUCATION

Bachelor of General Studies, Kent State University, 1986

Completed 350+ hours of continuing professional training in Security and Intelligence. Program included scientific and technical intelligence collection/analysis, leadership, and supervisory skills.

Security Management   *Available: January 20XX*

WARREN THOMAS
2480 Davis Circle
Washington, DC 29036
H: (202) 111-2222 / W: (202) 222-3345
ThomasW@aol.com

OBJECTIVE   An organizational development position with a security company requiring discipline, strength, and management expertise.

SUMMARY   Motivated, charismatic leader who seeks responsibility and accomplishes tasks in a professional, timely manner. Strong interpersonal skills have been demonstrated in a range of security-related assignments. Quickly adapt to new and physically challenging environments. Strong leadership skills were refined throughout Army service.

EXPERIENCE   <u>Leadership</u>. Responsible for the well-being, discipline, morale, and readiness of a 30-member unit. Set and enforced high standards in the areas of personal appearance, physical fitness, and weapons qualifications. Demonstrated leadership, supervision, management, and team building skills.

<u>Training</u>. Assisted in developing weekly training and development plans. Helped establish and conduct training programs in the areas of nuclear, biological, and chemical protection, physical fitness, land navigation, weapons qualifications, and equipment maintenance.

<u>Management</u>. Organized and led a 10-member team through numerous missions. Planned team work schedules and training for accomplishing mission objectives. Set and enforced high standards of performance.

<u>Supervision</u>. First line supervisor responsible for the productivity of a four-man team. Organized training, planned daily activities, and supervised team members.

**WORK
HISTORY**   **Platoon Sergeant**, 3rd US Infantry, Fort Myer, VA, 2003-present
Training Supervisor, 3rd US Infantry, Fort Myer, VA, 1999-2002
Infantry Squad Leader, 3rd US Infantry, Fort Myer, VA, 1996-1998
Team Leader, 197th Infantry Brigade, Fort Benning, GA, 1993-1995

TRAINING   - Infantry Advanced Noncommissioned Officers Course, 1999
- Infantry Basic Noncommissioned Officers Course, 1997
- Leadership Development Course, Noncommissioned Officers Academy, 1995
- Infantry Basic Training, 1989

Senior Electrician   *Available: August 20XX*

CHRISTOPHER BRADLEY
2813 Lincoln Lane
Las Vegas, NV 98031
W: (206) 918-7623 / H: (206) 231-8710

OBJECTIVE

Senior electrician position for a commercial aircraft manufacturer seeking to benefit from the experiences of a highly trained and motivated aircraft electrician.

QUALIFICATIONS SUMMARY

Air Force electrician with over 8 years of first-hand experience in the installation and maintenance of electrical systems on jet aircraft. Trained in effectively troubleshooting electrical systems using specialized diagnostic and test equipment. Dependable, hard-working professional who perseveres until all tasks are successfully accomplished. Recipient of numerous military awards.

WORK HISTORY

Electrical Supervisor, Nellis Air Force Base, NV, 2002-Present

Oversaw the electrical maintenance activities in a large Air Force maintenance shop. Designed and implemented maintenance procedures for fellow electricians. Performed numerous quality control checks. Trained electricians on various electrical maintenance activities. Improved aircraft readiness level by 32%.

Senior Electrician, Kelly Air Force Base, 1999-2001

Responsible for maintenance of all electrical components in the C-5 aircraft. Supervised nine electricians in all facets of operations. Developed maintenance checklists to ensure major electrical components were 100% operational before release. Used computer-based diagnostic tools to rapidly isolate deficiencies. Repaired electrical components, including generators and electric motors.

Electrician, Travis Air Force Base, CA, 1991-1994

Used wiring diagrams in the maintenance of various electrical components in the U.S. Air Force's F-16 jet fighter. Repaired or replaced various electrical instruments, including tachometers, temperature gauges, and altimeters. Used soldering equipment to solidify electrical connections. Replaced faulty wiring.

EDUCATION & TRAINING

A.A., Electrical Theory, Community College of the Air Force, 2003
Fundamentals of Electricity, 1995

Senior Operations Manager

Available: February 20XX

MARK FRANCIS
Box 900
APO AE 09120
011-49-711-678-1234
FrancisM@aol.com

OBJECTIVE

Senior operations manager for a Defense-related firm where discipline, drive, energy, and innovation will contribute to improved organizational performance.

CAREER PROFILE

Distinguished military career leading the planning, staffing, budgeting, technology and operations of organizations throughout the U.S. and abroad. Expert in cross-functional team building and leadership, multi-cultural communications, change management, organization development and quality/performance improvement. Traveled, lived and/or worked in more than 30 countries worldwide.

PROFESSIONAL EXPERIENCE

UNITED STATES MARINE CORPS   1984 to Present

Branch Chief / Commanding Officer / Executive Officer
Operations Officer / Logistics Officer / Safety Director

Fast-track career promotion through a series of increasingly responsible management positions leading large-scale operations worldwide. Currently hold the rank of Lieutenant Colonel. Received numerous commendations and awards for leadership.

Operations Management

- More than 20 years' management experience in the strategic planning, staffing, budgeting, resource allocation and leadership of administrative, field, flight, maintenance equipment, technology, training and logistics operations worldwide. Skilled policymaker.
- Direct and decisive leadership qualifications with particular strengths in planning, performance improvement, quality improvement and productivity gain.
- Experienced in the start-up and leadership of new operations and organizations.

Human Resources Affairs & Team Leadership

- Led teams of up to 500 personnel with full responsibility for work assignments, scheduling, performance review, disciplinary action and long-term career planning/development/ promotion.
- Expert qualifications in evaluating personnel needs and developing responsive training programs.
- Managed the audit and examination of personnel records to ensure regulatory compliance.

Budgeting & Financial Management
- Administered up to $50 million in annual budgets to support operations worldwide.
- Expert in evaluating organizational funding requirements, preparing/leading formal budget presentations, allocating the distribution of funds, and managing complex financial analysis and reporting functions.

Safety Management
- Extensive qualifications in the planning, development and leadership of occupational, workplace, transportation and aviation safety programs supporting operations throughout the U.S. and abroad.
- Equally extensive qualifications in safety training program design and instruction.

Technology Management
- Spearheaded the operational test, analysis and review of advanced navigational, telecommunications and operating support systems to evaluate performance and reliability.
- PC skills in word processing, database and spreadsheet applications.

Flight Operations
- Planned, staffed, budgeted and directed flight transportation operations worldwide.
- Directed flight planning and scheduling, aircraft operations, aircraft maintenance, aviator training and flight instructor training programs.
- Designated Naval Aviator with over 6100 hours of total flight time with no incidents.
- Four-year tenure as Presidential Command Pilot.

Project Coordination & Leadership
- Planned and directed cooperative operations between the U.S., France, Germany and the United Kingdom through direct leadership of multinational teams.
- Led joint efforts on behalf of the U.S. Government, U.S. embassies, Pentagon and State Department to facilitate emergency relief, assistance and humanitarian programs.

Communications
- Strong written communication, public speaking, and senior-level presentation skills.

EDUCATION & TRAINING

M.A., International Relations, University of Southern California, 1992
B.A., History, Indiana University, 1984

Graduate of numerous management and leadership training programs.

Senior Program Administrator

Available: June 20XX

SAMUAL MATTISON
10 Parkwood Lane
Groton, CT 06300
(860) 412-3456 / MattisonS@aol.com

OBJECTIVE

A Senior Program Administrator position where knowledge and technical expertise in facilities management will improve the efficiency of a firm's manufacturing operations.

PROFESSIONAL EXPERIENCE

UNITED STATES NAVY, 1981-Present

Project/Program Manager

- Managed a $200 million budget in an increasingly constrained and technically complex environment. *Saved $6 million in maintenance resources through skillful fixed-price negotiations.*
- Monitored General Electric operations of four Nuclear Propulsion Prototypes ensuring compliance with Naval Reactors, OSHA and EPA procedures for training and test requirements. Graded satisfactory on annual audits.
- Directed multiple industrial activities: job scoping and sequencing; quality control procedures; and personnel training. Ensured best product, least cost, shortest time.

   Special recognition: *"The success of the NR-1 $80 million Refueling Overhaul is due to LCDR Mattison's superior management and attention to detail."*—J. P. Smith, Vice Admiral, Navy Commendation Medal

Supervisor/Trainer

- Directed and supervised 40 technical writers in preparation of detailed, step-by-step, user friendly preventive and corrective maintenance procedures (3M) for a 1000-man production work force.
- Assessed department needs and problems, identified and recommended solution, developed realistic and achievable goals, and designed on-the-job training programs to eliminate discrepancies, increased productivity and enhanced skills of employees (e.g., revised the Basic Nuclear Electrician's Rate curriculum). *Reduced attrition by 23%.*
- Evaluated personnel semiannually: focused on contributions, character and accomplishments; counseled on ways to increase skills and advance in career. *Achieved a 95% success rate for electricians' advancement to E-5. Eighteen students were selected for officer commissioning programs.*
- Administered and implemented preventive and corrective maintenance program (3M), assigned and scheduled technicians based on skill and experience, inspected work ensuring compliance with regulations and technical specifications, and verified accurate documentation into records.

SAMUAL MATTISON   Page 2

Technical

- Researched, compiled and evaluated data and statistics to write reports and make formal presentations, with decision points to department heads and Chief Executive Officers. *Saved $2 million by identifying and eliminating an outdated time phased hydraulic control valve maintenance program.*
- Planned, scheduled and directed attack submarine employment, resulting in on-time departure and electronic suite certification.
- As quality assurance officer, continuously inspected Naval equipment to ensure operational readiness in a safe manner.

Quality Control

- Implemented radiological controls, nuclear work practices, radiographic operations and quality control procedures. Identified and developed solutions to resolve work practices discrepancies, before they impact production.
- Sent weekly letters to the Director, Naval Nuclear Propulsion Program, on mechanical and fluid systems compliance, with recommended solutions. *One recommendation to a nuclear valve was incorporated locally and fleet-wide, saving an estimated $1 million in corrective maintenance.*

EDUCATION & TRAINING

B.S., Nuclear Engineering Technology, Thomas Edison State College, Trenton, NJ, 2003

PROFESSIONAL AFFILIATIONS

American Nuclear Society
American Society of Mechanical Engineers

HONORS/AWARDS

Numerous awards and citations for leadership, supervision, and project management.

"Singled out by Squadron Four Commanding Officers and the Force Commander for timely and expert preparation of four SSN's for deployment."—A. W. Adams, Commodore, Navy Commendation Medal

"Conceived and implemented a harbor tug overhaul plan with a cost savings of $750,000. The success of this project was due to his thorough planning and resourceful initiatives by obtaining a harbor tug from Naval Station Rota, Spain."—M. D. Frank, Commodore

Senior Welder   *Available: January 20XX*

DANA WILLIAMS
100 Berry Drive
Groton, CT 05500
(860) 432-1066 / WilliamsD@hotmail.com

OBJECTIVE

Senior welder position for a large shipbuilding company where demonstrated expertise can
be used to expand the range of client services.

SUMMARY OF QUALIFICATIONS

- 8 years of military service as a welder, pipefitter, shipfitter, instructor, and supervisor.
- Experienced working from complex plans, blueprints, and sketches in conjunction
  with fabricating or repairing existing or new equipment of steel structures.
- Excellent interpersonal communication skills.
- Work well independently and as a team member.

WORK EXPERIENCE

United States Navy, Naval Station Norfolk, 1999-Present

- Identify metals using a variety of methods from continuous identification system to
  spark configuration.
- Strictly adhere to all safety procedures and regulations associated with cutting,
  welding, and with all shop equipment.
- Administer and perform formal preventive and corrective maintenance program which
  decreased maintenance cost and equipment failures by 50%.
- Hands-on supervisor and senior technician directly responsible for all aspects of
  safety, repair, maintenance of 17 different types of steel structures and piping.
- Assess job order and assign personnel according to capabilities, ensuring all work is
  completed in a timely and professional manner.

EDUCATION AND TRAINING

Bachelors Degree (Candidate, 2009), Liberal Arts, Norfolk State University
Welder, Journeyman License, 2000

Software Engineer   *Available: May 20XX*

DAVID M. JACKSON
8841 Greensboro Drive
Bedford, MA 01755
617-232-3212 / DavidJ@aol.com

OBJECTIVE

Software engineering position for a small to mid-sized firm where information technology skills can be used in all phases of software development life-cycle.

SUMMARY OF QUALIFICATIONS

Software Engineer with over 10 years experience in the U.S. Air Force. Skilled in the design and development of large-scale, object-oriented software applications. Demonstrated expertise in C, C++, and SQL programming languages. Experience includes systems analysis and programming in hardware environments ranging from desktops to IBM mainframes. Expert software trainer with strong interpersonal and communication skills. Recognized as a skilled programmer who can rapidly adapt to a variety of challenging environments.

PROFESSIONAL EXPERIENCE

Software Engineer, Hanscom Air Force Base, MA, 2006-Present
> Developed custom software applications using 3rd and 4th generation programming languages (e.g., C, C++). Hands-on experience in the use of CASE and other information engineering tools. Reduced projected software development time 25% through effective software module reuse.

Senior Computer Programmer, Travis Air Force Base, CA, 2002-2005
> Designed and developed complex software applications involving the transport of air passengers using the "C" programming language. Innovative software design was credited for decreasing development time by 23%. Assisted in the implementation and fielding of the software modules at over 15 Air Force bases where manifests had previously been done manually. Provided training to over 225 users at bases worldwide.

Computer Programmer, Travis Air Force Base, CA, 1999-2001
> Designed and developed COBOL-2 software applications that increased the efficiency of personnel processing actions affecting the records of approximately 8,000 military personnel. Programming was done on an IBM 3090 mainframe running MVS/TSO. Received Air Force commendation medal for saving the government over $25,000 in labor costs annually.

EDUCATION AND TRAINING

A.A., Computer Programming, College of the Air Force, 2003
Special Courses and Seminars: Systems Analysis, Programming in "C++," Object Oriented Programming and Design, 1998

Staff Recruiter *Available: June 20XX*

Mary Tyler
2122 Maryland Avenue
Fort Meade, MD 20311
W: (333) 222-3334 / H: (333) 555-4444
TylerM@aol.com

OBJECTIVE

In-house staff recruiter for an international consulting firm needing assistance in attracting and recruiting high quality professional staff.

SUMMARY OF QUALIFICATIONS

Resourceful military recruiting specialist with over 7 years experience. Exceptional interpersonal skills demonstrated in several successful assignments as a recruiter. Adept salesperson accustomed to meeting and exceeding demanding recruitment targets. Strong communicator with polished interpersonal skills.

PROFESSIONAL EXPERIENCE

Senior Recruiter, Baltimore, MD, 2004-Present

Exceeded target enlistment goals by 23%. Recruited high quality (Category I) candidates at the highest rate ever recorded in the state of Maryland. Recognized by the Eastern Region recruiting officer for the outstanding results attained. Received Navy Recruiter of the Year award for 2000.

Recruiting Specialist, Dallas, TX, 2002-2005

Totally revamped the Dallas recruiting program. Aggressively identified and recruited candidates from diverse ethnic backgrounds. Ensured recruitment candidates understood the responsibilities and rewards of Naval service. Raised percentage of recruits with high school degrees by 21% over 3 years.

Personnel Specialist, Naval Air Station, Oceana, VA, 1998-2001

Assisted in the coordination and distribution of Naval policies related to recruiting. Quickly learned all facets of the recruitment business. Rapidly comprehended complex personnel matters in minimal time. Recommended for early promotion and assignment as a Naval recruiter.

EDUCATION & TRAINING

A.A., Personnel Administration, Towson State University, MD, 2004
Naval Recruiters School, Norfolk, VA, 2002
Basic Training, Charleston, SC, 1996

Systems Engineer   *Available: July 20XX*

JEFFREY P. McCORMICK

1900 Novak Street   Office: (703) 903-2245
Carlton, Virginia 22400   Residence: (703) 432-1234

Objective:

Systems engineering position for an engineering consulting firm where technical skills
and proven management expertise will further enhance the firm's reputation for
excellence.

Summary of Qualifications:

Talented executive with proven skills in systems engineering, design engineering,
installation team supervision, and budget management. Extensive experience working
with leaders of key organizations to facilitate project implementation. Superb negotiating
skills to resolve issues and ensure successful project implementation. Ability to hire and
supervise large, talented, and motivated staff. Aggressive at identifying and resolving
inefficient procedures.

Professional Experience:

Computer Network Systems Analyst
Pentagon, Washington, DC, 2004-Present
Office of Secretary of Defense
  Responsible for computer network management and data traffic analysis for a computer
  networking system consisting of a fiber optic baseband Ethernet backbone supporting 10
  subnets arranged in a star/bus topology. System provides office automation, file transfer,
  electronic mail, calendar, and various other functions, to over 4,000 users, through four
  communications protocols: Transmission Control Protocol/Internet Protocol (TCP/IP),
  Xerox Network System (XNS), Novell Interpacket Exchange (IPX), and Digital Network
  (DecNet). Directly responsible for monitoring system errors and difficulties, engineering
  solutions, ordering equipment, and working with commercial vendors to implement.

Deputy Commander
Osan Air Base, Korea, 2001-2003
  Directed operation and maintenance (O&M) of vital communications and computer
  systems supporting 15,000 people. Managed 680 people, $2.5 million budget, and equip-
  ment assets worth $200 million. Developed emergency evacuations and operational plans
  for imminent natural disaster—subsequent implementation proved flawless. Planned and
  supervised removal of Department of Defense communications assets after volcanic
  eruptions. Involved planning to satisfy ongoing communications requirements, developing
  removal schedules, making team assignments, identifying budgeting methods, and arranging equipment transportation. Directly supervised 230-person workforce consisting of
  civilian contractors, foreign nationals, and military personnel.

Director of Communications
New Boston Air Force Station, New Hampshire, 1997-1998

Directed operations and maintenance of communications and computer systems supporting satellite operations. Directly supervised 23 people. Managed annual budget of $1.5 million and equipment assets worth $10 million. Developed and implemented plan to merge two organizations. Reduced manpower by 10% and administrative costs by 20% by upgrading computer systems. Worked with home office to validate requirement for new telephone switching equipment. Engineered solution, identified acquisition methods, obtained funding, and resolved contracting issues.

Commander
Zweibrucken Air Base, Germany, 1993-1996

Responsible for engineering, procurement, manufacturing, and installation of command post voice and data communications throughout Europe. Controlled annual budget of $2 million and warehouse stock exceeding $2 million. Supervised 150 employees. Turned a faltering, inefficient organization around in 3 months with dedicated group of professionals. Ensured functional integration of all communications systems, including VHF, UHF, and HF radios, telephone systems, secure communications systems, and teleconferencing equipment. Developed and implemented extensive quality assurance program and created specialized manufacturing and installation teams. Results: quality product, manufacturing costs cut by 30%, travel expenses reduced by 50%.

Executive Officer/Chief of Staff
Tinker Air Force Base, Oklahoma, 1992-1993

Responsible for tasking management staff directing 29 organizations involved in engineering, manufacturing, installation, and maintenance of communications systems throughout the world. Systems included VHF/UHF radios, radio control tower consoles and communications, computer systems, weather equipment and satellite terminals. Developed and implemented procedures for installation team deployment and progress reporting. Increased on-time starts by 20% and eliminated work stoppages. Directed implementation of systems engineering approach for all large projects, eliminating engineering errors and duplication. Provided customers with high quality communications systems.

Communications Systems Engineer
Griffiss Air Force Base, New York, 1990-1991

Designed, procured, and installed complex communications systems using a systems engineering approach. Handpicked as part of elite team of system engineers tasked with upgrading Berlin radar approach control facility and communications systems; served as on-site engineer during installation efforts. Supervised on-site installation teams and developed standard engineering procedures for over 100 locations.

Education:

M.S., Aviation Science, Embry-Riddle Aeronautical University, AZ, 1997
B.S., Electrical Engineering, University of New Hampshire, NH, 1987

Telecommunications Manager   *Available: July 20XX*

LISA JONES
4321 Sheppard's Landing
Fort Lewis, WA 99999
(999) 111-2222 / JonesL@hotmail.com

PROFILE

Intelligent, technology-savvy professional with strong technical background. Experienced leading classified technical projects of significant importance. Top Secret clearance.

EDUCATION & TRAINING

U.S. Military Academy, West Point, New York
  B.S. Computer Science, 1999; 3.6 GPA; Dean's List all 4 years

MILITARY EXPERIENCE   Captain, Signal Corps, U.S. Army

Communications Staff Officer, 12th Signal Brigade, Fort Lewis, WA, 2005-Present. Design, develop, and recommend plans to ensure continuous, secure communications between ground and sea-based units. Key responsibilities include:

- Design and engineer voice and data communication circuits
- Provide expert advice to senior management regarding the most cost-effective manner to deploy secure mobile communications systems.

Communications Company Commander, C Company, 50th Signal Battalion, Fort Bragg, NC, 2002-2004.

Led 110 telecommunications specialists in successfully performing a variety of communications-related missions under challenging and stressful conditions. Organized and planned all activities associated with the installation, operation, and maintenance of voice and messaging systems in support of Army units distributed throughout central Germany. Accomplishments included:
- Consistently attained 100% communications within 24 hours of arrival at field site.
- Rated best Company Commander of 12 in the brigade.

Platoon Leader, B Company, 220th Signal Battalion, Fort Bragg, NC, 1999-2001.

Skillfully planned and supervised installation of cable and radio communications systems. Accomplishments included:
- Safeguarded communications equipment valued at approximately $1.5 million from loss or inadvertent destruction.
- Trained 23 telecommunication specialists in all facets of day-to-day operations.
- Received Army award for achieving readiness rate of 98%.

PERSONAL: Enjoy basketball and other team sports. Member of IEEE since 2000.

Telecommunications Specialist   *Available: July 20XX*

CHRIS R. KELLY
112 Oleander Road
Quantico, VA 21221
(777) 795-1467 / KellyC@hotmail.com

OBJECTIVE

Local Area Network administrator position where LAN skills and knowledge will improve the range of services offered by a small to mid-sized telecommunications firm located in the East.

HIGHLIGHT OF QUALIFICATIONS

- Telecommunications professional with more than 12 years experience in the installation, operation, and maintenance of local area networks.
- Demonstrated knowledge of telecommunication protocols, including TCP/IP and IPX.
- Designed and installed LANs of various configurations and topologies.
- **Microsoft Certified Systems Engineer (MCSE).**

AREAS OF EXPERTISE

Network Administration: Installed and administered Banyan Vines LANs that interconnected 100 microcomputer users in an MS Windows environment. Expertly employed network management software to optimize network performance. Upgraded communications equipment and operating system software in a manner that minimized disturbances in LAN operations. Maintained accurate list of authorized users. Controlled passwords for direct and remote access to the LAN. Hands-on experience with many communication protocols.

Communications Training: Provided classroom and 1-on-1 telecommunications training for the organization's 200+ computer users. Instructed staff on the use of various applications, including electronic mail (cc:Mail), Internet/World Wide Web, and office automation software (Microsoft Office). Developed curriculum and taught specialized courses. Received top performance awards.

Computer Operations: Maintained large tape and disk library for 300-staff organization in an IBM mainframe environment. Coordinated activities and briefed senior operations managers on key issues. Interfaced with the organization's staff members to answer computer-related questions. Facilitated mainframe connection by installing Etherlink card in personal computers. Maintained accurate inventory of computer and peripheral equipment valued at $1.5 million.

EMPLOYMENT HISTORY

Computer Operations Supervisor, Henderson Hall, VA, 2005-Present
Network Supervisor, Cherry Point, NC, 2001-2004
Computer Network Specialist, San Diego, CA, 1998-2000

EDUCATION
B.S. (Candidate, 2009), Information Systems, George Mason University, Fairfax, VA
A.A., Computer Technology, North Carolina State University, 2004

Trainer   *Available: July 20XX*

KELLY RODRIGUEZ
100 Packard Dr.
Groton, CT 06300
(860) 213-4657 / RodriguezK@aol.com

OBJECTIVE

A training position where a strong blend of technical expertise and propensity to train will enable a firm to rapidly enhance the technical depth of its staff.

SUMMARY OF QUALIFICATIONS

- Over 8 years training and experience operating and maintaining Naval nuclear propulsion plants and electrical generation/distribution systems.
- Experience in adult education, technical training, and program management/development.
- Outstanding technical background in power plant operations and maintenance supervision.
- Strong interpersonal skills, meticulous administrator, and an enthusiastic instructor.
- Excel in individual and team-based settings.
- Fluent in Spanish.

WORK EXPERIENCE: United States Navy, 1999-Present

Instructor

- Train junior and senior staff in electrical theory, operating procedures, maintenance techniques, and safety precautions.
- Compile a comprehensive exam bank, write and administer exams, report results to department head.

Program Manager/Developer

- Assess division's training needs, identify weaknesses, develop and implement short-range and long-range training plans.
- Administer qualification program, assign goals, track progress, and verify individuals' compliance with qualification requirements.
- Confer with chain of command and administrators of local community college, arrange for college level English course to be taught to crew members, expanding crew's educational opportunities.

"His meticulous administration and outstanding effort as Electrical Division Training Petty Officer ensured the highest quality training."—Rear Admiral A. C. Hogan

EDUCATION

B.S., Education, Southern Illinois University, 1999

Transportation *Available: June 20XX*

JOHN BECKETT
123rd Street
Las Vegas, NV 12345
(333) 123-4567 / BeckettJ@aol.com

OBJECTIVE

Facilities Director for a large manufacturing plant where the application of experience-proven management expertise will result in improved operating efficiency and profit margins.

SUMMARY OF QUALIFICATIONS

Twenty-year Naval career with expertise in personnel management within large organizations. Experience in executive leadership positions managing organizations up to 300 people with total budgets in excess of $3 million annually. Extensive hands-on experience in facilities maintenance, organizational development, training, and time management. Strong communication skills.

PROFESSIONAL ACHIEVEMENTS

Chief, Sealift Transportation, U.S. Atlantic Command, 2005-Present

- Planned and executed strategic sealift throughout the Atlantic region. Efficiently managed annual sealift exercise of $13 million.
- Coordinated with military and commercial shipping industry to successfully demonstrate intermodal transportation and significantly improved U.S. strategic deployment capabilities.

Senior Staff Officer, Logistics Squadron One, 2000-2003

- Directed executive staff of 35 employees. Responsible for training and evaluating ships' operational readiness and engineering.
- Hands-on engineering training experience with various classes of Navy ships.

Executive Officer, 1997-1999

- Directed the planning, scheduling, and tracking of day-to-day operations for a large ship with five departments and 300 personnel.
- Guided and trained ship's crew on the proper use of Personnel Qualification System and Maintenance Materiel Management.

Developmental assignments: 1987-1996

EDUCATION

M.S., Organizational Effectiveness, University of Southern California, 2002
Naval Postgraduate School, Monterey, CA, 1996

Transportation Management   *Available: July 20XX*

PATRICK M. SIMMONS
2913 West Broad St.
Fairfax, VA 22313
(703) 888-3333 / SimmonsP@erols.com

OBJECTIVE

Transportation Management position where long-haul transportation experience can be fully utilized to the benefit of a national trucking company.

QUALIFICATIONS SUMMARY

TRANSPORTATION
- Directed the daily planning, coordination, and supervision of a 177-person transportation unit.

OPERATIONS
- Efficiently managed a 100-vehicle fleet, whose value exceeded $5 million, with no measurable losses.
- Planned, coordinated, and controlled the pickup and delivery of over 3 tons of cargo on time and under stressful conditions.
- Managed hazardous cargo certification requirements, vehicle maintenance, and safety deadlines with ease.

MANAGEMENT
- Supervised staffs of from 5 to 177 personnel involved in various transportation activities. Effective management resulted in successful accomplishment of projects within budgetary and time constraints.
- Focus on team building and unit esprit increased staff retention rates from 30% to 60% over a two-year period.
- Evaluated individual and team performance, providing positive reinforcement and constant encouragement.

TRAINING
- Revised curriculum of transportation training program, improving the student pass rate by 20%.
- Delivered educational presentations for audiences ranging from 10 to 200; consistently rated as "excellent" guest lecturer.

EMPLOYMENT HISTORY

Transportation Director, Fort Eustis, VA, 2004-Present
Transportation Staff Officer, Fort Bragg, NC, 2000-2003
Transportation Officer, Fort Eustis, VA, 1997-1999
Student, Fort Eustis, VA, 1996

EDUCATION & TRAINING

M.A., Transportation Management, University of Southern California, 2003
B.S., Statistics, University of Maryland, 1996

Warehouse Supervisor   *Available: February 20XX*

DANA PHILLIPS
2813 Lincoln Lane
Madison, CT 02521
(206) 918-7623 / PhillipsD@aol.com

OBJECTIVE

Position in inventory management for a large department store where skills and experience in warehouse operations can be used to improve efficiency and profitability.

QUALIFICATIONS SUMMARY

- Skilled inventory stocking specialist with over 6 years experience.
- Disciplined, dedicated supply professional trained in proper procedures for shipping, receiving, storing, and issuing stock.
- Extensive experience handling medicine, food, and other perishable supplies.
- Knowledgeable about stock control and accounting procedures.
- Effective in team or individual-based settings.

EMPLOYMENT HISTORY

Stock Control Specialist, 9th District, Cleveland, OH, 2004-Present

Locate and catalog supply items in a timely manner using computer-based tracking system. Improved stock verification procedures, resulting in no discrepancies found over a two-year period. Load, unload, and move stock using forklifts and hand trucks. Maintain accurate records on incoming and outgoing stock, which comprises over 1,000 line items.

Stock Control Clerk, Support Center, Elizabeth City, NJ, 2000-2003

Designed innovative system to better organize storage space for incoming stock of 5,500 line items. Closely followed established procedures for shipping, receiving, storing, and issuing stock. Verified quantity and description of stock received against bills of lading, ensuring 100% accuracy. Maintained accurate records of quantities on hand. Received commendation medal for results achieved.

EDUCATION & TRAINING

A.A., Business Administration, Ohio State, 2005
Materials Management Course, Fort Lee, VA, 2001
Army Basic Training, Fort Lee, VA, 2000

7

Electronic Resumes and Job Search Effectiveness

M OST OF THE PRINCIPLES and examples presented in this book apply to 95 percent of all resumes written and distributed today. Many of the remaining resumes, follow other important principles. This chapter examines the special case of electronic resumes, which come in a variety of different forms: plain text, formatted, PDF, web page, web portfolio, video, and multimedia. In addition, we include many useful websites for conducting an Internet-based job search as well as emphasizes the realities of using the Internet in your job search, with cautionary notes about being seduced by over-hyped resume distribution technology.

Since you will most likely send your resume via email, post a version of it on an employment website, or produce a video or multimedia resume, you should find this chapter especially useful. If you are in a remote location that does not permit you to meet employers face-to-face through job fairs or informational interviews, your long-distance Internet and email job search activities will greatly enhance your employability.

Electronic Distribution

Today, nearly 95 percent of Fortune 500 companies solicit online resumes and most companies either request or accept emailed resumes. Job seekers, employers, and recruiters increasingly use of the Internet and other electronic communication media. For you, the job seeker, the Internet offers a tremendous opportunity to efficiently advertise your skills and qualifications to prospective employers worldwide. As corporations increasingly rely on such technology to find qualified candidates and manage resumes, you must understand how to use electronic media to gain maximum advantage. In this chapter we explain how to create and distribute an electronic resume in its myriad forms to prospective employers as well as identify the best Internet employment sites to incorporate into a well organized job search.

Enter the Information Age

Using the Internet, we can now inexpensively engage in job hunting activities that span the globe in a matter of seconds rather than days, weeks, or months. This ability to quickly, easily, and cheaply transmit one's qualifications has important ramifications. Above all, it has expanded the pool of candidates vying for open positions. No longer are employers constrained to advertise in local newspapers or magazines. Now they can broadcast opportunities to a much larger audience using a company website or Internet job site. With this enhanced exposure comes increased competition for available jobs.

The increased reliance by companies on web-based technology requires that job seekers understand and properly use this technology. Fortunately, the technology is not difficult to learn and the tools you need to effectively advertise your skills and qualifications are readily available. To begin with, the key questions you need to ask yourself are these:

- Is my resume appropriate for online consumption?
- Does my resume have the right buzzwords (keywords) to satisfy the software used by human resources personnel who electronically screen candidates?

Essential Equipment

To participate in today's electronic job market, you will need access to four items – a computer, a modem, a word processing program, and a printer. If you don't have this equipment at home, don't despair. There are several free or low-cost alternatives available to you as a transitioning service member. We suggest starting at your local military transition assistance office (ACAP, Family Service Center, Career Resource Management Center, or Family Support Center). Most will have the necessary equipment in their facility. If not, or if you do not have authorized access, visit a local office store such as FedEx Kinkos, a One-Stop Career Center (www.careeronestop.org), or your local library. As for work processing programs, the two most widely used packages are MS Word™ and WordPerfect™. Either can be used to transform your conventional resume into an electronic resume. Later we'll describe how to accomplish this transformation. If you need help in using the word processing software, we suggest asking a friend or a military career counselor for assistance.

Conventional vs. Electronic Resumes

As previously discussed in Chapter 6, a conventional resume follows a traditional resume format, the most common being improved chronological, or combination. It's often rich with action verbs and includes special formatting and emphasizing elements to make it look attractive to the eye. An electronic resume, as its name implies, is a resume that's in electronic form. It's an electronic document that can be sent by email or uploaded to an e-form – an employer's version of an online fill-in-the-blacks application form. As we discuss below, an electronic resume can take several different forms. However, whether a resume is in a conventional or electronic form, the purpose is the same – to accurately and succinctly convey your skills, abilities, and interests to prospective employers in a manner that will motivate them to learn more about you through a personal interview.

The comparison between conventional and electronic resumes varies depending upon the form of the electronic resume. The **plain text resume**, which is commonly referred to as an ASCII resume, is designed without formatting elements. While these resumes are no longer as important as they were a few years ago, nonetheless, you may still need to send an ASCII resume to some recruiters and employers. Conventional and electronic resumes are similar in structure, both containing the core subcategories of header, work history, professional accomplishments, and education. The two types of resumes differ primarily in how one's work history/accomplishments are presented. In the conventional resume, most sentences or phrases start with an action verb. In the ASCII formatted electronic resume, the focus is on the selective use of **keywords**, which tend to be nouns. Additional differences are discussed later when we discuss ASCII text resumes in depth.

When compared in this context, the four major advantages electronic resumes have over conventional resumes follow:

1. **Speed:** Whereas sending a conventional resume through a mail service such as the U.S. Postal Service will take one or more days, an electronic resume can be sent almost anywhere worldwide in a matter of seconds. Using keyword searches, employers can quickly sore hundreds of resumes to narrow the field of candidates.

2. **Cost:** Assuming you have access to the Internet and the computer equipment listed above, the cost of sending an electronic resume is minimal. If you have a personal Internet account through an Internet service provider, your monthly Internet access costs will be in the vicinity of $10 to $20; transmitting a resume to an Internet site is usually free. Military transition sites do not charge for transmitting a resume via the Internet.

3. **Extended presence:** Because of the global array of interconnected networks that exist today, you can send your electronic resume almost anywhere worldwide. Once received at an Internet website, hiring managers, regardless of physical location, can access your resume over an extended period.

4. **Ease of access:** Because the resume information is stored in electronic form, hiring managers or recruiters can use specially designed search software to identify those candidates whose resume matches one or more search criteria. Then with the high quality automated applicant tracking systems available today, hiring managers can easily store and retrieve the entire resume on their desktop for viewing, sharing with others, or printing.

Resumes in an Electronic Job Market

Automated applicant tracking systems, employment databases, the Internet, videos, and multimedia have transformed the resume writing, production, distribution, and screening processes. These technologies are changing the methods by which employers arrive at screening and hiring decisions. While only a few years ago employers primarily asked for mailed, faxed, and scannable ASCII resumes, today more and more employers require applicants to submit their resumes by email or to go to company websites where they are requested to complete online forms (e-forms) that produce profiles of candidates in lieu of a resume. Consequently, job seekers need to become Internet-savvy in terms of how they both write and distribute their resume, especially their format options.

The Internet and computerized applicant tracking systems are increasingly responsible for linking candidates to employers, especially for entry-level positions in large companies. These and related technologies are significantly altering the way individuals write and distribute resumes as well as how employers initially screen candidates. In today's job market, you need to become acquainted with these technologies since your next resume may be initially "read" by computers before it gets passed on to the people who have the power to hire. Before mailing, faxing, emailing, or uploading your resume to an employer's website, you need to know the specific submission requirements of an employer. For

> *Your resume must first satisfy technological requirements before it has the opportunity to grab the attention of employers.*

example, does Employer X want you to email a plain text or formatted resume, complete an online resume form, or submit a PDF resume, web resume, or web portfolio? If you don't know the answer to this question, or if you can't provide your resume in a requested or acceptable electronic format, you may not be considered for a position. Above all, your resume must be appropriate for online consumption, whether it be dropped into an employer's online e-form or emailed as an ASCII document or an email attachment.

The Changing Electronic Resume

During the past few years, electronic resumes were primarily defined as scannable and emailable resumes. When advised to write an electronic resume, job seekers were given lists of do's and don'ts on how to write a scanner-friendly resume (eliminate special emphasizing elements) as well as one that could be emailed as an ASCII or plain text document (eliminate standard formatting). As a result, job seekers often wrote two types of resumes: (1) a pretty paper resume that could be mailed, faxed, or transmitted by email as a Word™ attachment or in PDF format, or (2) an "ugly duckling" resume to be transmitted virus-free in the body of an email message as an ASCII or plain text document. They also were alerted to posted resumes – complete forms for entering their resume into online searchable resume databases operated by such commercial employment sites as Monster.com, CareerBuilder.com, and Hotjobs.Yahoo.com. The result was often a mini-resume or resume profile that could be periodically updated online. All you needed to do was to follow the online instructions for completing each section of an online resume template or form.

How times have changed within just a few years. Today, given the widespread use of the Internet and recent changes in email programs and software, the era of the scanned and "ugly duckling" resume is about over. Scanning technology is now old and inconvenient technology for employers who increasingly rely on the Internet for applications and communications. However, it is still used at job fairs to scan paper resumes into databases. Very few employers scan resumes and fewer and fewer employers request that resumes be transmitted as ASCII or plain text documents. The issue for employers, especially those with large companies, is one of volume: they are inundated with resumes. Many resumes come from Internet-savvy students and recent graduates who blast their resumes to numerous employers via the Internet. Unable to handle the sheer volume of resumes they receive by mail, fax, and email, employers have decided to more efficiently manage this process by primarily relying on the Internet for acquiring resumes and screening candidates. As a result, many employers now refuse to accept mailed or faxed resumes. Instead, they require candidates to submit their resumes to a specific email address in a variety of alternative forms: plain text, formatted, PDF, and HTML. The use of online e-forms has become a standard way of acquiring resumes from candidates. Savvy job seekers respond to such forms by cutting and pasting sections of their plain text resume into the forms.

The current, and perhaps long-term, trend is to require applicants to post their resumes to a company website which automatically places resumes into a searchable database. Similar to rigid application forms, where one must complete each pre-defined section, many of these websites have their own resume format requirements. They require some effort on the part of the applicant to meet the specific resume standards of the employer. By requiring candidates to complete an online resume form, employers are able to eliminate many not-so-serious "copy and paste" and "resume blasting" candidates, acquire all requested qualifying data, and efficiently search and retrieve resumes in the company's own online database. In many cases, the online resume form produces a **candidate profile** rather than a standard resume. This website-generated profile becomes the key to getting screened in or screened out of consideration for a position.

Types of Electronic Resumes

In today's job market you will encounter several different types of electronic resumes that are more or less accepted by employers, depending on their particular requirements:

1. **ASCII or plain-text resumes:** These are the original "ugly duckling" emailable resumes shorn of standard formatting and highlighting elements. They also are known as text-only, simple-text, or unformatted resumes. Candidates send a text-only version of their resume in the body of an email message. Such unadorned resumes are virus-free and can be easily forwarded to others as well as entered into

resume databases. Since these resumes are not easy to read given their lack of standard formatting and highlighting elements, readers tend to focus on the language and content of such resumes. Writers of such resumes should pay particular attention to the use of keywords.

2. **Formatted resumes:** These resumes are produced in a standard word processing program and transmitted as an email attachment. Similar to resumes outlined in this book, they look like standard formatted resumes and include all the "dress for success" elements associated with traditional resumes. Writers of such resumes should focus on all resume elements, from format and emphasizing techniques to keywords and language, outlined in this book.

3. **PDF resume:** This type of resume is similar to the formatted resume, but it is saved in PDF (Portable Document Format) form. Such resumes can be emailed, posted on websites, viewed online, or submitted to resume databases. The recipient must be able to open and view such resumes using Adobe Acrobat Reader or PDF viewer. While these resumes look nice since they are in a graphic format, they limit the ability of the end-user to automatically enter them into a resume database without first printing and scanning the document.

4. **HTML or web page resume:** This type of resume actually becomes a web page with its own unique URL. It can be produced with a variety of graphic and color elements as well as incorporate photos, video clips, audio files, and hyperlinks. It can be easily designed using such popular, inexpensive, or free web page development programs as FrontPage, Dreamweaver, or Netscape Composer.

5. **Online portfolio:** This is the ultimate online resume website and marketing tool. Similar to a paper portfolio but functioning as a website, the online portfolio includes a web resume with hyperlinks to a variety of sections that emphasize qualifications and provide proof of performance: objectives and/or philosophy, photos, video clips, audio files, letters of recommendations, work samples, and testimonials. Going far beyond a standard resume format, the online portfolio attempts to provide a complete career profile of a candidate's background and qualifications.

6. **Posted resumes:** Required by online employment sites and employer websites, these are basically fill-in-the-template resumes. Just follow the instructions and complete each section accordingly. You may be able to copy and paste much of the required information from your standard resume. However, some of these forms may require a great deal of original writing. The end result is often a mini-resume or candidate profile rather than a full-blown standard resume. Such forms enable employers to quickly enter information into a searchable company resume database. The key to writing these resumes is to follow the instruments and include lots of keywords in the resume since resumes will be searched by keywords.

Whatever you do, make sure you understand the resume requirements of each employer. Expect large employers to primarily accept resumes entered into their online resume form. On the other hand, small employers may accept formatted resumes sent as email attachments. The new rule for writing and submitting electronic resumes is simple: Make no technology assumptions about employers; know the electronic resume requirements of each. When in doubt, ask about the organization's preferred format.

Electronic Mediums

There are several mediums for creating and distributing electronic resumes. Here we discuss four types of electronic resumes, starting with the scanning of a printed resume and ending with a high-tech multimedia resume. In the subsections that follow, we review the chronology of the electronic resume and show how improvements in information technology are continually making the job search "matching" process ever more efficient.

Scanning

Beginning in the mid-1980s, a popular method for creating an electronic resume was to scan a conventional resume in paper form into an electronic file. In the late 1980s, OCR (optical character recognition) software was introduced. After the printed text was scanned, the file would be passed through OCR software, which would attempt to interpret the printed text and convert it into a word processable file. To increase the likelihood of the OCR software working as intended, the resume writer was strongly encouraged to modify his or her resume to enhance readability. These changes would include:

- removal of special (non-ASCII) characters, such as italics and bold
- use of a plain font like Helvetica
- use of a larger font size such as 12 or 14 point
- deletion of boxes or shading
- use of high quality paper conducive to scanning
- re-writing one's work history and professional accomplishments using keywords

The resume format would continue to contain the same subcategories found in conventional resume formats. For resumes that were to be scanned into a job bank database, the "Objective" subcategory was often replaced with a "Keyword Preface," which was chock-full of keywords in the form of nouns or noun-centric phrases.

Once the resume information was successfully stored in the database, specially written software programs would be used to search for keywords of interest to prospective employers. Such an approach had the appeal of using computer technology to efficiently search large numbers of resumes in a matter of seconds. However, there were obvious drawbacks. Most significant was the limited matching ability of this technology since it was based almost exclusively on the use of simple keyword matches. Nonetheless, some companies were able to build successful businesses as "job banks" that stored and retrieved scanned resumes for employers. However, with the explosion of the World Wide Web in the mid-1990s, most offline resume database services using scanned resumes went out of business.

One should not deduce, however, that companies no longer scan resumes – many do but in a very different manner. What has changed is the scanning of paper resumes – few companies still engage in this increasingly archaic approach to resume management. Given the high volume of solicited and unsolicited resumes received by many medium- to large-sized companies, numerous Human Resources departments scan resumes in order to better manage the resume screening, storage, and retrieval processes. Since OCR technology is now obsolete (an exception being for job fair use), because of the advantages of emailing resumes, these companies only accept electronic (emailed) resumes for their databases. Such resumes get scanned when an employer searches for particular candidates by keywords. Since you may not know whether or not your resume will be scanned, it's safe to assume that it will if you are sending an electronic resume. Therefore, you should prepare your resume so it will be scanned to your advantage. The following rules-of-thumb should assist you in creating such a resume.

ASCII Text Files

With the advent of user-friendly word processing software and the increased use of electronic mail (thanks in large part to the reduced cost and ease-of-use of the Internet), a popular distribution method in the early 1990s was to send an electronic resume in ASCII text format. Since these are still required by some employers and recruiters and you will probably post your resume to job databases of third party sites (save as ASCII file and copy and paste), you need to know how to convert your conventionally formatted resume into an ASCII text file. Assuming you already created a conventional resume using a standard word processing program, the steps in transforming your resume into an ASCII text file are relatively straightforward:

1. **Open your current conventional resume using your word processing software.** Using the "File" pull-down menu and "Save As" option, save the file as a standard DOS text file under a different name, e.g., resume.txt. The most recent versions of both MS Word and WordPerfect allow you to save a file in ASCII format. The analogous word processing programs for Macintosh computers work the same way.

2. **Strip the resume of those special characters not supported by the ASCII character set, i.e., bold, italics, lines, shading, boxing, etc.** Use characters such as an "*" or ">" to set off your work history or professional accomplishments entries. If you are uncertain as to which characters are included in the ASCII character set, simply look at your keyboard. Any of the keys you can press (except for the function keys) are part of the ASCII character set.

3. **Make good use of white space.** As with a conventional resume, it's important that your resume not appear cluttered. To help achieve this effect, use paragraphs. Remember to move text using the space bar rather than tabs, which will disappear when your file is saved in text format.

4. **Limit the number of characters per line to 60.** By pressing the Enter or Return key instead of allowing the characters to wrap to the next line, you can cause the line to break where desired. In so doing you will ensure that the ASCII resume looks good when received at the other end.

5. **As with the conventional resume, we recommend limiting the length of the resume to two pages.** Given that the resume may be viewed electronically, it's important also that the resume break by page where intended. You may need to do some experimentation to achieve the desired effect.

The ultimate success of the resume in ASCII text file rests not in its format but in its substance. The proper selection of keywords to describe your work accomplishments and skills is particularly important. To enhance your probability for success, you must build on your networking and research activities to select keywords that are common to your desired industry and appropriate for your background. An aesthetically pleasing electronic resume that uses industry-common words that accurately reflect your background will give you the competitive edge.

When you have finished developing your ASCII text resume file, we recommend sending it to a friend and asking him or her to review it for content and confirm that it retained its format. Such testing is the only foolproof method of guaranteeing you have correctly formatted the ASCII file for transmission. Once you have proven that the electronic resume file displays as intended, you can send it to a prospective employer via electronic mail. Remember, however, to precede your resume with an electronic cover letter just as you would if sending the resume via regular mail. (We talk more about the cover letter in the next chapter.) In addition to sending the prospective employer the electronic resume, we also recommend sending your conventional resume on bond paper through the postal service. While it may take a couple days to reach the hiring manager, you will be reminding him or her of your interest in the position and providing a more attractively formatted resume for review.

The two versions of the resume (Samuel Adams) presented on pages 171-172 show how a conventional resume (page 171) can be transformed into an resume in ASCII text format (page 172). While the conventional resume is more aesthetically pleasing, the ASCII resume contains the same substantive information.

In addition to the rules-of-thumb for developing and distributing ASCII formatted resumes, the following "do's" and "don'ts" are relevant to electronic resumes:

SAMUEL ADAMS
2913 West Broad Street
Fairfax, VA 22313
H: (703) 888-3333 W: (202) 123-4567
AdamsS@aol.com

OBJECTIVE   Supervisory position where aviation maintenance experience can be used to improve the effectiveness and quality of a commercial airline's maintenance operations.

QUALIFICATIONS SUMMARY

MAINTENANCE
- Extensive maintenance experience on a variety of jet aircraft, including the B-1, C-117, and C-130.
- Innovative problem solver who developed efficient methods for ensuring aircraft were maintained at peak levels. Recommended cost cutting measures that saved the Air Force $1.5 million over a 3-year period.
- Developed maintenance checklists and enforced compliance, resulting in a near perfect safety record for all assigned aircraft.

MANAGEMENT
- Evaluated performance of 15 maintenance technicians on a daily basis.
- Developed customized maintenance training program, which resulted in a 98% pass rate for staff under my supervision.
- Executed action-oriented plans, ensuring assigned missions were accomplished on time and within budget.

COMMUNICATION
- Effectively communicated aircraft maintenance tasks to fellow teammates.
- Briefed senior leaders on the readiness status of aircraft.
- Developed innovative plans for repairing defective components.
- Taught aviation maintenance courses to newly assigned staff.

EMPLOYMENT HISTORY

Assistant Director, Maintenance, 79th Tactical Air Wing, Hanscom AFB, 2003-Present
Manager, Aircraft Maintenance, 339th Fighter Squadron, Nellis AFB, NV, 1998-2002
Staff Non-Commissioned Officer, Andrews AFB, MD, 1996-1998
Leader Development Positions, 1985-1995

EDUCATION & TRAINING

A.S. Aircraft Maintenance, Community College of the Air Force, 2002
Aircraft Maintenance Training, Nellis AFB, NV, 1999 ·
Basic Training, Randolph AFB, TX, 1985

SAMUEL ADAMS
2913 West Broad St.
Fairfax, VA 22313
H: (703) 888-3333; W: (202) 123-4567

AdamsS@aol.com

OBJECTIVE

Supervisory position where aviation maintenance experience can be used to improve the effectiveness and quality of an airline's maintenance operations.

QUALIFICATIONS SUMMARY

MAINTENANCE
> Extensive maintenance experience in a variety of jet aircraft, including the B-1, C-117, and C-130.
> Innovative problem solver who developed efficient methods for ensuring aircraft were maintained at peak levels. Recommended cost cutting measures that saved the Air Force $1.5 million over a 3-year period.
> Developed maintenance checklists and enforced compliance, resulting in a near perfect safety record for all assigned aircraft.

MANAGEMENT
> Evaluated performance of 15 maintenance technicians on a daily basis.
> Developed customized maintenance training program, which resulted in a 98% pass rate for staff under my supervision.
> Executed action-oriented plans, ensuring assigned missions were accomplished on time and within budget.

COMMUNICATION
> Effectively communicated aircraft maintenance tasks to fellow teammates.
> Briefed senior leaders on the readiness status of aircraft. Developed innovative plans for repairing defective components.
> Taught aviation maintenance courses to newly assigned staff.

EMPLOYMENT HISTORY

Assistant Director, Maintenance, 79th Tactical Air Wing, Hanscom AGB, 2003-Present
Manager, Aircraft Maintenance, 339th Fighter Squadron, Nellis AFB, NV, 1999-2002
Staff Non-Commissioned Officer, Andrews AFB, MD, 1996-1999
Leader Development Positions, 1985-1995

EDUCATION & TRAINING

A.S. Aircraft Maintenance, Community College of the Air Force, 2002
Aircraft Maintenance Training, Nellis AFB, NV, 1996
Basic Training, Randolph AFB, TX, 1985

Electronic Resume "Do's"

- **Do** use 12 to 14 point monospaced fonts, such as Arial, Bookman, Courier, Helvetica, or Times.
- **Do** limit the electronic resume length to two pages.
- **Do** put the most important information first.
- **Do** use industry-common keywords.
- **Do** use synonyms where appropriate.
- **Do** left-align headings and indent and align the remainder of the text.
- **Do** set off major sections by capitalizing.
- **Do** include your name on the second page.
- **Do** keep individual lines to 60 characters or less to accommodate differences in screen width.
- **Do** experiment with asterisks, hyphens, and other characters appearing on your keyboard for optimal appearance.
- **Do** use high quality, lightly colored paper, if the resume is to be scanned.

Electronic Resume "Don'ts"

- **Don't** fold the resume. Send it in a 9" x 12" envelope.
- **Don't** use action verbs to emphasize experience and capabilities.
- **Don't** stretch the truth when trying to match your capabilities with industry-common buzzwords.
- **Don't** underline, italicize, or shade words.
- **Don't** misspell words.
- **Don't** use fancy fonts.
- **Don't** use boxes.
- **Don't** use columns.
- **Don't** waste space with personal data or a reference statement.

Development of an effective, ASCII-based electronic resume is not difficult. Simply convey your qualifications using keywords common to the industry and structure your resume so that it highlights your strengths. If you follow this guidance and the formatting rules above, we're confident your resume will look good when received by the company or its hiring manager.

At the same time, an increasing trend is toward the return of what Joyce Lain Kennedy calls the "beautiful resume" – the paper resume in a more eye-pleasing format, such as the PDF formatted resume. For more information on the latest trends in electronic resumes among employers, see the newest edition of Joyce Lain Kennedy's *Resumes for Dummies* (John Wiley & Sons, 2007). For examples of electronic resumes, see Susan Britton Whitcomb's and Pat Kendall's *e-Resumes* (McGraw-Hill, 2001) and Pat Criscito's *e-Resumes* (Barron's Educational Services, 2004).

Electronic Mail Attachment

Up to this point we've discussed sending the resume to a prospective employer as an electronic mail message. Another option is to send your resume as an email attachment. When sending a word processed resume file in this manner, you are actually sending a binary file. All this means is that your resume file has been formatted in a particular way, using such program as MS Word or WordPerfect.

When you send your resume as an attached binary file, the distinction between the conventional resume and electronic resume disappears – it's the same file. However, when you send your resume as an attached file, you risk the recipient not being able to open it for two reasons. First, he or she may not have compatible word processing software and hence cannot open the file. Second, he may use a different online services network (for example, you may send the resume using America Online, and he may attempt to open it using a different online service or a different Internet service provider and have difficulty reading the file because of file encoding/decoding complexities. One way to avoid this problem is to ask the recipient ahead of time whether he has the ability to read a particular file format. However, this approach might be inappropriate or not feasible. Bottom line: even in this technologically sophisticated age, there are still many conditions that can preclude a seamless transmission of an attached file. We suggest sending the ASCII formatted resume in the body of the electronic mail message and attach the conventional file, preferably using MS Word. In addition, we recommend sending the hiring manager your conventional resume on bond paper using regular mail. Such redundancy will keep your employment candidacy at the forefront of the prospective employer's mind.

Internet/Web

While you will use the Internet to send your resume by email, the distribution method described here differs in that you enter the contents of your resume electronically into an Internet/Web site job database while connected online. There are two basic alternatives – entering your resume information directly into a particular company's online database or entering your resume information into commercial online employment databases, such as Monster.com, HotJobs.Yahoo.com, or CareerBuilder.com.

When sending your electronic resume to a particular company, you can naturally send it to them using the distribution methods discussed above, i.e., ASCII text file or electronic mail attachment. Another option not discussed above, though less common, is to send your electronic resume to them on disk. However, many companies now offer (and prefer) a more high-tech alternative that enables you to enter your resume information directly into their candidate database while connected to their website through a series of interactive HTML forms, which guide you through the process. While it may sound complicated, in actuality the process is quite simple. What makes this option so appealing to individual companies is that resume information entered in this manner can be easily and rapidly searched across multiple criteria by hiring managers sitting at their desks.

Hence, if a company hiring manager was looking for someone with a B.S. degree in Operations Research from Penn State with a graduation year of between 1998 and 2003, the system would display the resumes of only those candidates who met all three conditions. Such a sophisticated approach represents a significant advancement over earlier days when a company would often pay an outside firm to find all candidates whose resume "hit" on a particular keyword or phrase. Now individual companies can perform this function in-house at a fraction of the cost and with better results.

It's important to note that many large defense contractors like SAIC, EDS, Northrop Grumman, General Dynamics, and Lockheed Martin increasingly use their own websites to facilitate the input and later retrieval of employment candidates' resumes. All you must do is know their Internet address, link to their employment page, and follow the instructions for entering your resume information. If you don't know the Internet address (technically known as the URL, or Uniform Resource Locator), simply use a search engine such as Google (www.google.com), Yahoo! (www.yahoo.com), MSN Search (www.msn.com), AltaVista (www.altavista.com), or AlltheWeb (www.alltheweb.com) and surf the Web for the company name of interest. You will most likely find a link to the company's home page. Once there, make sure you add the website to your personal list of URLs using your browser's "Bookmark" or "Favorites" feature.

While many companies have websites with links to their employment page, others rely on large, online career centers, such as **Monster.com** (www.monster.com), **HotJobs Yahoo** (http://hotjobs.yahoo.com), and **CareerBuilder** (www.careerbuilder.com), for recruiting personnel. Monster.com alone claims to have nearly 70 million resumes in its database! Using these online services, more and more employers post job announcements and search online resume databases for candidates with particular education, skill, and experience profiles. A few sites, such as **Indeed.com** (www.indeed.com), troll the Internet for job listings found on the websites of thousands of employers. **Employment911.com** (www.employment911.com), claims to search more than 3 million jobs on over 300 major career sites.

Each day thousands of hiring managers access these online databases in search of candidates meeting their criteria. There is normally no cost to you, the individual job seeker. However, companies almost always pay a fee to gain access to these sites. Consequently, we strongly encourage you to visit their websites and learn more about their services. For a comprehensive listing of career-related websites, see the following books which are available through Impact Publications (see order form at the end of this book):

- *America's Top Internet Job Sites* (Ron and Caryl Krannich)
- *The Guide to Internet Job Searching* (Margaret Riley)
- *Job Hunting on the Internet* (Richard Nelson Bolles)

Transitioning military personnel should visit several websites specifically designed to deal with their employment needs, such as www.corporategray.com, www.taonline.com, and www.vetjobs.com. Most of these sites allow you to post your resume, apply for jobs online, and research various military-friendly companies. We include these websites, along with several other employment sites, in the final section of this chapter.

Multimedia Resumes

The final and most advanced resume format is the multimedia resume. Such a resume format requires knowledge of a special computer language called HTML (HyperText Markup Language), the base language of the Internet's World Wide Web. While not overly complex, HTML is foreign to most job seekers and will take some time to learn should you elect to do so. To assist you in converting your current electronic resume into HTML form, there are several software utilities on the market. For example, Microsoft Corporation offers "Internet Assistant," which converts a resume in MS Word format to HTML. Another well known package is titled *FrontPage*. Through HTML you can add interest and zest to your resume by including pictures, photos, graphics, sounds, etc. But do you really want to do so? Probably not. Unless you are in search of a high-tech, software-related job, we would discourage you from enriching your multimedia resume to such a degree. For those who are pursuing such a position, we recommend a well designed HTML document that uses only text to describe your interests and qualifications. You can still include hot links to a more detailed textual description of some aspect of your background. Such a resume would demonstrate your above-average knowledge of the Internet and its usage.

Such a multimedia resume is normally distributed on the Web as a personal home page. This means that you would require an Internet Service Provider capable of providing you with the technical facilities needed to host your resume on their server. The cost for having such a high-tech rendition of your electronic resume varies by provider. We suggest looking in the business or technology section of your local newspaper for companies advertising such services. While the cost of Internet service varies, expect to pay between $10 and $25 per month. Often, the provider will give you a limited amount of storage space as part of this monthly fee. You could then use this space to store your personal home page, where it could be accessed by anyone worldwide.

If you should elect to create a home page and make it accessible via the Web, we recommend including the Internet address on your paper resume. For example, your Internet address (URL, or Uniform Resource Locator) might appear as follows on your resume:

http://www.aol.com/~adamss.html

It shows a prospective employer that you are probably Internet savvy. However, for most of our readers, we would not recommend investing the time or resources needed to develop a good looking multimedia resume. We include it here only as an option.

Privacy

Our high-technology world offers us many ways to reveal our employment interests, skills, and abilities to prospective employers worldwide. For people who are currently employed by a private sector firm but interested in seeking greener pastures elsewhere, privacy may be a major concern. The ramifications of having a current employer inadvertently discover you are seeking employment outside the firm could be ugly. What precautions should you consider under these circumstances? For starters, you would want to protect your identity by not publishing your name, address, phone numbers, employer's name, or easily recognizable screen address, e.g., JenkinsT@aol.com. Well then, how can anyone send a resume? Here are a few options to consider. First, you could use a Post Office box, which we earlier did not recommend for other reasons. Second, you could have your resume faxed to a commercial business such as Mail Boxes Etc., which offers this service at a minimal fee (approximately $1 per page). Third, you could use an unrecognizable screen name or alias as your Internet address. CompuServe, for example, has for many years used numeric User IDs and alpha characters. If you are an America Online subscriber, you are offered multiple screen names for a given account. What you may not know is that they also offer an alias capability, which allows you to take on an unrecognizable name as another User ID at no additional charge. Fourth, you could go through a private placement service such as JOBTRAK (800-999-8725), which protects the confidentiality of job seeker who are currently employed.

Keep Electronic Resumes in Perspective

The electronic resume can take many forms and be distributed in multiple ways. As you explore the many options available to you, we advise you to take a conservative, yet forward-looking approach. As with the conventional, paper-based resume, make sure you do your homework upfront and carefully think through all the details required to make your electronic resume as powerful in content as your conventional resume. Remember, the intent of an electronic resume is the same as the paper resume – to motivate a prospective employer to learn more about you through a face-to-face interview.

Because of the more intricate nature of the electronic resume, we recommend that you take extra precautions when developing it. If you're creating an ASCII text resume, remember to follow the "do's" and "don'ts" on page 173. Check to ensure that the key-words you have chosen accurately reflect your background and are terms common to the industry in which you are seeking employment. It's also important to check that your electronic resume retains its intended appearance when sent over the Internet. If you elect to send your resume in conventional form as an email attachment, we suggest you consider calling the intended recipient ahead of time to check the compatibility of word processing software and Internet service provider. While MS Word is the standard these days, you don't know unless you first contact your recipient for information and permission to submit your resume as an attachment. Because email transmission across different networks is not without some degree of risk, we also recommend sending the ASCII formatted resume in the text of the message. Such redundancy will be appreciated and is in your favor.

The Internet is and will continue to be an important venue for distributing your electronic resume. We encourage you to explore the many Internet sites that host employment databases and seek those sites most applicable to your qualifications and job interests.

Always make sure to follow up by sending your electronic resume or entering the information online through the company's or online career service's employment web page. And should you be seeking a job in a high-tech field, don't forget to explore the potential advantages of posting a multimedia-type resume on your own home page.

Key Websites You Should Visit and Use

Numerous websites include useful information for transitioning military personnel. For example, ambitious sites such as **Military.com** (www.military.com) function as portals for capturing the attention and purchasing power of the military community. Casting a broad net, they focus on numerous issues relevant to the military community as a whole, from history, family, and finance to jobs, travel, shopping, relocation, and networking. These sites attempt to become one-stop shops for military personnel and veterans. Other community-wide sites are primarily designed to market services to the military community, such as **Military-Net.com** (www.military-net.com) and Military Exits (http://militaryexits.com). Many other military-specific sites primarily focus on job and career issues for transitioning military personnel and veterans. Most of these sites include information, advice, job listings, and resume database. The major military transition websites include:

- **Corporate Gray Online**   www.greentogray.com
- **TAOnline**   www.taonline.com
- **VetJobs.com**   www.vetjobs.com

Other websites focusing on transitioning military personnel include the following:

- **Army Times**   www.armytimes.com
- **Bradley-Morris, Inc.**   www.bradley-morris.com
- **Cameron-Brooks**   www.cameron-brooks.com
- **CareerCommandPost.com**   www.careercommandpost.com
- **Civilian Readiness**   www.civilianreadiness.com
- **ClearanceJobs.com**   www.clearancejobs.com
- **Defense Talent Network**   www.defensetalent.com
- **DOD Transportal**   www.dodtransportal.org
- **G.I. Jobs**   www.gijobs.net
- **Helmets to Hardhats**   www.helmetstohardhats.org
- **Hireveterans.com**   www.hireveterans.com
- **HireVetsFirst**   www.hirevetsfirst.gov
- **IntelligenceCareers.com**   www.intelligencecareers.com
- **Lucas Group**   www.lucasgroup.com
- **Military.com**   www.military.com
- **Military Candidates**   www.militarycandidates.com
- **Military Exits**   www.militaryexits.com

- Military Family Network   www.emilitary.org
- MilitaryHire.com   www.militaryhire.com
- MilitaryJobHunts.com   www.militaryjobhunts.com
- MilitaryJobZone.com   www.militaryjobzone.com
- Military Outplacement Post   www.midwestmilitary.com
- Military Partners   www.militarypartners.com
- MilitaryResumes.com   www.militaryresumes.com
- MilitaryStars.com   www.militarystars.com
- Military Times   www.militarytimes.com
- Military Transition Times   www.militarytransitiontimes.com
- Orion International   www.orioninternational.com
- RecruitMilitary.com   http://recruitmilitary.com
- TekSystems.com   www.teksystems.com
- SmartStart for New Vets   www.smartstartvets.org
- VeteranJobs.com   http://veteranjobs.com
- VeteranEmployment.com   www.veteranemployment.com
- Veterans' Employment
  and Training Service (DOL)   www.dol.gov/vets
- VeteransWorld.com   www.veteransworld.com

Transitioning members of the Guard and Reserve, who are often overlooked by both government and commercial career transition services, now share with Active Duty members of the various services the following transition assistance site:

- TurboTAP   www.TurboTAP.org

Post Your Resume Online

The Internet has quickly become the best friend of both employers and headhunters who can recruit personnel much faster and cheaper than through more traditional recruitment channels. Even small companies, with fewer than 10 employees, now use the Internet to advertise jobs and search resume databases for qualified candidates. At the same time, the Internet offers job seekers an important tool to add to their job search arsenal. Make sure you include the Internet in your job search by posting your resume on numerous sites, conducting research, and networking for information, advice, and referrals. In so doing, you'll acquire lots of useful information for enhancing your overall job search.

Over 25,000 websites in the United States deal with employment. Yes, there's a jungle out there in cyberspace as many job seekers face a daunting task of deciding which sites to visit and possibly use. A good starting point for making such decisions is the AIRS gateway site to job boards, which you download for free by going to this website:

www.airsdirectory.com/directories/job_boards

This site includes over 6,500 job boards which are classified by industry, function, occupations, and other useful categories. In the end, however, you'll probably want to concentrate on several of the most popular employment websites and then select a few sites from the AIRS directory that specialize in your occupational field:

■ Monster.com	www.monster.com
■ JobCentral	www.jobcentral.com
■ America's Job Bank	www.ajb.dni.us
■ CareerBuilder	www.careerbuilder.com
■ NationJob	www.nationjob.com
■ Hot Jobs Yahoo	http://hotjobs.yahoo.com
■ Jobs.com	www.jobs.com
■ JobSearch	http://jobsearch.monster.com
■ CareerJournal	www.careerjournal.com
■ CareerFlex	www.careerflex.com
■ Employment911.com	www.employment911.com
■ EmploymentSpot	www.employmentspot.com
■ Indeed	www.indeed.com
■ SimplyHired	www.simplyhired.com
■ WorkTree	www.worktree.com
■ Job Sniper	www.jobsniper.com
■ Vault	www.vault.com
■ WetFeet.com	www.wetfeet.com
■ PlanetRecruit	www.planetrecruit.com
■ BestJobsUSA	www.bestjobsusa.com
■ MRI Network	www.mrinetwork.com
■ Career Shop	www.careershop.com
■ CareerSite	www.careersite.com
■ MonsterTrak.com	www.monstertrak.monster.com
■ ClearChannel	www.clearchannel.com
■ Brass Ring	www.brassring.com
■ Career.com	www.career.com
■ JobBank USA	www.jobbankusa.com
■ Net-Temps	www.net-temps.com
■ CareerTV.net	www.careertv.net
■ American Preferred Jobs	www.preferredjobs.com
■ ProHire	www.prohire.com
■ CareerExchange	www.careerexchange.com
■ Career Magazine	www.careermag.com
■ Employers Online, Inc.	www.employersonline.com
■ EmployMax	www.employmax.com
■ EmploymentGuide	www.employmentguide.com
■ WantedJobs	www.wantedjobs.com
■ Arbita	www.recruitusa.com

- **Recruiters Online Network**   www.recruitersonline.com
- **kForce.com**   www.kforce.com
- **Dice.com**   www.dice.com
- **Washington Post**   www.washingtonjobs.com/wl/jobs

While you should visit the large employment websites, don't put much hope in locating a job or employer through them. Large employment websites such as Monster.com, HotJobs.Yahoo.com, and CareerBuilder.com offer a wealth of information and services to both employers and job seekers. However, these sites are primarily run for the benefit of the paying customers – employers. Job seekers can post their resumes online, browse job postings, and apply for jobs through these sites, but few ever get jobs this way. The most valuable aspects of these sites for job seekers are the peripheral services which are designed to keep you coming back again and again (in this online business, you're known as "traffic" when sites set their advertising rates for employers):

- Job Search Tips
- Featured Articles
- Career Experts or Advisors
- Career Tool Kit
- Career Assessment Tests
- Community Forums
- Discussion or Chat Groups
- Message Boards
- Job Alert ("Push") Emails
- Company Research Centers
- Networking Forums
- Salary Calculators/Wizards
- Resume Management Center
- Resume and Cover Letter Advice
- Multimedia Resume Software
- Job Interview Practice
- Relocation Information
- Reference Check Checkers
- Employment or Career News
- Free Email for Privacy
- Success Stories
- Career Newsletter
- Career Events
- Online Job Fairs
- Affiliate Sites
- Career Resources
- Featured Employers
- Polls and Surveys
- Contests
- Online Education and Training
- International Employment
- Talent Auction Centers
- Company Ads (buttons & banners)
- Sponsored Links
- Special Channels for Students, Executives, Freelancers, Military, and others

Huge mega employment sites such as Monster.com include over 80 percent of these add-on services. That site alone is well worth visiting again and again for tips and advice. Most sites, however, only include job postings and resume databases and maybe a newsletter designed to capture email addresses of job seekers, who must register in order to receive the newsletter. Again, don't expect too much from these sites in terms of connecting with employers who will invite you to interviews. After all, they have millions of resumes in their databases, which makes them especially attractive to employers and recruiters in search of a large pool of qualified candidates. What's good for employers is not necessarily good for you. Your chances of getting a job interview based on your presence in such huge databases are probably not very good because of the high competition. However, your chances may improve considerably if you post your resume online with various niche sites related to your skills set. Junior officers and those with security clearances also do well through various military transition sites that are used extensively by military-friendly employers in search of such individuals.

Indeed, you are well advised to focus on smaller specialty websites relevant to your occupation and industry. Many users of Internet employment websites focus most of their attention on a few huge employment sites, such as <u>Monster.com</u> and <u>HotJobs.Yahoo.com</u>. However, they would be better off using employment websites that specialize in their industry. For example, if you are an IT professional, your chances of connecting with an employer are much greater on <u>Dice.com</u> and <u>ItCareers.com</u> than on the top 10 mega employment sites. In fact, employers interested in hiring IT professionals are more likely to use these specialty sites than the more general mega employment sites.

Our advice is to post your resume on many such websites and see what happens. Pay particular attention to niche sites and military transition sites where you are more likely to stand out from the crowd. Make sure your resume includes lots of job-specific keywords – 25 is a good number – descriptive of your skills, accomplishments, and work history, including your military rank, since employers will search resume databases based upon keywords related to their hiring needs.

Using the Internet in your job search is relatively easy once you have some basic guidance on where to go and what to do. The following books provide details on using the Internet for finding a job. Several of these resources go through the whole process of using the Internet for conducting employment research, posting resumes, and communicating by email. Others primarily annotate the best sites on the Internet:

> *America's Top Internet Job Sites* (Ron and Caryl Krannich)
> *The Guide to Internet Job Searching* (Margaret Riley Dikel)
> *The Job Hunter's Online Goldmine* (Janet E. Wall)
> *Job-Hunting on the Internet* (Richard Nelson Bolles)
> *Weddle's Job-Seeker's Guide to Employment Web Sites* (Peter D. Weddle)

Also, be sure to examine these Internet resources on writing electronic and Internet resumes:

> *Electronic Resumes and Online Networking* (Rebecca Smith)
> *e-Resumes* (Pat Criscito)
> *e-Resumes* (Susan Britton Whitcomb and Pat Kendall)

Explore Military-Friendly Employer Websites

Most employers recognize the value of hiring ex-military. However, certain companies hire a large number of individuals with military backgrounds. For example, most transitioning military are familiar with the eight largest military contractors:

- Boeing
- General Dynamics
- General Electric
- General Motors
- Northrop Grumman
- Lockheed Martin
- Raytheon
- United Technologies

However, few people are knowledgeable about smaller contractors that do work with various military-, intelligence-, and security-related agencies of the government. Many of these companies specialize in such critical technology areas as chemical and biological systems, electronics, guidance and navigation control, information warfare, marine systems, nuclear systems, sensors and lasers, signature control, space systems, and weapons effects and countermeasures. In addition, many nonmilitary-related employers, including such large retailers as Wal-Mart, Target, and Home Depot, are eager to hire ex-military because of the positive attitudes, work habits, skills, and learning and leadership abilities they bring to the job.

The following companies, most of which recruit in the Washington, DC metropolitan area, regularly seek ex-military through classified ads, websites, and job fairs. Many of these companies also have operations elsewhere in the country as well as abroad. If you are interested in working for a military-friendly employer, visit the websites of these companies for information on what they do and how to apply for positions:

- **AAI Corporation** — www.aaicorp.com
- **Advanced Resource Technologies** — www.team-arti.com
- **AFLAC** — www.aflac.com
- **Alban Caterpillar** — www.albancat.com
- **Alion Science and Technology** — www.alionscience.com
- **Altarum** — www.altarum.org
- **American Casino and Entertainment Properties** — www.stratospherehotel.com/employment/
- **American Systems Corporation** — www.2asc.com
- **Anteon Corporation** — www.anteon.com/careers
- **ARAMARK – Healthcare** — www.aramark.com
- **Argon ST Inc.** — www.argonst.com
- **ASM Research** — www.asmr.com
- **Atlas Van Lines International** — www.atlasintl.com
- **BearingPoint** — www.bearingpoint.com
- **Bell Helicopter Textron** — www.bellhelicopter.textron.com
- **Beta Analytics International** — www.betaanalytics.com
- **Blackwater USA** — www.blackwaterusa.com
- **Booz Allen Hamilton** — www.boozallen.com
- **Burlington Northern Santa Fe Railway** — www.bnsf.com
- **CACI** — www.caci.com
- **CALIBRE** — www.calibresys.com
- **Camber Corporation** — www.camber.com
- **Carson Solutions, LLC** — www.carsonsolutionsllc.com

- Centennial Contractors
  Enterprises — www.cce-inc.com
- COLSA Corporation — www.colsa.com
- Computer Sciences Corp. — http://careers.csc.com
- Comtech Mobile Datacom — www.comtechmobile.com
- CVS Pharmacy — www.careers-cvs.com
- DaimlerChrysler — www.cap.daimlerchrysler.com
- Daston Corporation — www.daston.com
- DCS Corporation — www.dcscorp.com
- Decisive Analytics Corp. — www.dac.us
- Defense Intelligence Agency — www.dia.mil/employment
- DESE Research — www.dese.com
- Dynamics Research Corp. — www.drc.com
- EAI Corporation — www.eaicorp.com
- EDO Corporation — www.edo-services.com
- EG&G Technical Services — www.egginc.com
- Federal Aviation Administration — www.faa.gov
- First Command Financial Planning — www.firstcommand.com
- GC Services — www.gcserv.com
- General Dynamics Network Systems — www.gd-ns.com/careers
- Global Professional Solutions — www.gps-hq.com
- GMRI — www.gmri.com
- Home Depot — www.careers.homedepot.com
- Honeywell Technology Solutions — www.honeywell-tsi.com
- Inova Health System — www.inova.org/careers
- Institute for Defense Analyses — www.ida.org
- IntelliDyne — www.intellidyne-llc.com
- International Development
  Resources (IDR) — www.idrnet.com
- JB Management — www.jbmanagement.com
- Jiffy Lube — www.jiffylube.com
- KBR — www.kbrjobs.com
- L-3 Communications GSI — www.L-3gsi.com
- Leads Corporation — www.LeadsCorp.com
- Lockheed Martin — www.lockheedmartin.com
- Logistics Management Resources — www.lmr-inc.com
- ManTech International — www.mantech.com
- Mastec Advanced Technologies — www.mastec.com
- Miele — www.miele.com
- Military Sealift Command — www.sealiftcommand.com
- MPRI — www.mpri.com
- MTC Technologies — www.mtctechnologies.com
- MTS Technologies — www.mtstech.com
- National Geospatial-
  Intelligence Agency — www.nga.mil
- Nortel PEC Solutions — www.nortelpec.com

- Northrop Grumman — http://careers.northropgrumman.com
- Northwest Federal Credit Union — www.northwestfcu.org
- Office of Naval Intelligence — www.nmic.navy.mil
- OMNIPLEX World Services Corp. — www.omniplex.com
- Overseas Military Sales Corp. — www.encs.com
- Pentagon Force Protection Agency — www.pfpa.mil
- Perot Systems Government Srvs. — www.perotsystems.com
- Pfizer Pharmaceuticals — www.pfizer.com
- Pragmatics — www.pragmatics.com
- PricewaterhouseCoopers — www.pwc.com
- Professional Services — www.profserve.com/careers.php
- Prudential Financial — www.prudential com
- Quantum Research International — www.quantum-intl.com
- Raytheon — www.rayjobs.com
- RDR — www.rdr.com/careers
- Ryan's Restaurant Group — www.ryans.com
- SAIC — www.saic.com
- Securitas Security Services USA — www.securitasinc.com
- Sentara Healthcare — www.sentara.com
- Southwest Airlines — www.southwest.com
- SRA International — www.sra.com/career/
- Stanley Associates — www.stanleyassociates.com
- State Farm Insurance — www.statefarm.com
- SY Coleman Corporation — www.sycoleman.com
- Systems Planning and Analysis — www.spa.com
- Target Corporation — www.target.com/careers
- Tidewater Skanska — www.usacivil.skanska.com
- The Titan Corporation — www.titan.com
- The Shaw Group — www.shawgrp.com
- U.S. Army Reserve — www.goarmy.com
- U.S. Coast Guard (civilian careers) — www.uscg.mil/hq/cgpc/cpm/jobs
- U.S. Secret Service — www.secretservice.gov
- United Laboratories — www.beearthsmart.com
- University of Maryland Department of Public Safety — www.umpd.umd.edu
- Verizon FNS — www22.verizon.com/fns
- Vinnell Corporation — www.vinnell.com
- Virginia Hospital Center — www.virginiahospitalcenter.com
- Virginia Linen Service — www.virginialinen.com
- VISTA Technology Services — www.vistatsi.com
- Weichert, Realtors — www.weichert.com
- Wexford Group International — www.thewexfordgroup.com
- Zel Technologies — www.zeltech.com/employment

Most state departments of corrections, local police departments, and local governments, as well as any company dealing with security issues, are very interested in recruiting ex-military personnel. Examples of such groups that regularly recruit transitioning military include:

- **Arlington (VA) County Sheriff's Office** — www.arlingtonva.us/departments/sheriff/Sheriffmain.aspx
- **Athens-Clarke County Unified Government** — www.athenshr.com
- **California Department of Corrections** — www.cdcr.ca.gov
- **County of Los Angeles** — http://lacounty.info
- **Fort Lauderdale Police Department** — www.flpd.org
- **Georgia Department of Correction** — www.dcor.state.ga.us
- **San Diego Sheriff's Department** — www.joinsdsheriff.net

The following 200+ companies recruit individuals with **military intelligence backgrounds**. Many – but not all – of the positions advertised with these firms require top secret clearances:

- **AboutWeb** — www.aboutweb.com
- **Accenture** — www.accenture.com
- **Acclaim Technical Services** — www.acclaimtechnical.com
- **ACS Defense Services** — www.acsdefense.com
- **Action Technologies** — www.actiontech.com
- **Advanced Concepts** — www.aci-hq.com/jobs.php
- **Aegis Research Corporation** — www.aegisresearch.com
- **Alion Science and Technology** — www.alionscience.com
- **All World Language Consultants** — www.alcinc.com
- **Alliant Techsystems** — www.atk.com
- **Alphainsight Corporation** — www.alphainsight.com
- **Analysis Group** — www.analysisgroup.com
- **Analytic Services** — www.anser.org
- **American Systems Corporation** — www.2asc.com
- **Applied Integrated Technologies** — www.applied-integrated-technology.us/
- **Applied Marine Technology** — www.amti.net
- **Applied System Technology** — www.ast.net
- **Applied Systems Research** — www.asr-reman.com
- **Applied Signal Technology** — www.appsig.com
- **Aerospace Corporation** — www.aero.org
- **AT&T Government Solutions** — www.att.com/hr
- **BAE Systems** — www.eis.na.baesystems.com
- **BAE Systems, North America** — www.baesystems.com
- **BAE Systems–Analytical Solutions** — www.mevatec.com
- **BAE Systems–Enterprise Systems** — www.esi.na.baesystems.com
- **Baer Group** — www.baergroup.com

- Ball Aerospace & Technologies
  Corporation   www.ballaerospace.com
- Battelle Memorial Institute   www.battelle.org
- Beta Analytics International   www.betaanalytics.com
- Blackwater   www.blackwaterusa.com
- Boeing–Advanced Info. Systems   www.conquestnet.com
- Boeing Company   www.boeing.com
- Boeing Satellite Systems   www.boeing.com/defense-space/space/bss
- Booz, Allen, Hamilton   www.boozallen.com
- CACI, International   www.caci.com
- Celerity IT   www.celerityit.com
- CENTRA Technology   www.centrava.com
- Central Intelligence Agency (CIA)   www.cia.gov
- Chenega Technology Services
  Corporation   www.ctsc.net
- CherryRoad Technologies   www.cherryroad.com
- Chugach Alaska Corporation   www.chugach-ak.com
- CGI   www.cgi.com
- Collaborx   www.collaborx.com
- Command Decisions Systems
  and Solutions   www.cds2.com
- COMSO   www.comso.com
- Computer Sciences Corporation   http://careers.csc.com/index.shtml
- Concurrent Technologies Corp.   www.ctc.com
- Executive Placement Associates   www.executive-placement. com
- CPSI   www.cpsinet.com
- CSSS.NET   www.csss.net
- CTGi   www.ctgusa.com
- Cubic Defense Applications Group   www.cubic.com/cda1/index.html
- Dahl Morrow International   http://dahl-morrowintl.com
- DanSources Technical Services   www.dansources.com
- Data Computer Corp. of America   www.dcca.com
- Dauntless   www.dauntless.com/dauntless/resume.do
- Delex Systems   www.delex.com
- Deloitte   http://careers.deloitte.com/gateway.aspx
- Design Staffing, LLC   www.designstaffing.com
- DFI Government Services   www.acticadfi.com
- Digital Receiver Technology   www.drti.com
- Diligent Consulting   www.diligent-us.com
- Dynamics Research Corporation   www.drc.com
- Dynetics   www.dynetics.com
- Eagle Alliance   www.eagle-alliance.com
- EAI Corporation   www.eaicorp.com
- Edge Technologies   www.edge-technologies.com
- EDO Corporation   www.edocorp.com
- EMW   www.emu.com

- ENSCO   www.ensco.com
- Esenai Corporation   www.esenai.com
- Essex Corporation   www.essexcorp.com
- ETG   www.etgtech.com
- Exceptional Software Strategies   www.exceptionalsoftware.com
- Force 3   www.force3.com
- Future Technologies   www.futuretechnologies.com
- General Dynamics-C4 Systems   www.gdc4s.com
- General Dynamics Advanced
  Information Systems   www.gd-ais.com
- General Dynamics Network Systems   www.gd-ns.com
- Geo-Centers   www.geo-centers.com/home.html
- Global Analytic Information
  Technology Services   www.gaits.com
- GLS Associates   www.gls.net
- GMRI   www.gmri.com
- Gray Hawk Systems   www.mantech.com/grayhawk
- Great-Circle Technologies   www.great-circletech.com
- Harris Corporation   www.harris.com
- Honeywell Technology Solutions   www.honeywell.com
- Houston Associates   www.hai.com
- Hewlett-Packard   www.hp.com
- IBM   www.ibm.com/planetwide/us
- iGov   www.igov.com
- IMSI   www.imsicorp.com
- Indus Corporation   www.induscorp.com
- Innovative Management and
  Technology Approaches   www.imtas.com
- Ingenium Corporation   www.ingeniumcorp.com
- Integic Corporation   www.integic.com
- IntelData   www.inteldata.com
- Intervise   www.intervise.com
- In-Q-Tel   www.in-q-tel.org
- Institute for Defense Analyses   www.ida.org
- IntelliDyne   www.intellidynellc.com
- Intelligent Decisions   www.intelligent.net
- ITT Industries   www.itt.com
- JIL Information Systems   www.jil-tsd.com
- Joseph Group   www.josefgroup.com
- Kepler Research   www.keplerresearch.com
- Kforce   www.kforce.com
- KPMG International   www.kpmg.com
- L-3 Communications
  Government Services   www.eer.com
- Lingual Information System
  Technologies   www.lingualistek.com

- Lockhead Martin Company   www.lockheedmartin.com/careers
- Lucas Group   www.lucasgroup.com
- Maden Technologies   www.madentech.com
- ManTech International Corp.   www.mantech.com
- Matrixx Group   www.matrixx-group.com
- MAXIM Systems   www.maximsys.com
- McClendon Corporation   www.mcc-corp.com
- McDonald Bradley   www.mcdonaldbradley.com
- Meridian KSI   www.meridianksi.com
- Milestone Group   www.milestonegroup.net
- Military Sealift Command   www.sealiftcommand.com
- Minerva Engineering   www.minervaengineering.com
- Mitretek Systems   www.mitretek.org
- Miltec Corporation   www.mil-tec.com
- Mitre   www.mitre.org
- Modern Technology Solutions   www.mtsi-va.com
- MTC Technologies   www.commtechinc.com
- National Security Agency   www.nsa.gov
- NCI Information Systems   www.nciinc.com
- NJVC   https://www.njvc-llc.com
- Nortel PEC Solutions   www.pec.com
- Northrop Grumman IT   www.it.northropgrumman.com
- NW Systems   www.nw-systems.com
- Oberon Associates   www.oberonassociates.com
- Observera   www.observera.com
- Oracle Corporation   www.oracle.com
- Perot Systems Government Services   www.perotsystems.com/government
- Pinnacle CSI   www.pinncsi.com
- Planned Systems International   www.plan-sys.com
- Pluribus International Corp.   www.pluribusinternational.com
- Praxis Engineering Technologies   www.PraxisEng.com
- Premier Technology Group   www.ptginc.net
- PriceWaterhouseCoopers   www.pwglobal.com
- ProObject   www.proobject.com
- PROSOFT Engineering   www.prosoft-eng.com
- Protelligent   www.protelligent.com
- Radiance Technologies   www.radiance.com
- Raytheon   www.rayjobs.com
- Red Mill Group   www.redmillgroup.com
- Riverside Research Institute   www.rri-usa.org
- RS Information Systems   www.rsis.com
- RTGX   www.rtgx.com
- SAIC   www.saic.com
- SBI Technologies Corp.   www.sbi-tech.com
- Sebenza   www.sebenzasource.com

- SI International
- Sierra Nevada Corporation
- Sikorsky Aircraft Corporation
- SM Consulting
- SOS International
- Southwestern Business Resources
- Sparta
- Spatial Data Analytics Corp.
- SPS Technologies
- SRA International
- Stanley Associates
- Strategic Data Systems
- Sun Microsystems
- SyColeman Corporation
- Sytex Group
- TechOpps
- Tenacity Solutions
- Texcom
- Thales Communications
- Titan Corp.
- Trinity Technology Group
- Triton Services, Inc.
- Triumph Technologies
- Trusted Computer Solutions
- Unisys Corporation
- US Investigations Services, LLC
- Vangent
- Vaxcom Services
- Verizon–Federal Network Systems
- Viatech
- Vision Systems & Technology
- Wallach Associates
- Wexford Group International
- WFI Government Services
- Windermere
- Winter, Wyman & Co.
- Xelas Systems Engineering
- Zel Technologies

www.si-intl.com
www.sncorp.com
www.sikorsky.com
www.smcteam.com
www.sosiltd.com
www.thinkingahead.com
www.sparta.com
www.spadac.com
www.spstech.net
www.sra.com
www.stanleyassociates.com
www.sdatasystems.com
www.sun.com
www.sycoleman.com
www.SytexGroup.com
www.techopps.net
www.tenacityinc.net
www.texcominc.com
www.thalescomminc.com
www.titan.com
www.trinitytechnologygroup.com
www.tritonsvc.com
www.triumph-tech.com
www.tcs-sec.com
www.unisys.com/public_sector/index.htm
www.usis.com
www.vangent.com
www.vaxcom.com
www.verizon.com/fns
www.viatechinc.com
www.vsticorp.com
www.wallach.org
www.thewexfordgroup.com
www.htshq.com
www.windermeregroup.com
www.winterwyman.com
www.xelas-systems.com
www.zeltech.com

Many of these and other employers interested in hiring ex-military with intelligence backgrounds can be found on Corporate Gray's, Intelligence Career's, and Security Clearance Expo's websites, which also include current job postings and sponsor "Security Clearance Only" job fairs:

www.corporategray.com
www.techexpousa.com
www.securityclearanceexpo.com

Individuals interested in starting a business or acquiring a franchise should investigate these military-friendly companies:

- **Chick-fil-A**   www.chick-fil-a.com
- **The Entrepreneur's Source**   www.theesource.com

Entrepreneur Magazine includes a FranchiseZone page on its website, which is a great gateway to the world of franchise opportunities. It includes the top 500 franchises as well as over 100 of the fastest growing franchises:

www.entrepreneur.com/franzone/listings/fastestgrowing/0,5844,,00.html

Use Your Internet Time Wisely

While the Internet is a great place to post resumes, research jobs and employers, and network for information and advice, it also can be very seductive and deceptive. Similar to shotgunning your resume to hundreds of employers, using the Internet to post resumes and respond to electronic job listings may give you a false sense of making progress with your job search. Like a big black sinkhole, it can eat up valuable job search time. Our advice: Set aside "Internet time" for your job search, but don't become obsessed by converting most of your job search time to "Internet time." A good rule-of-thumb is to spend no more than 30 percent of your job search time on the Internet.

As you incorporate the Internet into your job search, don't neglect some of the more traditional job search methods that continue to prove effective for transitioning military personnel. Indeed, there's a very high probability your first post-military job will come through your network of former military associates and buddies who have successfully transitioned to the civilian world. Above all, **you need to talk with people** by phone and in person about what appears on your resume – your objective, skills, and accomplishments. **Networking** with former friends, colleagues, and commanders continues to yield some of the best job search results.

While the Internet can assist you with several networking activities, such as finding individuals in your network and communicating your interests, skills, and qualifications by email, it doesn't result in many jobs for the job seeker (at best nearly 15 percent of all job seekers find their job via Internet employment sites). Just don't let the Internet become your major approach to the job search. For more details on how to integrate the Internet into a well organized and effective job search, see Ron and Caryl Krannich's latest edition of *America's Top Internet Job Sites: The Click and Easy™ Guide to Finding a Job Online* (Impact Publications, 2004).

Electronic Distribution and Resume Blasting

If you enter your resume into an online resume database, it will be automatically distributed to employers who access the database by using keywords. However, this is a relatively passive and ineffective form of resume distribution which requires being "discovered" by employers. Few job seekers report success using this distribution method.

Several resume entrepreneurs offer resume blasting services that appear to be quick and easy ways of distributing resumes to employers and recruiters. These companies would make you believe this is an effective way to market your resume. They usually charge anywhere from $19.95 to $199.95 to email ("blast") your resume to thousands of employers and recruiters; a few charge thousands of dollars for more specialized blasting services. Many of them post testimonials from satisfied clients who claim great success using this approach. But as any direct-mail specialist will tell you, response rates are largely determined by the quality of both the mailing list and the mailing piece. When the two come together, expect a good response rate. The problem is that you never know the quality of the email lists of these companies until **after** you use them.

We still remain skeptical about using this approach to marketing your resume. In fact, we have yet to meet any employers who would subscribe to such a questionable service. Few reputable recruiters actually use such services. While blasting your resume by email may make you initially feel good – because you are doing something and have high hopes of reaching many potential employers and recruiters – motion does not equate momentum. In the end, it may be a waste of time and money, accompanied by dashed expectations. Indeed, if you want to quickly experience the highs and lows of conducting a job search, this approach will surely provide such an experience. Resume blasting largely violates a key principle of conducting an effective job search that leads to an excellent job "fit" – target specific employers around your specific career goals, skills, and experience. Shooting a resume en masse to hundreds of employers and recruiters is not a very targeted approach. It's a "potluck," and sometime desperate, approach to finding any job you think you might be able to fit into. We strongly recommend that you find a job that is fit for you, but you do this with a more targeted approach.

Having said all of this as a cautionary note for taming your expectations, you may still want to blast your resume for under $50, just to see if you get any "nibbles" on this type of fishing expedition. If you are executive-level material who wants to get your resume into the hands of many recruiters in your industry, you might get lucky with this approach. If you are an experienced professional, go ahead and spend $19.95 with www.resumeblaster. com to blast your resume to thousands of recruiters in your industry. At that price you don't have much to lose and perhaps you'll actually make a few useful contacts with recruiters. But again, don't believe all the hype surrounding this approach, and have realistic expectations of what you are likely to get for only $19.95, or even $199.95. The old adage that you usually get what you pay for is equally valid for the job search.

Chances are your greatest success with this approach will come in having reached key recruiters or headhunters rather than specific employers – individuals who are primarily interested in marketing candidates who are skilled and experienced enough to make over

$60,000, but preferably over $100,000, a year. These recruiters are in constant need of new resumes to refresh their pool of fast-aging resumes and candidates who have found jobs. Indeed, some recruiters and headhunters welcome the receipt of such blasted resumes which they, in turn, can "flip" to employers for hefty finder's fees, if and when one of the candidates gets a job through their "recruiting" efforts. Their sourcing "commission" is usually 20 to 30 percent of the candidate's first-year salary, which is paid by the employer. In other words, you need to be the perfect candidate for this approach. If, for example, you are making under $50,000 a year, this approach is probably a waste of time and money. Most recruiters simply don't have time, nor a market, for such candidates. This approach is one way to quickly reach hundreds of recruiters whom you might not reach by other means, such as putting your resume online with www.mrinetwork.com or www. recruitersonline.com. Indeed, if you are a near or over six-figure job seeker, you can quickly ratchet up your job search, as well as go global, by using these services to contact thousands of headhunters or executive recruiters who are always looking for high quality resumes and candidates they can market to their high-paying clients. The approach does work, but it works best for only certain types of candidates who fit the needs of recruiters and headhunters.

Are You Feeling Lucky?

If and when you decide to play this resume blasting game – knowing full well the odds are probably against you – start by investigating the following fee-based resume distribution firms (your cyberspace "blasters"). Try to find out the relative mix in their database of recruiters versus actual employers who might be looking for someone with your quali-fications. These sites know the mix since they require employers and recruiters to sign up or register to receive "free" resumes from these services. For example, one of the largest such firms, Resumezapper.com, tells you up front that they only work with third-party recruiters and search firms – no employers; they primarily appeal to candidates who prefer being marketed through an executive recruiter. The recipients of these free resumes usually specify filters, so they only receive resumes that meet their marketing criteria. Not surprisingly, most of these resume distribution sites will blast your resume almost solely to recruiters or headhunters. Some sites, such as www.resumerabbit.com, will blast your resume to numerous sites that have resume databases, thus saving time in entering your resume into each unique resume database.

▪ Allen and Associates	www.resumexpress.com
▪ CareerXpress.com	www.careerxpress.com
▪ E-cv.com	www.e-cv.com
▪ Executiveagent.com	www.executiveagent.com
▪ HotResumes	www.hotresumes.com
▪ Job Search Page	www.jobsearchpage.com (international focus)
▪ ResumeBlaster	www.resumeblaster.com

- ResumeBroadcaster   www.resumebroadcaster.com
- ResumeMachine.com   www.resumemachine.com
- Resume Rabbit   www.resumerabbit.com
- ResumeZapper   www.resumezapper.com
- RocketResume   www.rocketresume.com
- See Me Resumes   www.seemeresumes.com

If you want to try your luck, for anywhere from $19.95 to over $199.95, these resume blasting firms will send your resume to 1,000 to 10,000 headhunters and employers who seek such resumes. While we do not endorse these firms – and we are often skeptical about what appear to be inflated claims of effectiveness – nonetheless, you may want to explore a few of these firms. Good luck!

Rocket Science and the 4P's for Effectiveness

While some individuals may try to turn this whole career transition process into rocket science, it's far from being very complicated. You can simplify it by focusing on what's really important and then taking the necessary actions to get job interviews and offers.

Always remember what employers want from candidates: good value, habits, and outcomes based upon an understanding of your past patterns of behavior and future goals. If you can clearly communicate your qualifications and goals via an employer-oriented resume based upon the principles outlined in this book, you should be able to get job interviews that will turn into job offers.

Once you've completed your resume, mail it, email it, hand it to lots of relevant individuals, and talk to key people about your interests, skills, and availability. Above all, follow our 4P's for job search effectiveness by always being:

- Patient
- Persistent
- Professional
- Personable

With a little help from a few friends in your network and perhaps a career professional, before long this so-called complicated process will work to your advantage!

8

Essential Letters for Job Search Success

HILE MANY JOB SEEKERS believe their resume is the key to getting a job, employers often report that a good cover letter is frequently more important to their screening and hiring decisions than the resume. Indeed, cover letters and other types of job search letters can play a critical role in getting invited to a job interview and offered a job. Neglect these letters and you very well may neglect some of the most important elements in your job search.

The most important job search letters are cover, "T," approach, thank-you, and resume. Each can be subdivided into additional types of letters. Let's survey these letters before we examine the details of writing and distributing job search letters to complement and enhance your resume.

Cover Letters

The cover letter is a special type of job search letter. By definition, it always accompanies a resume and usually is targeted toward potential employers. Employers regularly receive two types of cover letters – targeted and broadcast. Each letter literally provides "cover" for an enclosed resume.

Targeted Cover Letter

The targeted cover letter is the most commonly written job search letter. It is addressed to a specific person and in reference to a position which may or may not be vacant. It may be written in response to a classified ad or vacancy announcement or in reference to a job lead received from a referral.

A targeted cover letter should be specific and oriented toward the needs of the employer. The content of this letter should reflect as much knowledge of the employer and the position as possible. You should emphasize your skills that appear most compatible with the needs of the employer and the requirements of the position. You should tell the employer why he or she should take time to talk with you by telephone or meet you in person to further discuss your qualifications. Your letter should communicate both professional and personal qualities about you – that you are first and foremost a competent **and** likable individual.

Always try to **address this letter to a specific person,** by name and title. A proper salutation should begin with Mr., Mrs., or Ms. If you are unclear whether you are writing to a male or female, because of the unisex nature of the first name or the use of initials only – Darrell Smith or L. C. Williams – use "Mr." or the full name – "Dear Darrell Smith" or "Dear L. C. Williams." Women should always be addressed as "Ms." unless you know for certain that "Mrs." or "Miss" is the appropriate and preferred salutation.

A targeted cover letter should be oriented toward the needs of the employer.

However, many classified ads and vacancy announcements only include an address. Some may appear to be blind ads with limited information on the employer – P.O. Box 7999, Culver City, CA. If you are unable to determine to whom to address your letter, use one of two preferred choices:

1. "Dear Sir or Madam" or "Dear Sir/Madam." This is the formal, neutral, and most acceptable way of addressing an anonymous reader.

2. Eliminate this perfunctory salutation altogether and go directly from the return address to the first paragraph, leaving three spaces between the two sections. We prefer this "open" style, since it directs your letter to the organization in the same manner in which the anonymous classified ad or vacancy announcement was addressed. Your opening sentence will indicate to whom the letter goes.

Whatever your choice, please do not address the individual as "Dear Gentleperson," "Dear Gentlepeople," "Dear Person," "Dear Sir," "Dear Future Employer," "Dear Friend," "Dear Company," "Dear Personnel Department," or "To Whom It May Concern." Employers are neither gentlepeople nor friends; a "sir" often turns out to be a female; you should not be so presumptuous to imply you'll be working there soon; and a company or department is not a person. Such salutations do nothing to elevate your status in the eyes of a potential employer. Several are negatives; most verge on being dumb! It's perfectly acceptable to follow the time-honored rule of *"When in doubt, leave it out."*

The targeted cover letter is designed to directly **connect** you to the needs of the employer. It is normally divided into three distinct paragraphs. In response to a classified ad or vacancy announcement, for example, the first paragraph of this letter should connect you to the advertised position by way of introduction. For openers, make your first sentence connect you directly to the employer's advertising efforts:

I learned about your sales and marketing position in today's <u>Record-Courier</u>.

The remaining sentences should connect your skills and goals to the position and organization:

I learned about your sales and marketing position in today's <u>Record-Courier</u>. I have seven years of progressive sales and marketing experience in pharmaceuticals, involving $3.5 million in annual sales. I'm interested in taking on new challenges with a highly respected and innovative pharmaceutical firm that values team performance and wishes to explore new markets.

Such an opening paragraph is short, to the point, grabs attention, and avoids the canned language and droning character of so many boring cover letters received by hiring personnel. Our letter emphasizes four key points:

1. Where and when you learned about the position – you make a logical and legitimate connection to the employer. Also, employers like to know where candidates learned about the vacancy in order to determine the effectiveness of their advertising campaigns.

2. You have specific skills and experience related to the employer's needs.

3. You are interested in this position because you want to progress in your career rather than because of need (unemployed) or greed (you want more money). Your purpose is both employer- and career-centered rather than self-centered.

4. Your style and tone are professional, personal, positive, upbeat, and value neutral. Most important, you appear likable. You avoid making canned, self-serving, or flattering statements about yourself and the employer. The reader is probably impressed so far with your skills, interests, and knowledge of his firm. The reader's initial response is to learn more about you by reading the rest of the letter as well as reviewing the enclosed resume.

If you send a cover letter and resume in response to a referral, the only change in reference to our first original targeted cover letter involves the first sentence. In this case, you may or may not be responding to a specific position vacancy. An employer may be surveying existing talent to see what's available to the organization for possible personnel expansion. This is an example of how an employer may hire someone without ever advertising a vacancy – behavior in the so-called "hidden job market." He or she may want to let the market determine whether or not the organization is interested in adding new personnel. In this cover letter, the emphasis again is on making a legitimate connection to the employer. The tone is more personal:

Jane Parsons, who spoke with you on Friday about my interests, suggested I contact you about my sales and marketing experience. She indicated you wished to see my resume.

I have seven years of progressive sales and marketing experience in pharmaceuticals, involving $3.5 million in annual sales. I'm interested in taking on new challenges with a highly respected and innovative pharmaceutical firm that values team performance and wishes to explore new markets.

This is the best type of referral you can receive – an intermediary already introduced you to a potential employer, who is requesting your resume. She has already legitimized your candidacy and screened your qualifications based on her own judgment and personal relationship with the employer. If she is highly respected by the employer for her judgment on personnel matters – or, better still, if the employer "owes her a favor" – you have an important foot in the door. At this point you need to reinforce her judgment with a well-crafted cover letter and resume immediately followed up with a phone call. In this case you need not mention a specific position being advertised since it may not actually be advertised. Include only the name of your referral as well as refer to those interests and skills you already know are compatible with the employer's interests. Keep in mind that the opening sentence – personal reference to your referral – is the most important element in this letter.

The remaining paragraphs in this type of targeted letter will follow the same form used for other kinds of cover letters – emphasize your relevant experience and skills, which are summarized in your resume, and call for action on your candidacy. We'll examine these other paragraphs later.

Broadcast Cover Letter

Similar to resume blasting in Chapter 7 (see pages 192-194), broadcast cover letters are the ultimate exercise in delivering job search junk mail to employers. These letters are produced by job search dreamers. These are basically form letters sent to hundreds, perhaps thousands, of employers in the hope of being "discovered" by someone in need of your particular qualifications and experience. This is a favorite marketing method used by job search firms that charge individuals to help them find a job. It is their single most important indicator – however ineffective – that they are performing for their clients. The broadcast cover letter and resume prove to their clients that they are doing something for them in exchange for their fees: *"This week we sent 1,500 copies of your resume to our in-house list of employers."* Many paying clients actually believe they are getting their money's worth. Perhaps in a few days a job will be in the mail for them!

Many job hunters resort to sending such letters because the broadcast exercise involves motion. It gives them a feeling of doing something about their job search – they are actually contacting potential employers with their resume – without having to go through the process of making personal contacts through referrals and cold calls. Like most direct-mail schemes engaged in by the uninitiated, this is the lazy person's way to job search riches. Just find the names and addresses of several hundred potential employers, address the envelopes, stuff them with your resume and letter, and affix postage. Presto! In a few days you expect phone calls from employers who just discovered your talents by opening their junk mail!

Let's speak the truth about going nowhere with this approach. Motion does not mean momentum. Anyone who thinks he or she can get a job by engaging in such a junk mail exercise is at best engaging in a self-fulfilling prophecy: it results in few if any responses and numerous rejections. If you want to experience rejections, or need to fill your weekly depression quota, just broadcast several hundred resumes and letters to employers. Wait a few weeks and you will most likely get the depressing news – no one is positive about you and your resume. At best you will receive a few polite form letters informing you that the employer will keep your resume on file:

> Thank you for your resume. While we do not have a vacancy at present for someone with your qualifications, we will keep your resume on file for future reference.

If after receiving several such replies you conclude it's a tough job market out there, and no one is interested in your qualifications and experience, you're probably correct. Such an approach to communicating your qualifications to employers simply sets you up for failure. You probably don't need this type of compounding experience!

This is not to say that this approach never works. Indeed, some people get job interviews from such broadcast letters and resumes. The reason they get interviews is not because of the quality of their resume, letter, or mailing list. It's because of dumb luck in playing the numbers game.

Direct mail operates like this. If you know what you are doing – have an excellent product targeted to a very receptive audience – you may receive a 2% positive response. Indeed, successful direct-mail campaigns use 2% as an indicator of success. On the other hand, if your product is less than exciting and is not well targeted on an audience, you can expect to receive less than 0.5% positive response. In some cases you may receive no response whatsoever. In fact, few direct-mail campaigns ever result in a 2% response rate!

Let's speak the truth about going nowhere with this approach. Motion does not mean momentum.

You should never expect to receive more than a 1% positive response to your broadcast letters and resumes. Translated into real numbers, this means for every 100 unsolicited resumes you mail, you'll be lucky to get one interview. For every 1,000 resumes you mail, you may get 10 interviews. But you will be lucky if you even get a 1% positive response. Chances are your efforts will be rewarded with no invitations to interview.

The reason for such meager numbers is simple: You don't have a receptive audience for your mailing piece. Employers are busy and serious people who seek candidates when they have specific personnel needs. If they have no vacancies, why would they be interested in interviewing candidates or even replying to an unsolicited letter and resume for a nonexistent position? Such mail is a waste of their time. Writing responses to such mail costs them time and money. Employers simply don't interview people based upon a survey of their junk mail.

If you do get an interview from a broadcast letter, chances are you got lucky: Your letter and resume arrived at the time an employer was actually looking for a candidate with your type of qualifications. This is your luck calling.

If you decide to engage in the broadcast exercise, please don't waste a great deal of time and money trying to produce the "perfect" mailing piece or acquiring a "hot" mailing list. It's wishful thinking that the quality of the mailing piece or your mailing list will somehow give you an "extra edge" in generating a higher response rate.

Simply write a short three-paragraph cover letter in which you generate interest in both you and your resume as well as demonstrate your enthusiasm, drive, honesty, goals, and performance orientation. The first two paragraphs introduce you to the employer by way of your experience, previous performance, and future goals. The final paragraph calls for action on the part of the receiver:

> I have seven years of progressive sales and marketing experience in pharmaceuticals. Last year alone I generated $3.5 million in annual sales – a 25% increase over the previous year. Next year I want to do at least $4.5 million.
>
> I'm interested in taking on new challenges with a firm that values team performance and is interested in exploring new markets. As you can see from my enclosed resume, I have extensive sales and marketing experience. For the past five years, I've exceeded my annual sales goals by 30%.
>
> If you have a need for someone with my experience, I would appreciate an opportunity to speak with you about how we might best work together in meeting your sales and marketing goals. I can be contacted during the day at 808-729-3290 and in the evening at 808-729-4751. My e-mail address is: RogerE@aol.com.

If this letter were received by an employer who had a specific need for an experienced and productive individual in pharmaceutical sales and marketing, chances are he or she would contact the writer. However, the chances are very slim that this letter would connect with an employer who just happened to have such an immediate and specific need. Therefore, this otherwise excellent letter is likely to result in numerous rejections because it has no audience on the day it arrives.

While it is always preferable to address your letter to a specific name and type each envelope rather than use computer-generated mailing labels, in the end it probably doesn't really make much difference if no position exists in reference to your letter and resume. It does make a difference if you are lucky to stumble upon a position through such a mailing effort. An employer either does or does not have a personnel need specifically coinciding with your qualifications and experience. The **content** of both your letter and resume is the most important element in this broadcast exercise. If an employer has a specific personnel need and your letter and resume indicate you fit those needs, you'll probably hear from the employer regardless of whether you have his or her correct name and title or if you used a computer-generated mailing label. The employer knows what you are doing regardless of any cosmetic pretenses to the contrary.

How effective this mailing piece becomes will depend on your luck. Whatever you do, don't expect to receive many positive responses. And be prepared for an avalanche of bad news – no one appears to want you! You will collect numerous rejections in the process. After you complete this direct-mail exercise, get back to what you should really be doing with your job search time: directly contacting potential employers through referral networks, cold- calling techniques, and in response to advertised vacancies. Cover letters targeted to employers with specific personnel needs will result in many more positive responses than the junk mail you generated. You will decrease your number of rejections with a higher number of acceptances.

The T-Letter – The Ultimate Weapon

The T-letter is the most powerful type of cover letter you can deploy in your job search. It targets your relevant skills, experience, and qualifications around an employer's specific job requirements. Organized in a two-column "T" format, with the employer's advertised requirements in the left column and your qualifications in the corresponding right column, it lists bullet by bullet the employer's requirements and your related qualifications. For example, you might respond to an advertisement for a Property Management position by targeting the employer's requirements with this type of letter. Be sure to carefully read and highlight the ad for specific required skills and experience, and then compose a letter that directly relates your skills and experience to those requirements. The most powerful type of letter in response to such an ad is the classic two-column T-letter:

As a Property Manager, I would bring to this job the following qualifications:

Your Requirements	My Qualifications
▪ Enjoy working with people	▪ Seven years of progressive experience in customer service.
	▪ Regularly cited in annual performance appraisal for "excellent people skills."
	▪ Serve as a volunteer to raise funds for the United Way.
▪ Energetic personality	▪ Recognized by current employer as a go-getter who maintains a high energy level, even in highly stressful situations.
	▪ Enjoy new challenges and meeting new people.
▪ Strong attention to detail	▪ Five years experience as a quality control inspector. Improved the quality of inspections by 40% within first six months.
	▪ Supervised housing inspection teams. Achieved a 97% rating for excellence.

You may or may not want to enclose a resume with this type of cover letter. If constructed properly, this T-letter can stand on its own as a combination letter-resume. Job seekers who write such letters report phenomenal results – a very high percentage of employers contact them for interviews. The reason for such a response is very simple. Over 90% of resumes and letters received by employers do not directly relate to their job requirements. The T-letter, by contrast, is 100% on target, because it is custom-designed around required skills and experience and may include interesting examples of performance. Easy to read and centered on the specific needs of the employer, this letter quickly moves to the top of the pile where it receives more attention than most other resumes and letters. Well constructed T-letters result in numerous job interviews.

For more information on how to write T-letters, including examples of T-letters used by hundreds of clients seeking high paying professional positions, see *Haldane's Best Cover Letters for Professionals* (Impact Publications). Indeed, if you learn to write only one type of letter or resume, make sure it's a T-letter (see our example on page 214). This type of letter really works. It's the perfect medium for communicating your military experience to civilian employers who may otherwise have difficulty translating military positions, experience, and language that appear on your resume.

Approach Letters

Approach letters are some of the most important letters you should write during your job search. The purpose of these letters is to approach individuals for job search information, advice, and referrals. They play a central role in your prospecting and networking activities. You write them because you need information on alternative jobs, the job market, organizations, potential employers, and job vacancies. You need this information because the job market is highly decentralized and chaotic, and because you want to uncover job leads **before** others learn about them. Approach letters help you bring some degree of coherence and structure to your job search by organizing the job market around your interests, skills, and experience.

> *If you write only one type of letter, make sure it's a T-letter. It's the perfect medium for communicating military experience to civilian employers.*

Approach letters are responsible for opening doors for informational interviews – one of the most critical interviews in your job search. Approach letters help give you access to important job information and potential employers. Failure to write these letters is likely to weaken your overall job search campaign.

One of the most important differences between approach letters and cover letters is that an approach letter should **never** be accompanied by a resume. The reason is simple: an enclosed resume implies you are looking for a job from the individual who receives your letter. You put responsibility on this individual to either give you a job or help you find one. Few individuals want such responsibility or are eager to become your job search helper. This pushy and presumptuous approach violates the most important principle of the approach letter – these letters are designed for gaining access to critical job search information, advice, and referrals. Such a letter should never imply that you are looking for a job with or through this individual. Only during an informational interview, preferably **after** you receive such information, advice, and referrals, should you share your resume with your letter recipient.

Time and again job searchers make the mistake of writing an approach letter but enclosing their resume. Such ill-conceived actions generate contradictory messages. While they may produce an outstanding approach letter, they in effect kill it by attaching a resume. The letter says they are only asking for information, advice, and referrals, but the enclosed resume implies they are actually looking for a job from the letter recipient. Job seekers who do this are unethical or dishonest. This puts the recipients on the spot and makes them feel uncomfortable.

You may want to write two different types of approach letters for different situations: referral and cold turkey. The **referral letter** is written to someone based on a referral or a connection with someone else. A friend or acquaintance, for example, recommends that you contact a particular individual for job search information and advice:

> Why don't you contact John Staples? He really knows what's going on. I'm sure he'd be happy to give you advice on what he knows about the pharmaceutical industry in this area. Tell him I recommended you give him a call.

This type of referral is **the** basis for building and expanding networks for conducting informational interviews that eventually lead to job interviews and offers. It's the type of referral you want to elicit again and again in the process of expanding your job search network into the offices of potential employers. When you receive such a referral, you have one of two choices for developing the connection.

First, depending on the situation and the individual's position, you may want to immediately initiate the contact by telephone. The use of the telephone is efficient; it gets the job done quickly. However, it is not always the most effective way of initiating a contact. The individual may be very busy and thus unable to take your call, or he may be in the middle of some important business that should not be interrupted by someone like you. When you telephone a stranger, you may face immediate resistance to any attempt to use his valuable time or schedule an informational interview.

Second, you may want to write a referral approach letter which can be sent as email or as a posted letter. While not as efficient as a telephone call, this letter may be more effective. It prepares the individual for your telephone call. Such a letter enables you to be in complete control of the one-way communication; you should be better able to craft an effective message that will lead to a productive telephone call and informational interview.

This type of approach letter should immediately open with a personal statement that nicely connects you to the reader via your referral and a bit of honest flattery. Start with something like this:

> John Staples suggested that I contact you regarding the local pharmaceutical industry. He said you know the business better than anyone else.

> When I spoke with Mary Thompson today, she highly recommended you as a source of information on the local pharmaceutical industry.

Such statements include two positives that should result in a favorable impression on the receiver: You've already been screened by the referral for making this contact, and this individual is recognized as an expert in the eyes of others who are important to him who, in turn, pass this recognition on to others.

The next two paragraphs should indicate your interests, motivations, and background in reference to the purpose of making this contact. It should clearly communicate your intentions for making this contact and for using the individual's time. You might say something like this:

> After several successful years in pharmaceutical sales and marketing in Boston, I've decided to relocate to the Midwest where I can be closer to my family. However, having moved to the East nearly 15 years ago, I've discovered I'm somewhat of a stranger to the industry in this area.
>
> I would very much appreciate any information and advice you might be able to share with me on the nature of the pharmaceutical industry in the greater Chicago Metro area. I have several questions I'm hoping to find answers to in the coming weeks.
>
> Perhaps, as John said, you could fill me in on the who, what, and where of the local industry.

Throughout this letter, as well as in your telephone conversation or in a face-to-face meeting, you should **never** indicate that you are looking for a job through this individual. You are only seeking information and advice. If this contact results in referrals that lead to job interviews and offers, that's great. But you are explicitly initiating this contact because you need more information and advice at this stage of your job search. This individual, in effect, becomes your personal advisor – not your future employer. Individuals who use the approach letter for the purpose of getting a job through the recipient abuse this form of communication. Their actions are exploitive, and they tend to become undesirable nuisances few people want to hire. Worst still, they give networking and informational interviewing bad names.

Whatever you do, make sure you are completely honest when you approach referral contacts for information and advice. You will get better cooperation and information as well as be seen as a thoughtful individual who should be promoted through referrals and networking. Therefore, the second and third paragraphs of your letter should indicate your true intentions in initiating this contact.

Your final paragraph should consist of an action statement which indicates what you will do next. Alerting the letter recipient that you will soon contact him or her, your concluding paragraph should specify a time and date for making contact:

> I'll give you a call Tuesday afternoon to see if your schedule would permit some time to discuss my interests in the local pharmaceutical industry. I appreciate your time and look forward to talking with you in a few days.

You – not the letter recipient – must take **follow-up action** on this letter. You should never end such a letter with an ostensibly action-oriented statement requesting the recipient to contact you (*"I look forward to hearing from you"* or *"Please give me a call if your schedule would permit us to meet"*). If you do this, you're unlikely to receive a reply. It's incumbent upon **you** to further initiate the contact with a telephone call. Assuming you sent the letter by regular mail or transmitted it by email, try to leave at least four days between when you sent the letter and when you make the telephone call. If you use special next-day delivery services, make your call on the same delivery day, preferably between 2pm and 4pm.

This action statement prepares the contact for your telephone call and subsequent conversation or meeting. He or she will most likely give you some time. However, please note that this action statement is also a thoughtful conclusion that does not specify the nature of your future contact nor is it overly aggressive or presumptuous (*"I'll schedule a meeting"*). The open-ended statement *"to see if your schedule would permit some time"* could result in either a telephone interview or a face-to-face meeting. In many cases a telephone interview will suffice. The individual may have a limited amount of information that is best shared in a 5-10 minute telephone call. In other cases, a face-to-face half-hour to one-hour informational interview would be more appropriate. By choosing such a closing action statement, you leave the time, place, and medium of the interview open to discussion.

The **cold-turkey approach letter** is written for the same purpose but without a personal contact. In this case you literally approach a stranger with no prior contacts. In contrast to the referral approach letter, in this situation you do not have instant credibility attendant with a personal connect. While cold-turkey contacts can be difficult to initiate, they can play an important role in your job search campaign.

Since you do not have a personal contact to introduce you to the letter recipient, you need to begin your letter with an appropriate "cold call" opener that logically connects you to the reader. Try to make your connection as warm, personal, and professional as possible. Avoid excessive flattery or boastful statements that are likely to make your motives suspect and thus turn off the reader. It's always helpful to inject in this letter a personal observation that gently strokes the ego of the reader. If, for example, you read a newspaper article about the individual's work, or if he just received an award or promotion, you might introduce yourself in this letter in any of the following ways:

> I read with great interest about your work with _____. Congratulations on a job well done. During the past twelve years I've been involved in similar work.

> Congratulations on receiving the annual community award. Your efforts have certainly helped improve the appearance of our base housing area. My interest in helping to improve the image of our community began nearly ten years ago when I was living in base housing outside Frankfurt, Germany.

> Congratulations on your recent promotion to Vice President of Allied Materials. I have been following your rapid rise through the corporate ranks ever since you left the 82nd Airborne Division. Your work in expanding Allied Materials' markets to Japan and China especially interests me given my fluency in Japanese and recent military assignment to the Far East.

Other openers might begin with some of the following lead-in phrases which help connect you to the reader:

I am writing to you because of your position as . . .

Because of your experience in . . .

We have a common interest in . . .

Since we are both alumni of Texas A&M, I thought . . .

As a fellow member of Delta Sigma Alpha sorority, I wanted to congratulate you on your recent election to . . .

Since we both served in Iraq during 2006 . . .

Whatever opener you choose, make sure you focus on making a **logical connection** that is both personal and professional. Inject some personality in this letter. After all, you want this stranger to take an immediate interest in you. Try to communicate that you are a likable, enthusiastic, honest, and competent person worth talking to or even meeting. The very first sentence should grab the reader's attention.

A strong opener in a cold-turkey approach letter can be nearly as effective as the personal contact opener in the referral approach letter.

The remaining paragraphs of the cold-turkey referral letter will be structured similarly to the referral approach letter – indicate your interests, motivations, and background in reference to your purpose in making this contact. Clearly communicate your intentions for taking the individual's time. Again, be perfectly truthful and tactful in what you say, but avoid making honest but stupid statements, such as *"I really don't know what's going to happen to me in the next three months."* Be sure to close with an indication of action – you will call on a particular date to see if the person's schedule would permit some time to discuss your interests.

If you incorporate these two types of approach letters in your job search, you will quickly discover they are the most powerful forms of communication in your job search arsenal. They must be written and targeted toward individuals who have information, advice, and referrals relevant to your job search interests. They are the bricks-and-mortar for building networks that generate informational interviews that lead to job interviews and offers. Resumes and telephone calls are no substitute for these referral letters. A resume **never** accompanies these letters, and a telephone call only follows **after** the recipient has received and read your approach letter. If you write these letters according to our suggested structure and content, and follow up with the telephone call, you will receive a great deal of useful job search information, advice, and referrals. You will learn about the structure of the job market, identify key players who can help you, and inject a healthy dose of reality into a job search that may otherwise be guided by myths and wishful thinking.

If for any reason you still feel compelled to sneak a resume in the envelope or as an email attachment with one of these approach letters, you will quickly discover few recipients want to see or talk with you. The enclosed or attached resume immediately transforms what was potentially an effective approach letter into an ineffective cover letter for a job application – something that is inappropriate in this situation. As we've already seen, an effective cover letter has a different purpose as well as follows other writing, distribution, and follow-up principles.

Thank-You Letters

Thank-you letters are some of the most effective communications in a job search. They demonstrate an important **social grace** that says something about you as an individual – your personality and how you probably relate to others. They communicate one of the most important characteristics sought in potential employees – **thoughtfulness**.

Better still, since few individuals write thank-you letters, those who do write them are **remembered** by letter recipients. And one thing you definitely want to happen again and again during your job search is to be remembered by individuals who can provide you with useful information, advice, and referrals as well as invite you to job interviews and extend to you job offers. Being remembered as a thoughtful person with the proper social graces will give you an edge over other job seekers who fail to write thank-you letters. Whatever you do, make sure you regularly send thank-you letters in response to individuals who assist you in your job search.

Many job seekers discover the most important letters they ever wrote were thank-you letters. These letters can have several positive outcomes:

- **Contacts turn into more contacts and job interviews:** A job seeker sends a thank-you letter to someone who recommended contacting a former college roommate; impressed with the thoughtfulness of the job seeker and feeling responsible for helping her make the right contacts, the individual continues providing additional referrals, which eventually lead to two job interviews.

- **Job interview turns into a job offer:** A job seeker completes a job interview. Within 24 hours, he writes a nice thank-you in which he expresses his gratitude for having an opportunity to interview for the position as well as reiterates his interest in working for the employer. This individual is subsequently offered the job. The employer later tells him it was his thoughtful thank-you letter that gave him the edge over two other equally qualified candidates who never bothered to follow up the interview.

- **A job rejection later turns into a job offer:** After interviewing for a position, a job seeker receives a standard rejection letter from an employer indicating the job was offered to another individual. Rather than get angry and end communications with the employer, the job seeker sends a nice thank-you letter in which she notes her disappointment in not being selected and then thanks him for the opportunity to interview for the position. She also reiterates her continuing interest in working for the organization. The employer remembers this individual. Rather than let her get away, he decides to create a new position for her.

- **A job offer turns into an immediate positive relationship:** Upon receiving a job offer, the new employee sends a nice thank-you letter in which he expresses his appreciation for the confidence shown by the employer. He also reassures the employer that he will be as productive as expected. This letter is well received by the employer, who is looking forward to working closely with such a thoughtful new employee. Indeed, he becomes a mentor and sponsor who immediately gives the employee some plum assignments that help him fast-track his career within the organization.

- **Termination results in strong recommendations and a future job offer:** An employee, seeking to advance her career with a larger organization, receives a job offer from a competing firm. In submitting her formal letter of resignation, she also sends a personal thank-you letter to her former employer. She sincerely expresses her gratitude for having the opportunity work with him and attributes much of her success to his mentoring. This letter further confirms his conclusion about this former employee – he's losing a valuable asset. While he cannot offer her a similar or better career opportunity in this organization, he will keep her in mind if things change. And things do change two years later when he makes a major career move to a much larger organization. One of the first things he does as Vice-President is to begin shaping his own personal staff. He immediately contacts her to see if she would be interested in working with him. She's interested and soon joins her former employer in making another major career move.

In these cases it was the job seekers' thank-you letters, rather than their cover letters and resumes, that got them job interviews and offers.

As indicated in the above scenarios, thank-you letters should be written in the following situations:

- **After receiving information, advice, or a referral from a contact:** You should always express your gratitude in writing to individuals who provide you with job search assistance. Not only is this a nice thing to do, it also is functional for a successful job search. Individuals who feel they are appreciated will most likely remember you and be willing to further assist you with your job search and recommend you to others.

- **Immediately after interviewing for a job:** Whether it be a telephone or face-to-face interview, always write a nice thank-you letter within 12 hours of completing the interview. This letter should express your gratitude for having an opportunity to interview for the job. Be sure to reiterate your interest in the job and stress your possible contributions to the employer's operations. The letter should emphasize your major strengths in relationship to the employer's needs. All other things being equal, this letter may give you an extra edge over other candidates. It may well become your most effective job search letter!

- **Withdrawing from further consideration:** At some point during the recruitment process, you may decide to withdraw from further consideration. Perhaps you decided to take another job, you're now more satisfied with your present job, or the position no longer interests you. For whatever reason, you should write a short thank-you letter in which you withdraw from consideration. Explain in positive terms why you are no longer interested in pursuing an application with the organization. Thank them for their time and consideration.

- **After receiving a rejection:** Even if you receive a rejection, it's a good idea to write a thank-you letter. How many employers ever receive such a letter from what ostensibly should be a disappointed job seeker? This unique letter is likely to be remembered – which is what you want to accomplish in this situation. Being remembered may result in referrals to other employers or perhaps a job interview and offer at some later date.

- **After receiving a job offer:** However well they think they hire, employers still are uncertain about the outcome of their hiring decisions until new employees perform in their organization. Why not put their initial anxieties at ease and get off on the right foot by writing a nice thank-you letter? In this letter express your appreciation for having received the confidence and trust of the employer. Reiterate what you told the employer during the job interview(s) about your goals and expected performance. Conclude with a reaffirmation of your starting date as well as a statement about how much you look forward to becoming a productive member of the team. Such a thoughtful letter will be well received by the employer. It could well accelerate your progress within the organization beyond the norm.

- **Upon leaving a job:** Whether you leave your job voluntarily or are forced by circumstances to terminate, try to leave a positive part of you behind by writing a thank-you letter. Burning bridges behind you through face-to-face confrontation or a vindictive, get-even letter may later catch up with you, especially if you anger someone in the process who may later be in a position to affect your career. If you quit to take a job with another organization, thank your employer for the time you spent with the organization and the opportunities given to you to acquire valuable experience and skills. If you terminated under difficult circumstances – organizational cutbacks or a nasty firing – try to leave on as positive a note as possible. Employers in such situations would rather have you out of sight and mind. Assure them there are no hard feelings, and you wish them the best as you would hope they would wish you the same. Stress the positives of your relationship with both the employer and the organization. Remember, your future employer may call your previous employer for information on your past performance. If you leave a stressful situation on a positive note, chances are your previous employer will give you the benefit of the doubt and stress only your positives to others. He may even commit a few "sins of omission" that only you and he know about: *"She really worked well with her co-workers and was one of our best analysts"* does not tell the whole story which may be that you couldn't get along with your boss, and vice versa. After having made peace with each other through the medium of the thank-you letter, what would your former employer have to gain by telling the whole story to others about your work with him? Your thank-you letter should at least neutralize the situation and at best turn a negative situation into a positive for your career. Indeed, he may well become one of your supporters – for other jobs with other employers, that is!

Examples of each type of letter, written according to our principles of effective thank-you letters, appear at the end of this chapter and are identified accordingly.

Thank-you letters should always be written in a timely manner – within 12 hours of the situation that prompted this letter. It should be mailed and/or emailed immediately so that it reaches the recipient within three to four days. If you wait longer, the letter will have less impact on the situation. Indeed, in the case of the interview thank-you letter, if an employer is making a final hiring decision among three candidates, your letter should arrive as soon as possible to have a chance to affect the outcome.

It's okay to email thank-you letters. However, don't treat this letter similar to an instant message or a quick and often sloppy email note. This letter should represent your very best effort at both thinking and writing. Carefully compose your message off-line, check your spelling and grammar, drop it into your email program, use an attention-grabbing subject line, and send it. Don't forget that your goal in writing this letter in a post-interview situation is to be **remembered** as someone who should be offered the job.

At the same time, we recommend mailing a paper copy of your thank-you letter. Since many individuals get flooded with emails, which can quickly get overlooked, deleted, or skimmed, a mailed paper letter will likely get read and remembered. Indeed, your mailed letter may stand out as unique and thoughtful. After all, you took the time to compose, produce, and mail this letter. Whether you handwrite or type this letter may not make a great deal of difference in terms of outcomes, but your choice says something about your professional style and mentality. Many people claim handwritten thank-you letters are more powerful than typed letters. We doubt such claims and have yet to see any credible data on the subject other than personal preferences and questionable logic. It is true that handwritten thank-you letters communicate a certain personal element that cannot be expressed in typewritten letters. If you choose to handwrite this letter, make sure you have attractive handwriting. Your handwriting form and style could be a negative.

The problem with handwritten letters is that they can express a certain nonprofessional, amateurish style. They also may raise questions about your motivations and manipulative style. They turn off some readers who expect a business letter, rather than an expression of social graces, in reference to a business situation. Furthermore, some readers may consider the handwritten letter an attempt at psychological manipulation – they know what you're trying to do by handwriting a letter. That's what real estate, insurance agents, and car salespeople are taught to do in their training seminars! When in doubt, it's best to type this letter in a neat, clean, and professional manner. If typewritten, such a personal letter also will express your professional style and respond to the expectations appropriate for the situation. It tells the reader that you know proper business etiquette, you know this is a business situation, you are equipped to respond, and you attempt to demonstrate your best professional effort.

Resume Letters

A resume letter is a special type of approach letter that substitutes for a formal resume. Merging the cover letter and resume into a single document, this type of letter is written when it is appropriate to target your qualifications in a format other than a separate cover letter and resume. It's most often used to approach employers with information on your experience and skills in the hope that they will have vacancies for someone with your qualifications.

Since it outlines your experience and skills, the resume letter is designed to get job interviews with employers. It, in effect, asks for a job interview rather than information, advice, or referrals for expanding your job search.

Similar to the cold-turkey approach letter, the resume letter should open with a logical connection between you and the employer. The second paragraph, however, is what defines this as a resume letter. This paragraph should summarize your major experience and skills in relation to the employer's needs. In fact, you may want to take this section directly from the "Areas of Effectiveness," "Experience," or "Work History" section appearing on your resume. For ease of reading, it's best to bullet each item, preferably including three to five items similar to the examples found at the end of this chapter. The final paragraph should call for action – you taking the initiative to call the recipient at a specific time for the purpose of scheduling a possible interview.

You should try to keep this letter to a single page. Remember, it is neither a cover letter nor a resume, but a combination of both which has a specific purpose – you are trying to invite yourself to a job interview. Since this type of letter tends to put employers on the spot – here's another "cold-caller" – it will probably generate few positive responses and numerous rejections. However well written this letter may be, few employers are prepared to give job interviews based on such a letter. Chances are most employers will not have vacancies available at the time you send this letter. What they may be able to do is give you referrals to other employers who may have vacancies – but only if you follow up this letter with a phone call. In the end, your resume letter may become an important prospecting letter for uncovering job leads.

COVER LETTER
Response to Advertised Position

724 Grand Avenue
St. Louis, MO 62345

July 15, 20__

Jeff Morris
Director of Personnel
GREATER CHICAGO BANK
245 LaSalle Street
Chicago, IL 60000

Dear Mr. Morris:

The accompanying resume is in response to your listing in yesterday's Chicago Tribune for a loan officer.

I am especially interested in this position because my experience as an Army Finance Officer has prepared me for understanding the budget issues associated with large organizations as well as the financial needs of a diverse array of individuals. I wish to use this experience with a growing and community-conscious bank such as yours.

I would appreciate an opportunity to meet with you to discuss how my experience will best meet your needs. My ideas on how to improve small business financing may be of particular interest to you. I will call your office on the morning of July 21 to inquire if a meeting can be scheduled at a convenient time.

I look forward to meeting you.

Sincerely yours,

Maurine Davis

Maurine Davis

COVER LETTER
Referral

2101 Terrace Street
Sacramento, CA 97342

May 3, 20____

Terry Ford
Vice President
Fulton Engineering Corporation
1254 Madison Street
Sacramento, CA 97340

Dear Mr. Ford:

John Bird, the Director of Data Systems at Ottings Engineering Company, informed me that you are looking for someone to direct your new management information system.

I enclose my resume for your consideration. During the past 10 years I have designed and developed a variety of information systems for the U.S. Air Force. I have worked at both the operational and managerial levels and know how to develop systems appropriate for different types of organizations.

I would appreciate an opportunity to visit with you and examine your operations. Perhaps I could provide you with a needs assessment prior to an interview. I will call you next week to make arrangements for a visit.

I look forward to speaking with you next week.

Sincerely,

Steven Paris

Steven Paris

T-LETTER
Response to Advertised Position

431 Wilson Street
Columbus, OH 53211

November 17, 20___

Mary Tilman
Director of Training
SITMORE ENTERPRISES
822 Liberty Street
Philadelphia, PA 17175

Dear Ms. Tilman:

I noticed with interest your ad in *Training Resources* for an experienced
Management Trainer. I would bring to this position these qualifications:

Your Needs	My Qualifications
▪ Five years training experience.	▪ Seven years of progressive experience as a management trainer in a variety of organizational settings.
▪ Strong writing and presentation skills.	▪ Annually produce 6-8 training manuals and conduct over 30 3-day training sessions on supervisory skills for senior entry-level to senior-level managers.
▪ Ability to supervise a group of training professionals	▪ Annually supervise 7 trainers who conduct more than 300 programs in 18 U.S. and European locations.

The enclosed resume further summarizes my qualifications. I would appreciate
an opportunity to speak with you about this position. I'll call your office next
Thursday morning to answer any question you may have about my candidacy.

Sincerely,

David Watson

David Watson

APPROACH LETTER
Referral

2931 Gadwall Place
Virginia Beach, VA 23462

November 3, 20___

Doris Leffert, Director
Architectural Design Office
ABC ENGINEERING COMPANY
213 Landmore Street
Cleveland, OH 44444

Dear Ms. Leffert:

Captain David Johns suggested that I write to you in regards to my interests in architectural drafting. He thought you would be a good person to give me some career advice.

I am interested in an architectural drafting position with a firm specializing in commercial construction. As a trained draftsman for the U.S. Navy, I have six years of progressive experience in all facets of construction, from pouring concrete to developing plans for $15 million in residential construction. I am particularly interested in improving construction design and building operations of shopping complexes.

Captain Johns mentioned you as one of the leading experts in this growing field. Would it be possible for us to meet briefly? Over the next few months I will be conducting a job search. I am certain your counsel would assist me as I begin looking for new opportunities.

I will call your office next week to see if your schedule permits such a meeting.

Sincerely,

Barry West

Barry West

APPROACH LETTER
Cold Turkey

881 Potomac Street
Quantico, VA 22222

August 9, 20____

Judy Zukaris, Director
NORTHEAST ASSOCIATION
    FOR SENIOR CITIZENS
1267 Connecticut Avenue
Washington, DC 20000

Dear Ms. Zukaris:

I have been impressed with your work with the elderly. Your organization takes a community perspective in trying to integrate the concerns of the elderly with those of other community groups. Perhaps other organizations will soon follow your lead.

I am anxious to meet you and learn more about your work. While serving in the U.S. Marine Corps, I used my off-duty hours as a volunteer working with senior citizens in my local community. From this experience I decided to pursue a career working with community organizations and the elderly.

However, before I pursue my interest further, I need to talk to people with experience in gerontology. In particular, I would like to know more about careers with the elderly as well as how my background might best be used in the field of gerontology.

I am hoping you can assist me in this matter. I would like to meet with you briefly to discuss several of my concerns. I will call next week to see if your schedule permits such a meeting.

I look forward to meeting you.

Sincerely,

Darrell Rutherford

Darrell Rutherford

THANK-YOU LETTER
Referral

3211 Fairview Blvd.
Ft. Lauderdale, FL 30000

June 16, 20____

Albert Bates
123 Riggs Drive
Miami, FL 30301

Dear Mr. Bates:

Thank you so much for putting me in contact with Jane Burton at Fordham Manufacturing Company.

I spoke with her today about my interest in technical training. She was most gracious with her time and provided me with a great deal of useful information on job opportunities in the Miami area. She even made some valuable suggestions for strengthening my resume and gave me a few names of individuals who might be interested in my qualifications.

I'll send you a copy of my resume once I revise it. Please feel free to make any comments or suggestions as well as share it with others who might be interested in my background.

Again, thank you for the Jane Burton contact. She spoke very highly of you and your work with the United Fund.

Sincerely,

Clark Owens

Clark Owens

THANK-YOU LETTER
After Informational Interview

2234 Taylor Drive
Cincinnati, OH 43333

January 5, 20 ____

Michael Marris, Director
OHIO FINANCE CORPORATION
1145 Davis Street
Columbus, OH 43380

Dear Mr. Marris:

Your advice was most helpful in clarifying my questions on careers in finance. I am now reworking my resume and have included many of your thoughtful suggestions. I will send you a copy next week.

Thank you so much for taking time from your busy schedule to see me. I will keep in contact and follow through on your suggestion to see Janet Olson about opportunities with the Cleveland-Akron Finance Company.

Sincerely,

Perry Wilson

Perry Wilson

THANK-YOU LETTER
Post Job Interview

421 Center Street
Denver, CO 82171

September 7, 20 _____

Fred Thomas
Director, Personnel Department
Coastal Products Incorporated
7229 Lakewood Drive
Denver, CO 82170

Dear Mr. Thomas:

Thank you again for the opportunity to interview for the marketing position. I appreciated your hospitality and enjoyed meeting you and members of your staff.

The interview convinced me of how compatible my background, interests, and skills are with the goals of Coastal Products Incorporated. As discussed, I am a fast learner with a strong propensity for sales. During my off-duty time in the military, I was very successful in selling long distance telecommunications services. This work required developing a marketing strategy and carefully following through with implementation. Combined with my military background in Asian and Pacific affairs and my fluency in Chinese, I am confident my skills and experience would increase market share for Coastal Products Incorporated in the rapidly expanding Pacific Rim market.

For more information on the new product promotion program I described, call Steve Barry in the evening at 333/411-2351. I talked to Steve this morning and mentioned your interest in this program.

I look forward to meeting you and your staff again.

Sincerely,

Mark Harris

Mark Harris

THANK-YOU LETTER
Responding to Rejection

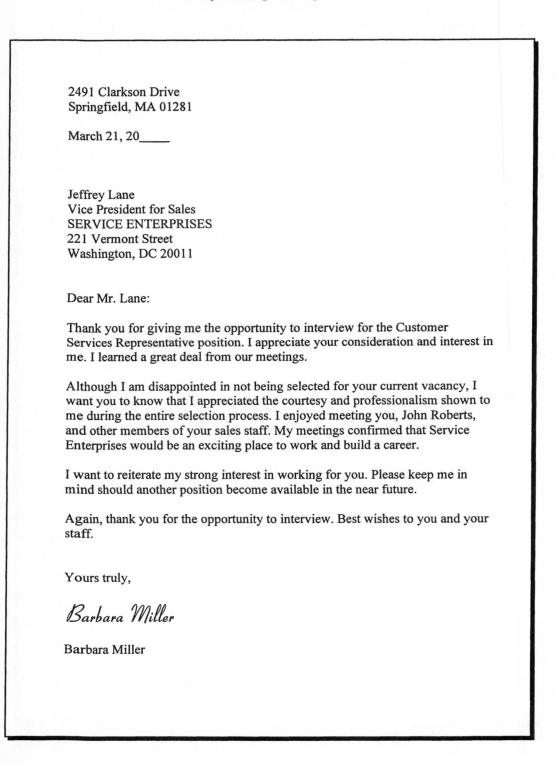

2491 Clarkson Drive
Springfield, MA 01281

March 21, 20____

Jeffrey Lane
Vice President for Sales
SERVICE ENTERPRISES
221 Vermont Street
Washington, DC 20011

Dear Mr. Lane:

Thank you for giving me the opportunity to interview for the Customer
Services Representative position. I appreciate your consideration and interest in
me. I learned a great deal from our meetings.

Although I am disappointed in not being selected for your current vacancy, I
want you to know that I appreciated the courtesy and professionalism shown to
me during the entire selection process. I enjoyed meeting you, John Roberts,
and other members of your sales staff. My meetings confirmed that Service
Enterprises would be an exciting place to work and build a career.

I want to reiterate my strong interest in working for you. Please keep me in
mind should another position become available in the near future.

Again, thank you for the opportunity to interview. Best wishes to you and your
staff.

Yours truly,

Barbara Miller

Barbara Miller

THANK-YOU LETTER
Withdrawing From Consideration

921 Peters Street
Williamsburg, VA 23512

February 9, 20____

Dr. Thomas C. Bostelli, President
Northern States University
2500 University Drive
Greenfield, MA 03241

Dear Dr. Bostelli:

It was indeed a pleasure meeting with you and your staff last week to discuss your need for a Director of Public and Government Relations. Our time together was most enjoyable and informative.

As I discussed with you during our meetings, I believe one purpose of preliminary interviews is to explore areas of mutual interest and to assess the fit between the individual and the position. After careful consideration, I have decided to withdraw from consideration for the position.

My decision is based upon several factors. First, the emphasis on fund raising is certainly needed, but I would prefer more balance in my work activities. Second, the position would require more travel than I am willing to accept with my other responsibilities. Third, professional opportunities for my wife would be very limited in northwest Massachusetts.

I want to thank you for interviewing me and giving me the opportunity to learn about your needs. You have a fine staff and faculty, and I would have enjoyed working with them.

Best wishes in your search.

Sincerely,

Edward Rollins

Edward Rollins

THANK-YOU LETTER
Accepting Job Offer

190 Wilson Blvd.
San Francisco, CA 94826

April 25, 20____

Martin Franks
Vice President
PACIFIC COAST AIRLINES
781 McDonnell Street
San Francisco, CA 94829

Dear Mr. Franks:

I am pleased to accept your offer, and I am looking forward to joining you and your staff next month.

The customer relations position is ideally suited to my background and interests. I assure you I will give you my best effort in making this an effective position within your company.

I understand I will begin work on July 1. If, in the meantime, I need to complete any paper work or take care of any other matters, please contact me at 377-4029.

I enjoyed meeting with you and your staff and appreciated the professional manner in which the hiring was conducted.

Sincerely,

Jennifer Nash

Jennifer Nash

THANK-YOU LETTER
Terminating Employment

914 Sixth Avenue
Pittsburgh, PA 43211

November 11, 20____

Kevin Wallace
Chief Engineer
PITTSBURGH CONSTRUCTION COMPANY
2111 Hillsborough Road
Pittsburgh, PA 43210

Dear Kevin,

I am writing to inform you that I will be leaving Pittsburgh Construction Company on December 12 to accept another position.

As you know, I have developed an interest in architectural drafting which combines my drafting skills with my artistic interests. While I was vacationing in Houston recently, a relative approached me about an opening for someone with my background with a large architecture and engineering firm. I investigated the possibility and, consequently, received an offer. After careful consideration, I decided to accept the offer and relocate to Houston. I will be working with Brown and Little Company.

I have thoroughly enjoyed working with you over the past two years, and deeply appreciate your fine supervision and support. You have taught me a great deal about drafting, and I want to thank you for providing me with the opportunity to work here. It has been a very positive experience for me both personally and professionally.

I wanted to give you more than the customary two weeks notice so you would have time to find my replacement. I made the decision to relocate yesterday and decided to inform you immediately.

Best wishes.

Sincerely,

Garry Slater

Garry Slater

RESUME LETTER

773 Main Street
Williamsburg, VA 23572

November 12, 20____

Barbara Thompson, President
SRM ASSOCIATES
421 91st Street
New York, NY 11910

Dear Ms. Thompson:

I just completed reading the article in <u>Business Today</u> on SRM Associates. Your innovative approach to recruiting minorities is of particular interest to me because of my background in public relations and minority recruitment.

I am interested in learning more about your work as well as the possibilities of joining your firm. My qualifications include:

- research and writing on minority recruitment in the military
- administered a major minority representation program for DoD
- published several professional articles on career development for minorities
- organized and led public relations, press, and minority conferences
- M.A. in Journalism and B.A. in English

I will be in New York City during the week of December 10. Perhaps your schedule would permit us to meet briefly to discuss our mutual interests. I will call your office next week to see if such a meeting can be arranged.

I appreciate your consideration.

Sincerely yours,

Chris Taylor

Chris Taylor

RESUME LETTER

3331 Taylor Road
Baltimore, MD 20000

April 4, 20____

Carol Watson
TRC CORPORATION
719 Olson Road
Rockville, MD 21101

Dear Ms. Watson:

TRC Corporation is one of the most dynamic computer companies in the nation. Its model employee training and development program makes it the type of organization I am interested in joining.

I am seeking a training position with a computer firm which would use my administrative, communication, and planning abilities to develop effective training and counseling programs. My experience includes:

Administration: Supervised instructors and counselors. Coordinated job vacancy and training information for military businesses and schools.

Communication: Conducted over 100 workshops on interpersonal skills, stress management, and career planning. Frequent guest speaker to various agencies and associations. Experienced writer of training manuals and public relations materials.

Planning: Planned and developed counseling programs for over 5,000 employees. Reorganized interviewing and screening processes and developed program of individualized and group counseling.

I am also completing my M.A. in industrial psychology with an emphasis on developing training and counseling programs for technical personnel.

Could we meet to discuss your program as well as how my experience might relate to your needs? I will call your office on Tuesday morning, April 12, to arrange a convenient time.

I especially want to show you a model employee counseling and career development program I recently developed. Perhaps you may find it useful for your work with TRC.

Sincerely,

Harold Haines

Harold Haines

9

Effective Letter Writing

SSUMING YOUR LETTER IS impressive enough to pass the five- to ten-second reading test, what you say and how you say it will largely determine if the reader will take desired actions. The power of your paper letters or email compositions must move the reader to action. You can best do this by observing the rules of effective letter organization and content.

Common Mistakes

Individuals who receive hundreds of letters from job seekers report similar problems with letters they receive. These problems can be corrected by following a few simple organization and content rules. Letters that don't pass the five- to ten-second test tend to include several of these errors:

- **Look unprofessional in form, structure, and design:** Many letters neglect the basic rules of form, structure, and design associated with writing effective letters. Mistaking the art of letter writing with quick email message exercises, many writers compose cryptic email notes that demonstrate their communication incompetence. Whether paper or electronic compositions, many letters look amateurish rather than reflect the professional competence of the writer. They simply don't demonstrate the writer's best professional effort.

- **Addressed to the wrong person or sent to the wrong place:** Many letter writers still forget to include proper contact information or send their letters to the wrong people and places. Make sure your letter includes a complete return address and a telephone number you can be reached at during the day. Also, closely check the name and address of your letter recipient.

- **Does not relate to the reader's knowledge, interests, work, or needs:** Many letter writers fail to research the needs of their audience and target them accordingly. They simply waste employers' valuable time. If you respond to a classified ad or vacancy announcement, make sure you address the requirements specified for submitting your letter and resume.

- **Includes spelling, grammatical, and punctuation errors:** The worst mistakes you can make in a letter are spelling, grammatical, or punctuation errors. These are unforgiving errors that clearly communicate your incompetence. Such mistakes demonstrate you are either careless or semi-illiterate – both deadly to a job search!

- **Uses awkward language and the passive voice:** Carefully watch your use of language and try to use the active voice. The active voice gives your writing more energy. Good, crisp, interesting, and pleasing language is something few readers experience in reading letters.

- **Overly aggressive, assertive, boastful, hyped, and obnoxious in tone:** Employers receive many letters from individuals who try to impress them with what is essentially obnoxious language. They think that telling an employer they are the "hottest thing since sliced bread" will get them an interview. These letters even appear in some books that claim they are examples of "outstanding letters"! We have yet to encounter employers who are impressed by such letters. They tend to be low-class letters that follow the principles of low-class advertising.

- **Self-centered rather than job- or employer-centered:** Too many job applicants still focus on what they want **from** employers (position, salary, benefits) rather than what they can do **for** employers (be productive, solve problems, contribute to organization, give benefits). Make sure your letters are oriented toward employers' needs. Tell them about the **benefits** you will give them. If you start referring to "you" rather than "I" in your letters, you will force yourself to be more employer-centered.

- **Poorly organized, difficult to follow, or wanders aimlessly:** Many letter writers still fail to plan the logic, sequence, and flow of their letters. They often begin with one idea, wander off to another idea, continue on to yet another disconnected idea, and then end the letter abruptly with no regard for transitions. Readers often must examine the letter two or three times to figure out what the writer wants. Such poor writing is inexcusable. If you can't say something in an organized and coherent manner, don't waste other people's time with your drivel!

- **Unclear what they are writing about or what they want:** Is there a goal or purpose to this letter? Many letters still lack a clear purpose or goal. Writers assume the reader will somehow figure out what they are writing about! Make sure your letter has a clear purpose. This should be revealed in the first paragraph.

- **Says little about the individual's interests, skills, accomplishments, or what he or she expects to achieve in the future:** Your job search letters should tell letter recipients what it is you can do for them. Unfortunately, many letter writers fail to communicate their strengths and benefits to potential employers.

- **Fails to include adequate contact information:** Be sure to include your complete address, including zip code, and a daytime and/or evening telephone number. Do not use a P.O. Box number.

- **Dull, boring, and uninspired:** Employers are looking for individuals who have enthusiasm, energy, and fire. However, most letters they receive give little indication of these critical characteristics. Try to use language that expresses your enthusiasm and energy. At least start with the active voice!

- **Too long:** Busy people don't have time to read long letters. Chances are you can say just as much, and more effectively, in a short letter. If you're writing a cover letter that accompanies a resume, be sure you do not repeat the same information that already appears on your resume. Follow the principle of "less is best."

- **Poorly typed:** We still receive letters from people who make typing errors and then try to correct them by hand. The result is an amateurish looking letter that reflects poorly on the professional style and competence of the letter writer. If you write a job search letter, make sure it reflects your **best** professional effort.

- **Produced on cheap and unattractive paper:** Professional correspondence should be produced on good quality paper. However, many letter writers cut corners and go with poor quality paper. Don't be cheap. Good quality paper only costs a few cents more than the cheap product, and it's easy to find at your local stationery or print shop. It more than pays for itself.

- **Lacks information on appropriate follow-up actions:** In addition to indicating the writer's purpose, the letter should include information on what actions should or will be taken next. This information normally appears in the last paragraph.

In other words, many letters aren't just poorly written; they make poor impressions on readers. Letters that avoid these errors tend to be read and responded to. Make sure your letters are free of such errors!

Principles of Good Advertising

Several principles of effective advertising can be adapted to business writing and the job search. Indeed, the advertising analogy is most appropriate for a job search since both deal with how to best communicate benefits to potential buyers and users. These principles should assist you in developing your creative capacity to get what you want through letter writing.

Job search letters should be written according to the key principles of good advertising copy. They should include the following principles:

- **Catch the reader's attention:** While advertising copy primarily captures attention through a visual (headline, photo, illustration), a job search letter can do the same. It should project an overall quality appearance and an opening sentence or paragraph that immediately grabs the reader's attention. Like any good presentation, an attention-grabbing opening can be a question, startling statement, quotation, an example or illustration, humorous anecdote, a suspenseful observation, or a compliment to the reader. You must do this at the very beginning of your letter – not near the end which may never get read or where the reader's attention span has dissipated. You should always present your most important points first.

- **Persuade the reader about you, the product:** Good advertising copy involves the reader in the product by stressing **value and benefits**. It tells why the reader should acquire the product. A good job search letter should do the same – the product is you and the letter should stress the specific benefits the reader will receive for contacting you. The benefits you should offer are your skills and accomplishments as they relate to the reader's present and future needs. Therefore, you must know something about your reader's needs before you can offer the proper mix of benefits.

- **Convince the reader with more evidence:** Good advertising copy presents facts about the product that relate to its benefits. An effective job search letter should also present evidence of the writer's benefits. Statements of specific accomplishments and examples of productivity are the strongest such evidence.

- **Move the reader to take action (acquire the product):** Effective advertising copy concludes with a call to take action to acquire the product. This usually involves a convenient order form or a toll-free telephone number. To stress the benefits of the product without moving the reader to take action would be a waste of time and money. When writing job search letters, you should conclude with a call to action. This is the ultimate power of paper. You want the reader to do something he or she ordinarily would not do – pick up the telephone to contact you, or write you a positive letter that leads to job search information, advice, and referrals as well as job interviews and offers. But we know few letters are so powerful as to move the reader to take initiative in contacting the letter writer. Simply put, the benefits are not as clear in a job search letter as they are in selling a product through advertising copy. Therefore, your call to action should mention that **you** will contact the reader by telephone at a certain time.

Form, style, content, production, and distribution all play important roles in communicating these persuasive elements in your letters.

Planning and Organizing

It goes without saying that you need to plan and organize your writing. By all means do not copy or edit a letter you think may be a good example of an effective job search letter. Canned letters tend to be too formal. Worst of all, they look and sound canned and thus they lack credibility.

Your letters should represent **you** – your personality, your credibility, your style, and your purpose. Start by asking yourself these questions **before** organizing and writing your letters:

- What is the **purpose** of this letter?

- What are the **needs** of my audience?

- What is a good opening sentence or paragraph for grabbing the **attention** of my audience?

- How can I maintain the **interest** of my audience?

- How can I best end the letter so that my audience will be **persuaded** to contact me?

- How much **time** should I spend revising and proofreading the letter?

- Will this letter represent my **best professional effort**?

After writing your letter, review these questions again. But this time convert them into a checklist for evaluating the potential effectiveness of your letter:

❑ Is the **purpose** of this letter clear?

❑ Does the letter clearly target the **needs** of my audience?

❑ Does the opening sentence or paragraph grab the **attention** of my audience?

❑ Does the letter state specific **benefits** for the reader?

❑ Does the letter sustain the **interest** of my audience?

❑ Will the letter **persuade** the reader to contact me?

❑   Have I spent enough **time** revising and proofreading the letter?

❑   Does the letter represent my **best professional effort**?

Always keep in mind what you want your audience to do in reference to your job search:

- Pay attention to your message.

- Remember you.

- Take specific actions you want them to take.

Content Rules

The body of the letter should clearly communicate your message. How well you structure this section of the letter will largely determine how much impact it will have on your reader.

The basic principles of effective communication are especially applicable to the body of your letter. In general you should:

1. **Have a clear purpose in writing your letter:** First ask yourself, "What message do I want to convey to my reader? What do I want him or her to do after reading my letter?" Your message should be directly related to some desirable action or outcome.

2. **Plan and organize each section:** Each paragraph should be related to your overall purpose as well as to each other. The message should be logical and flow in sequential order. Start with a detailed outline of your message.

3. **Put your most important ideas first:** Since readers' attention decreases in direct relation to the length of a message, always state your most important points first.

4. **Keep your paragraphs short and your sentences simple:** Your reader is most likely a busy person who does not have time to read and interpret long and complex letters. The shorter the letter the better. Plain simple English is always preferred to complex verbiage which require the reader to re-read and decode your language. Three to four paragraphs, each three to five lines in length, should be sufficient. Keep sentences to no more than 25 words. Avoid including too many ideas in a single sentence.

5. **Your opening sentence should get the attention of the reader:** Your first sentence is the most important one. It should have a similar function as an advertisement – get the interest and involvement of your audience. Avoid the standard canned openers by making your sentence unique.

6. **Your opening paragraph should clearly communicate your purpose:** Get directly to the point in as short a space as possible. Remember, this is a business letter. Your reader wants to know why he should spend time reading your letter. Your first sentence should tell why and begin motivating him or her to take actions you desire.

7. **Your letter should convince the reader to take action:** Most letters attempt to inform and/or to persuade. In either case, they should lead to some action. Incorporate these four principles of good advertising in your letter writing:

   - Catch the reader's attention.
   - Persuade the reader about you or your product – establish your credibility.
   - Convince the reader with more evidence and benefits.
   - Move the reader to acquire the service or product.

8. **Follow the rules of good grammar, spelling, and punctuation:** Grammatical, spelling, and punctuation errors communicate a lack of competence and professionalism. Always check and re-check for such errors by (1) proofreading the letter yourself at least twice, and (2) asking someone else to proofread it also.

9. **Communicate your unique style:** Try to avoid standard or canned business language which is found in numerous how-to books on business writing and sample letters. Such language tends to be too formalistic and boring. Some examples go to the other extreme in presenting excessively aggressive and obnoxious letters that would turn off any normal employer. Write as if you were talking to a reader in a natural conversational tone. Be honest and straightforward in your message. Use your imagination in making your letter interesting. Put your personality into this letter. Try to demonstrate your energy and enthusiasm through your writing tone. For example, what impression does this letter leave on a reader?

> I'm writing in response to your recent ad for an assistant manager at your Great Falls Super Store.
>
> Please find enclosed a copy of my resume which outlines my experience in relationship to this position.
>
> Thank you for your consideration.

While this letter is short and to the point, it doesn't grab the reader's attention, sustain interest, nor lead to desirable action. It screams "b-o-r-i-n-g!" It sounds like hundreds of canned letters employers receive each day. Why not try writing with more personality and energy? Consider this more energetic and action-oriented alternative:

> Last year I decreased the unit's operating expenses by 15%. It was a tremendous challenge, but the secret was evaluating the existing processes and re-engineering them to make the new processes more efficient. By going through this exercise, we eliminated two full-time employees and dramatically improved customer service.
>
> I'm now interested in taking on another challenge that requires a similar type of thought-leadership and creativity. When I saw your ad in Sunday's <u>Toledo Star</u>, I thought we might share a mutual interest.
>
> If you're interested in learning more about my experience, let's talk soon on how we might work together. I'll call you Thursday afternoon to answer any questions. In the meantime, please look over my enclosed resume.

Which letter do you think will grab the attention of the employer and lead to some action? The first letter is both standard and boring. It asks the recipient to take action, if he or she so desires. The second letter, equally true, incorporates most principles of effective letter writing – and advertising! In this case, the writer will take action – make a follow-up phone call – to get a response from the letter recipient.

10. **Be personable by referring to "you" more than "I" or "we":** Your letters should communicate that you are other-centered rather than self-centered. You communicate your awareness and concern for the individual by frequently referring to "you."

11. **Try to be positive in what you say:** Avoid negative words and tones in your letters. Such words as "can't," "didn't," "shouldn't," and "won't" can be eliminated in favor of a more positive way of stating a negative. For example, instead of writing:

> I don't have the required five years experience nor have I taken the certification test.

Try putting your message in a more positive tone by using positive content:

> I have several years of experience and will be taking the certification test next month.

12. **Follow the basic ABC's of good writing:** <u>A</u>lways <u>B</u>eing:

- Clear
- Correct
- Complete
- Concise
- Courteous

- Considerate
- Creative
- Cheerful
- Careful

Inclusions and Omissions

What should be included and omitted in your cover letters? This question depends on your purpose and your audience. If you are responding to a vacancy announcement or a classified ad, you need to address the stated requirements for submitting an application. This usually involves a resume and sometimes information on your "salary requirements."

Use the following general guidelines when trying to decide what to include or omit in your letters:

Things you should include:

- Positive information that supports your candidacy.

- Information on your skills, abilities, strengths, accomplishments, interests, and goals.

- Examples of your productivity and performance.

- Benefits you can offer the reader.

- A daytime contact telephone number.

Things you should omit:

- Any extraneous information unrelated to the position, the employer's needs, or your skills.

- Any negative references to a former employer, your weaknesses, or the employer's organization and position.

- Boastful statements or proposed solutions to the employer's problems.

- Salary requirements or history.

- Personal information such as height, weight, marital status, hobbies – information that should not appear on a resume.

- References.

One major question concerning many job applicants is whether or not to include salary information in their letter. Our general rule is to omit such information in letters; never volunteer salary information unless asked for it, since this is the last question you want to deal with **after** you have demonstrated your value in job interviews. However, it is not always possible to avoid the salary question. In certain situations you must address this question in your letter. Job ads or vacancy announcements, for example, often request a statement about your salary requirements or salary history. If you don't respond, you may be eliminated from consideration. Be careful in how you respond to this requirement. When asked, state a **salary range** rather than a specific salary figure. If, for example, you currently make $40,000 a year but you expect to make $50,000 in your next job, you might state your salary expectation is *"in the range of $48,000 to $54,000."* When stating your salary history, make sure to include your **total compensation package** – not just your monthly salary figure.

The basic rule for including information in cover letters is to include only positive information that stresses your skills and abilities in reference to the employer's needs. Never, never, never volunteer your weaknesses or negatives. These are subjects which may be discussed during a job interview, but you should never put them in writing.

The biggest problem facing most job seekers is keeping focused on their goal and maintaining their self-esteem. The job search is an intensely ego-involved activity that often goes awry due to a combination of wishful thinking and bouts of depression attendant with rejections. If you keep focused on your goals, what you include or omit in your cover letters will come naturally. You will know what should be communicated to employers as your qualifications.

Evaluation

Evaluate the quality of the organization and content of your letters by responding to the following evaluation criteria. Circle the numbers to the right that best describe your letter.

	Characteristic	Yes	No
1.	Immediately grabs the reader's attention.	1	3
2.	Presents most important ideas first.	1	3
3.	Expressed concisely.	1	3
4.	Relates to the reader's interests and needs.	1	3

5.	Persuades the reader to take action.	1	3
6.	Free of spelling, grammatical, and punctuation errors.	1	3
7.	Incorporates the active voice.	1	3
8.	Avoids negative words and tones; uses positive language throughout.	1	3
9.	Expresses the "unique you."	1	3
10.	Employer-centered rather than self-centered.	1	3
11.	Stresses benefits the reader is likely to receive from the letter writer.	1	3
12.	Demonstrates a clear purpose.	1	3
13.	Sentences and paragraphs flow logically.	1	3
14.	Includes complete contact information (no P.O. Box numbers).	1	3
15.	Expresses enthusiasm, energy, and fire.	1	3
16.	Follows the ABC's of good writing.	1	3

TOTAL

Add the circled numbers to arrive at your composite score. If you incorporate the principles identified in this chapter into the organization and content of your writing, your letter should score a perfect "16."

10

Creating Your Resume Database

T HE FOLLOWING WORKSHEETS are designed to help you systematically generate a complete database on yourself for writing each resume section. We recommend completing the forms **before** writing your resume.

Generate the Right Data on Yourself

You will be in the strongest position to write each resume section after you document, analyze, and synthesize different types of data on yourself based on these forms. Each form will assist you in specifying your accomplishments and generating the proper resume language. Since your experience/education may exceed the number of worksheets provided here, make several copies of these worksheets if necessary to complete the exercises.

Try to complete each form as thoroughly as possible. While you will not include all the information on your resume, you will at least have a rich database from which to write each resume section. Our general rule is to go for volume – generate as much detailed information on yourself as possible. Condense it later when writing and editing each resume section.

The final worksheet focuses on detailing your **achievements**. This may be the most important worksheet since it will help you speak the language of employers. Make multiple copies of this worksheet. Try to identify your seven key achievements. The language generated here will be important to both writing your resume and handling the critical job interview.

Employment Experience Worksheet

1. Name of employer: _____

2. Address: _____

    _____

3. Inclusive dates of employment: From _____ to _____ .

                                          month/year   month/year

4. Type of organization: _____

5. Size of organization/approximate number of employees: _____

6. Approximate annual sales volume or annual budget: _____

7. Position held: _____

8. Earnings per month/year: (not to appear on resume) _____

9. Responsibilities/duties: _____

    _____

    _____

    _____

10. Achievements or significant contributions: _____

    _____

    _____

    _____

    _____

11. Demonstrated skills and abilities: _____

    _____

    _____

12. Reason(s) for leaving: _____

    _____

    _____

Educational Data

1. Institution: _____

2. Address: _____

    _____

3. Inclusive dates: From _____ to _____.

    month/year   month/year

4. Degree or years completed: _____

5. Major(s): _____ Minor(s): _____

6. Education highlights: _____

    _____

    _____

7. Student activities: _____

    _____

    _____

8. Demonstrated abilities and skills: _____

    _____

    _____

9. Significant contributions/achievements: _____

    _____

    _____

10. Special training courses: _____

    _____

    _____

11. G.P.A.: _____ (on _____ index)

Community/Civic/
Volunteer Experience

1. Name and address of organization/group: _____

   _____

   _____

2. Inclusive dates: From _____ to _____.

                       month/year   month/year

3. Offices held/nature of involvement: _____

   _____

   _____

   _____

   _____

   _____

4. Significant contributions/achievements/projects: _____

   _____

   _____

   _____

   _____

   _____

5. Demonstrated skills and abilities: _____

   _____

   _____

   _____

   _____

   _____

Additional Information

1. Professional memberships and status:

    a. _____

    b. _____

    c. _____

    d. _____

    e. _____

    f. _____

2. Licenses/certifications/security clearance:

    a. _____

    b. _____

    c. _____

    d. _____

3. Expected salary range: $ _____ to $ _____ (do not include on resume)

4. Acceptable amount of on-the-job travel: _____ days per month.

5. Geographical areas of acceptable relocation:

    a. _____   c. _____

    b. _____   d. _____

6. Date of availability: _____

7. Contacting present employer:

    a. Is he or she aware of your prospective job change? _____

    b. May he or she be contacted at this time? _____

8. References: (name, address, telephone number – not to appear on resume)

    a. _____   b. _____

    _____   _____

    _____   _____

    c. _____   d. _____

    _____   _____

    _____   _____

9. Foreign languages and degree of competency:

   a. _____

   b. _____

10. Interests and activities: hobbies, avocations, pursuits

    a. _____

    b. _____

    c. _____

    d. _____

Circle letter of ones which support your objective.

11. Foreign travel:

	Country	Purpose	Dates
a.	_____	_____	_____
b.	_____	_____	_____
c.	_____	_____	_____
d.	_____	_____	_____
e.	_____	_____	_____

12. Special awards/recognition:

    a. _____

    b. _____

    c. _____

    d. _____

13. Special abilities/skills/talents/accomplishments:

    a. _____

    b. _____

    c. _____

    d. _____

Detail Your Achievements

Definition: An "Achievement" is anything you enjoyed doing, believe you did well, and felt a sense of satisfaction, pride, or accomplishment in doing.

ACHIEVEMENT # _____: _____

_____

1. How did I initially become involved? _____

   _____

   _____

   _____

   _____

2. What did I do? _____

   _____

   _____

   _____

   _____

3. How did I do it? _____

   _____

   _____

   _____

   _____

4. What was especially enjoyable about doing it? _____

   _____

   _____

   _____

   _____

11

Resumes and Letters
From Career Professionals

THE FOLLOWING COLLECTION of military-to-civilian resumes and letters comes from the files of several talented professional resume writers and career coaches who regularly work with transitioning military personnel. In contrast to principle-driven resumes in Chapter 6 – organized by occupations and of similar style – here we group resumes by individual authors and include many different styles and formats. Thus you'll be able to see the diverse approaches, styles, and formats to resume writing. Once you've had a chance to explore these samples, you may want to contact individual authors about their fee-based services. They can save you a great deal of time and effort as well as show you what might work best for you. Best of all, you'll be putting yourself in the hands of a professional who has a track record of success.

Whatever you do, don't hesitate to contact a career professional for assistance when it comes time to write your resume and letters or complete other steps in your job search (see our 10-step process on page 9). What little money you spend on their services will more than pay for itself when your expertly crafted documents turn into invitations to job interviews that eventually result in job offers. We further address this important "professional help" issue for transitioning military personnel in Chapter 12.

Different Approaches

The resumes and letters presented in this chapter are both similar and dissimilar in many ways. Most share the major principle stressed throughout this book – clearly communicate your skills, accomplishments, and results to the reader. How they present this principle varies from writer to writer. For example, Don Orlando's three targeted resumes and cover letters on pages 249-258 represent one of the most innovative approaches to resume and letter writing. Thinking outside the traditional generic resume and letter writing boxes, his clients speak directly to the needs of employers by targeting skills and accomplishments as "payoffs" and "examples." Indeed, their use of **examples and/or stories** is one of the most powerful techniques for communicating skills and accomplishments to prospective employers. Their engaging letters open the door to unique resumes that grab the attention of readers rather than merely rehash what appears on the resume. This approach results in compelling letters and resumes that also communicate the **personality and style** of the candidate to prospective employers. Most important of all, these resumes and letters simply stand above many other resumes and letters employers are likely to receive from perhaps equally or even more qualified candidates. Look at these examples carefully and ask yourself these two question: Would you want to interview this person? Are you writing equally compelling resumes and letters?

While most examples in this chapter give the reader a sense of what the individual can do and wants to do by initially stating an objective, desired position, occupational specialty, capabilities, competencies, career profile, highlights, or summary, a few examples may be difficult to interpret, because they are primarily summaries of many different experiences. Lacking a central organizing concept yet rich with keywords, these are essentially exploratory resumes that attempt to pull together in the space of one to two pages many different skills, experiences, and positions without stressing a pattern of accomplishments or telling the reader what the individual really wants to do. In these cases, the individuals may not know what they want to do other than find a job compatible with some of their strengths. To be most effective, these resumes will require a powerful cover letter to focus the individuals' qualifications around the particular needs of employers. These also tend to be general all-purpose resumes that have yet to be targeted on specific positions and employers.

Most of the examples in this book are taken from transitioning U.S. military personnel, encompassing both enlisted personnel and officers. However, in this chapter three examples presented by George Dutch (pages 294-299), including a powerful T-letter, are taken from transitioning Canadian military personnel. Regardless of nationality, most principles of good resume writing tend to cross national borders with relative ease, especially if you are looking for a position that directly relates to your goals and major strengths. For an interesting compilation of powerful international resumes, which follow the same principles outlined in this book, see Ron Krannich's and Wendy Enelow's *Best Resumes and CVs for International Jobs* (Impact Publications).

Our Contributors

The following 18 career professionals contributed the 58 resume and letter examples appearing in the remainder of this chapter. Most of them are Certified Professional Resume Writers (CPRW) and are active in several professional career groups, such as the

Professional Association of Resume Writers and Career Coaches (see pages 340-341). For your convenience, we've included email addresses and telephone numbers for contacting the contributors. In many cases, you can visit their websites.

Don Orlando, MBA, CPRW, JCTC, CCM, CCMC
Tel. 334-264-2020
yourcareercoach@charterinternet.com

▪ Charles Milverton (letter)	IT Consulting Practice Manager	page 249
▪ Charles Milverton (resume)	IT Consulting Practice Manager	pages 250-251
▪ Harold Wilson (letter)	Vice President for Construction	page 252
▪ Harold Wilson (resume)	Vice President for Construction	pages 253-254
▪ Charles W. Marklin (letter)	Industrial Security Manager	page 255
▪ Charles W. Marklin (resume)	Industrial Security Manager	pages 256-258

Louise Garver, CMP, CPRW, CEIP, MCDP, JCTC, CPBS, CLBF
Tel. 860-623-9476
LouiseGarver@cox.net   CareerDirectionsLLC.com

▪ Lawrence Williams (resume)	Maintenance Technician	pages 259-260
▪ Elaine Erickson (resume)	Security Site Manager	pages 261-262
▪ Stephanie A. Johnson (letter)	Medical Laboratory Supervisor	page 263
▪ Stephanie A. Johnson (resume)	Medical Laboratory Supervisor	pages 264-265
▪ David A. Jones (resume)	Maintenance/Operations	page 266
▪ Robert Murray (resume)	Maintenance Management	page 267
▪ Fredrick Smith (resume)	Sales Training	page 268
▪ Mary Sullivan (resume)	Licensed Professional Nurse	page 269

Phyllis Houston
Tel. 202-361-0847 or 301-574-3956
phyllis_houston@msn.com

▪ Barry Campbell (letter)	K-9 Program Administrator	page 270
▪ Barry Campbell (resume)	K-9 Program Administrator	pages 271-272
▪ Elaine Charleston (letter)	Senior Paralegal	page 273
▪ Elaine Charleston (resume)	Senior Paralegal	page 274
▪ Sheila D. Cook (letter)	Information Technology	page 275
▪ Sheila D. Cook (resume)	Information Technology	pages 276-277
▪ Beck O. Cooper (letter)	Hospitality Services Manager	page 278
▪ Beck O. Cooper (resume)	Hospitality Services Manager	pages 279-280
▪ Sharon A. Jones (letter)	Personnel Operations Manager	page 281
▪ Sharon A. Jones (resume)	Personnel Operations Manager	pages 282-283
▪ Matthew Rice (letter)	General inquiry (executive)	page 284
▪ Matthew Rice (resume)	General inquiry (executive)	pages 285-286

Melanie Noonan
Tel. 973-785-3011
PeriPro1@aol.com

▪ Kenya Brown (resume)	Paralegal	pages 287-288
▪ Hernando Chavez (resume)	Front Line Investigator	pages 289-290
▪ Ian J. Parker (resume)	Special Agent	pages 291-292
▪ Robert K. Williams (resume)	Incident Management Specialist	page 293

George Dutch, BA, CMF, CCM, JCTC
Tel. 613-563-0584
george@jobjoy.com   **www.JobJoy.com**

Billie Ruth Sucher, MS, CTMS, CTSB, JCTC
Tel. 515-276-0061
billie@billiesucher.com   **www.billiesucher.com**

Jean Cummings, M.A.T., CPRW, CPBS, CEIP
Tel. 978-371-9266 or 1-800-324-1699
jc@YesResumes.com   **www.aResumeForToday.com**

Debra O'Reilly, CPRW, CEIP, JCTC, FRWC
Tel. 1-800-340-5570
debra@resumewriter.com   **www.resumewriter.com**

Don Goodman, CPRW, CCMC
Tel. 1-800-909-0109
success@GotTheJob.com   **www.GotTheJob.com**

Laurie Berenson, CPRW
Tel. 201-573-8282
laurie@sterlingcareerconcepts.com   **www.SterlingCareerConcepts.com**

Rita Fisher, CPRW
Tel. 812-342-7978
RitaFisher33@comcast.com   **www.career-change-resume-help.com**

Beth Colley, CPRW, CFJST
Tel. 410-533-2457
resume@chesres.com   **www.chesres.com**

Erin Kennedy, CPRW
Tel. 1-866-793-9224
ekennedy@proreswriters.com   **www.proreswriters.com**

- Griffin M. Hankerd (letter)   Chief Financial Officer   page 318
- Griffin M. Hankerd (resume)   Chief Financial Officer   pages 319-320

Jennifer Bloom, CPRW
jbloom@accepted.com   **www.accepted.com**

- John B. White (resume)   Environmental Resource Manager   page 321
- John L. Smith (resume)   Operations Manager   page 322

John Femia, BS, CPRW
Tel. 518-872-1305
Customresume1@aol.com   **www.customresumewriting.com**

- Louis G. Smith (resume)   Electronics Professional   page 323
- Martin F. Robinson (resume)   Logistics Professional   pages 324-325
- Robert F. Henderson (resume)   Security and Surveillance   pages 326-327

Angela S. Jones, CPRW
Tel. 1-866-695-9318
angie@anewresume.com   **www.anewresume.com**

- David Brown (resume)   Information Technology   pages 328-329

Doris Appelbaum,
Tel. 1-800-619-9777 or 414-352-5994
dorisa@execpc.com   **www.appelbaumresumes.com**

- Matthew O'Doul (resume)   Management   pages 330-331
- Kevin O'Donnell (resume)   General   pages 332-333
- Theodore Turnbull (resume)   Human Resources   pages 334-335

Carl Bascom, MA
amainfo2@yahoo.com   **www.resumewinners.com**

- Benjamin T. Evans (resume)   General   page 336
- Lyle S. Evans (resume)   General   page 337
- Mark A. Evans (resume)   General   page 338

One important theme runs throughout these examples – there are no hard-and-fast rules on resume and letter writing. For example, while we prefer using an objective on all of our resumes in Chapter 6, most examples in this chapter tend to use a career summary, qualifications summary, career profile, keyword summary, or bulleted list of career highlights in lieu of an objective. Examples in this chapter also showcase a variety of attractive layouts.

But most important of all, in this chapter you'll see what talented professional resume writers and career professionals produce for their clients – stand-out resumes that grab the attention of potential employers. And that's exactly what **you** want to do!

CHARLES MILVERTON
1500 Felder Avenue
Montgomery, AL 36100
☎ 334.555.5555 (Direct office line) — 334.555.6666 (Home)
charles.milverton@gunter.af.mil

May 30, 2008

Ms. Lauri O'Brien
Recruiting Coordinator
The Revere Group
1751 Lake Cook Road
Suite 600
Deerfield, Illinois 60015

Dear Ms. O'Brien:

If you could "design" the perfect senior IT consulting practice manager for your clients, would
the following specs meet their most demanding needs?

- ❑ Documented experience transforming large groups of narrowly focused professionals
  into problem-destroying teams that trust one another.
- ❑ A solid track record applying creative, mutually profitable, advocacy models across
  entire organizations.
- ❑ Expertise in managing change — even cultural change — using technology to model
  business and social systems in new, persuasive ways.

You have just read the 49-word version of my résumé. You'll find the details in the full-length
version on the next pages. That document may not look like others you have seen. I wanted you
to have more than the usual sterile lists of job titles and responsibilities. And so, you will find
nine examples of payoffs I've gotten for organizations large and small. As you read, I hope a
central idea stands out. I thrive by transforming new concepts into effective solutions to real life
problems.

My employer, the United States Air Force, has promoted me rapidly. And I find my work
greatly rewarding because the new Air Force now aligns so closely with private sector business
models. However, I want to return to the Deerfield area to help corporate organizations.
Perhaps a good way to start is to explore how I might serve The Revere Group's special needs.
May I call in a few days to arrange an interview?

Sincerely,

Charles Milverton

Charles Milverton

Encl.: Résumé

CHARLES MILVERTON

1500 Felder Avenue
Montgomery, AL 36100   charles.milverton@gunter.af.mil

☎ 334.555.5555 (Direct office line)
334.555.6666 (Home)

WHAT I OFFER THE REVERE GROUP AS YOUR NEWEST SENIOR IT CONSULTING PRACTICE MANAGER:

❑ **Customer focus** that lets clients think my solutions are their own good ideas,

❑ **Communications skills** that help people break down barriers to productivity, and

❑ **Experience** to transform groups of strangers into smoothly running teams.

RECENT EMPLOYMENT HISTORY WITH SELECTED CONTRIBUTIONS TO PRODUCTIVITY:

More than 18 years of increasingly responsible managerial positions as a commissioned Air Force officer, including these most recent assignments:

❑ *Promoted to* Chief of **Client Support** *and* Director of **IT Operations Planning** (VICE PRESIDENTIAL POSITIONS), Standard Systems Group, Gunter Air Force Base, Montgomery, AL   Jun 03 – Jun 07

The Standard Systems Group is the Air Force's largest, central IT systems design center. The Group develops, validates, tests, installs, maintains, and upgrades complete networking and IT-based solutions for thousands of users around the world. Manages $10B in software.

Supervise four senior and mid-level mangers directly and 200 mid-level executives and specialists indirectly. Build and defend a growing budget (currently $11M) annually.

Transformed a corporate vision of improved customer service into a responsive help desk that serves more than 8,000 diverse users. Guided employees to change their outlook from "turf protection" to team building. *Payoffs:* **Productivity rose** and stayed high across the board. Expensive specialists freed to make **maximum contributions** to our mission.

Guided a **major technology changeover**. Designed, advocated, and tested new ways to help hundreds of people work much more collaboratively. *Payoffs:* New tools make us focus on solving problems, not react to symptoms. **Costs reduced 60%** in only eight months. Our work became the **corporate standard worldwide**.

Chosen to "bullet proof" the Air Force's Y2K plans—six months before the deadline. Led 130 customers to build solutions they could own. Then **made the tough sell** that persuaded **20 CEO-equivalents** (and their CIO's) to relinquish some control of their proprietary data for the greater good. *Payoffs:* Y2K transition **trouble-free** at over 300 locations around the globe.

Converted part of a 40-year-old building into one of most advanced communications and business innovation centers in the world—in six months. Worked with customers to produce pioneering software in 15 days. *Payoffs:* Our center featured in Internet World. Our software now **the standard for** Air Force **network status reporting**.

Found an incipient problem by "wandering around:" the need for new expertise to push our R & D forward. Drew on experience to find just the right contractor. Then used my **ROI analysis** to persuade management to fund them. *Payoffs:* **Captured a multi-million dollar "account"** with the fresh insights we gained.

❑ *Promoted to* **Chief of Analysis** *promoted to* Deputy **Chief Information Officer** (ASSISTANT VICE PRESIDENTIAL POSITIONS), National Guard Bureau, Washington, D.C.   Aug 00 – Jun 03

More indicators of performance to support The Revere Group's missiony

Charles Milverton   **Senior IT Consulting Practice Manager**   334.555.5555 (Office)

Applied **technology** in **completely new ways**: helped change how a 50-year-old corporate culture valued diversity. Led **large group interventions** (up to 250 people) to **produce everything** from strategies to metrics to tools. *Payoffs:* Employers, diversity leaders, managers, and entry-level workers came together as a team. Worldwide implementation, ownership, and QA **all Internet based.**

Realigned corporate and production **goals** that had drifted us into conflict. Got team members recommitted to our mission. *Payoffs:* **108,000 people** focused on just 14 goals and 22 objectives.

❑ In-residence Student, U.S. Naval War College, Newport, RI   Aug 99 − Aug 00

Chosen among the top two percent of senior executives to attend this 10-month school. Showed senior leadership the benefits of electronic brainstorming. **Pulled together 25** of the **best minds** from academia and the private sector to validate and improve my work. *Payoffs:* CEOs built facilities still dedicated to this method.

❑ *Promoted to* **Chief of Analysis** *promoted to* Director, Air **Operations** and **Contingency Support** Centers *promoted to* Manager of **Business Process and Data Modeling** (ASSISTANT VICE PRESIDENTIAL POSITIONS), Andrews Air Force Base, MD   Jul 95 − Aug 99

Overhauled the inefficient way we served our customers' most pressing needs. **Defined** the **best practices**. Designed a tailor-made facility to exploit the right worker competencies. *Payoffs:* New **single point of service** got users information they needed: fast and right.

COMPUTER SKILLS:

❑ Proficient in Remedy (a software suite than manages **trouble-ticketing, assessment,** and **customer relationships**), BusinessObjects (**business intelligence software** that provides **on-line, analytical processing**), System Dynamics business modeling and simulation software. Word, Excel, Outlook, PowerPoint, Access, MS Project, Internet search protocols, and Palm OS.

❑ Working knowledge of SQL, VMS, UNIX, Mac OS, HP OpenView, Axent Enterprise **Security Manager,** Sidewinder (**firewall**), Tivoli, group facilitation software and CA Unicenter (both software suites **manage large enterprises** from one location).

RELEVANT PROFESSIONAL DEVELOPMENT:

❑ **MBA**, Kenan-Flager Business School, University of North Carolina, Chapel Hill, NC, 92

❑ BS, U.S. Air Force Academy, Colorado Springs, CO, 77 *Dean's List five out of eight semesters. Commandant's List (of top 25% of students).*

❑ Certificate in **Advanced Studies in Systems Dynamics**, Massachusetts Institute of Technology, Cambridge, MA, Dec 04.

❑ "Managerial Statistics," National Guard Bureau, three days, 04

❑ "Process and Data Modeling," Dacom, one week, 02

❑ "Quality Management for Managers," United States Air Force, two weeks, 99 *Chosen by senior management as one of 16 (from 2,000 eligibles) to build our first quality team.*

❑ Regular, recurring training in combating sexual harassment and drugs in the workplace, **ethical contracting, leading diverse workforces,** and **computer security.**

Harold Wilson

1112 Norton Road ✦ Scott Air Force Base, Illinois 62225 ✦ hw2@yahoo.com ✦ ☎ [618] 555-5555

May 28, 2008

Mr. John W. Woodall
Senior Executive Vice President
PJM
Box ENR-195
340 East 93rd Street, Suite 12B
New York, NY 10128

Dear Mr. Woodall:

From the first day I started managing projects, my customers always cited a single standard: bring it in on time and on budget. I never thought those criteria—as good as they are—were good enough. If you agree that well-managed projects should boost productivity before, during and long after construction, we should talk. Specifically, I want to translate that vision into reality by joining the your firm team your Vice President for Construction.

I have been working as a project manager with the broadest responsibilities for several years. My employer, the United States Air Force, consistently rewards me for my work. However, I think I can make an even better contribution elsewhere.

To help you learn more about my track record, I have enclosed my résumé. A résumé can illustrate capabilities you can use, but it cannot show you *how* I get consistent results my customers like. I bind myself with this professional creed:

   ✦ It is the *customer's* project. I do what it takes to please him now and in the future.
   ✦ Contractors, sub-contractors and craftsmen are also customers. I must stay close to them if the right things are to be in the right place at the right time.
   ✦ Saving time is not good enough; "banking" time is the minimum requirement.

I am ready to put my drive, energy, and experience to work for you. May I call in a few days to explore the possibility of an interview?

Sincerely,

Harold Wilson

One enclosure: Résumé

Harold Wilson

1112 Norton Road ✧ Scott Air Force Base, Illinois 62225 ✧ hw2@yahoo.com ✧ ☎ [618] 555-5555

Value to PJM: As your **Vice President for Construction**, bring in profit building ventures on time and within budget.

Capabilities you can use

- Translating plans into projects that satisfy demanding customers

- Negotiating contracts to increase profits and keep top subcontractors

- Keeping capability high; life-cycle costs low

Work History

Nearly 20 years as an Air Force civil engineer accountable for all project management functions. (01 – 08) This partial list of my current responsibilities typifies the kind of work I have done for the last five years:

- Build, defend and administer annual budget of $60 million,

- Lead teams drawn from 450 engineers, craftsmen, administrators and service providers,

- Guide maintenance of 511 buildings covering 5,000,000 square feet of office space, restaurants, meeting rooms, shopping malls, a supermarket, 884 homes and apartments, industrial plants, an airport, and academic facilities,

- Maintain plants used by a communications center, a fire department, a police force, and a full-service medical center,

- Keep water and sanitary distribution systems within tight standards,

- Keep electrical and steam generation plants fully operational, and

- Build, pave, and repair nearly 50 miles of road.

Selected examples of success

SATISFYING THE CUSTOMERS

Asked to **turn** 50-year-old **derelict building into major corporate headquarters** - in six weeks! Contract I inherited allowed over-extended contractor to "bail out" without penalty. Customers were on site every day.

Payoffs: Customer *very* satisfied. Done **on time; on budget**.

When customer asked me to repair underground utilities fast, I found ways to **save him lots of future dollars**. Made inevitable upgrades **faster** and **cheaper** and **improved** the road surface above the junctions at the same time.

Payoffs: Senior decision-maker spent scarce extra money and coped with road detours because he liked the **long-term savings** I gave him.

More indicators of performance that might benefit PJMγ

Harold Wilson   Vice President for Construction   ℘ [618] 555-5555

Selected examples of success (continued)

MATCHING THE
RIGHT CONTRACTOR
TO THE RIGHT JOB AT
THE RIGHT COST

The challenge: overhaul ceiling of 700-seat lecture hall between courses. Offered an alternative to the contractor's very costly method of reaching the 30-foot ceiling.

> *Payoffs:* Innovative, untried method worked beautifully. **Saved 20%** including proration for material contractor could use on other jobs. Done **on time**. Customer pleased.

GETTING THE MOST
FROM EVERY DOLLAR

Just as I took over a project to build a child development center planned at $2.6 million, **funds** were **cut by $1.0 million** even as **cost factors rose 14%.** Met with customer to find new ways to fill the need.

> *Payoffs:* **Project on track**, even though I have 10% fewer people, 5% smaller operating funds.

Education and Training

+ "Executive Leadership Course on Environmental Protection," 2002

+ Master of **Public Administration**, Central Michigan University, 2000
  Attended nights and weekends despite very pressing professional schedule

+ B.S. **Electrical Engineering**, Virginia Military Institute, 1985

Professional Associations

+ Society of American Military Engineers: Past President and Secretary of local chapter

2

Requisition number: 605473   *Relocating to Ft. Worth*

Charles W. Marklin
Industrial Security Manager
2217 Wilmore Drive St. Louis, Missouri 63101
✉ CWM110@aol.com – ☎ 314.555.5555 (cell) – 314.555.6666 (home)

25 October 2008

Steve Johnston
Director of Security
Lockheed Martin Corporation
Lockheed Boulevard
Fort Worth, Texas 76100

Dear Mr. Johnston:

I've entered my résumé into Lockheed's system and I'm forwarding this copy for consideration to be Lockheed Martin's Industrial Security Manager.

As I put this package together, I knew there is important information no résumé could communicate well. In the next paragraph, I'll lay out those facts. After that, I'll explain out how I tailored my document to Lockheed's needs.

If I were in Lockheed's shoes, I'd probably wonder why someone with my background would apply for a job that seems more administrative than operational. The reason is simple: I've been a "chief" and the attraction of serving at that level has dimmed a little. I am extremely proud of my operational background and accomplishments both in, and outside, the cockpit. And so, I'll approach my work as I always have, doing the best job I can possibly do as a point of personal honor. And I'll have the work-life balance that will let me enjoy, and be proud of, my service for years to come.

As to my résumé, I wanted to spare you the usual, tired objective statement, fuzzy summary of qualifications, and sterile lists of responsibilities. Instead, right at the top, are actions I want Lockheed to hold me responsible for. Normally, I'd follow those up with tightly integrated proofs of performance. But the stories that best illustrate my success come with a clearance level and a need to know. That's why the few I was able to include might seem less than specific.

I've always thrived on learning about the mission very well. I'd like to continue on that path, hearing about your team's special industrial security challenges in your own words. May I call in a few days to arrange a time to do that?

Sincerely,

Charles W. Marklin

Encl.: Résumé

Requisition number: 605473   *Relocating to Ft. Worth*

Charles W. Marklin   2217 Wilmore Drive
                                                 St. Louis, Missouri 63101
Industrial Security Manager   ✉ CWM110@aol.com
                                    ☎ 314.555.5555 (cell) – 314.555.6666 (home)

WHAT I OFFER THE LOCKHEED MARTIN TEAM

❑ The fluency to **speak the operators' language** so well that synergy becomes the norm,

❑ The experience to build in **"bullet-proof" accountability** without slowing down the most sensitive, fast-moving contracts and missions,

❑ The passion to persuade others to see **security as a way of life,**

❑ The international background that lets me **adapt to the diverse cultures** of our customers quickly and seamlessly, and

❑ The poise to **establish the right course** of action, even under the most stressful conditions.

CURRENT SECURITY CLEARANCE

❑ TS – SCI   As of Jun 08

RECENT WORK HISTORY WITH SELECTED, UNCLASSIFIED EXAMPLES OF CONTRIBUTIONS TO THE MISSION

More than 30 years' service as a commissioned officer, and for the past seven years as a Colonel, in the United States Air Force including these most relevant assignments:

| **Special note: You can read about contributions involving security on pages two and three. They are marked with this special symbol: ✪** |

❑ *Sought out to by name to serve as* **Special Assistant** to the Commander of Air Mobility Command, Scott Air Force Base, Illinois   Sep 08 – Present
Air Mobility Command is the global reach of the Air Force. With 140,000 team members, AMC provides airlift and air refueling capability worldwide.

Tapped to **guide the greatest change** to AMC since its inception 15 years ago. The challenges: reduce the Commander's span of control, accommodate a projected 12 percent manpower cut and reduction in funding, all while insuring our mission supports every educational need the Air Force has and will have.

❑ *Recruited by the Center Commander to be* **Director of Doctrine Deployment,** Air Force Doctrine Center, *while also serving as* Adjunct Professor of Leadership, Air War College, Air University, Maxwell Air Force Base, Alabama   Jun 07 – Sep 08

❑ *Chosen specifically by the Commandant to be* Dean of Students, Air Command and Staff College, Air University, Maxwell Air Force Base, Alabama   Jun 04 – Jun 07

    ❑ *Selected for a* **special assignment** *while still Dean of Students to be* **Expeditionary** Air Base Group **Commander,** Tuzla Air Base, Bosnia-Herzegovina   Jan 02 – Jun 04

    Served as direct reporting official for 15 intelligence, civil engineering, weather, services, and airfield management professionals. For 250 employees (including some 60 foreign

More indicators of return on investment **Lockheed Martin** *can use …*

Charles Marklin	**Industrial Security Manager**	314.555.6666 (Cell)

nationals), provided many of the services available in a small US city. Compiled and defended an annual budget of $4.4M.

❑ *Selected for a special assignment while still Dean of Students to be* **Battle Staff Commander**, Southeast Air Defense Sector, Tyndall Air Force Base, Florida
Apr 00 – Jan 02

Responsible for the defense of one-third of our nation's air space soon after 9/11.

❑ *Chosen at the Chancellor level to serve as* Professor, Department of **Leadership and Ethics,** Air Command and Staff College, Air University, Maxwell Air Force Base, Alabama
Jun 98 – Jun 00

Served as the primary educational advisor to 5 groups of 15 mid -level students, including representatives of the Thai, Zimbabwean, and Slovakian governments. Managed two courses (totaling 6 contact hours) and leadership electives (totaling 30 contact hours).

❑ **Student**, Air War College, Air University, Maxwell Air Force Base, Alabama Jul 97 – May 98

❑ **Deputy Operations Group Commander,** Davis-Monthan Air Force Base, Arizona
Jan 95 – Jul 97

❑ **Operations Officer** *promoted to* **Commander,** 33rd **Airborne Command and Control** Squadron, Condon Air Force Base, Montana   Jan 92 – Jan 95
Responsible for a diverse mix of 400 people, from high school graduates to college educated professionals, from skilled laborers to mid-level executives.

✪Integrated every detailed aspect of missions so sensitive and so potentially visible that I could be the only member of the organization who understood the link between our taskings and our tactics. **Accommodated** our **ever-changing** list of **customers**, each with their own corporate culture, smoothly. *Outcomes:* Consistently completed the most demanding tasks. Morale in my squadron was very high—even though **no single crewmember was allowed to see the link between** his or her **actions and** our **success.**

✪Maintained and protected one of **the most complex, fluid crypto accounts in the world**—20 filing cabinets worth of highly classified information crews needed to fly securely anywhere in the world. Each mission required a huge, unique set of documents and there was **absolutely no room for error**, even when our crews moved from base to base constantly. *Outcomes:* Made **my contributions durable** by training a younger communications officer in every aspect of the task. **Seamless control and accountability on a massive scale.**

✪Built **"bullet-proof" security** every day in such a state-of-the-art operation that we often flew with untested, prototype equipment **in a combat zone.** *Outcomes:* My teams were very proud that their **actions could be reviewed** at every level from research engineers, to senior staff officers, to general officer commanders.

❑ Executive Officer to the Director, Air Forced Reserve, Pentagon, Washington, DC
Jun 89 – Jul 92

❑ F-4G and RF-4C Force Programmer, Pentagon, Washington, DC   May 87 – Jun 89

Recruited by a four-star officer to be the only operator helping to build the influential Imagery Architectural Study, an effort that affected every user of intelligence from the uniformed

Charles Marklin   **Industrial Security Manager**   314.555.6666 (Cell)

services to the CIA, to the Defense Mapping Agency, to the Departments of State and Energy.

✪Stepped in often to articulate the users' requirements—a role that required a very steep learning curve to be sure I **understood the potential of highly classified programs**, especially when used in mix and match roles. Built the presentation the Director of Central Imagery used to **brief at the highest levels**. *Outcomes:* The Assistant Chief of Staff, Intelligence, wrote, "…(Major Marklin's) ability to **grasp complex system information** and articulate the user environment to national-level systems developers…left a highly positive impression. Without his dedication and ability to look forward, the Imagery Architectural Study would have failed to consider…the user."

OPERATIONAL BACKGROUND

❏ Qualified in three aircraft with 3,300 hours, all as pilot-in-command, instructor pilot, or flight examiner. Experience in **operational test and evaluation**. Produced nearly all of the RF-4C's **classified tactics, techniques, and procedures manual**.

EDUCATION AND PROFESSIONAL DEVELOPMENT (LAST FIVE YEARS ONLY)

❏ M.S.S., **Strategic Studies**, Air War College, Air University, Maxwell Air Force Base, Alabama, GPA 3.77   98

❏ M.A., Higher Education Administration, Creighton University, Omaha, Nebraska   95
Earned this degree while working 60 hours a week and carrying a full academic load. GPA 4.0.

❏ M.A., **Management**, Centralia University, Centralia, Illinois   81
Worked 60 hours a week and carried a full academic load. GPA 3.8.

❏ B.A., History, Texas University, Del Rio, Texas   76
Attended under a full scholarship. Worked about 30 hours a week. Inducted into the Freshmen Men's Honor Society. Received the Academic Leadership Award from the College of Professional Studies. Distinguished Graduate, AFROTC

❏ **Information Assurance Awareness**, United States Air Force, two hours   Annually

❏ **Records Management** General Awareness, United States Air Force, two hours   Annually

❏ Supervisor Negotiation and **Conflict Resolution**, United States Air Force, four hours   05

IT LITERACY

❏ Comfortable with PowerPoint, Word, Excel, and advanced Internet search protocols.

LAWRENCE P. WILLIAMS

34 Sullivan Avenue   Fairfax, VA 22313
☎703.878.2299   🖳 williams@net.com

MAINTENANCE TECHNICIAN

Ten years of experience in the maintenance, repair, troubleshooting and operation of highly complex electronics equipment. Technical skills include maintaining hydraulic, pneumatic, mechanical, electrical and electronic systems. Proficient in repairing hydraulic cylinders and motors, water breaks, sealing devices, O and V rings, gaskets, valves, and filters, and in using inside/outside micrometers and tools. Demonstrated ability to train and lead others to perform productively. Comfortable in fast-paced, high-stress environments requiring attention to detail, ability to meet deadlines and quick adaptation to constantly changing priorities.

ACCOMPLISHMENTS

➢ Completed and achieved the highest number of technical qualifications out of 22 people within division.
➢ Selected by senior management as Employee of the Quarter twice in the last year for "superior performance, dedication, professionalism and positive attitude."
➢ Recognized as a team player who requires minimum supervision, is motivated to the highest performance standards and committed to excellence.
➢ Displayed "unequaled troubleshooting skills in maintenance activities," resulting in the flawless execution of 50+ critical maintenance actions for the safe launch of 10,000+ aircraft.

EMPLOYMENT HISTORY

UNITED STATES NAVY   1994 to Present
Aircraft Equipment Maintenance Technician

Advanced through increasingly responsible positions in aviation equipment operation, maintenance, quality assurance and safety. Selected by supervisor out of 22 technicians to handle one of the most complex assignments in the entire division.

Equipment Repair & Maintenance

• Experienced in the operation and maintenance of multimillion-dollar aircraft launching and recovery equipment.
• Performed troubleshooting and/or repair of electrical, electronic, hydraulic, pneumatic, and mechanical systems.
• Ensured and documented safe equipment operation and work practices within work center; oversaw proper handling, storage and disposal of hazardous materials to meet compliance standards.

Quality Assurance & Inspection

• Accurately calibrated and installed 70+ precision-measurement tools valued at over $250,000.
• Accountable for quality assurance of all tools, parts and materials to maximize safety of all personnel and equipment.
• Supervised all maintenance checks to monitor accuracy and adherence to precise procedures.

continued...

LAWRENCE P. WILLIAMS • Page 2

Employment _continued..._

Training & Team Leadership

- Trained and oversaw 40-member work center in the operation, maintenance and repair of various equipment.
- Trained and advanced the skills of new personnel, quickly advancing the qualifications of over 15 team members who subsequently contributed to 15,000+ safe, error-free aircraft operations.
- Coordinated technical reference manuals on electrical and hydraulic systems and mechanical operations of equipment to update staff on new parts, materials and maintenance procedures.

EDUCATIONAL TRAINING

Successfully completed specialized training programs in:

- Maintenance Equipment and Operations
- Aircraft Firefighting
- Catapult Hydraulics
- Arresting Gear Hydraulics
- Quality Assurance
- Damage Control

ELAINE ERICKSON
Box 9004
APO AE 09220
011-972-4499-3267
Elaine_Erickson@net.com

CAPABILITIES OFFERED AS SITE MANAGER

Offering B.A. in Criminal Justice and 4 years of progressive experience in the U.S. military in protective services and security operations in hostile environments. Hold Secret Security Clearance - Protective Services Qualified.

✓ Solid qualifications in supervision and personnel training, contributing to operational readiness/success.
✓ U.S. citizen; born and raised in Russia; Russian Linguist; Scored 4/4 on Defense Language Proficiency Test.
✓ Recognized by supervisors as a highly self-motivated, efficient professional who delivers outstanding results through problem-solving, communications and interpersonal strengths.
✓ Personal qualities include reliability, trustworthiness, sound judgment and strong work ethic.

EXPERIENCE

U.S. NAVY COMMANDER FLEET, U.S. NAVAL CENTRAL COMMAND   2003 to Present
Protective Service Agent

Handpicked as the first woman to represent Naval Support Activity as a Protective Service Agent in the Gulf. Conducted more than 100 VIP movements without any incidents.

- Plan, coordinate and provide security, administrative and logistics support to the Commander of the U.S. Fifth Fleet and visiting dignitaries who are high-risk targets of terrorism.

- Entrusted to coordinate monthly Motorcade Operations detail for the Commanders of Joint Chiefs of Staff and U.S. Naval Central Command.

- Range of experience includes protective service tactics, anti-ambush operations, counter surveillance operations, evasive driving techniques and providing physical security.

- Execute and monitor force protection level training for the Command with an emphasis on crime prevention, port security, public relations and language instruction.

- Train security staff in force protection, anti-terrorism, threat collection, information security, crisis management, terrorist and weapons of mass destruction response, mass casualty and physical security planning.

Accomplishments & Awards

- Liaised with numerous U.S. protection agencies and host nations, playing a key role in the successful protection of the Vice Admiral, 20+ visiting Flag Officers and dignitaries.
- Recognized for successful results in planning and coordinating physical fitness assessment program for 50 Central Command personnel.
- Earned the National Defense Service Medal, 2003; Armed Forces Expeditionary Medal, 2003; Navy and Marine Corps Achievement Medal, 2002; and Meritorious Unit Commendation, 2002.

Supervisor's Evaluation Comments: *"Sandra is a key member of the Commander's Executive Protection Detail. One of the go-to sailors when things need to get done. A self-starter who rapidly established herself as a leader in the work center; both junior and senior personnel look to her for direction. Her knowledge and drive have reinvigorated the Executive Protection Detail She is essential to its success."*

ELAINE ERICKSON - PAGE 2

NAVAL SECURITY FORCE
Training Officer   2003 to 2003

Promoted to Master-at-Arms Second Class and assigned to Protective Service Detail in Bahrain following closure of Roosevelt Roads Naval Base.

- Planned and coordinated bi-monthly training schedules for new Security Personnel in all aspects of force protection and security issues.
- Taught courses in Security Department operations and job duties, Crime Prevention, Search and Seizure, Jurisdiction, Public Relations, Uniform Code of Military Justice, Use of Force, Report Writing, Perimeter Searches, Interview and Interrogation, Crime Scenes and Preservation of Evidence and CPR.

Accomplishments

- Trained and ensured that all personnel were properly trained and qualified in Search and Seizure procedures, vehicle and personnel searches, and detention and apprehension of suspects.
- Initiated the Naval Security Force Bahrain CPR Program, certifying over 150 security personnel and maintaining 300 records.

Patrol Officer / Training Coordinator   2001 to 2003

Supervised a team of 15 personnel on Vieques Island during quarterly military exercises. Scheduled work assignments/rotations and acted as liaison between military and local authorities.

- Evaluated daily operations of Force Protection and Physical Security. Analyzed and reviewed complex security issues. Recommended action steps to ensure appropriate implementation of security measures in response to threat assessment and intelligence.
- Acted as a liaison for the Naval Security Department with Marine Support Units and the Coast Guard for safeguarding the Live Impact Area during exercise operations.
- Ensured that Security Force personnel were properly equipped and briefed on threat level during protests.
- Performed additional responsibilities as Dispatcher, Incident Report Writer, DWI Patrol Officer, security and riot support, protective service volunteer, range support and base security.

Accomplishments

- Developed and coordinated security policy and procedures for assigned security programs.
- Trained over 300 Naval Security Force Personnel on all aspects of law enforcement and force protection, ensuring their qualification in Search and Seizure procedures, vehicle and personnel searches, detention and apprehension of suspects, CPR and weapons.
- Prepared and implemented automated presentations in classroom settings during the Department of Defense Joint Service Integrate Vulnerability Assessment briefings.
- Assisted in the safe removal of 16 anti-Navy protestors on the island, enabling Joint Forces and U.S. Naval Battle Groups to maintain operational readiness.

EDUCATION

B.A. in Criminal Justice, emphasis in Policing, Excelsior College (military distance learning program), 2004
Courses include: Criminal Investigation, Corrections, Deviant Behavior, Juvenile Delinquency, Forensic Science

MILITARY TRAINING

Naval Security Force Field Training Officer Academy, Protective Training and Antiterrorism Evasive Driver Course, Protective Service Detail School, Executive Protection Driver School, Naval Criminal Investigative Service Surveillance Course, Executive Protective Services, Emergency Medical Technician and Law Enforcement Apprentice Course.

Stephanie A. Johnson

203 Marler Boulevard • San Diego, CA 92100 • (619) 514-5569 • sajohnson@net.com

September 10, 2007

Terrance Wilson, Director
Med Lab Systems
2971 O'Donnell Blvd.
San Diego, CA 92111

Dear Mr. Wilson:

Your requirements for a Medical Laboratory Supervisor are a perfect match with my background. As a medical laboratory management professional with a 10-year record of successful performance, I offer the following qualifications:

- B.S. degree in laboratory science combined with advanced training in laboratory procedures, techniques and operations.
- Well-rounded hands-on and management experience in all aspects of medical laboratory operations in major medical centers in the U.S. and overseas.
- Certification as a Laboratory Technician.

Throughout my career, I have achieved recognition for my expertise, leadership, team-building strengths and focus on quality standards. Recent examples of my accomplishments include:

- Start-up and management of multiple medical laboratory operations, including coordination of personnel recruitment, training and equipment implementation.
- Development and implementation of consistent policies and procedures, as well as staff training on best practices, resulting in efficient operations with 100% safety record.
- Planning and coordinating educational programs launched organization-wide that have been touted for excellence.

I will be completing my service with the United States Navy next month and would welcome the opportunity to discuss the contributions I would make to your medical lab operations. Thank you for your consideration.

Very truly yours,

Stephanie A. Johnson

Stephanie A. Johnson

Stephanie A. Johnson

203 Marler Boulevard • San Diego, CA 92100 • (619) 514-5569 • sajohnson@net.com

Medical Laboratory Management

Certified Medical Laboratory professional with 10 years of progressive team leadership, policy development and management experience in major medical center, clinic and field environments. Solid background in staffing, training, developing and supervising emergency and lab personnel. Budget planning and administrative expertise includes successes in cost reductions while maintaining highest quality standards. Proven analytical, problem solving and organizational abilities resulting in effective approaches in operations and administration.

Career Milestones

- **Selected to establish, staff and manage medical lab operations at an overseas clinic. Developed policies/procedures and led operations to attain licensure and certification in only 14 months.**
- **Chosen to lead the start-up of medical laboratory functions at naval hospitals in 2 states, coordinated staffing and procurement of state-of-the-art equipment.**
- **Achieved and maintained 100% safety record in laboratory operations through effective staff training, team building and supervision in all clinical areas.**
- **Initiated the first blood DNA collection program for Naval Academy and Department of the Navy to be launched organization-wide. Credited by senior management for "phenomenal planning, meticulous attention to detail and flawless program execution."**
- **Annually awarded and achieved 5 promotions for superior performance record and initiative in the development of staff educational and other programs.**

Experience & Accomplishments

UNITED STATES NAVY (1988–present)
Assistant Medical Laboratory Supervisor, Naval Hospital, San Diego (1999–present)
Sr. Medical Laboratory Technician, Clinic & Naval Hospital, New Mexico (1993–1999)

Lab Operations & Management

- Supervise medical laboratory operations and staff of 24 technicians in performing over 2,000 procedures weekly, utilizing state-of-the-art equipment.
- Plan and administer $150,000 annual budget for laboratory operations, successfully reducing costs and maintaining budget well under 20% through training and accountability.
- Involved in administrative functions, including medical billing, patient medical records, purchasing, and inventory/stock control.
- Coordinate and prepare all documentation required by JCAHO and OSHA regulatory agencies.
- Develop, implement and monitor adherence to laboratory department policies and procedures.
- Ensure stringent compliance to standards on quality control, infection control, safety, and disposal of hazardous materials.

Staff Training, Development & Supervision

- Supervise and develop teams of up to 45 personnel, motivating and evaluating performance to maximize efficiency and productivity.
- Train staff on laboratory equipment procedures and protocols to improve productivity while maximizing safety.
- Develop and conduct training programs for new recruits on infectious diseases and preventive medicine.
- Implement training curriculum for health science students on nursing, laboratory policies, procedures and operations.

continued...

Stephanie A. Johnson   **Page 2**

Experience & Accomplishments continued...

Patient Technician, Naval Medical Center, Germany (1991–1993)
Emergency Medical Technician, Naval Hospital, Persian Gulf (1988–1991)

Lab Procedures/Emergency Medicine

- Performed hematology, blood banking, chemistry, microbiology, urinalysis, phlebotomy, serology, specimen collection and other lab procedures.
- Diagnosed and provided routine/emergency medical care to broad range of patients (ICU, CCU, neuro ICU, geriatric, and pediatric) in emergency/trauma, home care and acute care environments.
- Prescribed medications and performed thorough patient assessments and medical procedures: taking vital signs, audiograms, IV and oxygen therapy, suturing, casting, venipuncture, starting arterial lines, EKGs and tracheotomies.
- Advocated and represented patients, effectively resolving issues to ensure quality care and excellent patients relations.

Education / Certifications

Bachelor of Science, Laboratory Science, 2000
University of California, San Diego, CA

Additional Training

UNITED STATES NAVY: **Advanced Laboratory School,** 1994; **Basic Laboratory School,** 1992; **Emergency Medical Technician School,** 1990; **Hospital Corpsman School,** 1988

Seminars

Leadership Development, Critical Care, Field Emergency Medicine, Bacteriology

Certifications

Laboratory Technician, Emergency Medical Technician, Phlebotomy, CPR/First Aid, Health Educator

DAVID A. JONES

85 Ellington Street • Groton, CT 06098 • (203) 437-6779

MAINTENANCE / MATERIALS / OPERATIONS MANAGEMENT
Transportation ~ Shipping Industry

"David is an exceptional planner, organizer and innovative problem solver who has succeeded where others have failed ... he has exceptional operations expertise, strong leadership skills and sound judgment."

Bertrand Fisher
Commanding Officer

Management Professional offering 15 years of experience in electronics equipment maintenance, materials, operations and security.

- Promoted through increasingly responsible technical and supervisory positions based on expertise, demonstrated initiative and contributions to operational efficiency.

- Effective trainer who develops and leads staff to peak performance.

- Expert in navigation and ship-handling operations and systems.

- Recipient of 15 achievement, commendation and distinguished service awards throughout naval career.

RELEVANT EXPERIENCE & ACCOMPLISHMENTS

Maintenance & Materials Management

- Improved operations through aggressive materials improvement and equipment refurbishment programs that were subsequently instituted throughout the organization.
- Supervised electronics technicians in maintenance/repair of various communications, radar and other electronics systems, ensuring peak efficiency and reliability.
- Led implementation of efficient purchasing and JIT inventory management system.
- Oversaw hazardous cargo certification requirements, equipment maintenance and safety deadlines.

Operations Management

- Managed the daily planning, coordination and supervision of 45 staff members, effectively ensuring stringent compliance with vessel safety standards.
- Developed and executed detailed operational review plans for command administrative inspection, resulting in timely problem identification and corrective actions.
- Recognized for instrumental role in achieving "excellent" ratings in all areas during plant inspections.

Staff Training & Management

- Trained more than 500 military and civilian personnel in maintenance procedures, navigation, fire fighting, damage control, security and other areas.
- Turned around an under-performing division to rank #1 in productivity by improving the training curriculum.

CAREER HISTORY

United States Navy • 1989 to Present
Patrol Boat Captain • 1989 to 1990; Legal & Administrative Officer • 1988 to 1989
Assistant Operations & Electronics Material Officer • 1986 to 1988

EDUCATION

B.E., Electrical Engineering, Connecticut College • New London, CT
Additional Training: Electronics Material Management Training Program
Boat Group Management Training Program, Military Justice Legal Training Program

ROBERT MURRAY

3345 Main Street • Fort Meade, MD 20311

(333) 222-4331   robertmurray@net.com

PROFILE

Maintenance Management professional experienced in leading efficient, cost-effective maintenance and repair functions through strong planning and organizational skills. Earned the trust and respect of senior management, associates and subordinates. Strong supervisory skills evident in building cohesive team spirit and developing staff to perform at peak levels. Proven ability to improve productivity, analyze problems and implement solutions that turn challenges into results and enhance organizational effectiveness.

EXPERIENCE

AIR NATIONAL GUARD—Field Maintenance Division
Recipient of 17 awards for exemplary performance, leadership and dedication.
Aircraft Systems Maintenance Supervisor   1996 to Present
Aircraft Maintenance Lead   1988 to 1996

Manage aircraft maintenance operations and inspections with accountability for strategic and financial planning, recruitment, training and development, purchasing, ground equipment and resources. Managed team of 6 supervisors, 50 technicians and 100 weekend air guard personnel. Planned and administered $800,000 annual budget to support operations. Instrumental member of continuous improvement and other initiatives impacting daily operations.

Accomplishments

▸ Significantly improved staff performance and skills by revamping the training and development program; passing rate on courses jumped from 74% over prior years to 94%.

▸ Consistently led unit to achieve top ratings from Air Force inspection team and increased division output 10% by introducing a quality assessment program.

▸ Increased efficiency in aircraft inspection preparation process by restructuring workflow, cutting prep time from 60 days to 8 days; commended as the "best seen to date" by inspection team.

▸ Enforced unit's adherence to stringent safety regulatory requirements and cited by the state DEP for having "the best safety program in the state."

▸ Created an evaluation rating system resulting in the selection of top-tier employees; program was adopted by other supervisors with similar positive results in candidate quality.

▸ Ensured smooth, day-to-day operating continuity by creating comprehensive operations and procedures manual for all unit functions that was adopted throughout Air Force.

▸ Maintained perfect record for no labor union grievances throughout 18-year management career by empowering staff and promoting positive morale through open communications.

Previously as Lead, managed 180 personnel and 15 different maintenance shops for aircraft systems such as hydraulics, electrical, sheet metal, machine, welding, and others.

EDUCATION / TRAINING / CERTIFICATIONS

Completed Instrument Ground School, Flight School, Air Service School, Airmotive School, Senior Non-Commissioned Officer Academy, Management for Air Force Supervisors and U.S. Air Force Air University Extension Institute

Special Training: ANG Chief Master Sergeant Executive Course, Senior Leader Awareness Course, Middle Management Course, Personnel Management for Managers, Hazardous Waste Management, Mediation Training and Aircraft Hydraulic Systems

Certifications: Aircraft Electrical Repair Technician, Maintenance Technician and Aerospace Ground Equipment Repair Technician

Fredrick Smith

678 Willow Lane • City, State • (555) 555-5555 • FredSmith@aol.com

CAREER OBJECTIVE

Sales training position for a technical products company seeking a motivating individual with dynamic presentation and leadership skills.

ACCOMPLISHMENTS

Program Design/Training
- Designed and conducted numerous training programs for 500+ employees and supervisory personnel, resulting in highly skilled, knowledgeable teams.
- Presented experiential workshops on operational procedures and related technical information, personnel policies, new program requirements on security and safety issues, and other topics.
- Researched and implemented several new programs on security, safety and occupational health, telecommunications system and other topics which were introduced organization-wide.

Operations & Maintenance/Technical
- Directed day-to-day operations and equipment maintenance/repair functions in several departments.
- Demonstrated technical knowledge in telecommunications, electronic/electrical systems and equipment,
nuclear power and strategic weapons.
- Supervised the operation and maintenance of a nuclear submarine power plant.

Management/Leadership
- Created two new departments, which included staffing, development of all policies/procedures and training subsequently instituted organization-wide.
- Supervised, developed and evaluated performance of up to 45 technical, maintenance, and administrative support staffs. Recognized for ability to motivate and build cohesive teams.
- Experienced in planning, implementing and managing large-scale projects which were completed ahead of schedule and consistently received outstanding evaluations.
- Orchestrated and supervised 3 shifts of 70 employees in the flawless installation and testing of more than $1 billion in sensitive technical equipment.

PROFESSIONAL EXPERIENCE

UNITED STATES NAVY (1982-XXXX)
Department Head (1991-XXXX)
Engineering Assistant/Division Supervisor (1989-1991)
Department Head (1986-1988)
Operations Assistant/Division Supervisor (1983-1986)

MANUFACTURING COMPANY, City, State (1981-1982)
Production Control Staff

EDUCATIONAL BACKGROUND

B.A. (Chemistry) College, City, State, 1982
Naval Nuclear Power School, City, State, 1989
Naval Nuclear Prototype, City, State, 1989
Naval Submarine School, City, State, 1987

Mary Sullivan, R.N.

54 Marlin Drive ● Newark, NJ 98556 ● Home: 555-555-5555 ● Mobile: 555-555-5555 ● MSullivan@msn.com

LICENSED NURSING PROFESSIONAL – MEDICAL/SURGICAL INTENSIVE CARE

Offering 10 years of experience in providing compassionate and quality nursing care to patients in ICU, Neuro ICU, Recovery, Surgical ICU and Surgical/Medical/ICU Step-down units at major trauma centers with up to 944 beds.

- **Complete patient charts/organizational documentation in a thorough, accurate and timely manner** in accordance with hospital protocol and procedures.
- **Work effectively both independently and as part of a multidisciplinary healthcare team.** Noted for attention to detail, while remaining empathetic and approachable.
- **Recognized by supervisors for dedication, initiative, organizational and problem-solving strengths.** Effective communicator who develops and maintains positive rapport with physicians, peers, patients and family members.

EDUCATION

TEXAS UNIVERSITY, DALLAS, TX: Bachelor of Science in Nursing (2002)

US ARMY, WASHINGTON, DC: Practical Nurse Program, Academy of Health Sciences (1998)

***

LICENSES

Registered Nurse – Licensed in New Jersey

***

AWARD

Army Commendation Medal for Meritorious Service while assigned as an RN at Army Medical Center.

"Your organizational skills and commitment to excellence contributed to mission accomplishment. Your exemplary performance of duty reflects great credit upon you, the United States Army Medical Command and the United States Army."

Colonel, Medical Corps, Commanding

PROFESSIONAL EMPLOYMENT

Sergeant; UNITED STATES ARMY; Europe, Middle East, United States (8/97 to 4/07); Honorable Discharge. Assignments include:

- Registered Nurse; Army Medical Center, Dallax, TX (2000 to 2007)
- Emergency Medical Technician in Middle East and Europe (1997 to 2000)

Summary of Nursing Experience & Clinical Skills

Developed, implemented and monitored nursing care plans including post-operative/trauma care and discharge planning for patients in medical, surgical, rehab, coronary and critical-care environments. Monitored nursing assistants and served as preceptor in training new staff and students. Educated patients and family members on home care and prevention. Well-rounded clinical skills and experience included:

- **Performing comprehensive patient physical assessments,** as well as EKGs, routine lab tests, chest compressions, catherizations, endotracheal and tracheostomy care, phlebotomy and IV therapy.
- **Administering medications** via PO, GT and IVs; assisted with insertion and removal of arterial lines; monitored and managed patients on ventilators, insulin therapy and infusion pumps; handled chemotherapy and pain management.
- **Conducting triage assessment and treatment;** maintaining heparin locks and central lines, treatments and dressings.
- **Performing hemodynamic/Swan-ganz/intracranial pressure monitoring;** crisis management (such as patients with arrhythmias); monitoring and managing patients on GT/ NGT tube feedings, ventilators and telemetry; wound care monitoring and management. Overseeing LPNs in the insertion of IVs, nasogastric tubes and dispensing of medications. Monitoring lab values. Interpreting ABGs.
- **Performing various medical procedures** including cystometricgrams, uroflows and bladder sonograms. Transfusing blood products.
- **Assisting physicians with** bronchoscopies, tracheoscopies, colonoscopies, intubations, endoscopies, arterial catheter insertions, internal/external pacemakers, cardioversions, Swan-ganz/central lines, as well as with prostheses, orthotics and other medical devices.
- **Presenting in-service training to LPNs and RNs** on Arterial Line Set-Up and Maintenance; Identification of Cardiac Dysrhythmias & Arrhythmias; Chronic Obstructive Pulmonary Disease; Swan Ganz Set-Up, Hemodynamic Monitoring, Establishing Manual Cardiac Output; Nasogastric Tube Insertion & Maintenance; Pulmonary Capillary Wedge Pressure; Calculating and Interpreting Arterial Blood Gases; Initiating, Monitoring, and Necessary Interventions of Blood Transfusions.

BARRY CAMPBELL

15917 Greens Drive
Frederick, MD 21740
(301) 356-6689
barryc@yahoo.com

21 Mar 2007

James Stone, Kennel Master
Uniden K-9 Training School
409 Butterscotch Drive
Hagerstown, MD 11507

SUBJECT: K-9 Program Administrator Opportunities

Dear Mr. Stone:

I attended the Montgomery County Police Force Job Fair held on 20 Mar 2007 in Rockville, MD, and found your exhibit on K-9 training to very informative. Mr. Billings, your agency representative was an inexhaustible source of knowledge. The wealth of information that he armed me with was the deciding factor that led me to pursue available employment opportunities with your company.

I have taken the liberty to attach my résumé with this cover letter detailing my multi-year military background with military working dogs. I have supplemented my hands-on experience with ongoing professional development.

I will follow up with you in a few days to confirm receipt and to discuss any specific needs that you may currently have or any that you have projected for your K-9 program.

Thank you in advance, for both your time and consideration.

Respectfully Yours,

Barry Campbell

Barry Campbell

Attachment: Résumé

BARRY CAMPBELL

15917 Greens Drive
Frederick, MD 21740
(301) 356-6689
barryc@yahoo.com

CAREER SUMMARY

Trained working dogs and handlers for patrol, officer protection, criminal apprehension, tracking, building searches, article / evidence searches, and narcotics detection. Taught techniques for setting up containment, backing up officers, tactical team movements, arrest techniques, and how to work with K9 teams in potentially lethal confrontations with suspects.

MILITARY PROFILE

U.S. Air Force
Security Forces Officer {K9 Handler}   Jan 1990-Aug 20--

- **K9 Program Administrator** with the responsibility for ensuring that K9 program was efficiently managed and all handlers were properly trained and equipped with the knowledge, skills, and abilities required to perform the duties of their position. Ensured that handlers were fully cognizant of operating procedures, instructions, appropriate provisions for health, safety, and care of assigned dogs, understood the physical and psychological characteristics and capabilities of their dog, and were properly trained to detect and interpret the dog's responses to persons, narcotics, or other stimuli.
- Conducted proficiency training with training exercises that closely simulated actual performance requirements. Instructional techniques consisted of classroom lectures, demonstrations, and practical exercises.
- Certified that handlers were capable of controlling the patrol dog and possessed the capacity to adjust commands to deal with situations in accordance with guidelines outlined in the **Working Dog Team Proficiency Standards.**
- Trained working dog teams on all aspects of:
    - **Alarm Responses**
    - **Narcotics / Contraband Detection**
    - **Bloodhound In-Service Training**
    - **Man-Trailing Training**
    - **Confrontation Management**
- Developed retrain modules for all phases of critical training when dogs did not consistently perform to minimum standards. Meeting proficiency standards were mandatory for retention of certification as a patrol dog.
- Managed career field education and training plans. Applied principles, practices, and techniques with regard to evaluation activities and performance measures. Created reporting documents to track performance improvement activities, trends, patterns, and identified opportunities for advancing proficiency.

BARRY CAMPBELL   **PAGE 2 OF 2**

EDUCATION

Baltimore City Community College, Baltimore, MD
AS, Criminal Justice   **Jul 1993**

PROFESSIONAL DEVELOPMENT

Criminal Justice Academy K9 Handlers In-Service Training, **Nov 96, Oct 93;** Man-Trailing Training
School, **Apr 96, Apr 95, Apr 94;** National Police Bloodhound Association Annual Seminar, **Oct 94, Oct
93;** North America Police Work Dog Association Workshop, **Sep 92;** Federal Law Enforcement Training
Center Mixed Basic Police Training Program, **Apr 91;** Federal Law Enforcement Training Center
Practical Pistol Course {**Expert**}, **Apr 91**

CERTIFICATIONS

Associate Instructor, **Apr 94**

HONORS & AWARDS

U.S Air Force Meritorious Medal, **May 99;** Kosovo Campaign Medal, **Oct 98;** U.S Air Force Aerial
Achievement 1st oak leaf Medal, **Sep 96;** U.S Air Force Aerial Achievement Medal, **Apr 95;** Global War
on Terrorism Medal, **Mar 94;** Outstanding Achievement, **Nov 93;** Air Force Achievement Medal, **Oct 92**

ELAINE CHARLESTON

elainec@comcast.net

25 January 2007

Gwynne Morrison, Human Resources Director
Jones, Justin, & Womble Law Associates
806 Green Street
Washington, DC 55587

SUBJECT: Available Employment Opportunities

Dear Ms. Morrison:

I am forwarding my résumé to you after researching multi-faceted law firms in the Washington, DC metropolitan area. Your association offering a broad range of services is where I would like to hang my hat. I will be relocating to your area in the upcoming months after an extended period of time in the U.S. Army.

A brief synopsis of my areas of professional responsibility as a Senior Legal Assistant is listed below:

- Performed legal research for government contract law, adversary proceedings, claims, standards of conduct, and investigations.
- Provided assistance to attorneys in the development and/or evaluation of litigation cases and other legal matters requiring the application of established legal principles/concepts, regulations, precedents, agency guidelines, and judicial/administrative proceedings.
- Maintained attorney calendar for trial preparation by arranging for documentary evidence, court reporters, and expert witnesses to appear at trials, hearings, and depositions. Prepared exhibits, charts, graphs, and other visual aids required for use in court.

I will be in your area February 10-17 and would welcome the opportunity for a brief face-to-face introductory meeting to discuss any current or anticipated openings that you may have that parallel the experience that I have documented on my résumé. I will call you in the upcoming week to coordinate a time that is convenient for you. Thank you, in advance for both your time and consideration.

Respectfully Yours

Elaine Charleston

Elaine Charleston

Enclosure: Résumé

6589 Blues Alley*New Orleans, LA 23308*887-944-3321 (H)*856-333-6599 (C)

ELAINE CHARLESTON

elainec@comcast.net

Career Objective

To secure a challenging **Senior Paralegal** position with a law firm in need of a dependable hardworking professional with excellent analytical and research skills; a broad knowledge of legal operations; and proven leadership abilities.

Military Profile

U.S. Army   **Dec 1993-Dec 20--**
Legal Services Specialist

♦ Research and analyze law sources to prepare drafts of briefs or arguments for review, approval, and use by attorney. Prepare affidavits. Maintain document files, and file pleadings with court clerk. Issue orders of the court, release documentation, sentencing information, and summonses. Amend indictments when necessary, and endorse indictments with pertinent information.

♦ Answer inquiries from eneral public regarding judicial procedures, forms, court appearances, trial dates, adjournments, summonses, and subpoenas. Search files, and contact witnesses, attorneys, and litigants, in order to obtain information for court hearings.

♦ Notarize wills, separation agreements, bill of sales, affidavits, powers of attorney, and other documents which require a notary seal.

♦ Senior Specialist on claims for and against the Government involving Permanent Change of Station moves, personal property loss/damage, Federal Tort Claims Act, Military Claims Act, recovery actions, and affirmative claims.

♦ Attend court-martials, pre-trail hearings, and other legal proceedings to assist attorney and ensure courtroom is prepared for applicable proceedings. Transcribe notes and tapes into final form; select, complete and attach applicable forms and documents to the record as required. Keep a running index of cases to include listing of witnesses and marking and listing exhibits. Assist trial counsel in the preparation of offers to plead guilty, stipulations, depositions, and other administrative documents. Ensure all timeline requirements imposed for record preparations are met.

Academic Achievements

Our Lady of the Lake College, Baton Rouge, LA
BA, Legal Studies
June 1994

Technical Proficiencies

Microsoft Word, LexisNexis, Legal Automation Army Wide System (LAAWS) and JAG Bulletin Board

Professional Development

Legal Specialist Course, **Apr 99;** Admin and Law for Legal Specialists, **Jul 95;** Legal Specialist/Court Reporter Course, **May 95;** Law for Legal Specialist Course, **April 94**

6589 Blues Alley*New Orleans, LA 23308*887-944-3321 (H)*856-333-6599 (C)

SHEILA D. COOK

1655 Poole Place
Orlando, FL 21889

cooksheilad@yahoo.com

123-987-6543 (H)
123-456-7890 (C)

Apr 21, 2007

Shirley Link, Personnel Operations Director
Benchmark Computer Systems
5689 International Drive
Orlando, FL 25897

SUBJ: Telephonic Request for Paper Copy of Résumé

Dear Ms. Link:

Thank you so much for your e-mail on Apr 20, 20--, expressing your desire to discuss my Information Technology credentials further. Enclosed, per your request is a hard copy of my résumé. Upon review you will see that I have an extensive background in Information Systems Security.

During my military career I was afforded the opportunity to work in areas that enhanced my ability to:

- Ensure the rigorous application of information security / information assurance policies, principles, and practices to the delivery of application software services.
- Conduct pre- and post-implementation evaluations of network software and utilities while providing technical and analytical guidance for all network operational functions.
- Implement security techniques, procedures, and guidance guaranteeing user access control (physical, personnel, software, and information security) and other security requirements were in place.
- Define and maintain network architecture and infrastructure; configuring and optimizing network servers, hubs, routers, and switches.

Now at the crossroads of my career, I am excited about my unlimited future possibilities. I am open to meeting with you and / or your representative to discuss this employment opportunity. I will follow up with you in the upcoming week to firm up a time that will fit into both of our schedules. Thank you in advance, for both your time and consideration.

Respectfully,

Sheila D. Cook

Sheila D. Cook

SHEILA D. COOK

1655 Poole Place	**123-987-6543 (H)**
Orlando, FL 21889	**123-456-7890 (C)**

cooksheilad@yahoo.com

Available Oct 20--

*****PROFESSIONAL OBJECTIVE*****

To offer broad-based knowledge, effective utilization of comprehensive methods to evaluate qualitative, comprehensive, complex system analysis, and program performance related to **Information Systems Management** to an organization that recognizes the value of the ability to provide core network services configuring, installing, and managing data services at the network, hardware, and software operating systems level.

*****MILITARY SERVICE*****

Senior Information Systems Security Analyst	**Jul 1986-Sep 20--**
U.S. Army	

Information Assurance Security Officer responsible for day-to-day security implementation and operations. Principal source of Automatic Data Processing (ADP) professional and technical information for all information system matters pertaining to communication, hardware, software, ADP security, networks, systems integration, and system operations.

Protected unclassified, sensitive, or classified information stored, processed, accessed, or transmitted using:
- **Virus Protection** - Scanned all files and software with anti-virus product before introducing them onto Information Systems or networks using the multilevel approach to virus detection.
- **Monitoring Networks** - Ensured proper performance and management.
- **Software Security** - Implemented controls to protect system software from compromise, unauthorized use, or manipulation. Maintained configuration management controls, including version controls, on all software.
- **Database Management** - Stored and managed all information and made certain that data was accurate, protected, accessible, and verifiable.
- **Hardware-Based Security Controls** - Incorporated security measures to safeguard information. Protected hardware from compromise, unauthorized use, removal, manipulation, modification, destruction, or disclosure.

Managed 25 multi-vendor and microcomputer systems via two master console systems and one system integration processor valued at over $700M. Provided direct computer and communications support to over 5000 consumers worldwide.

NT System Administrator for 10 Microsoft Windows NT servers and multiple client workstations. Oversaw internal software update and security patch programs. Resulted in zero deficiencies. Investigated and resolved computer software and hardware problems of users as **Help Desk Leader**. Performed diagnostic procedures, using software to troubleshoot automation equipment and systems for isolation of malfunctions to specific hardware or software. Collaborated with programmers to explain software errors or to recommend changes to programs.

Congressional Nominee for White House Communication Agency providing engineering support and technical assistance for communications systems and circuits supporting the President and Vice President of the United States, White House Staff, and United States Secret Service. Safeguarded diagrams for over 5,000 circuits.

Investigated and resolved computer software and hardware problems of users as **Chief of System Operations**. Designed, edited, and tested computer programs. Authored associated technical documentation for program reference and maintenance purposes. Modified existing application packages using application and operating system software and appropriate computer language commands and files.

*****EDUCATION*****

University of Phoenix, Phoenix, AZ
BS, Computer Systems Technology   **May 2001-Jun 2004**

*****PROFESSIONAL CERTIFICATIONS*****

Information Assurance Security Phase II Certified, **Jun 00;** Fiber Optic LAN Specialist, **Sep 90**

*****CAREER DEVELOPMENT/MILITARY TRAINING*****

System Administrator Security Course, **Dec 04;** Network Manager Security Course, **Sep 02;** Information Assurance Security Awareness Training, **Apr 00;** The Army Materiel Command's Information Assurance Conference, **Jan 95;** Introduction to Computer Networking-Part I/II, **May 90**

*****MILITARY AWARDS*****

Certificate of Appreciation, **Feb 03, Sep 02;** Joint Meritorious Unit Award, **Dec 01;** Good Conduct Medal, **Jul 01, Jul 98, Jul 95, Jul 92, Jul 89;** Army Commendation Medal, **Dec 98, Dec 93, Dec 90;** Joint Service Commendation Medal w/1 oak leaf cluster, **Mar 94;** Army Achievement Medal, **May 92;** Certificate of Recognition, **Nov 91**

BECK O. COOPER

beckocooper@comcast.net

8888 Hope Well Drive*Arlington, VA 98765*703-123-4567 (H)*703-987-5687 (C)

****

Feb 05, 2007

Brook Webster, Human Resources Director
Regency Plaza Resorts
6987 Gray Worthy Place
Washington, DC 26839

SUBJECT: Requested information for "Hospitality Services Manager" listed on your company website on Feb 03, 2007

Dear Mr. Webster:

I am providing you my résumé in response to our conversation on last week in regard to the Hospitality Services Manager employment opportunity with your firm. To further expound on my professional profile, I have just recently transitioned from an exciting career with the U.S. Air Force. My immediate professional objective is to secure a position with a company where I will be able to fully utilize the core competencies that I acquired during my career.

I offer a background of versatile experience, distinctive qualifications, accomplishments, and reputation in:

- Decisive leadership, keen assessment and problem-solving techniques, key motivational strategies, and performance/productivity improvement.
- A passion for the hospitality industry, qualified with specialized hospitality education and extensive quest services knowledge.
- The capacity to multitask, meet deadlines, delegate appropriate support roles, and respect for both colleagues and customers.

I welcome the opportunity to meet with you or your designated agency representatives to discuss my qualifications and your objectives further. I will follow up with your office in the upcoming week to discuss interviewing possibilities. Thank you, in advance for both your time and consideration.

Respectfully Yours,

Beck O. Cooper

Beck O. Cooper

BECK O. COOPER
beckocooper@comcast.net

8888 Hope Well Drive*Arlington, VA 98765*703-123-4567 (H)*703-987-5687 (C)

****

Professional Objective

Food Services Manager offering a background of excellence based on hands-on experience dedicated to providing quality service and performance in high-volume operations, exploring opportunities to secure a management level position in a challenging environment where my professional expertise can be effectively utilized.

Areas of Expertise

- Menu Planning/Food Preparation
- Performance Optimization
- Accountability
- Lodging & Dining Operations

- Vendor Sourcing/Negotiations
- Food Sanitation Practices
- Resource Management
- Public & Guest Relations

- Hospitality Industry
- Staff Supervision
- Needs Assessment
- Inventory

Military Profile

Food Services Specialist
U.S. Air Force   **Jan 1998-Jan 2007**

Scope of Work Performed

FOOD SERVICES OFFICER

Provided efficient administration of food service activities including administration and nutrition aspects of food preparation and service. Exercised management control over operation, maintenance, and sanitation of all food service spaces, equipment, supplies, and provisions. Assembled, measured, weighed, and mixed ingredients for basic formulas and other supplemental feedings in accordance with Armed Forces Recipe Service (AFRS). Reviewed menus, work sheets and recipes. Determined type and quantities of items required for number of persons to be served. Skilled in planning, coordinating, and timing the sequences of steps needed to have menu items ready for serving without overcooking or wasting. Experienced in the full range of food preparation principles, including the techniques and procedures necessary to develop new or revise current recipes. Knowledge of the characteristics of various raw and cooked foods in deciding if raw materials are fresh; and judging the final product by its color, consistency, temperature, odor, and taste. Ensured food service staff practiced and maintained high standards of personal hygiene and sanitation. Made certain food service spaces and associated equipment was in clean and sanitary condition.

INVENTORY MANAGEMENT

Determined current and future subsistence requirements. Considered demand trends, procurement, lead-time, essentiality, authorizations, changes in mission, and operational plans. Received and counted stock items. Packed and unpacked items to be stocked on shelves in stockrooms. Verified inventory computations by comparing them to physical counts of stock, and investigated discrepancies or adjusted errors. Determined proper storage methods, identification, and stock location based on turnover, environmental factors, and physical capabilities of facilities. Collaborated with vendors to coordinate delivery details, requirements, and to resolve discrepancies or eliminate delays. Upon receipt, examined documents, materials, and products, to assess completeness, accuracy, and conformance to standards and specifications. Full understanding of well-established and commonly applied food services principles, concepts, and methodologies used in budget preparation and acquisition of food preparation equipment.

_____**Academic Credentials**_____

The Art Institute of Washington, Arlington, VA
B.A., Culinary Arts   **May 00-Dec 04**

_____**Professional Development**_____

Introduction to Food Preparation, Food Service Techniques, Consumer Services Management, Services Readiness Operations, Services Operations

SHARON A.
JONES

3616 M Street
Charleston, SC 20002
345-488-1235 (H) 345-688-9875 (C)
sajones@yahoo.com

Mar 30, 2007

Carl Isaac, Director, Human Resources Division
Personnel Strategy & Planning Agency
2255 Wise Ave
Charleston, SC 26839

SUBJECT: "Personnel Operations Manager" listed on your company website on Mar 29, 2007

Dear Mr. Isaac:

In response to the employment opportunity listed on your web posting, I am submitting this cover letter and accompanying résumé for consideration. I have just recently transitioned from 20 years of excitement with the U.S. Air Force. Upon perusal of my résumé, you will find that my previous experience effectively parallel the skill set stated as required for your position.

My added values and transferable skills consist of my demonstrated ability to:

- Administer decisive leadership to drive organizational change, process reengineering, and performance/productivity improvement.
- Provide overall expert knowledge of regulatory requirements concerning military personnel administration.
- Counsel careerists on training needs and all other aspects of their mandatory/optional career program requirements necessary to achieve career objectives.

As requested, my previous position commanded an annual salary of $80K in addition to a full benefit package. I have no doubt that your company offers a salary that is both fair and competitive. My salary requirement, not including benefits, or agency supplements, is flexible and negotiable.

I welcome the opportunity to discuss my qualifications and your objectives further. I will follow up with you early next week to discuss interviewing possibilities. Thank you, in advance for both your time and consideration.

Respectfully Yours,

Sharon A. Jones

Sharon A. Jones

SHARON A.
JONES_____

3616 M Street
Charleston, SC 20002
345-488-1235 (H) 345-688-9875 (C)
sajones@yahoo.com

_____Military Profile_____

U.S. Air Force	**Jan 1986-May 2007**
	Secret Clearance

Career Summary_____

Solutions-oriented **Human Resources Professional** with a reputation for "superior performance." Career field professional offering consistently outstanding time management, excellent organizational, multiple task/project coordination, and critical thinking skills to an organization that recognizes the value of the contributions that I will be able to make as a member of their team.

Areas of Professional Responsibility_____

PROGRAM MANAGEMENT

- Principal advisor to Unit Commander, 900 military service members, civilian personnel, and family members on health, moral, and welfare issues. Resolved issues that adversely impacted troop readiness. Advised on management/employee relations, discipline, management/employee rights, adverse actions, grievances, performance management and recognition, employee counseling, and related functions promoting awareness of human needs and reactions of employees, and suggested constructive methods for dealing with problems arising from indifference, personality conflicts, and poor work habits or behavior problems.

  - Enlisted Performance Reports, Awards, & Decorations
  - Weight Management, Fitness, & Family Care
  - Urinalysis Drug Testing

PERFORMANCE OPTIMIZATION/COMPENSATION

- Provided direction for Professional Military Education. Identified developmental needs of staff that supported/facilitated professional growth. Determined methods and procedures for conducting military career guidance and counseling to ensure personnel had optimal and established career pattern.

  - Created competency-based performance analysis and appraisal system to identify top performers and facilitate progressive career development.
  - Established "Stellar Troop Award" for on-the-spot recognition of superior performers.

ORATORY AND WRITING ABILITY

- Practical knowledge and understanding of advanced concepts required to be able speak and write well. Ability to select precise format, organization, and style based on the nature of the topic and needs and interests of the intended audience.

  - Authored guidelines for administrative actions related to Weight and Body Fat Program.
  - Mistress of Ceremony for 50 farewell and 10 wing promotion ceremonies, volunteer recognition event, and 4 Quarterly award ceremonies.
  - Wrote, "Leading our Troops" and inspirational article for the base newspaper that inspired supervisors to re-evaluate their work ethic and incorporate changes.
  - Guest Speaker at Senior Non Commissioned Officer Course graduation.
  - Conducted 2-day Suicide Intervention Skills Training course to cultivate critical skills required for crisis situations.
  - Led writing sessions for Enlisted Performance Ratings and recognition processes. Efforts resulted in immediate improvement, preserved integrity, and ensured consistency.

INFORMATION MANAGEMENT

- Chief Administrator, with oversight responsibility for branch administrative functions.

  - As Functional Areas Records Manager performed staff assistance visits. Decision-making authority on file plans for 9 offices. Ensured timely and accurate submission of 600+ suspense's annually.
  - Information Taskmaster for programs, policies, and procedures directly impacting publications, forms, office systems, records, and administrative communications. Introduced paperless forms and publications storage and retrieval systems. Saved countless man-hours.
  - Developed systematic process to identify and analyze communication requirements that resulted in critical upgrades and equipment purchases valued at more than $200K as Work Group Information Systems Officer.

Academic Credentials

Villanova University, Villanova, PA
Masters Certificate, Human Resource Management   **May 2006**

Columbia Union College, Columbia, MD
B.S., Human Resource Management   **May 2003**

Professional Development

Dispute Resolution Course; Business Ethics; Introduction to Guidance and Counseling; Senior Seminar in Human Resources Management; Senior Seminar in Management; Principles of Management; Labor Relations; Organizational Development and Change; Compensation Management; Interpersonal Communication I; Quality Force Management; Leadership/Management II

MATTHEW RICE

2357 Durby Dae Place*Hampton, VA 12345*336-333-9999 (H)*336-633-222-8888 (M)
colriceret@yahoo.com

Mar 07, 2007

Maxine Shaw, Director, Policy and Planning Division
Bureau of International Planning
2587 Barron Avenue
Norfolk, VA 25897

SUBJECT: Consideration for Known or Anticipated Employment Opportunities

Dear Ms Shaw:

Recently, Pat Cummings recommended that I contact you regarding any known or anticipated employment opportunities with your firm or any of the organizations with which you partner. I am a career officer retiring after more than 25 years of service with the U.S. Marine Corps. I am exploring opportunities to secure an executive-level opportunity with domestic and/or international responsibilities. Upon perusal of my resume you will see experiences that will contribute to my being able to be a tremendous asset to your organization; in addition to a record of constant success associated with a diverse range of functions.

Augmenting my education, military training, and character are skills that demonstrate my leadership ability to:

- Set priorities and manage time in accordance with agency goals.
- Perform well under pressure, where precision and choices are critical to positive outcomes.
- Identify objective, organize resources, and direct efforts to achieve desired results.
- Share a vision, communicate goals, and delegate tasks to appropriate individuals to generate success.
- Anticipate needs/problems, assess progress, evaluate results, and apply required knowledge for an efficient operation.
- Enforce compliance with policy and procedures to maintain departmental credibility.

I welcome the opportunity to meet with you or your designated agency representatives to discuss my qualifications and your objectives further. I will follow up with your office in the upcoming week to discuss interviewing possibilities. Thank you in advance for both your time and consideration.

Respectfully yours,

Matthew Rice

Matthew Rice

COL MATTHEW RICE, RET

2357 Durby Dae Place*Hampton, VA 12345*336-333-9999 (H)*336-633-222-8888 (M)
colriceret@yahoo.com

EXECUTIVE QUALIFICATION STATEMENT

OBJECTIVE: Career Marine Corps Officer exploring opportunities to secure an executive level position offering more than **25 years** of professional responsibility in the diverse and complex areas of:

* Policy Planning & Implementation
* Strategic Thinking / Logistics
* Performance Optimization
* Organizational Improvement
* Contingency / Wartime Platform
* Leadership Development

Top Secret / Secret Compartmentalized Information Security Clearance - (Active through Jan 20--)

CAREER HIGHLIGHTS

Program Plans Officer

Handpicked to become Chief of Strategic Policy Division. Provided unsurpassed vision and analytical insight into nation's most important policy issues.

- **Challenge:** Implementation of the Joint Staff Strategic Communication Secretariat
- **Action**: "Key Player" in development of instructions, policies and execution mechanisms that served as the foundation of the Chairman of the Joint Chiefs of Staff and Combatant Commanders Strategic Communication Doctrine.
- **Result:** Successful integration of the Joint Staff and the Office of the Secretary of Defense Strategic Communication Secretariat with the State Department Public Diplomacy Committee.

Logistical Responsibility

Compiled, analyzed, and evaluated information concerning staff actions and made recommendations regarding possible course(s) of action, including justification and/or impact statements to ensure that plans met mission requirements.

- **Challenge:** To procure pre-fabricated armor for over 1,500 Marine Corps tactical vehicles for units directed to deploy to Iraq one month ahead of schedule.
- **Action**: Consolidated vehicle requirements by model and type to ensure correct size and shape of steel would be fabricated. Collaborated with the Marine Corps Systems Command, the Marine Corps Logistics Command, the Marine Corps Headquarters Personnel, Plans, and Policies Directorate and the Unit Logistics Officers.
- **Result:** Units received all required armor prior to deployment. Normal delivery time was decreased by 60 percent. Mission accomplished without any unforeseen increases in cost or incurring the 25 percent additional expense for rush delivery.

Strategic Organizational Expertise

Developed long-range strategy for headquarters and subordinate elements. Oversight responsibility for installation of timetables and milestones. Prepared briefings and correspondence and distributed command policy and guidance on strategic planning processes.

- **Challenge:** To train Naval Service Officers in the rapid planning processes required developing a course of action in a compressed time frame based on mission directed deployments overseas.
- **Action:** "Major Contributor" in development of instructions, policies, and execution mechanisms utilized for training multi-service officers on development of crisis action plans to provide continuity of operations.
- **Result:** Increased number of qualified operational planning team officers within the Staff of Third Fleet by 50 percent.

Civil Military Operations

Principal authority on the relationship between military forces, civil authorities, and local nationals. Combined regional expertise, political-military awareness, cross-cultural communication, and professional military skills to direct, guide, and manage 3 separate civil affairs organizations responsible for regional stability in Iraq.

- **Challenge:** To ensure local populace in Iraq would provide support and cooperation to US and Coalition Forces.
- **Action:** Coordinated with unit level Civil Affairs teams and local leaders to identify areas where local civilians would benefit from short-term projects that would show commitment to rebuilding country.
- **Result:** Restored infrastructure that included an inoperable power station, a police station, local schools, and a water pipeline. Finished projects gave local community a sense of pride and solidified allegiance to US and Coalition Forces.

ACADEMIC CREDENTIALS

BS, Business Administration, Morgan State University, Baltimore, MD

POSITION SPECIFIC EMPLOYMENT PROFILE

Chief, Strategic Policy Division - The Joint Staff, Pentagon, Washington, DC	**2005-2007**
Fleet Marines Officer/Plans Officer - US Third Fleet, San Diego, CA	**2003-2004**
Future Operations Officer - 1st Marine Expeditionary Force, Camp Pendleton, CA	**2002**
Chief of Operations, - US Army 352nd Civil Affairs Command, Kuwait/Iraq	**2001**
Regional Desk Officer - Marines Forces Pacific, Camp Smith Hawaii	**2000**
Asst. Operations Officer - Marine Forces Reserve Headquarters, New Orleans, LA	**1999**
Detachment Commander - 3rd Civil Affairs Group, Camp Pendleton, CA	**1995**

KENYA BROWN

7296 Matthews Avenue   843.555.0001
Charleston, SC 29406   kenyabrown126@roadrunner.com

OBJECTIVE

To enter the paralegal profession following an outstanding 16-year career in the U.S. Navy.

EDUCATION/TRAINING

THE PARALEGAL INSTITUTE INC., PHOENIX, ARIZONA

Associate of Arts degree in Paralegal Studies
ABA approved distance learning program; current overall GPA 3.6   December 2006

Concentration: **Real Estate and Litigation Law**

Coursework included:

- The Professional Paralegal
- Substantive Law I and II
- Civil Litigation
- Criminal Law and Procedures
- Legal Research
- Legal Analysis and Writing

- Ethics and Professional Responsibility
- The Court System and Alternative Dispute Resolution
- Administrative Law and Governmental Regulation
- Trial Procedures
- Conducting Interviews and Investigations
- Computer Assisted Legal Research

NAVY LEADER DEVELOPMENT PROGRAM (NAVLEAD) FOR LEADING PETTY OFFICERS

PROFESSIONAL AFFILIATIONS

- Student Member, National Association of Legal Assistants
- Student Member, National Paralegal Association

SKILLS & TRANSFERRABLE EXPERIENCE

Administration/Organization
- Organized a large volume of paperwork and computerized files
- Demonstrated computer proficiency with MS Word and Excel programs
- Coordinated, scheduled, and administered assignments
- Extracted and summarized information and prepared reports
- Established daily operating procedures
- Trained and supervised personnel

Communication
- Interacted with persons of diverse backgrounds
- Conducted briefings and interviews
- Provided assistance and information within scope of authority
- Drafted written instructions and notices
- Handled sensitive and confidential information with discretion

Personal Attributes
- Cordial and well-mannered; positive attitude; strong work ethic; eager to learn and grow
- Unrivaled in customer service; give 110% effort to satisfy client needs
- Extremely dependable and take on additional tasks without hesitation
- Confident, self-motivated, and resourceful in handling routine assignments as well as the demands of adverse situations
- Highly organized, accurate, and efficient in meeting or exceeding production expectations and deadlines
- Willing to travel and/or relocate

PROFESSIONAL EXPERIENCE

UNITED STATES NAVY   1990 to Present

ADMINISTRATIVE SUPPORT CLERK

Educational Support Supervisor (1998 to present)
Naval Weapons Station, Charleston, South Carolina

Customer Services Supervisor (1994 to 1998)
Personnel Support Activity, Naples, Italy

Records Clerk (1990 to 1994)
USS Shreveport LPD12

Highlights of Accomplishments (As noted from performance evaluations)

- Selected as Division Training Officer, a duty normally assigned to senior level petty officers.
- Supervised up to 12 subordinates; directed their production and efficient performance of their administrative duties.
- Effectively counseled personnel in preparation for promotion exams, resulting in a 35% advancement rate.
- Restructured the division training format, achieving a 45% increase in personnel qualification.
- Skillfully managed a $7.5K training budget while ensuring a cost-effective means of attaining and enhancing required skill levels.
- Initiated new procedures to improve the tracking of personnel qualifications.
- Engineered an audit of personnel service records consisting of over 2,500 crewmembers.

HONORS

- Navy Achievement Medal, two-time recipient for outstanding professional achievement
- Three Good Conduct Medals
- Numerous Letters of Appreciation

Hernando Chavez

222 East 19th Avenue, Allentown, PA 18101 ■ ■ ■ ■ ■ ■ ■ ■ ■ ■ ■ ■ ■ ■ ■ ■ ■ ■ (484) 555-1212

GOAL

Front Line Investigator with the County Prosecutor's Office

PROFILE

Strong interest in the preservation of law and security from an early age, combined with active military duty concentrated in the police sciences. Extensive training and exposure to law enforcement techniques as well as the leadership of others.

Demonstrated skills in the following areas:

Civilian disturbance investigations — Instructor for all Eastern Pennsylvania Reserve Units in special assault tactics and survival skills in an urban and combative environment.

Narcotics detection — Trained to recognize and apprehend suspect persons and vehicles. Conducted searches with canine assistance. Applied forceful techniques and made one of the largest seizures of marijuana on the base.

Firearms and weapons handling — Classified as expert or sharp shooter in the use of M92F 9mm Beretta pistol, M1911 .45 caliber pistol, M6A1 and A2 rifles. Also skilled in the use of explosive grenades, chemical agents and pain-inflicting weapons for riot control.

Self defense — Well-developed "street smarts" from having grown up in a crime-ridden neighborhood, plus almost 10 years of martial arts training to earn First Class Black Belt in karate.

Physical fitness — Held record for 3 years at Fort Knox, KY for fastest completion of their obstacle course, requiring top strength and endurance.

Emergency medical techniques — Knowledge of basic life support systems, first aid, CPR, and underwater rescue. Passed EMT certification requirements at age 17, the first in the area to qualify at such a young age.

Defensive and offensive driving — Selected for bodyguard duties and transport of high-ranking military officers.

Leadership and communication — Advanced in status quickly by displaying ability to act decisively without intimidation, uphold the highest standards, and instruct others by example. Fluent in Spanish.

EXPERIENCE

UNITED STATES ARMY   2000–Present
Military Policeman, Fort Knox, KY and Fort Dix, NJ
Attained rank of Corporal, honorably discharged from active duty in 2004. Selected for rank of Sergeant while continuing military service in the Army Reserves.

AWARDS & CITATIONS

- **Soldier of the Year,** 2002: Selected for this honor out of 150 soldiers in the unit for highest standards of physical fitness, dress, behavior, verbal communications, preparation for inspections, marksmanship, protection of officers, and involvement with the community.

- **Army Commendation Medal** for getting prompt medical attention, which saved the life of another soldier who was injured during training.

- **Recruiters Award** for encouraging Army enlistment as a career direction for 36 urban youths following their high school graduation.

Hernando Chavez ■■

COMMUNITY SERVICE

ALLENTOWN CORPS OF CADETS   2003–Present
Co-Founder

- With Army colleague, conceived and organized a co-ed program for urban youth, ages 12 to 17, based on military disciplines.
- Developed in these adolescents a sense of self-esteem, respect for authority, better study habits, awareness of the dangers of substance abuse, and the importance of keeping physically fit.
- Secured initial funding through the National Guard, and as program expanded from originally 6 participants to currently over 180, solicited support from local police department, fire marshal, educators, merchants, and family service agencies.
- Received commendations from both city mayor and state governor.

EDUCATION

LEHIGH COUNTY COMMUNITY COLLEGE   2004–Present
Major: Criminal Justice, specializing in law and order.
Minor: Emergency Medical Technology

DEPARTMENT OF BASIC MILITARY POLICE TRAINING,
Fort Knox, KY   2002
Concentration in Military Police and Military Law

Ian J. Parker
112 Penny Lane, Providence, RI 02911
Home: (401) 999-8888   Mobile: (401) 333-0000

Expertise and Qualifications
for position of United States Government Special Agent

▶ Four years of service with the U.S. Marine Corps, attaining rank of Master Sergeant
▶ Team leadership proven in multiple challenging situations
▶ Surveillance, sniper operations, reconnaissance and related reporting procedures
▶ Expert marksmanship with a variety of firearms and grenade/anti-armor weapons
▶ Instruction of others in weapons and tactical maneuvers
▶ All forms of communications systems, including use of field expedient antennae
▶ Day/night all-terrain land and maritime navigation
▶ Information collection/undercover intelligence activities
▶ Operating and survival techniques in combat and extreme environmental conditions
▶ Observation, identification and deterrence of threatening circumstances
▶ Top physical condition/endurance in severely rigorous situations
▶ Recognized for responsibility, dedication and efficiency of service
▶ U.S. Top Secret clearance

Highlights of Leadership and Operations Experience

U.S. MARINE CORPS   1995–1999

Observer NCO (Camp Lejeune, NC):
Participated in Marine Corps urban warfare experiment. Advised a non-infantry squad on how to conduct operations in an urban setting using lethal and non-lethal experimental weapons.

Chief Instructor at battalion level scout school (Parris Island, SC):
Led staff of 4 in training 30 recruits in basic scouting techniques, enabling them to operate effectively in the absence of sniper and reconnaissance teams. Recommended eligible candidates to join the Scout Sniper Community.

Squad Leader for an infantry platoon (Fort Story, VA):
Participated in Operation Cooperative Osprey, which included 5 weeks of cross-training with 15 non-NATO former Soviet Bloc countries. Explored operations and overall cultural differences among these nations.

Radio Communications Operator for Operation Quick and Assured Response (Africa):
Kept a detailed intelligence daily logbook during the evacuation of U.S. and British Embassies in Sierra Leone, Liberia, and Central Republic of Africa. Briefed the battalion intelligence officer on all operations being conducted in the platoon's vicinity. Took charge of the platoon headquarters in the absence of the commander.

Sniper Team Detachment Leader for Operation Provide Hope (Albania):
Reported to company commander during the air war in Kosovo. Participated in providing 24-hour surveillance on the camp's perimeter. Conducted recon patrols and pattern analysis around camp to identify/defer terrorist activities directed toward U.S. Marines and construction workers as well as Albanian refugees.

Scout Sniper Team Leader in support of Peace Keeping and Enforcement Operations (Kosovo): Conducted sniper/counter-sniper defense overtly and clandestinely in wooded and urban terrain. Watched over ground infantry operations, which greatly reduced the threat of violence and looting. Routinely briefed officers ranging in rank from Brigadier General to Captain on all operations.

Military Training

Camp Lejeune, NC:
   Basic training
   Marine Corps Scout Sniper course

Quantico, VA:
   Graduated School of Infantry
   Basic Recon course and indoctrination to Platoon Camp

Camp Butler, Okinawa, Japan:
   Group Coxswain course
   Special Operations training
   Jungle Warfare training

MCCDC, Bridgeport, CA:
   Mountain Warfare course in cold weather

MCAGCC, Twentynine Palms, CA:
   Sniper and recon operations in a desert environment

Non-Military Service

Participated in Humanitarian Relief, providing food, water, medical supplies, and
shelter for earthquake survivors in Turkey.

Decorations

National Defense Medal
Humanitarian Service Medal
NATO Medal
Navy Achievement Medal (Kosovo)
Good Conduct Medal
Kosovo Campaign Medal
Armed Forces Service Medal
Combat Action Ribbon
Navy Unit Commander Ribbon
Joint Meritorious Unit Commander Ribbon
Sea Service Deployment Ribbon
Meritorious Unit Citation Ribbon
2 Meritorious MASTS

Current Status

Honorably discharged; Inactive Reserve

ROBERT K. WILLIAMS

6334 Cherokee Avenue, Oklahoma City, OK 73105 ♦ (405) 555-1212 ♦ rkwilliams@questnet.com

Incident Management Specialist / U.S. Department of Homeland Security
Qualified to provide immediate incident management capabilities to ensure seamless integration of threat monitoring and strategic operational response activities.

PROFILE
Resourceful leader with proven skills in high-risk situations. Courageous, loyal and mission oriented, with high level of ethics and performance standards. Excellent physical condition. Accept all assignments with enthusiasm and a positive attitude. Working knowledge of the Spanish and Arabic languages. Recognized for responsibility, dedication and efficiency of service. Extensive training and practice in:

♦ Advanced special operations/counterterrorist activities
♦ Surveillance, reconnaissance and reporting procedures
♦ Expert marksmanship with M-16 and anti-armor weapons
♦ Freefall and static line parachute jumping

♦ Instruction in weapons and tactical maneuvers
♦ Field craft/survival techniques
♦ Map reading/orienteering
♦ Identification of unusual details or circumstances

CAREER HIGHLIGHTS

OKLAHOMA ARMY NATIONAL GUARD, SPECIAL FORCES UNIT   2004 – Present
Drill Sergeant
♦ Tested and evaluated enlistees' mastery of challenging field maneuvers and their understanding of Army values, with emphasis on personal courage.
♦ Deployed to assist in air rescue of 60 Hurricane Katrina victims from hotel rooftop in New Orleans.

U.S. ARMY   1989 – 2004
Active duty in Iraq, Egypt, Saudi Arabia, and Kuwait
Command Sergeant Major, Training and Operations, Special Forces Detachment (1998 – 2004)
♦ Conducted tactical simulation exercises to prepare reserve personnel for combat duty, both as individuals and as a unit.
♦ Participated in Operation Iraqi Freedom, employing strategic initiatives to counter the crude warfare and deceptive practices of Islamic insurgents.

Special Operations Weapons Sergeant, Special Forces Detachment (1989– 1998)
♦ As leader/instructor of small unit light infantry tactics, prepared detachment for certification.
♦ Assisted in the initiation and running of combat operations as well as the planning and execution of training for conventional and special purpose weaponry.
♦ Trained foreign personnel on weapons during Outside Continental U.S. (OCONUS) exercises.
♦ Served as detachment static line/military freefall jumpmaster and held responsibility for all personnel and equipment within aircraft.

During mobilization for Gulf War:
♦ Prepared and instructed detachment in use of heavy and special purpose weaponry.
♦ Planned for employment of large calibre and indirect fire weapons.
♦ Supervised transportation, storage, security, and maintenance of weaponry.
♦ Served as instructor and tactical leader for conventional and unconventional tactics as well as decontamination team, and spotter for detachment sniper team.

During Operation Desert Shield/Desert Storm:
♦ Served as Light Weapons Leader with responsibilities as overseas advisor to Commander and advisor to Saudi Arabian Special Forces teams.
♦ As vital trainer of Host Nation Forces, assured that Saudis received technically sound instruction in the use of machine guns, night view goggles, and basic radio procedures.
♦ Patrolled Saudi Arabian-Kuwaiti border, updating intelligence on a daily basis.
♦ Received citation for outstanding performance in reconnaissance mission within Iraq.
♦ Promoted to Weapons NCO with added responsibility of rifle company advisor.

DECORATIONS
♦ Saudi Arabia Kuwait Liberation Medal
♦ Southwest Asia Service Medal w/3BSS
♦ Bronze Star Medal w/V Device
♦ National Defense Service Medal
♦ Combat Infantryman Badge
♦ Master Parachute Badge

EDUCATION
B.A. 1998 — American Intercontinental University
      Major: Criminal Justice. Minor: Geography.

Robert Normand, CD, OMM, MA

Tel: 509-877-2607   email: rnormand@roberts.com

6 September 2007

DIRECTOR - TRAINING & ORGANIZATIONAL DEVELOPMENT

My relevant experiences are highlighted in the enclosed resume, and I hope that you will agree; my candidacy should be given careful consideration.

YOUR REQUIREMENTS	MY CAPABILITIES
Minimum Bachelor's Degree in a training related field.	✓ Bachelor of Science (Mathematics), Maritime University of Newcastle (1976) ✓ Bachelor of Education, Maritime University of Newcastle (1976)
Master's degree in Organization Development, Human Resources Development, Change Management or related discipline is preferred.	✓ Master of Arts (Education), University of Uclulet (1989), specializing in Adult Training & Education Development.
Knowledge of training methodologies, delivery and media is required.	✓ 10+ years delivering training programs and professional development in the National Forces and the Navy.
Minimum of ten years experience in a combination of human resources generalist, training, and/or organization development, with a minimum of three years organization development/consulting.	✓ 10+ years of developing numerous occupation specifications in the NF and Navy; developing training programs for these occupations; and implementing budgets, resource allocation, and training standards.
Experience with e-learning tools is preferred.	✓ E-learning instructor for 4 years at the NF Fleet School in Halifax ✓ Project Manager for the $68M Computer Assisted Learning Project for 3 years
Proven effective leadership skills in HR or line organizations, including local and remote teams and external consultant management.	✓ Management of the Naval Training System, involving 9 schools, 1100 staff, and a $14M budget, including management of several multimillion-dollar contracts with various training institutes across the country.
Demonstrated ability to create a high performance team that is results oriented and performance driven.	✓ Managed a $25 M budget with 80 military, civilian, & contract personnel in MOS project to analyse and redesign the new military occupational structure and develop policies to support the new structure.

I look forward to the opportunity to discuss with you how I can best contribute to your team. Thank you for your consideration.

Sincerely,

Robert Normand

Robert Normand, CD, OMM, MA

Home phone: (509) 877-2607
Email: rnormand@roberts.com

DIRECTOR - TRAINING & EDUCATION

Specializing in design and development of programs to support large HR systems

Performance-driven professional offering 25+ years of comprehensive achievements in managing and implementing significant portions of the National Forces budget of $2.5B to train over 60,000 members each year on courses ranging from technical skills to leadership and ethics. Wide experience in the development of business cases to achieve best value through cost-efficient training strategies.

Relevant professional proficiencies:

✓ Expert knowledge of adult learning principles and experience with the National Forces Individual Training And Education System (NFITES).

✓ Innovative resource management techniques, and varied expertise in qualitative process--analysis, design, development, conduct, evaluation, and validation).

✓ Proven change agent, gaining cross-functional collaboration through teams during several transformations in the National Forces to achieve desired results.

✓ Exceptional director, flourishing in turn-around situations, transforming HR policies and procedures to meet new goals and objectives.

✓ Commendations for team building and working with others.

Strong competencies in:

Operations & Change Management	Recruiting & Training	Computer-Assisted Training
Organization Development	Team Building & Leadership	Work, Budget & Resource Planning
Corporate Vision & Strategy	Training Program Evaluation	Information Technology & Systems
Procurement & Tendering Acumen	E-learning Programs	Giving Presentations

Secret Security Clearance

NOTABLE STRENGTHS AND CAREER ACHIEVEMENTS

♦ Spearheaded restructuring of the HR management system for the National Forces to achieve a more flexible and versatile work force involving 90,000 regular and reserve members in 105 occupations.

♦ Managed a multi million dollar out-service training program, involving the purchase of training and education services from foreign militaries and from various civilian companies and agencies.

♦ Developed business cases to support the implementation of establishing training contracts with various training and education institutions in Canada, including the Marine Institute in St Joseph, NL and Marine College in Renardo, CO.

♦ Established education programs for military officers in various universities across the nation.

♦ Developed and implemented computer-assisted learning programs to convert all NF electronic training from stand-up classroom instruction to self-paced computer-assisted training for $18M.

♦ Involved with the acquisition and implementation of $1B worth of trainers and simulators for the Navy during the process of changing its fleet to new frigates, submarines, patrol boats, and updating its fleet of destroyers.

♦ Implemented the NF Harassment and Racism Prevention Program for 13,000 Navy personnel, as well as Harassment Advisor and Harassment Investigator training programs.

Robert Normand, CD, OMM, MA

CAREER HIGHLIGHTS

DEPARTMENT OF NATIONAL SECURITY   1977–2006

➤ National Forces Expeditionary Force Command Headquarters   Current
Joint Force Manning Branch Head (14 military and civilian personnel)
• Responsible for all HR issues for 21 National Forces missions around the world, including Afghanistan.

➤ Military Occupational Structure Analysis & Redesign and Project   2002 - 2005
Operations Section Head/Deputy Project Director (80 military, civilian, & contract personnel)
• Analyse and redesign the new military occupational structure, including development of new NF policies to support the new structure as the foundation of the HR management system for the entire National Forces.
• Defined all the work performed by the 90,000 members of the Regular and Reserve members of the National Forces by identifying the tasks, skills and knowledge for each and ensuring that the jobs are grouped appropriately into 105 different occupations

➤ Maritime Staff, National Security Headquarters (NSHQ), London   2001 - 2002
 Director of Maritime Training and Education (50 military personnel)
• Manage the Naval Training System, involving nine (9) schools, 1100 staff, 200 training programs, and a $14M budget, including management of several multimillion-dollar contracts with various training institutes across the country.

➤ Coastal Command Headquarters, Maritime Staff, NSHQ   1995 - 2001
Senior Staff Officer Training Development/Senior Staff Officer Training Support & Official Languages
• Develop and implement National Forces Naval strategic training and education policies; develop and implement Naval official language policies; develop business plans for the Naval Training System; and manage of financial resources assigned to the Naval Training System.
• Provide direction and guidance to schools on all aspects of training and education--from initial analyses to final program evaluations and course validations.

EARLY CAREER PROGRESSION

1992 - 1995	Operations Requirement Manager and Project Manager for the Computer Assisted Learning Project - National Security Headquarters London
1991 - 1992	Senior Staff Officer Training Technology - National Forces Fleet School London
1988 - 1991	Computer Assisted Learning Officer - National Forces Fleet School London
1987 - 1988	Graduate Training - University of Uclulet
1985 - 1987	Standards Officer - Naval Officer Training Centre
1984 - 1985	Instructor - National Forces Training Development Centre
1982 - 1984	Weapons Officer - Command Ship Robillard
1980 - 1982	Above Water Weapons Officer - Command Ship Terra Nova

EDUCATION

• Master of Arts (Education), University of Uclulet (1989)
• Bachelor of Education , Maritime University of Newcastle (1976)
• Bachelor of Science (Mathematics) Maritime University of Newcastle (1976)

Advanced leadership courses and certifications including:

• French Language Training   (2005/2006) • Advanced Military Studies Course (1999) • Training Development Officer Basic Qualification Course (1984) • Naval Weapons and Electronic Warfare Officer Course (1982) • Naval Operations Course (1980) • Maritime Surface Officer/Naval Officer (1978-1979) • Warranty Clerk (1977)

Robert Normand, CD, OMM, MA

ADDENDUM - Samples of additional projects

Training & Development

Military Branch Advisor, NF Training Development Branch

• Guide the professional development, training and employment of 150 Training Development Officers.

Director of Maritime Training and Education

• Formulation and coordination of naval individual training and professional development policies and plans and provision of input to the National Forces Professional Development System.
• Provided coordination and advice on the individual training and professional development requirements associated with the introduction of new fleet assets and new shipboard equipment.
• As chairman of the assessment and interview team, co-ordinated the selection of applicants for naval officer training and assigned their subsequent naval occupation.

Senior Staff Officer Training Development

• Managing the Navy's outsourcing of training and education programs, which included drafted contractual documents, evaluating bid proposals and overseeing the implementation of the contracts.
• Coordinating the marketing of excess training capacity in the naval training establishments to non-DSD agencies.

Project Director and the Operations Requirements Manager for the Computer Assisted Learning (CAL) Project.

• Omnibus project valued at $68M, involving five sub-projects: one for each of the Training Managing Authorities in the NF (Navy, Army, Air Force, Training Group and a special project for the National Forces School of Communications and Electronics (NFSCE)).

Organizational Development

Director of Maritime Training and Education

• Development of occupation specifications and occupation specialty specifications for all assigned naval occupations, the development and implementation of training programs for these occupations in accordance with the National Forces Individual Training and Education System (NFITES).
• Budgeting, resource allocation, and training standards were implemented for both individual training and professional development programs for the occupations.

Senior Staff Officer Training Development

• Served on 10 committees and working groups which directed the training and professional development of personnel in the National Forces and the Navy.
• Assisted National Security Headquarters (London) in the development of specifications for the acquisition and the implementation of various instructional strategies, including generic trainers, simulators, and distributed training programs. This included establishing and maintaining the policy for in-service support requirements for naval trainers and simulators.
• As coordinator of the naval recruiting program, directed all naval recruiting activities and projects across the country that were organized by regional supervisors.

PATRICIA E. NICHOLSON

• Tel: 314-424-0244 • Email: patenich@lycos.com

PARTS MANAGER • SERVICE MANAGER • SHOP MANAGER

Strong planning, organizing, and troubleshooting skills under pressure

Former National Forces Vehicle Technician with 20+ years of proven success in the management and delivery of repair and maintenance services to a large fleet of vehicles in a constant state of readiness. Highly organized and efficient when managing shop and warehouse environments. Energized by challenges, steep learning curves and high-pressure deadlines. Strong, decisive, and highly qualified worker with outstanding hands-on competencies. Regular training, instruction and supervision of young personnel. Solid team player with effective conflict resolution skills. Honest and ethical in demanding situations.

Areas of Strength:

◆ Mechanical Repair	◆ Customer Interaction	◆ Supply & Parts Ordering
◆ Shop Management	◆ Inventory Control	◆ Problem Solving
◆ Scheduling & Service	◆ Communication Skills	◆ Customer Satisfaction

Bilingual in English & French with conversational Spanish.

KEY SKILLS & EXPERTISE

✓ **Fleet Management:** 17 vehicles, 13 trailers, 5 of which have generators installed and 2 portable generators and 4 portable combustion heaters for a squadron specializing in tactical and strategic communication. *Result*: Unit was continuously commended for having the best fleet and equipment within our group, operational vehicles of the highest standard.

✓ **Shop Management:** Planned and designed a new maintenance shop. Set-up a functioning vehicle maintenance bay with a very limited budget and very few tools, equipment, spare parts, or reference materials. *Example*: Shop had a special A-frame used for towing disabled vehicles but could not use it on public roads because it did not have specialized military towing lights, considered too expensive. Manufactured towing light using odds and ends from scrap and supply. *Result:* Having a good stock of tools, parts and equipment contributed to a productive and efficient shop that was the envy of other visiting units.

✓ **Team-Building Skills:** As a small, versatile group, we worked together in order to make deadlines in preparing for exercises and training. Important to motivate others by being enthusiastic, and providing guidance and encouragement when needed. *Example*: Students who were learning to back up trailers for driver training often got frustrated. Was patient and praised them for little accomplishments which motivated them to try harder.

✓ **Leadership Style**: Earned respect of others by working along side them or lend a helping hand when they need it even if it isn't in my job description. *Example*: When I first joined the unit, I noticed on the first driving exercise I attended, there was no clear instruction on what is going on. So, on my first driver training course as an instructor, I taught a lesson on how to read and follow a route card, driver discipline and briefing before departing using a Movement Order. This material was then used in future driving exercises.

✓ **Computer Skills:** Microsoft Office Suite applications. *Example*: Maintain Fleet Management System with MS Access, including dispatching vehicles, issuing work tickets, updating driving records, issuing permits, and controlling fuel cards and credit cards.

PATRICIA E. NICHOLSON

Page 2

CAREER EXPERIENCE

➤ **NATIONAL ARMED FORCES**   **1977 - 1989, 1993 - 2005**
(Served as Master Corporal in Regular Force & Full-Time Reserve, as Sergeant in Part-Time Reserve.)

Vehicle Technician

• Perform inspections, first line repairs on all unit fleet of vehicles, trailers, generators and heaters.
<u>Sample Achievement</u> *Problem*: Reserves are mostly young part-time soldiers who continuously train on many different subjects, and quickly forget some things, e.g. a requirement to perform a daily inspection, before, during and after operations on vehicles, and write down any problems on a defect slip. Very rarely were defect slips turned in. *Action*: Created a detailed checklist for each type of vehicle in our unit, and attached it to every work ticket, so that each user knew exactly what to check during inspections. They listed defects or problems on the same form. *Result*: Repaired vehicles in a timely manner thus eliminating any last minute surprises when the previous user didn't report faults and the new user required the vehicle for an exercise or an important task. Other units incorporated this checklist system into their inspection routines.

• Prepare and submit work requests, technical orders, and demands for spare parts, consumable items and petroleum requirements to appropriate authority.
<u>Sample Achievement</u> Problem: Recurring mechanical failure related to a modification to electronic fuel pumps on a fleet of support vehicles. Action: Diagnosed the problem after examining numerous repairs. The modifications had been done according to the manufacturer's instructions that did not take into account the correct placement of a fuel line. I explained the situation to the main repair facility. Necessary parts were ordered. Modifications were done correctly to the fleet. *Result*: Saved $3000 per vehicle.

• Acted as Support Troop Warrant in his absence, overseeing sub-sections.
<u>Sample Achievement</u> *Problem*: Our unit received a brand new issue of containers to transport food to the field. Unfortunately, they didn't come with the stainless steel steam table pan insert which rendered them useless. These pans had to be bought locally but there weren't sufficient funds. *Action*: I called a local supplier for a quote and substantiation, then navigated a request through the chain of command, until it was approved. *Result*: Saved our unit $1100 from a $30K annual budget.

OTHER WORK EXPERIENCE

➤ Self-employed, Kanata City Area   1990 – 1993
• Residential housecleaning and odd jobs. Performed odd jobs including minor plumbing, small appliance repair and residential house painting.
• Summer help for packing furniture and effects.

EDUCATION & TRAINING

• First Aid and CPR training • WHMIS training • Conflict Resolution Center "Supervisor Course"
• Completed formal vehicle technician QL3, QL5 and QL6A training. • Completed Junior Leaders Course. • Completed Aircraft Airfield Ground Support Equip (AAGSE) course. • Completed Land Maint Management Asistance (LMMA) course
• Secondary School Diploma, Center Washington District H.S., Kanata, KS (1974)

PERSONAL INTERESTS

Curling, cross-country skiing, camping, jogging, weight training, gardening, home renovating. travelling

ALFONZO T. BACHE

555 Trevor Expressway   555-555-5555
Baton Rouge, LA 70823   atbache@macx.com

Focus: Wheeled and Tracked Vehicle Maintenance - Military Environment
— Recipient of numerous Certificates of Recognition for performance excellence —

PROFILE

- Certified A&P Mechanic with 12 years' experience in wheeled and tracked vehicle maintenance and repair of military vehicles in the Middle East, Europe, and United States of America.
  - — HMMWV   — 2.5 - 5 ton military trucks
  - — HEMMT   — Bradley Fighting Vehicles
  - — PLS   — M113
- Welding background includes MIG, TIG and all ferrous and non-ferrous metals; supervisory experience.
- Accustomed to working in demanding, high stress, and dangerous military environments.
- Produce work that is high quality, accurate, thorough and completed in an expeditious manner.
- Have earned a reputation as the "*go-to-guy*" regarding maintenance and welding matters.

EXPERIENCE

VHLDR, INC, Detroit, MI *Corporate Headquarters USA*   **2003 - Present**
Engineering Mechanic – IRAQ
- Maintain and repair road building equipment, graders, scrapers and other heavy equipment.
- Perform welding duties as needed to ensure equipment is operating efficiently.
- Supervise work crew of 10 to 15 mechanics, welders, and specialists, earning their trust and respect.
- Routinely work 10 to 12 hour days in a high-stress, fast-paced, and ever-changing environment.
- Constantly monitor work quality to ensure highest standards, safety, and compliance.

FAXLER ENTERPRISES, Houston, TX *Corporate Headquarters USA*   **2001 - 2003**
Site Welding Shop – Armor Installation/Welding/Repair - KUWAIT
- Installed ballistic armor kits on HEMMT, PLS, HETT, and 5 ton trucks; supervised 12 welders.
- Repaired armor defects and adapted kits for vehicles to ensure compliance with stringent standards.
- Utilized skills in fabrication, welding, and installation of manufactured and custom truck armor.

JOHNS GRIEG, INC., Dallas, TX *Contract Assignments*   **1995 - 2001**
Wheeled and Tracked Vehicle Mechanic – Combat Equipment Battalion - Europe
- Served as a mechanic for M113 and Bradley Fighting vehicles including pack removal, ground hop, and 10/20 repair of these vehicles. Originally hired to repair Bradley Fighting Vehicles, then asked to supervise base welding shop and welders. Operated 40-ton crane. Repaired floating bridges for military maneuvers.

Wheeled and Tracked Vehicle Mechanic, 1995 - 1996
U.S. Naval Ship – Persian Gulf
- Maintained and repaired all wheeled and tracked vehicles loaded aboard pre-position ship deployed to the Persian Gulf. One of nine mechanics residing aboard the ship. Satisfactorily fulfilled one-year contract commitment with Johns Grieg, Inc. with contract renewal to European base of operation.

MILITARY

United States Army – Honorable Discharge, 1991 - 1995
- Field Maintenance Division, Germany – Supervising Crew Lead; Maintenance Technician Certification.
- Supervisory Leadership Course – Four weeks, Fort Bragg, North Carolina.
- Numerous specialty training programs – engineering; mechanical; maintenance; repair; supervision.
- *Received five awards for exemplary service, supervisory leadership, and performance excellence.*

EDUCATION & TRAINING

- Certificate - Heavy Equipment & Power Plant Mechanic, Winslow Aero Tech, Boulder, CO, 1991
- Certificate - Bridgewater Welding School, Denver, CO, 1991
- Brewer College of Technology, Denver, CO, 1990, 60 credit hours

George D. Hanson

MANAGEMENT CONSULTING
EXPERTISE: OPERATIONS / STRATEGY / SUPPLY CHAIN

100 Central Street
Tampa, FL 55555
555.555.5555
george.hanson55@gmail.com

Core Strengths
- ☑ **Strategize at the big-picture level; execute at the detail level**
- ☑ **Cut costs by restructuring operations & streamlining processes**
- ☑ **Manage large programs on time & ahead of budget**
- ☑ **Provide creative, cost-conscious leadership to people & programs**

Transitioning US Army Major with extensive civilian-side management experience in a range of high-profile leadership positions. Consistently deployed to turn around underperforming projects and divisions. Led large cross-functional teams in the US and globally. Leveraged strong collaborative, political, communication, and customer service skills to achieve buy-in from diverse constituencies. Master of Public Administration degree.

Expertise in:

- ☑ **Large program management**
- ☑ **Managing culturally diverse staff**
- ☑ **Research & analysis**

- ☑ **Public presentations & reporting**
- ☑ **Budgeting & financial management**
- ☑ **Business software**

Professional Highlights

Assistant Professor / Deputy Department Chairman
University of South Florida, Tampa, FL

2006-Present

Oversee budgeting, scheduling, and facilities management. Teach and mentor students. Rewrote curriculum in 45 days.

Deputy Director, Strategic Plans
Coalition Provisional Authority, Baghdad, Iraq

2003-2006

Held top planning position for Office of Strategic Communications. Supervised and coordinated efforts of 26 ministries, 2 multinational military organizations, and 6 non-governmental organizations. Created/delivered reports to National Security Council and White House staffs.

Challenge #1: Create a communications plan within 90 days to communicate all activities of the multinational forces in Iraq to the people of Iraq and the national, regional and international media. Implement plan in a physically hostile environment with an austere logistics and electronic communications infrastructure (with technology from the 1960s). Plan alternative communication channels to reach a population with a 50% literacy rate.

Strategy: Established crisis action team to integrate planning efforts with the interim Iraqi government and the Coalition Provisional Authority. Created 5 broad themes with 102 sub-messages. Managed 6 cross-functional, multicultural teams in plan execution. Achieved approval from U.S. Presidential envoy, National Security Council Staff, White House Staff, and other national and multinational stakeholders. Hired and managed consultants to rebuild Iraqi technical infrastructure.

Results:
- Produced the plan that was credited with the 100% successful turnover of pre-war "Saddam" currency.
- Achieved 100% consensus on the communications plans despite communications disruptions.
- Continuous polling (by Gallup and others) showed attitudes toward the Coalition improved by 10% on average.

Challenge #2: Communicate the meaning of democracy to Iraqis in time to impact the first national elections.

Strategy: Hired/managed an advertising agency. Planned 18 regional educational forums (~4000 attendees each) and 3 national conferences. Coordinated complex logistics and security issues across multinational military and civilian organizations.

Results:
- Successfully led the largest communications program of its kind ever, paving the way for the unprecedented national elections in Iraq that exceeded all global expectations.

Regional Recruiting Director
U.S. Army Cadet Command, Fort Dix, NJ

2000-2003

Oversaw all training programs in PA, NJ, and NYC. Directed 22 area managers. Administered $11.5 million budget.

GEORGE D. HANSON – PAGE 2

U.S. Army Cadet Command, continued...

Challenge #1: Develop formal system for tracking $9.5 million in ROTC scholarship money within 2 weeks.

Strategy: Created efficient accounting processes. Established quality measures to ensure optimal candidate selection.

Results:
- Achieved the distinction of being one of only two business units out of 14 to achieve 100% utilization of scholarship dollars. Captured an additional $2 million in scholarship incentives above budgeted amount.
- Reduced attrition by 16%, thereby eliminating workload and costs associated with finding new candidates.

Challenge #2: Turn around 7-year decline in recruitment levels for Army ROTC programs in 3 NYC schools.

Strategy: Conducted comprehensive market analysis and developed marketing plan, including media strategies. Sought and obtained other funding sources valued at $1 million.

Results
- Increased enrollment in metro NYC schools by 17%.
- Increased personnel recruiting by 10%, exceeding tough recruiting goals for 2 consecutive years.

Director, Support Operations
U.S. Army, Fort Riley, KS   1999-2000

Managed and planned services delivery for a 3,700 person organization. Oversaw medical care and medical supply, general supply, transportation, and heavy maintenance. Administered $15 million annual budget.

- Produced $2 million in savings by establishing rigorous cost recovery measures.
- Trained and prepared a unit for a major exercise within 60 days.
- Produced a streamlined operation that was acknowledged to be the most successful out of 4 units deployed.
- Reduced backlog of customer service issues by 66%.

Executive Director, Logistics
U.S. Army, Fort Riley, KS   1998-1999

Member of the senior management team challenged to develop, implement and manage a unique logistics infrastructure for an operating unit with 17,000 personnel in 7 states to increase combat readiness of the Army National Guard.

- Authored logistics plan for unit roll-out. Reorganized staff to deliver programs with 66% fewer personnel.
- Refocused staff on core business functions. Eliminated inefficiencies. Improved coordination.
- Established internal training and evaluation programs for 27 units in 5 states.
- Delivered project on time and under budget, meeting all Congressional timelines. Increased fleet readiness by 8%.

Program Analyst / Program Manager
The Pentagon, Washington, DC   1996-1997

Recruited to provide econometric analysis in support of a $1.3 trillion Future Year Program to address Army fiscal spending. Liaised with House National Security Committee and the Senate Armed Services Committee.

- Wrote *The Army Strategic Management Plan* for tracking performance.
- Gained Congressional acceptance. Successfully implemented plan.

Executive Fellow
The Pentagon, Washington, DC   1995-1996

Directed the federal legislative program for 3 offices.

- Personally commended by the U.S. Secretary of Defense for analytical work on issues concerning the Czech Republic. Made recommendations that were all subsequently adopted.
- Achieved 90% success rate writing programs that passed into law.

Education & Certification

University of South Florida, Tampa, FL: **Master of Public Administration with Honors**

Trinity College, Hartford, CT: **Bachelor of Arts in History**

U.S. Naval War College, Newport, RI: **Master of Arts, National Security & Strategy with Distinction**

Boston University, Boston, MA: **Project Management Certificate**

MARC GREEN

1717 Elm Avenue, Arboria, VA 23003 ♦
H: 703.122.1717 ♦ C: 703.002.9101 ♦
green_m@usb.com ♦

AIRCRAFT TEST & EVALUATION / SYSTEMS ENGINEERING / PROGRAM MANAGEMENT

LEADERSHIP: *20+ years of operational excellence, coupled with:*

♦ Expertise in management of flight test & systems engineering for highly sophisticated, mission-critical aircraft.

♦ Consistently rapid delivery of time-sensitive projects/programs with high customer-satisfaction ratings.

♦ Proficient in the employment of weapons systems in all mission environments; 1900+ flight hours in both fleet and test aircraft.

♦ Top-level Acquisition Career Field Certifications: *Test and Evaluation; Systems, Planning, Research, Development and Engineering* (SPRDE).

♦ Top Secret Security Clearance/SCI eligible. Graduate, United States Naval Academy.

Core competencies:
Program Management ... Human Resource Management ...Operations Planning ...Command and Control ... Acquisition ... Budget Management ...Team-building ...Test and Evaluation ... Joint Battlegroup Tactics ... Communications (all levels)

Technologies:
Tactical data links .. radio communications ... networks ... active and passive sensor systems ... simulations ... information processing ... software ... combat identification systems

---

HIGHLIGHTS OF EXPERIENCE AND ACCOMPLISHMENTS

UNITED STATES NAVY 1982–2007
Assistant Program Manager for Projects (2004–2007)

As **Integrated Test Team Leader,** directed a composite department of 100+ military, civil-service and contract employees in hardware and software testing for five aircraft and $300 million inventory. Managed $50+ million operations budget. Oversight included creation and evaluation of specifications, development of test plans, and writing/distribution of test reports for science and technology, system functionality, and airworthiness testing.

Highlights:
• Managed all test projects on the most complex aircraft. Team executed 100+ ground/flight test plans, accruing 1,200 flight hours and 13,000+ ground test hours. Staff performed nearly 2000 maintenance actions, 10,000+ labor hours, and more than 450 aircraft configuration changes in support of ongoing military operations.
• Led composite team to *Test Team of the Quarter* three times in less than three years.
• Successfully gained buy-in for new-facility construction to replace outdated rental structures. Projected construction cost will save taxpayers $10+ million over planned rental fees within the next five years.
• Earned top-tier Acquisition Career Field Certification in Test and Evaluation.

H: 703.122.1717 ♦ C: 703.002.9101 ♦ green_m@usb.com

Assistant Program Manager for Systems Engineering (2001–2003)

Oversaw all development and in-service engineering efforts for fleet of 75 aircraft. Supervised several engineering teams in providing safe, mission-critical assets to Fleet Commanders. Responded to myriad engineering challenges in both in-service and new-production aircraft.

Highlights:

- Post-9/11, successfully fielded new aircraft configuration to fleet, from evaluation of specs, through all ground and flight tests, to post-release technical instructions. Challenged to spearhead urgent fixes to numerous engineering defects to meet critical operational commitments safely. Coordinated with federal and civilian entities, resolving defects well ahead of schedule and enabling the concurrent deployment of 6 squadrons during Operation Iraqi Freedom.
- Led team in rapid implementation of 1000+ changes to Aircrew Operator's Manual. Team completed (normally) 9-month project in 6 weeks.
- Achieved Level 3 Acquisition Career Field Certification in Systems, Planning, Research, Development and Engineering (SPRDE).

Department Head (1999–2001)

As **Operations Officer,** orchestrated operations (20 months) for a 145-person squadron. Led squadron in achieving 1300 flight hours and 79 support missions while enforcing the No Fly Zone over Iraq.

As **Maintenance Officer** (six months), despite crippling parts shortages, led Maintenance Department to supply two fully mission-capable aircraft to meet critical operational commitments on schedule.

Naval Flight Officer (NFO) Instructor (1996 - 1999)

In addition to NFO instruction, served as Aviation Department Head School Coordinator. Taught a variety of tactical and mission systems courses as well as providing mentorship.

AFFILIATIONS

Boy Scout Leader, United States Naval Academy Alumni Association,
Association of Naval Aviation

EDUCATION

Naval Postgraduate School
Master of Science: System Technologies

United States Naval Academy
Bachelor of Science

William Leon

16 Mansfield Way
Hartfield, CT 06001

860-555-9669
wm.leon@usb.com

SENIOR SECURITY MANAGER

Nearly ten years of exemplary experience in **security,** including four years of active duty in U.S. Marine Corps. Trained to be exceptionally observant, attentive to detail, highly disciplined and self-reliant. Analytical problem-solver with excellent interpersonal and negotiation skills; able to defuse tense situations. **Held Secret security clearance.**

PROFESSIONAL EXPERIENCE and ACHIEVEMENTS

HARTFIELD AMUSEMENT PARK, South Hartfield, CT   4/02 - Present
Services Manager (1/05 - Present)
Security Manager (3/03 – 1/05)
Security Supervisor (4/02 – 3/03)
 Fast-track advancement through increasingly responsible positions to senior Security position in park.
Budgetary, supervisory and operational responsibility for Public Service / Security department, as well as oversight of First Aid, Housekeeping, Parking Lot and Risk Management divisions (85 employees overall). Supervise 25 security personnel throughout park to maintain safety, control losses and assist guests. Respond to all emergency medical calls and security problems. Provide documentation and follow-up concerning accidents on park grounds; manage insurance claims and settlements. Schedule and coordinate employee orientation and training.

- Developed evacuation plan for park rides; re-designed parking-lot roadways to improve efficiency.
- Negotiate cost-effective annual hospital contract for First Aid services.
- Lead special security detail for all celebrity visits.
- Created / implemented integrated reporting and follow-up procedure for park incidents and accidents.
- Through meticulous management of human resources, consistently remain within operational budget.
- Eliminated overtime in Housekeeping and Parking Lot staffs while retaining healthy employee relations.
- Implemented checkpoint policy that cut internal losses 50% in first year and has remained effective.

U.S. MARINE CORPS   1/98 - 12/01
Security Force
Advanced rapidly to team leader, directing up to ten personnel. Provided training, scheduling and oversight of activities. **Held Secret security clearance.** Selected to serve as Custodian of Armory: Responsible for maintenance, repair and distribution of over $1 million in arms inventory.

- Analyzed / revised inspection procedure. Reduced monthly armory inspection time by 75%.
- In four years, only member of company to earn two Navy Achievement Medals.

EDUCATION / PROFESSIONAL DEVELOPMENT / CERTIFICATIONS

Hartfield Community College, Hartfield, CT   Ongoing
 Over fifty credit hours. Courses have included: Introduction to Criminal Justice, Forensics, Psychology, Business Management, Financial Accounting, Managerial Accounting, Business Ethics, Business Law (I and II), Marketing, English and Sociology.

Additional:
 Hartfield Park: Management of Aggressive Behavior. Coaches (Supervisory) Training.
 U.S. Marine Corps: Non-Commissioned Officer Training. Machine Gun training.

Certifications:
 Emergency Medical Technician, Healthcare Provider, Basic Security Guard Certification, U.S. Marine Corps Security Force Battalion, Forklift Operator

BILL WARREN

212 South Green Circle • Mt. Pleasant, SC 29466
843.856.5301 Res • 843.412.6543 • Bill Warren@charleston.af.mil

EXECUTIVE PROFILE

Retiring USAF Lieutenant Colonel with a sterling track record of superior performance. Recognized for outstanding leadership for mission-critical operations and logistics. Consistently ranked as Top Performer based on leadership, performance improvement, innovative and strategic thinking. Winner of numerous awards and accolades – selected to manage President Clinton's travel into Bosnia. Held both field management positions as well as strategy development roles at Pentagon. Visionary and dynamic leader, able to build high-performance teams that consistently exceed targets.

PROFESSIONAL EXPERIENCE

UNITED STATES AIR FORCE   1983–PRESENT

Successively promoted to positions of increasing responsibility based on consistently exceeding goals and objectives.

COMMANDER, 437 OPERATIONS SUPPORT SQUADRON ✧ MAY 2003–PRESENT
CHARLESTON AFB, SC

Lt. Colonel accountable for all aspects of airfield management, life support services, flight records management, weather/intelligence support, airlift scheduling, tactical employment of major weapons systems, aircrew training, information technology, and mission launch and recovery operations for approximately 1,400 active duty and reserve personnel. Managed initial $3M budget, documented need and secured additional funding as needed. Challenged to turnaround performance of stagnant unit that had received "Marginal" in recent audit.

- Reviewed personnel skill sets of over 200 on-loan and assigned personnel and reallocated staff resulting in increasing number of operational units from 9 to 11 to develop areas of expertise.
- Built and managed largest C-17A aircraft staging operations in Air Mobility Command history. Recognized for ensuring success of approximately 6000 missions key to operations in Iraq and Afghanistan.
- Achieved stellar 95% mission reliability rate versus approximately 85% average.
- Reengineered unit manning process by hiring civilian employees in critical positions to drive 100% continuity. Eliminated 40% staff shortfall by architecting first ever local aircrew upgrade program and reduction in training time by 51 days.

"Squadron Commander with Midas touch, turned average unit into Charleston AFB's flagship and breathed life into stagnant unit." – Brigadier General James L. Buck

OPERATIONS OFFICER, 16TH AIRLIFT SQUADRON ✧ JUN 2000–MAY 2003
CHARLESTON AFB, SC

Lt. Colonel challenged to develop new, leading edge C-17A squadron and ensure readiness to support war efforts in Iraq and Afghanistan. Oversaw daily operations including training, readiness, scheduling and execution.

- Successfully managed over 8,000 accident-free flying hours and 1, 050 worldwide airdrop, transport, and training sorties. Delivered 643K lbs of cargo and 200 packages to fighting personnel in Iraq.
- Streamlined processes and implemented improved practices that reduced mission-ready time by 25%.
- Credited for training 130 crew members in 6 months less time than budgeted.
- Selected as Mission Commander responsible for transporting Chairman of the Joint Chiefs of Staff into combat areas.
- Worked with HQ to maintain manning levels and succeeded in securing 20 personnel to meet requirements.

"An honest to goodness, hands-on leader.. touched every aircrew… #1 of 90 Officers!" – Lt. Colonel Larry Smith

BILL WARREN

EXECUTIVE OFFICER, DIRECTORATE OF STRATEGIC PLANNING
DEPUTY CHIEF OF STAFF, PLANS AND PROGRAMS ✧ JUN 1997–JUN 2000
US AIR FORCE HEADQUARTERS ✧ PENTAGON, WASHINGTON DC

Lt. Colonel assigned to Headquarters to provide all administrative and support needs for 2 Major Generals at the Pentagon. Noted for overseeing needs of 2 Generals versus normal standard of 1. Challenged to coordinate fast-paced schedules and correspondence, prepare briefings, exchange information with Generals and serve as their representative in liaisons with high-ranking government officials.

- Selectively staffed unit that develops and implements Air Force long-range strategic planning through merging of 2 Air Staff directorates of 110 personnel into 1.
- Recognized for assisting the most senior Air Force leaders in making strategic decisions, integrating long-range planning initiatives and studies into Air Force planning.
- Instrumental in establishing administrative policy and procedures for 5 Divisions.

"My most trusted confidant, advisor, and sounding board—gives right advise…on target and in time. Top 1% of Officers I have known in my 34-year career. Brilliant, loyal and effective." – Major General Donald R. Larson

EXECUTIVE OFFICER, OFFICE OF THE ASSISTANT VICE CHIEF OF STAFF OF THE US AIR FORCE
QUADRENNIAL DEFENSE REVIEW ✧ JUN 1994–JUN 1997
US AIR FORCE HEADQUARTERS ✧ PENTAGON, WASHINGTON DC

Promoted to Lt. Colonel and hand-picked by Major General to be airlift Subject Matter Expert for mobility as part of very select team to advocate Air Force best practices to support the future of national security.

- Facilitated input from 8 Divisions and worked closely with 2 Major Generals to drive decisions and consensus.
- Interacted daily with Air Force and Department of Defense leaders, ensuring quality and timely completion of Office of Secretary of Defense, Joint Chiefs of Staff, Secretary of the Air Force, and Chief of Staff of the Air Force assignments.
- Expertly prioritized workload, juggling multiple "hot" senior level taskings while keeping unit morale high during long work hours.
- Recognized for tact, diplomacy and ability to successfully work sensitive issues across multiple Air Staff Directorates. Served as focal point for all responses to Secretary of Defense directed defense studies.

"I trust Bill implicitly…no issue comes the Director's way prior to his review and comment—brilliant judgment. My #1 of 9 "superstar" Majors." – Major General Joseph A. Siroca

COMMANDER, AIRCREW STANDARDIZATION & EVALUATION DIVISION
437 OPERATIONS GROUP ✧ APR 1990–JUN 1994
CHARLESTON AFB, SC

Major assigned to improve Group performance and quality control of 1,062 aircrew members. Directly supervised 5 officers, 6 Non-commission Officers and 1 civilian.

- Automated and standardized wing's aircrew evaluation database dramatically reducing time to collate data.
- Deputy Commander for first-ever Expeditionary Airlift Squadron that significantly improved combat capabilities in the face of force reductions.
- Credited for effectively expediting evacuation and safeguarding of over $5B in assets during major hurricanes.

"His decisiveness was pivotal to the 100% success of new concept. No better Officer anywhere!" – Brigadier General Paul B. Ayers

EDUCATION

Master of Science, Major in Operations Management ✧ University Of Arkansas ✧ 1991

Bachelor of Science, Behavioral Sciences ✧ United States Air Force Academy ✧ 1985

DARREN M. THOMAS

29 Mountain Road • Rockville, MD 20852
Res: (301) 885-5636 • dmthomas@excite.com

Strategic Intelligence Professional

More than five years of experience in civil government, military, and business intelligence.
Known for technical expertise in national security decision-making • TOP SECRET/SCI security clearance

Core competencies: Client Needs Assessment • Research Skills • Leadership Ability • Writing & Presentation Skills
Information Filtering • Managing Information Security Programs • Promoting Partnerships between Organizations

PROFESSIONAL EXPERIENCE

McGuireWoods Consulting, Washington, DC   2006-Present
Intelligence Analyst
Compose strategic-level threat assessments for information operations (IO), including computer network operations
(CNO). Analyze how threats would use IO in combination with other strategic capabilities to achieve national
objectives. Participate in intelligence community (IC) and high-level military outreach campaign to raise awareness of
threat CNO capabilities.

- Produced threat analysis documents regarding computer network attack and exploitation (CNA/CNE) for
  Defense Intelligence Agency client, making a technical topic accessible to less technically-oriented intelligence
  professionals, military officers, and civil government decision-makers
- Won praise from technical experts with the Office of Naval Research for bridging the gap between capability
  development and opponent strategy in CNA/CNE as well as for organizing and editing data from varied
  sources into coherent and usable intelligence documents.

US Army, Washington, DC & Kuwait   2004-2005
Captain, Military Intelligence
Highest intelligence officer for the Army Central Command (ARCENT) Theater Signal Command, consisting of
more than 3,000 soldiers, military civilians, and contractors. Oversee all intelligence activities (collection, analysis,
and production) within the command and coordinate with other Army units for additional intelligence support.
Keep personnel assigned to the Theater Signal Command informed of kinetic and cyber threats to the
communications network in the Middle East. Write policy for the Command concerning intelligence support
activities, physical security, information security, personnel security, anti-terrorism, and force protection.

- Completely transformed unit intelligence website, creating a new intelligence support page easily accessed and
  used by unit personnel, including keeping the command informed of on-going political developments in the
  Middle East and terrorist threats in various countries as well as providing threat briefings on travel destinations.
- Built an information-assurance intelligence support page to keep the command informed of threat capability
  studies and the latest threats to Army networks, when the command had received no actual intelligence support
  from predecessor.
- Created and defined intelligence support mission for the command by interviewing customers, determining
  needs, building new relationships between intelligence producers and customers, and ultimately dramatically
  increasing the level of intelligence support received by soldiers in the unit.

Prior to mobilization, conducted research and analysis in support of counter-terrorism operations for National
Ground Intelligence Center (NGIC). Also analyzed threat IO and CNO capabilities, disposition, future potential,
and intentions.

McKinsey & Company, Washington, DC   2003-2004
Business Intelligence Analyst
Analyzed proposed legislation, administration policy changes, and general trends in national security field to guide
government consulting marketing investment choices. Researched and analyzed trends and diverse fields including
electronic warfare and public health surveillance. Analyzed competitor and potential teaming partner capabilities,
presence, and intentions in varied consulting markets, including the intelligence community, Department of
Defense, Department of Health and Human Services, and Department of Homeland Security.

DARREN M. THOMAS

McKinsey & Company *(Continued)*

- Consistently praised by clients for useful products, the result of working with them and taking the time to determine their exact needs.
- Initial participant of a "loan" program from the intelligence community team to assess whether effective intelligence analysts made effective business intelligence analysts. Based on my success, program expanded after six months with approximately 10 intelligence "fellows" firm-wide on one-year rotations in business intelligence.

Boxwood Research Group, Washington, DC   2000-2003
National Security Analyst
Composed strategic-level conflict scenarios and wargames used by major military commands (MACOMs). Analyzed how threats would use ballistic missile assets in combination with other strategic capabilities to achieve national objectives.

- Led a team of four analysts to dramatically change wargame presentations by incorporating full, self-running briefings with narrated movies. Briefs were lauded by client as the "new standard" for wargame and conflict scenarios and were shared with contractors on other projects as benchmarks for the future.

US Army, Fort Irwin, CA   1995-2000
Captain, Signal Corps (1997-2000)
Commanded communications platoon of 60 soldiers on annual training exercises.

- Served as primary communications officer for an elite 300-soldier airborne artillery battalion, a position normally occupied by an officer one rank higher.

First Lieutenant, Infantry (1995-1997)
Commanded platoon of 20 elite, anti-armor soldiers in the 82nd Airborne Division.

- Graduated Army Ranger School, the Army's premier close-combat leadership school which includes sleep and food deprivation and incorporates three graduation-determining peer evaluations.

EDUCATION

George Washington University, Washington, DC   2003
Master of Arts in Political Management
Thesis: American Strategy and Untraditional Warfare
Coursework included: Net Assessment and Strategic Intelligence; Terrorism and Political Violence; Information Operations and Warfare; and Energy and National Security.

- Achieved highest score possible on comprehensive exams.

University of Chicago, Chicago, IL   1995
Bachelor of Arts in Political Science
Undergraduate thesis: Inadequacies of Intelligence Support to Military Operations, 1991-1995

- Distinguished Military Graduate (top third of Army ROTC class).

AWARDS & HONORS

Army Ranger Tab • Army Commendation Medal • Army Achievement Medal

COMPUTER SKILLS

Proficient in the following applications: Microsoft Office, Microsoft Front Page, Adobe Acrobat and Premier.

ERIC C. LANDON
45 Storrey Court
Princeton, NJ 08540
Home (609) 579-3789 Cell (609) 307-1145
eric_landon@optonline.net

QUALITY ASSURANCE SPECIALIST

Detailed, dedicated professional with solid contractor, military and federal government experience.
20+ years of service with the United States Air Force. Retired with numerous accolades.
IATA Certified in the Technical Transportation of Hazardous Materials.
Proven record of outstanding work performance across multiple environments.

PROFESSIONAL EXPERIENCE

Quality Assurance Evaluator   November 2001–February 2006
United States Federal Government   Maxwell, AL
Managed the receipt, storage, segregation and inspection of all explosives entering and leaving this
2,500 personnel Air Force base. Reported directly to the Base Commanding Officer.
- Provided input for 14 quality assurance safety plans to remain current with changes to the
  Base Operating Services Contract and subsequent changes in fleet posture and
  commitments.
- Developed comprehensive training and testing program to certify personnel in the safe
  handling and transportation of ammunition and explosives.
- Hand-picked to serve as a member of five-person Ordnance Certification Board.

Quality Assurance Inspector   April 2000–November 2001
Capital Factors Applications   Maxwell, AL
Secured the safe loading, receipt, segregation, issue and grading of all ammunition and explosives
leaving the base. Reported directly to company project manager.
- As wharf supervisor, personally responsible for the safe loading of over 7,000 lifts of
  ammunition and explosives over a four-month period without incident.
- Noted by military command ships USNS Flint and USNS Kiska as having exceptional
  foresight contributing to complete consumer satisfaction.

Quality Assurance Supervisor   1989–February 2000
United States Air Force   Tampa, FL & Maxwell, AL
Also **Full Systems Quality Assurance Representative** (1979–1988)
Supervised 13 senior personnel in Quality Assurance and reported directly to the Manager of the
Quality Assurance Management Program for the entire base. The department managed seven of its
own programs and audited an additional 13 quality assurance programs throughout the base.
- Managed and monitored programs with an overall grade of Outstanding in Commander
  Naval Air Forces Pacific inspection three consecutive years.
- Developed and implemented quality assurance safety plans for aviation safety through field
  research and technical expertise.
- Promoted through superior knowledge, technical skill and dedication to duty.

Continued...

ADDITIONAL AIR FORCE EXPERIENCE

Search and Rescue (SAR) Instructor E-6   1989–2000
- Managed the training and flight schedules for more than 70 crewmen.
- Managed daily mandatory physical training sessions for 70 SAR crewmen in the squadron.
- Tracked and assured all qualifications were current to facilitate full-mission capability.
- Hand-picked for instructor duty and independent duty requiring no supervision.

Air Crewman   1989–2000
Graduated number one from Air Crew Candidate School–1989
- As Operations Manager, supervised the maintenance and upkeep of 24 aircraft. Managed more than 270 maintenance personnel during high-tempo operations.

Aviation Electrician   1979–1988

QUALITY ASSURANCE TRAINING

- Quality Assurance Evaluator course (40 hours), U.S. Federal Government–March 2002
- Instructor Training course (120 hours), U.S. Air Force–November 1990
- Quality Assurance Supervisor course (40 hours), U.S. Air Force–June 1986

LICENSES AND CERTIFICATES

- Inspector, Technical Transportation of Hazardous Materials, International Air Transport Association (IATA)–March 2002; *Ranked number one in a graduating class of 35 (75% attrition rate)*
- Naval Motor Vehicle and Railcar Inspector, U.S. Federal Government–March 2002
- Facilities Services Support Contract Evaluator, U.S. Federal Government–February 2002
- National Registered EMT–July 1993 (160 hrs)
- American Heart Association CPR Instructor–September 1991 (80 hrs)

SELECTED MILITARY HONORS

- Air Force Achievement Medal–1992, 1996 and 1999
- Rescue of the Year–1996
- Air Force Commendation Medal–1993 and 1996
  Rated Outstanding Inspector for Search and Rescue
- Humanitarian Service Medal–1994
- Air Force Unit Commendation–1985/'86
- Meritorious Unit Commendation–1980/'81

COMPUTER SKILLS

Proficient in Microsoft Word and Excel.

JARROD NOBLE

Award winning and highly accomplished Network Administrator with proven track record of reducing operating expenses and administration costs and increasing productivity

HIGHLIGHTS OF QUALIFICATIONS

◆ Seven years of experience in network administration & technical troubleshooting.
◆ Outstanding record of resourceful cost reduction.
◆ Known for exceptional leadership and for consistently performing at highest levels.
◆ Knowledgeable in wide variety of networking environments and applications.
◆ Team player with excellent interpersonal and communication skills.

COMPUTER SKILLS

Operating Systems: Windows NT 4.0 and 3.51, Windows for Workgroups 3.11, WANG Cobol
Software Applications: MS Office 2000, MS Exchange and MS Outlook, MS Internet Explorer, Netscape, Norton AntiVirus, Adobe Acrobat Reader, Jet Form Flow
Networking Protocols: TCP/IP, NetBui
Hardware: Personal computers and laptops (Dell, Micron, Zenith), backup domain controllers, print servers, HP laserjet printers HPIII, HPIV and HPV, high speed band printers and all related peripherals: CD-ROM's, CD-Writers, Scanners, Modems, Network Interface Cards, Tape backup units, Zip Drives

RELEVANT SKILLS & ACCOMPLISHMENTS

NETWORK ADMINISTRATION
▪ In charge of all software and hardware utilized by squadron personnel.
▪ **Successfully maintained, troubleshot and repaired vast array of hardware and software applications.**
▪ Oversaw entire line of user accounts, assigned security rights and provided desktop support.
▪ Prepared and coordinated all data file transfers with local and outside agencies.
▪ **Fully accountable for over 400 pieces of computer equipment, valued at over $1.5 million.**
▪ Provided PC configuration, procurement and installation.
▪ **Saved over $30,000** as result of transferring 10 computer systems to support and troubleshoot system deficiency.
▪ Demonstrated solid expertise during four infrastructure upgrade projects worth over $200.000.
▪ Oversaw multiple distribution hubs, six network servers, and miles of network cable supporting over 200 workstations and network peripherals.
▪ Developed and implemented equipment-tracking database in order to accurately monitor computer usage.
▪ **Dramatically improved computer peripheral inventory by introducing aggressive inspection schedules. Results: 100% item accountability compared with previous 80%.**

MANAGEMENT & TRAINING
▪ **Currently manage mainframe and Windows NT computer systems supporting 150 users.**
▪ Supervised and trained over 50 individuals in Mainframe Information Management Systems.
▪ **Saved thousands of dollars by establishing training classroom and revitalizing productivity levels of numerous employees.**

5555 First Dr., Fairland, IL 55555 ● 555-555-5555 ● E-mail address

Jarrod Noble   **Page two**

(Management & Training continues)
- **Exceeded facility's goals by training 98% of squadron personnel.**
- In charge of scheduling and overseeing all utility work crews during equipment testing.
- **Trained all users and wrote over 100 pages of operating manual including maintenance schedules and guidelines.**
- Managed all phases of work order-completion from receipt of order to finished project.

OPERATIONS
- **Full profit & loss management responsibility for strategic planning, schedule coordinating, material & equipment handling, labor & materials cost estimating for 400-employee facility.**
- Coordinated and scheduled jobs with customers and craftsmen.
- **Successfully handled large number of job orders, resulting in timely completion of nearly 100% of approximately 1,000 monthly work orders.**
- Instrumental in facility's Y2K preparations; single-handedly coordinated with 218 facility managers to ensure smooth operations along with quick & effective troubleshooting of possible problems. Results: no incidents reported.
- Strategically located craftsmen throughout base for immediate Y2K crisis response.

PROFESSIONAL BACKGROUND

1999 – Present	**15th Civil Engineering Squadron**, City, State, *Job title*
1992 – 1999	**514th Civil Engineering Squadron**, City, State, *Job title*

COURSES ATTENDED
Computer Courses: Windows NT, Desktop & Server

Management Courses: Non-Commissioned Office Management Seminar. Topics included:
Effective Communication, Time Management, Employee Motivation & Supervision

AWARDS
Received award for outstanding professional skills and technical knowledge
as Network Administrator at the XYZ Civil Engineering Squadron, City, State

Employer comments:
"Sergeant Noble systematically maintained a stellar Information Protection Program enabling the unit to secure 100 percent electronic data integrity while maintaining an extremely high level of customer awareness. His wealth of knowledge proved critical during the XYZ Air Support Group's successful transition from the Wang Information Management System to a newer year 2000 compatible system. He enforced an automated anti-virus protection program blanketing 300 computer systems that included immediate virus eradication and near real-time up-channel virus reporting."
Citation to accompany award of The Air Force Commendation Medal (Fourth award received).

5555 First Dr., Fairland, IL 55555 • 555-555-5555 • E-mail address

Rodger L. Michaels
555 Magnolia Street ● Jackson, MS ● h.601.555.1234 ● w. 601.555.1234 ● rodlmichaels@email.com

April 7, 2007

Company U.S.A.
Attn: John Smith, Program Director
123 Main Street
Jackson, MS 39211

Dear Mr. Smith,

We are working in an environment where managers and employees are often required to perform to higher levels of expectation with fewer and fewer resources. The military is finding itself in a similar situation. More is expected of our military volunteers in an environment where there are more demands on our time, personnel, and resources, and there are fewer people to go around.

As your new project manager, I will bring strong people and budget management skills, discipline, ingenuity, and most importantly decisiveness to your organization. My experience with the Mississippi Army National Guard has given me the opportunity to coordinate large scale operatives and military initiatives with little notice. Being able to meet these expectations requires extensive pre-planning and communication between other leaders in the Unit to ensure that we CAN be ready at a moment's notice. This is project management at its utmost level.

Additionally, I have had to analyze numerous Department of the Army (DOA) policies to ensure compliance and plan creatively to adjust our strategies to meet DOA regulations. This has sometimes required extensive career strategizing and mentoring with personnel to incorporate military service expectations into a civilian lifestyle. I have always provided hands-on leadership and exemplified the kind of commitment that I expected from the individuals in my Unit.

I am interested in this position with Company U.S.A because I want to transition into the private sector with a new set of challenges. I believe that your company's mission and goals match my professional and personal goals. Once we talk, I'm sure that you will agree I am the right candidate for this position.

I would like to meet with you so that we can discuss the special needs of Company USA. We should discuss exactly how my experience and qualifications would best contribute to your success. I will contact you by April 15, to confirm that you received my résumé and discuss how I can fit into your organization. Thank you for your time and consideration.

Sincerely,

Rodger L. Michaels

Rodger L. Michaels

Rodger L. Michaels

555 Magnolia Street ● Jackson, MS ● h.601.555.1234 ● w. 601.555.1234 ● rodlmichaels@email.com

---

Project Manager / Policy Analysis

Decisive, action-oriented leader with more than 20 years of experience as a principal Noncommissioned Officer in the Mississippi Army National Guard. Proven ability to excel under tight deadlines and utilize available resources to the fullest extent.

SECRET CLEARANCE, CURRENT
Areas of Proficiency

Communication	Problem Solving	Logistics
Strategic Planning	Motivation	Policy Formulation/Analysis
Management	Budget Oversight	Safety & Risk Management

Key Strengths
- Experience commanding and directing over 100 people
- Devise tactical strategies and logical steps for completing complicated projects on time and on budget
- Evaluate and Analyze operational effectiveness/readiness and streamline operations for efficiency
- Budget management – up to$6 Million.
- Review new and standard policies and interpret/strategize various implementation options

Career Progression

Aviation Operations Sergeants Major, 155th Combat Aviation Brigade   2005 to present
Hattiesburg, MS
- Successfully executed official response to assist with the Hurricane Katrina emergency, transporting personnel and supplies during a time of limited communication and extensive confusion at local and national levels.
- Determined individual training initiatives for nearly 1000 people, coordinated classes within budget guidelines, and increased combat readiness preparation over 300%.
- Established timelines and program schedules, clearly communicating specific desired outcomes to unit leaders, and measured actual performance against expectations.
- Generated quarterly and annual comprehensive reports incorporating topics such as budgetary needs, training requirements, and emergency/combat preparedness, accurately illustrating the "state of readiness" of the unit, and submitted them to the Department of the Army.
- Increased personnel retention by 94% through careful planning, clear and concise communication, flexible scheduling, and career mentoring which significantly improved morale and dedication to the unit.

Battalion Operation Sergeants Major, 1st Squadron 158th Cavalry   1999 to 2005
Grenada, MS
- Reviewed and analyzed directives from the Department of the Army and formulated polices and requirements for fulfilling and executing specific demands.
- Increased performance awareness among personnel and devised extensive resource management and training plans that improved operational performance and readiness from 100 to over 300 soldiers.
- Prepared and enforced Standard Operating Procedures (SOP) within battalion resulting in improved consistency, order, and discipline among all personnel.
- Briefed personnel on operational procedures, critical mission objectives, cultural populations and customs, geography, and climate prior to deployment.

Readiness NCO (Services Support Company) HHC 1st Squadron 158th Calvary   1995 to 1999
Grenada, MS
➢ Instructed and trained up to 125 personnel on various military strategies, tactics, and specialty skills detailing progress and readiness of the company.
➢ Informed superior officers of completed training requirements, future training plans, equipment inventory, and personnel readiness status of company.
➢ Developed logistics plans, recommended task organization, and assignment of missions for unit.

Readiness NCO (Combat Arms Company) Troop A 1st Squadron 158th Calvary   1989 to 1995
Grenada, MS
➢ Assimilated and recruited numerous volunteers within four hours to provide extensive assistance to medical, police, and civilian personnel during an official state of emergency response.
➢ Assisted unit commander in carrying out and implementing professional development and training plans by coordinating, organizing, and requesting classes.
➢ Streamlined weapons and equipment inventory/checkout procedures facilitating training and military operations.

Training & Professional Development
Participated in several hundred hours of professional development and training related to military tactics and leadership training equivalent to 62 hours of college credit.
Served as an instructor for Professional Development in Bosnia and Estonia
Sergeants Major Academy
Advanced Noncommissioned Officer Course
Risk Management Orientation Course
Sales & Management Training
TQM Awareness Seminar
OSHA Compliance Training
Total Quality Leadership Course (TQL)

Awards & Commendations
Recipient of numerous military awards and commendations throughout career. Among the most notable:
Army Commendation Medal
Army Achievement Medal
Army Good Conduct Medal
Army Reserve Components Achievement Medal
National Defense Service Medal
Armed Forces Reserve Medal
Mississippi National Guard Recruiting Medal
Reckord Award (Most Combat Ready Unit in First Army Area)
Walter T. Kerwin Award (Most Combat Ready Unit in US Army Reserve)
State of Mississippi Military Department's Employee of the Quarter
Certificate of Appreciation Inaugural Ceremonies President Bush
Letter of Commendation from President Senate of MS for support during Tornado Emergency Operations

Jeffrey P. Jacobs

123 Oak Street, Annapolis, MD 21401 ◆ h 410-555-1234 ◆ c 410-555-1234 ◆ jpj123@email.com

SUMMARY

➢ Four years Active Duty U.S. Army – Sergeant E-5, Team Leader (Honorably Discharged)
➢ Strong leadership qualities; Ability to take charge and manage projects to completion
➢ Creative and resourceful in generating new ideas and solving problems
➢ Excellent communication skills
➢ Takes initiative; Motivates others to perform to excellence
➢ Background and experience in construction and demolition – military certified heavy equipment operator

---

Quotes from recent Army Service Performance Evaluation
"Outstanding leader; able to accomplish any mission. Possesses the moral courage to do the right thing. Places unit's mission and the welfare of his Soldiers above personal needs." *1st Lieutenant Salinas, U.S. Army*

SKILLS & EXPERIENCE

SUPERVISORY/LEADERSHIP

➢ Immediately promoted upon passing the rigorous Sergeant's Board evaluation process by demonstrating self-discipline and initiative in acquiring the specified number of hours of army education/training.
➢ Directly supervised, trained, and mentored two to six soldiers – Initiated weekly classes/drills with team to ensure constant readiness for any situation.
➢ Consistently advocated high safety standards among soldiers resulting in an accident-free safety record.
➢ Assisted the Platoon Leader in the writing of new platoon Standard Operating Procedures (SOP); Mentored and trained new soldiers in the SOP's and policies of the unit.
➢ Led team on over 200 combat patrols during Operation Iraqi Freedom III, earning the respect and loyalty of soldiers by constantly leading from the front.
➢ Maintained direct accountability for more than $300K in military supplies and equipment.

COMMUNICATION/TRAINING

➢ Conducted classes for the 3rd Brigade Combat Team, including officers and enlisted personnel, on military weapons training to review/learn the maintenance, care, and handling of the M2 machine gun.
➢ Coordinated/conducted briefings to unit regarding daily mission, tasks, and objectives. Provided clear and concise direction, instruction, and objectives for the mission.
➢ Maintained open door policy to enhance communication.
➢ Cross-trained personnel to effectively operate multiple stations on military vehicles as a means of enhancing security and military/emergency readiness.

WORK HISTORY

United States Army	Combat Engineer, Sergeant E-5, Team Leader	05/02 to 05/06
Rentals Plus	Customer Associate – Lot Worker/Delivery	01/02 to 05/02
United Parcel Service (UPS)	Package Sorter	05/01 to 12/01
Konnarock Volunteer – repaired parts of the Appalachian Trail in five states over two weeks		June 1999

EDUCATION

Millersville University, Millersville, PA	3 Credit hours
Anne Arundel Community College, Arnold, MD	6 Credit hours
Shenandoah University, Winchester, VA	14 Credit hours
Arundel High School, Gambrills, MD	Graduate

AWARDS & HONORS

Received two Army Commendation Medals – Awarded for performance above & beyond the call of duty during combat.
Army Good Conduct Medal
Presidential Unit Citation – Awarded to the 3rd Infantry Division
National Defense Service Medal – Awarded for joining the Army and serving during a time of war
Global War on Terrorism Expeditionary Medal – Participated in the march to and takeover of Baghdad
Global War on Terrorism Service Medal

GRIFFIN M. HANKERD

1732 Resort Rd.   gmhankerd1@aol.com   313-732-5302
Utica, MI 48233   787-443-8100

August 7, 2007

Emily Thomas
L. T. Silver Associates
392 West Motors Blvd.
Detroit, MI 48888

Dear Ms. Thomas:

With over 25 years of success in linking finance to business operations, the value I bring to L.T. Silver Associates extends far beyond that of your typical Chief Financial Officer. Not only am I effective in developing strategic plans, budgets and forecasts, I know what it will take for operations, marketing and sales to successfully execute on them to deliver strong and sustainable revenue, profit and performance results.

My career has included CFO roles in $140 million base operations, impacting a Joint Task Force and over 2000 personnel. I provide a unique combination of tools and direction to continuously navigate financial, market and operational transitions to ensure the long-term success as measured by:

- **Best Practices Implementation** to enhance the value of employee productivity and process improvements.

- Managing the **payroll and travel expenses** for US Army personnel and Joint Task Force in Baghdad, Iraq.

- **Project Manager** for Air Force Defense Team, completing 135 sites (originally designed for 100) on time and $750,000 under budget.

- **Driving change** through analyzing full scope of organizational structure and executing plans for success.

I have succeeded in building financial teams from the ground up, implementing financial systems and facilitating merger integration and change management initiatives that have directly impacted the top and bottom-line. My ability to build key relationships with executive leadership and personnel is exceptional, and has been essential to positioning finance as a key business partner.

Aware of the caliber and reputation L.T. Silver Associates holds in the marketplace, I would welcome the opportunity to meet with you, discuss your needs and further demonstrate the value I offer. Thank you in advance for your consideration. I look forward to the first of many positive communications.

Sincerely,

Griffin M. Hankerd

Griffin M. Hankerd

Enclosure

GRIFFIN M. HANKERD

1732 Resort Rd.   gmhankerd1@aol.com   313-732-5302
Utica, MI 48233   787-443-8100

CHIEF FINANCIAL OFFICER

Chief Financial Officer with over 20 years experience managing US Army's fiscal operations. Offer a unique blend of business, financial and military experience, backed up by practical actions and programs that have been a vanguard for change management. Expertise in strategic planning, project management, department/organization reengineering, and staff development. Exceptional financial analysis, planning and accounting skills with a track record of success working at the top levels of a global organization down to niche operating units. Additional qualifications include:

- Financial Analysis/Reporting
- Financial Controls
- Operational Budgets
- Strategic Planning
- Project Accounting
- Treasury

PROFESSIONAL EXPERIENCE

UNITED STATES ARMY, Active Duty, Baghdad, Iraq   1994 to Present
Chief Financial Officer, Colonel (2003 to Present)
Transferred to Joint Task Force headquarters to take over more than $180 million in base operations, joint military intelligence, and various other operations, maintenance funding and resources for over 2,000 personnel. Primary Financial Advisor to Joint Task Force Commanding General. Managed daily operations and a staff of 11, strategic planning, programming and budgeting to meet the demands of the ever-changing resource requirements. Governed payroll and travel reimbursement for US Army personnel and Joint Task Force.
- Hand-selected by the Assistant Secretary of the Army (Financial Management & Comptroller) to receive the prestigious "Annual Resource Management Award" for FY 2003, in the Comptroller/Deputy Comptroller MAJCOM category.
- Led the team that completed a project slated for one year, in just six months, cutting human resource expenses by 43%.

US ARMY RESERVES HEADQUARTERS, Boulder, CO
Chief Financial Officer, Colonel (2002 to 2003)
Managed the financial activities of the medical brigade including 22 units, 6 hospitals and support units of logistics, chaplain, public affairs, medical evacuation, dental services, veterinary services, surgery and sanitation/entomology.
- Created the financial management course "Resource Management for AMEDD Officers", utilized by over 10,000 officers to balance finances.

US ARMY RESERVES, FORT CUSTER, Olympia, WA
Hospital Administrator/Executive Officer (2000 to 2001)
Brought onboard to direct the daily operations of 600 personnel, 21 vehicle medical facility with over $12 million in equipment and 340 beds. Interpreted and ensured active duty/reserve regulations and HQ Army policies. Defined administrative requirements / procedures for managing a multi-component unit.
- Governed strategic planning, performance measurements, and established goals objectives and long-range plans for a newly activated unit.
- Created and implemented "Best Practice" local policies and procedures.
- Principal Advisor to Commander for administrative personnel, manpower, training, logistics, operations, patient administration, regulatory compliance resource utilization, and financial stewardship.

GRIFFIN M. HANKERD

JEFFERSON AIR FORCE BASE, San Antonio, TX
Chief Systems Accountant (1994 to 2000)
Managed e-senior system accountants and e-senior computer specialists. Contracting Officer's technical representative for worldwide information technology projects. Drafted statements of work for proposals and determined project training requirements. Budgeted worldwide implementation projects and Agency. ADPE acquisitions.

- Analyzed and instituted improvements to Air Force services financial systems.
- Successfully performed global implementation for Air Force: $6 million dollar 'Time Management System' in 1,600 activities; $1.6 million for "Advance" at 100 bases; $10 million for "American Food and Beverage" point of sale system (POS), and Lunchies, $10 million; $5 million dollar internet-based purchasing system (IBPS); and over $5 million for "Oasis", a hotel property management system.
- Played a key role in the development, testing and evaluation of automated systems for Air Force Services activities globally.
- Spearheaded effective and economical ways to use automation to process data and prepare comprehensive management reports.
- Launched a $7.5 million worldwide Air Force Services Core Management Information System (MIS).
- Served as Project Manager for $4.5 million Jones Hardware Replacement, completing project $500,000 under budget and on schedule.

EARLY MILITARY CAREER (1975 to 1994)

Began military career in roles as Chief of Health Care Operations, Supervisory Systems Accountant, and Computer Specialist. Gained valuable experience in all aspects of finance departments, payroll, budgeting, and accounting.

EDUCATION, TRAINING & CERTIFICATIONS

MBA, Emphasis in Accounting, MICHIGAN STATE UNIVERSITY, Lansing, MI
BS, Accounting, MICHIGAN STATE UNIVERSITY, Lansing, MI

<u>**Trained in:**</u>

→ **Project Management** (Fundamentals, Initiation and Startup, Scope, Communications, Control, Estimating, Human Resources, Procurement, Quality, Risk, Scheduling and Cost Control)
→ **Project Management for IT**
→ **Professionals Managing Multiple Projects**; Managing Project Teams, Planning, Programming
→ **Budgeting System Command and General Staff College**

Certified Public Accountant   **Certified Systems Professional**
Certified Data Processor   **Certified Computer Professional**
          Commercial Pilot with commercial, instrument, multi-engine ratings.

AWARDS & AFFILIATIONS

· US Army's "Comptroller of the Year" under MACOM for FY02
· Comptroller's "Comptroller of the Year, 2002"

JOHN B. WHITE

FSSG UNIT 12345 / FPO AP 12345-6789 / Telephone: 123-456-7890 / johnbwhite@hotmail.com

CAREER TARGET:
BIODIVERSITY CONSERVATION
AND ENVIRONMENTAL RESOURCE MANAGEMENT

**Committed to collaborating with international organizations, governments, and citizens
to protect biological diversity and optimize limited natural resources**

Proven leader and team player recognized for infusing ethic of hard work into teams and partners. Excellent oral and written communication skills honed through years of training groups and producing formal written reports and bulletins. Ten years' experience living around the globe (Germany, Thailand, Japan, Africa). Fluent German.

"I have set implausible goals for myself throughout my life, and I have met every one of them, succeeding in the most physically and mentally challenging international environments imaginable. Now, I want to return to the environmental field to work toward a diverse, healthy, and sustainable planet for future generations."

Core Competencies Include:

Resource Management:	Planned and executed transfer, scheduling, and utilization of human and aircraft resources, including movement of 250 personnel and equipment from Miramar to Afghanistan, and preparing, coordinating, and routing daily flight schedule for 30 aircraft, 63 pilots, and 80 crew.
Leadership:	Foster team ownership not strict delegation to ensure excellent results. In only five months led planning and execution of aviation-specific training for over 450 Marines, 50 Convoy Commanders and Senior Enlisted Marines, through 5 separate training evolutions.
Project Management:	Simultaneously assumed two officer positions, formerly held by two separate officers, coordinating 6 ground training exercises monthly and 8 major operational training operations for 1800 Marines in 8 squadrons.
International Humanitarian Aid:	Flew over 8 hours and assisted in scheduling and executing many more to bring relief and reconstruction supplies to East Timor following its United-Nations-sponsored split from Indonesia. Awarded Humanitarian Aid Medal approved by US Secretary of Defense.
Investigation and Reporting:	Served as Safety Team first responder following helicopter crash with 4 deaths and over $5 million in damage in San Diego, CA. Conducted a month-long investigation to determine cause of accident, and drafted reports, evaluations, and corrective policies for review by entire Marine Corps Chain of Command and Naval Aviation Safety Center.

PROFESSIONAL EXPERIENCE

UNITED STATES MARINE CORPS   1998-present
Aviation Liason Officer, Okinawa, Japan (2005-present). **Future Operations and Ground Training**, San Diego, California (2004-2005). **Aviation Safety Officer & Fleet Pilot**, San Diego, California (2003-2004). **Current Operations Schedule Writer & Fleet Pilot,** San Diego, California; Djibouti, Africa; and Asia (2001-2003).

EDUCATION

Certificate of Aviation Safety, Naval Postgraduate School, Ranked 3rd of 30 with GPA of 3.9, 2003

Marine Corps Flight School, Earned Academic Excellence Award, 1999-2001

Leadership Training, Marine Corps Officer Basic School, 1998

Bachelor's Degree in Environmental Science, University of Virginia, 1998
Relevant Coursework Includes: Chemistry for Engineers; Physics; Biology; Physical Geology; Ecology; Hydrology; Atmosphere and Weather; Beaches, Coasts, Rivers; Coastal Processes

JOHN L. SMITH

123 Main Street   Cellular: 123-456-7890
San Francisco, California 94100   Email: johnlsmith@aol.com

OPERATIONS MANAGER
Expertise in Devising Solutions and Leading Teams to Accomplish Missions

PROFESSIONAL PROFILE
Proactive, Detail-Oriented Manager

Accomplished operations manager with Secret security clearance. Proven leader of individuals and departments to accomplish missions in rapidly changing environments. Professional renowned for integrity and ability to judge short- and long-term ramifications of decisions and actions. Possesses positive attitude and endurance, able to work 15-hour days for months with no days off. Big picture perspective: determine goals, manage assets, and mentor subordinates to achieve optimal performance.

CAREER HIGHLIGHTS

◆ **Leadership:** Selected for battle staff to task and execute over 3800 helicopter sorties for four US Marine squadrons during Operation Iraqi Freedom. Extensive mission planning and leadership in flights involving up to sixteen aircraft of five different types. Awarded with **Navy Commendation Medal** for service.

◆ **Results Under Pressure:** Led and/or flew in more than 75 combat missions as a CH-46E Aircraft commander to move personnel throughout hostile territory in Iraq with near 100% success rate of avoiding insurgent attacks. Safely delivered all troops, cargo, wounded personnel, and enemy prisoners to their destinations without loss of aircraft or crew. Awarded 4 **Air Medals** for performance.

◆ **Initiative:** Re-built Ground Training Program for squadron of 500 Marines and developed most aggressive pre-Combat Training Program in the history of the squadron. Instituted standardization of study, evaluation, and promotion that eliminated formerly-rampant favoritism.

◆ **Operational Re-engineering:** Led successful move of combat operations command center from sea (USS Boxer) to land (Jalibah, Iraq) during heavy period of combat in the country. Selected to enter Iraq ahead of staff and establish base and maintenance facilities under grueling conditions in the middle of the desert, enabling aircraft to become land-based and reduce each flight to the frontlines by 300 miles.

◆ **Safety Management:** Liased across 6 command and control agencies and developed multilayer system to establish redundant, failure-resistant communication networks. Enabled constant contact for approximately 30 flight missions throughout Iraq daily.

◆ **Integrity:** Conducted internal audit of Government Travel Credit Card Program to eliminate thousands of dollars in abuses. Identified misuses of government funds, brought program to zero balance, and counseled staff in acceptable use of government credit to replace squadron in good graces of external auditors.

◆ **Organization:** Currently responsible for operational tasking of all U.S Marine West Coast helicopter assets, comprised of 9 squadrons and 150 tactical aircraft. Serve as sole Marine representative on Governor Schwarzenegger's Firescope Committee creating guidelines and streamlining processes for use of military aircraft in fighting natural and terrorist disasters.

PROFESSIONAL EXPERIENCE

UNITED STATES MARINE CORPS   1997 – PRESENT
Helicopter Operations Tasking Officer (2005-present), **Special Projects Officer** (2004-2005), **Ground Training Officer** (2004), **Current Operations Watch Officer** (2003), **Airframes Maintenance Officer** (2001-2003), **Assistant Administrative Officer** (2000-2001), **Student Naval Aviator** (1998-2000)

EDUCATION

Marine Corps Basic School, 1997
Leadership training; Graduated in top 10% of class of 230 people

Marine Corps Officer Candidate School, 1997

University of Virginia, Charlottesville, Virginia, 1996
Bachelor of Science, Criminal Justice, Minor in Business Administration

Louis G. Smith

122 Canton Street ♦ Gettysburg, PA 12345
Home: (515) 244-5433 ♦ Work: (515) 438-1234 ♦ Cell: (515) 346-2356 ♦ LouisG@yahoo.com

SUMMARY OF QUALIFICATIONS

Well qualified and highly skilled Electronics Technology professional with more than 3 years of field experience performing installations, repairs, modifications, and maintenance of electronics equipment on various projects. Skilled at analyzing and troubleshooting to card and component level, testing equipment. and following safety procedures. Proven leadership and communication skills with ability to work independently or as member of team. Strong organizational skills; capable of prioritizing, scheduling, and managing work flow. Experienced at driving heavy trucks and machinery.

Technical Skills & Abilities:

► Soldering	► Schematics	► Quality Control	► Troubleshooting
► Oscilloscopes	► Cabling Systems	► Transistors & Diodes	► Power / Electrical Wiring
► RF Generators	► Power Meters	► Ammeters	► Audio Signal Generators
► Frequency Analyzers	► Calibrations	► Radio Systems	► Multimeters

COMPUTER SKILLS

Microsoft Office, CAD, FTP Programs, Internet Applications

EDUCATION & PROFESSIONAL DEVELOPMENT

United States Air Force Technical School, Keesler AFB, Biloxi, MS   2003
Certified 3 Level Maintenance Technician (Received award as Distinguished Graduate with 97% average)

Air National Guard Lightning Force Academy, Annville, PA   2003
Certification course in Electronics Standard Installation Practices and Techniques

United States Air Force Technical School, Keesler, AFB, Biloxi, MS   2002
Certification in Electronic Principles (Received award as Top Graduate with 99% average)

Additional Certifications:
Siemons Certification — Certified to install and terminate Siemons connector blocks   2005
Avaya Certification — Certified to install and terminate Avaya gigaspeed fiber optics connectors and cabling   2003
Avaya Certification — Certified to install and terminate Avaya category 5/6 cabling   2003

Possess Current Secret Security Clearance and U.S. Civilian Passport

RELEVANT EXPERIENCE

Pennsylvania Air National Guard – 211 Engineering and Installation Squadron, Annville, PA   2002 – Present
Ground Radio Systems Journeyman

- Perform installations, repairs, modifications, and maintenance of fixed, mobile, and transportable transmitters, receivers, transceivers, and related equipment at various locations worldwide as assigned to engineering section.
- Install and repair radio communications equipment, including transmitters, power supplies, and antenna assemblies.
- Pinpoint cause of malfunctions using checking procedures, test equipment, diagrams, and operating characteristics.
- Conduct tests, tuning, adjustments, and alignment on all installed equipment to ensure proper operation.
- Troubleshoot and resolve problems associated with ground radio communications equipment.
- Utilize layout drawings, schematics, and pictorial diagrams to repair maintenance problems.
- Conduct intricate alignment and calibration procedures to maintain optimal operating efficiency of equipment.

ADDITIONAL EXPERIENCE

ESCM Utilities Contracting, Carlisle, PA   2005 – Present
Data Entry and Technical Support

- Compile and process GIS and electrical testing data using Excel program in support of utilities contracting projects.
- Work on project that tests every traffic pole, power transmission pole, and traffic light pole in state of New York; create maps of locations for completed and future tests in field utilizing Excel and MS Streets and Trips.
- Audit information provided from field testers to ensure accuracy.

United States Air Force, Germany & North Dakota   1998 – 2002
Spangdahlem Air Force Base, Spangdahlem, Germany (2000 – 2002)
Minot Air Force Base, Minot, ND (1998 – 2000)
Munitions Systems Journeyman

- Worked in Precision Guided Munitions shop serving on various assignments worldwide. Operated heavy equipment, including fork lifts, tractor trailers, bomb lift trucks, Bobcat utility vehicles, and munitions handling trailers. Handled and transported hazardous materials in safe manner. Served as Senior Crew Chief as Minot Air Force Base.

Martin F. Robinson

444 Maplewood Street
Chicago, IL 12345

Home: (209) 355-1644
Cell: (209) 123-1234
Martin F@yahoo.com

PROFILE

Results-oriented and well-qualified Logistics professional with over 30 years of experience in logistics, supply-chain management, inventory control, and shipping / receiving. Decorated military career comprised of continuous promotions and awards / recognition for performing top-quality work. Detail oriented with track record of managing logistics / inventory with high degree of accuracy in timely manner within deadline-oriented work settings. Skilled in project management and managing logistics / inventory during large-scale operations. Proven leader experienced in training and motivating team members in meeting or exceeding targeted goals and objectives. Outstanding communication, organizational, and follow-through skills. Extensive experience in safe handling and management of hazardous materials and implementing safety rules and regulations. Skilled problem solver who works well in challenging situations. Possess Active Secret Security Clearance.

► Inventory Control / Management
► Material Handling
► Product Merchandising
► Purchasing Management
► Team Building / Management
► Technology Integration
► Quality Assurance / Control

► Warehousing
► Order Management
► Shipping & Receiving
► Supply Processing
► Cost Containment / Control
► Database Management
► Project Management / Planning

► Logistics / Supply Chain Management
► Product Distribution & Tracking
► Inventory Replenishment
► Project Management / Planning
► Vendor Relations / Negotiations
► Staff Training & Development
► Budget Management

PROFESSIONAL EXPERIENCE

UNITED STATES AIR FORCE   1977 – Present
Material Handler (1998 – Present)

- Oversee all personnel during mobility exercises and special mobility tasking; evaluate and monitor mobility planning, dispersal, special exercises and procedures for logistics support and maintain inventory.
- Manage Mobility Inventory Control and Accountability System: **ensure 100% accuracy** that all inventories for entire base enters system correctly and successfully meet demand for supplies and fill all shortages.
- **Helped prepare 300 personnel for deployment to Iraq in 2003.**
- Operate material-handling equipment and general-purpose vehicles.
- Function as Head Trainer on use of material-handling equipment, including 4,000, 6,000, and 10,000 lb. forklifts and Rider Reach forklift and train new staff on use of Standard Base Supply System.
- Utilize technology and software programs to manage inventory databases and research federal logistics.
- Maintain physical security of Inspection Computer system and hold training for subordinates.
- Inspect condition of inventory and identify shelf-life items, health-hazard items, and hazardous materials.
- Designed PowerPoint presentations to assist supervisors with training of subordinates.
- Process off-line requisitions and handle depot requisition reconciliation.
- Prepare annual financial budget, compile and submit supply cost data reports to base funds management activities for cost projections, and resolve inventory discrepancies promptly.
- Assist with planning, conducting, and monitoring mobility exercises and training for staff and equipment.
- Obtain automated data processing output products for stock-funded items.
- Serve as Bench Stock Supervisor: establish and oversee inventory and replenish Bench Stocks.
- Monitor shipment-tracing programs and requisitions, and receipts for serialized items.
- Create logistics documents and evaluate, monitor, and inspect logistics activities.
- Implement and adhere to Air Force Office of Safety and Health program rules and regulations.
- Identify and report unsuitable materials, monitor health-hazard issues, and dispose of hazardous waste.

Continued...

Martin F. Robinson   Résumé / Page 2

Noncommissioned Officer in Charge of Mobility Section (1993 – 1998)
- Directed Load Crews during mobility exercises and special mobility tasking and oversaw safe handling of all chemical warfare gear as well as small warehouse in box containers in preparation for deployments.
- Evaluated and monitored mobility planning, dispersal, special exercises and procedures for logistics support.
- Developed and maintained mobility personnel and equipment listings and prepared logistics documents.
- Played active role in conducting and monitoring mobility exercises and training.
- Worked on installation surveys to determine support capabilities.

Supervisor of the Receiving Section of the Warehouse (1980 – 1993)
- Received and processed incoming shipments of parts and equipment, ensuring that incoming materials matched accompanying documentation; inspected shipments for shortages, overages, and obvious damage.
- Supervised moving and shipment of materials and equipment and performed quality control measures.
- Provided secure storage and handling of classified and sensitive items and documented all shipments.
- Stored in-warehouse assets and supplies and ensured proper tracking and identification of all items.

Supply Technician (1979 – 1980)
- Controlled and initiated inputs to add or delete exception codes pertaining to requisitioning, shipping, and related issues and prepared responses to messages, letters, and inquiries regarding inventory.
- Examined unserviceable items for possible repair; prepared documents and recorded items sent for repair.
- Ensured timely processing of priority requisitions by use of computerized systems, machine inquiries, and telephone contacts with system managers and transportation offices.
- Headed lateral supply support by maintaining contacts with military command, Defense Logistics Centers, and other military bases and trained and supervised all personnel in section.
- Reviewed unfavorable inventory control trends and made recommendations to appropriate authorities.
- Collected and entered data into computer system and maintained high-priority checklist, management reports, and priority-status board.

EDUCATION & TRAINING

Community College of the Air Force, Montgomery, AL   *To be completed* Fall 2007
Associate's degree in Logistics, 3.5 G.P.A.

Illinois Central College, East Peoria, IL   1995
Associate's degree in General / Liberal Studies, 4.0 G.P.A.

Specialized Training:
Supply Management Specialist
Material Facilities Specialist
Material Facilities Manager
Mobility Inventory Control & Accountability System
Explosive Safety Orientation Course

AWARDS

Air Reserve Forces Meritorious Service Medal (9)
Air Force Achievement Medal (3)
Air Force Outstanding Unit Award (2)
National Defense Service Medal (1)
Air Force Longevity Service (6)
Illinois Long and Honorable Service Medal (6)

COMPUTER SKILLS

Microsoft Word, Excel, PowerPoint

Robert F. Henderson

22 Miller Road
Schenectady, NY 12052

Residence: (318) 123-1844
Office: (318) 321-4888
robert.henderson@us.army.mil

PROFESSIONAL PROFILE

Successful 17-year military career comprised of continuous promotion and recognition with career encompassing broad range of security and surveillance capabilities. Proven ability to develop creative, common-sense solutions to complex problems and situations. Master team builder and motivator with outstanding communication skills: verbal, written, interpersonal, and rapport building. Self-directed leader capable of training, developing, and managing team of security / intelligence professionals and coordinating joint efforts of multiple agencies. Accomplished management professional with competency areas in:

Security / Surveillance ... Intelligence / Operations Analysis ... Homeland Security

Emergency Management ... Interagency Coordination ... Information Collection / Analysis

Program / Project Management ... Event Planning & Management ... Training & Development

Multi-Company Operations & Procedural Integration ... Sensitive Information Management

PROVEN RESULTS

➢ **Security / Surveillance Expert** — Active Top Secret / SCI security clearance with current background investigation; over 13 years' experience in positions of increasing leadership duties.

➢ **Enthusiastic & Proven Leader** — Captain in U.S. Army and NY Army National Guard; coordinated intelligence operations for approximately **24,000 square miles** in Iraq during Operation Iraqi Freedom III (OIF III); conducted security and threat assessments and coordinated support for 2001 World Trade Center Bombing Operations; implemented security / surveillance programs.

➢ **Skilled Trainer** — Certified Military Instructor; taught basic intelligence analytical techniques to Saudi Military during training mission to Saudi Arabia; trained units for deployment in OIF III and OIF II; instructor in nuclear, biological, and chemical threats, and intelligence analysis.

➢ **Experienced Manager** — Operated Logistics Watch Desk for New York State's Joint Operations Center in support of military operations for 2001 World Trade Center bombings.

➢ **Influential Leader** — Lead teams of up to 60 professionals and synchronize efforts of multiple units and organizations during joint efforts and operations in various security / surveillance activities.

➢ **Seasoned Intelligence Analyst** — Human Intelligence, Signals Intelligence, Measures and Signatures Intelligence, and Imagery Intelligence; able to use technology in managing intelligence / surveillance operations; expertise in gathering intelligence and generating analytical reports.

➢ **Quality Control / Safety**— Inspected units and personnel mobilized for Operation Enduring Freedom and OIF; served as Battalion Assistant Safety Officer, overseeing safety of team members; introduced unit safety protocols and standard operating procedures.

➢ **Master Team Builder & Motivator** — In-depth experience training, developing, planning, and motivating highly effective teams of security / surveillance professionals.

➢ **Emergency Response Expert** — Conducted training for U.S. Department of Defense personnel on reaction to chemical environment and use of protective equipment for disaster relief and security.

➢ **Polished Communicator** — Strong public speaking and presentation skills; communicate well and build solid working relationships with all team members, including management and staff.

➢ **Technology / Computer Expertise** — Proficient in Microsoft Office, Classified Intelligence Software, Single Source Processing Systems, Intelligence / Surveillance Databases.

Continued...

Robert F. Henderson   **Résumé / Page 2**

PROFESSIONAL EXPERIENCE

UNITED STATES ARMY   1988 – Present

Directorate of Logistics, Divisions of Military and Naval Affairs, Latham, NY (2001 – Present)
Administrative / Logistics Officer
➤ Oversee unit's logistical activities, inspection of supply and services operations, and analyze authority for Unit Status Reports Equipment on Hand section before report submission to national agencies.
➤ Managed Logistics Watch Desk and inspected units prior to deployment in Iraq.

642 Military Intelligence Battalion, 42 Infantry Division, Troy, NY / Tikrit, Iraq (2004 – Present)
Collection Manager / Tactical Intelligence Officer / Operations Officer
➤ Coordinate planning, collection, evaluation, fusion, analysis, production, and dissemination of all source intelligence and counter intelligence at multiple units and groups. Manage preparation of intelligence.
➤ Deployed for active duty for Operation Iraqi Freedom III (2004 – 2005), serving in Tikrit, Iraq, coordinating intelligence operations for approximately **24,000 square miles.**

642 Military Intelligence Battalion, 42 Infantry Division (Garrison), Troy, NY (2001 – 2004)
Collection Manager / Operations Officer
➤ Supervised intelligence operations and up to 60 team members and executed security and threat assessments at Ground Zero and critical military installations after 2001 World Trade Center bombings.

642 Military Intelligence Battalion, 42 Infantry Division (Garrison), Troy, NY (2000 – 2001)
Assistant S-4 / Logistics Officer
➤ Controlled logistics and implemented standardized safety procedures for members of unit.

Directorate of Recruiting and Retention, Div. of Military and Naval Affairs, Latham, NY (1999 – 2001)
Liaison Officer
➤ Supported 2 interrelated state-level task forces assigned to improve retention rates in NYARNG.

D Company, 201 Military Intelligence Battalion, Gordon, GA (1998 – 1999)
Squad Leader / Mission Manager / Senior Intelligence Analyst / Reporter
➤ Led up to 25 team members in Analysis section at collection facility. Instituted safety protocols.

United States Military Training Mission, Riyadh, Saudi Arabia (1997 – 1998)
Intelligence Analyst Advisor / Trainer
➤ Trained Saudi Military on response to chemical environment and use of protective equipment.

D Company, 201 Military Intelligence Battalion, Fort Gordon, GA (1996 – 1997)
Intelligence Analyst

42 Infantry Division (Garrison), Troy, NY (1991 – 1996)
Intelligence Analyst / Squad Leader / Order of Battle NCO

748th Military Intelligence Battalion, San Antonio, TX (1988 – 1991)
Intelligence Analyst

EDUCATION & SPECIALIZED TRAINING

B.A., Political Science, Siena College, Loudonville, NY

A.A., Liberal Arts, Hudson Valley Community College, Troy, NY

Specialized Training: Foreign Disclosure Officer Course • High Value Target Course • ASAS-ACE Block II (Data Processing & Command) • Collection Manager Course • 98C Intel Analyst Basic Noncommissioned Officer Course • Primary Leadership Development

AWARDS & RECOGNITION

Bronze Star • Army Commendation Medal (3) • Joint Service Achievement Medal • Army Achievement Medal (2) • Joint Meritorious Unit Award (2) • Army Good Conduct Medal (2) • National Defense Service Medal (2) • Armed Forces Expeditionary Forces Medal • Non-Commissioned Officer Professional Development Ribbon (2) • Armed Forces Reserve Medal with M Device • Global War on Terrorism Service Medal • Iraq Campaign Medal

David Brown
352 March Lane SW, Bolling AFB, District of Columbia 20032
202-536-4593
dbrown@hotmail.com

INFORMATION TECHNOLOGY/SYSTEMS ANALYST

Confident, dependable, versatile information technology professional with
extensive diverse experiences enhanced by graduate-level studies. More than
10 years of experience in system analysis and programming for the US Air Force.
Experienced in major programming languages, network administration, database
management, operating systems, hardware and software. Certified Capability
Maturity Model Integrated inspector. Possess active *DoD – Top Secret Clearance*.

SKILLS SUMMARY

Strong background in user training and support documentation. Experience in major
programming languages, operating systems, hardware and software.

Networks/Operating Systems
WINDOWS XP, 2000, NT – Experienced in creating accounts, developing account
policies, implementing user rights, installing and configuring network printers,
providing application support, installing and configuring network protocols,
managing clients, and performing maintenance upgrades.

Hardware
A+ CERTIFIED – Proven ability to perform tasks such as installation, configuration,
diagnosing, preventive maintenance and basic networking.

Database Administration
MICROSOFT ACCESS, SQL SERVER

Programming Languages
ASP, ASP.NET, SQL, C++, JAVA, VISUAL BASIC, VISUAL BASIC.NET, IBM
ASSEMBLER

PC Software
MICROSOFT WORD, EXCEL, ACCESS, POWERPOINT, PROJECT

EXPERIENCE

US Air Force, Washington, DC   4/06-present
Superintendent Senior Leader, Operations Branch
- Oversight of $3.9 million budget for hardware, software and other IT related
  expenses.
- Project manager, developer and administrator of the Air Force *Senior Leader
  Career Management System* an intranet and secure extranet for access by
  authorized military personnel.
- Direct daily operations of one military member and four contractors, analyzing
  workflow, establishing priorities, developing standards and setting deadlines.
- Administrator for the Air Force's E-Mail for Life program; responsible for e-mail
  efficiency, security and stability.
- Responsible for SQL server administration, writing complex data mining queries,
  and other assignments as necessary.

US Air Force, Offutt AFB, NE   11/03-04/06
SACCS Programmer Analyst
- Researched, planned, installed, configured, troubleshot, maintained and
  upgraded hardware and software interfaces with the operating system.

Analyzed and evaluated present or proposed business procedures or problems to define data processing needs.

- Conducted technical research on system upgrades to determine feasibility, cost, time required, and compatibility with current system.

- Conferred with users to gain understanding of needed changes or modifications of existing programs. Resolved questions of program intent, data input, output requirements, and inclusion of internal checks and controls.

- Designed software requirements and implemented code for Strategic Automated Command Control system. Participated in software testing and code inspections. Eliminated redundancies saving more than $78 thousand per year.

- Coded, tested and troubleshot programs utilizing the appropriate hardware, database, and programming technology.

- Trained and managed a team of four programmers in Quality Assurance of the software lifecycle and saw significant improvement in their performance.

- Orchestrated $100 thousand SACCS migration of multiple systems into one multi-function system. Acted as facilitator coordinating between various teams ensuring a successful migration.

- Oversaw a $1.9 million purchasing budget for hardware, software and other expenses. Authored $500 thousand Program Objective Memorandum.

US Air Force, Elmendorf AFB, AK   8/00-8/03
Computer Security Systems Officer / Database Administrator

- Analyzed, planned, designed and installed new personal computer systems and reviewed, monitored and upgraded existing personal computer systems.

- Investigated hardware problems and performed minor system hardware and communication connection repairs.

- Designed Access database solutions and maintained SQL databases.

US Air Force, Elmendorf AFB, AK   11/96-8/00
Computer Security Systems Officer / Database Administrator

- Liaised extensively with internal clients and translated client requirements into highly specified project briefs.

- Worked closely with developers and a variety of end users to ensure technical compatibility and user satisfaction.

- Assisted User Acceptance Training team in testing new Military Immunization Tracking System (MITS).

EDUCATION

Master of Science Program   2006 to
Information Technology Management   Present
Tourou University, Cypress, CA
Completed 8 credit hours towards Masters Degree
3.83/4.0 GPA   2006

Bachelor of Science
Computer Information Systems Programming
Bellevue University, Bellevue, NE
3.84/4.0 GPA

Associate Degree(s)
Computer Science and Health Care Science
Community College of the Air Force, Maxwell AFB, AL

Certificate, Software Engineering
Air Force Institute of Technology

MATTHEW O'DOUL

5139 North Cumberland Boulevard
Whitefish Bay, WI 53217
414-964-6275
matthewodoul@worldnet.att.net

SUMMARY OF QUALIFICIATIONS

Seasoned *upper/middle management professional* with 25 years of experience. Recipient of many management and leadership awards through the United States Armed Forces. Skilled in long term planning, multi-million dollar budgeting, contract administration, public relations, international relations, Special Operations and crisis management. Master of Science in Management.

SUMMARY OF ACHIEVEMENTS

- Productively initiate and monitor long range planning and multi-million dollar budgets for day-to-day/Special Operations, purchasing, strategizing, relocation, and training.
- Efficiently administer internal controls for 41 facilities and personnel.
- Successfully direct the hiring, training, and management of 200+ civilian and military staff (to include Officers and Recruiters).
- Effectively plan, coordinate, and implement quarterly media campaigns for recruitment.
- Selected and authorized to perform staff studies for approval by the Secretary of Defense and Chairman of the Joint Chiefs of Staff.
- Chosen to provide independent support to multiple governmental inter-agencies for special projects in coordination with several departments within the Pentagon and Washington DC area.
- Achieved cultural diversity through multiple international tours of duty and life in Germany, Lebanon, and Haiti.
- Recipient of numerous management and leadership awards and the following: Joint Meritorious Service, Armed Forces Expeditionary, Berlin Occupation Service, Army Meritorious Service, Army and Joint Commendation and Achievement medals.
- Attained Master of Science, Bachelor of Arts, and Associate of Arts while working full time.
- Developed computer proficiency and a working knowledge of German language.

OPERATIONS/ADMINISTRATION

Human Resources: Provide final interviews and decision-making for hiring civilians (one-third of staff annually) throughout the year. Establish training programs, ensure standards are met, determine training sites (in-house or off-site), and monitor same.

Operating Budget: Establish and monitor $1.5M annual budget (excluding payroll) for training, equipment, supplies, transportation, and daily operations. Generate long range planning two to three quarters in advance and execute same. Supervise Executive Officer in Charge of Purchasing. Administer all internal controls for 41 facilities and personnel.

Public Relations: Coordinate advertising and public relations with staff, to include print, Internet, radio, and television. Plan and execute quarterly media campaign. Speak to business organizations, colleges, high schools, veterans' groups, Chambers of Commerce, etc.

Resume of MATTHEW O'DOUL

INTERNATIONAL RELATIONS

Europe: Accountable for selected Secretary of Defense-approved special operations activities in locations throughout Europe, including NATO and former Warsaw Pact countries, as well as security operations for special security events.

Africa: Integrated, synchronized and developed staff of 50+ to support deployment of an isolated support group of 400 for crisis intervention and joint training with numerous African nations. Staff managed personnel, intelligence, training, maintenance, medical, and logistics within a $2.0M annual budget. (1996-1997) Also commanded unit of 100, prepared for contingencies, crisis intervention, and training for 15 African nations. (1994-1996)

Haiti: Commanded units in Haiti to provide peacekeeping functions and stabilization of a new government. (1994-1995)

Lebanon and Beirut: Commanded unit in this region during the crisis years (1984-1985).

CIVILIAN EDUCATION

Webster University, St. Louis, MO
MASTER OF SCIENCE – MANAGEMENT (1994)
Edison State College, Trenton, NJ
BACHELOR OF ARTS – HISTORY (1987)
Campbell University, Buies Creek, NC
ASSOCIATE OF ARTS – GENERAL STUDIES   (1980)

MILITARY EDUCATION

Armed Forces Staff College, Norfolk, VA
COMPLETED: 1998
Command and General Staff College, Fort Leavenworth, KS
COMPLETED: 1994
Numerous Military Schools: Pre-1990

MILITARY SERVICE

United States Army (March 1976-Present)
LIEUTENANT COLONEL – O/5

- **Recruiting Battalion Commander (Regional Manager) – Regular Army and Reserves – State of Wisconsin and Upper Peninsula of Michigan** (July 1999-Present)
- **Operations Officer for Chairman of Joint Chiefs of Staff – Pentagon** (1997-1999)
- **Commander – Special Forces Command - NC** (1994-1997)
- **Scenario Developer/Warfighter Exercise Controller – Battle Command Training Center – Fort Leavenworth, KS** (1992-1994)
- **Operations Officer/Observer Controller – Joint Readiness Training Center - Fort Chafee, AK** (1990-1992)
- **Pre-1990:** Enlisted in the Army in 1976, progressed to Commissioned Officer and received promotions regularly thereafter. Commanded Special Forces and Infantry Units, attended numerous military schools, and was stationed in Europe and various states.

KEVIN O'DONNELL
4515 South Whitnall Avenue, Apartment 18
St. Francis, Wisconsin 53235
KOtt@wi.rr.com

414-489-0267 (h)   **414-482-5374 (o)**

INVESTIGATOR GS-1810 QUALIFICATIONS
Skilled in application of investigative skills and techniques while investigating the character, practices, appropriateness, or credentials of persons. Knowledgeable about civil and administrative aspects of law. Knowledge of laws of evidence, rules of criminal procedure, precedent court decisions, maintaining surveillance, and performing undercover work. Expertise in decision-making relating to national security, subversive organizations and their methods of operation, security issues, and record-keeping. Proficiency in evaluating reliability and credibility, gaining confidence and cooperation, and making positive decisions while distinguishing between conclusions and facts.

EDUCATION
Civilian
Concordia University, Mequon, WI
BACHELOR OF ARTS – MANAGEMENT AND COMMUNICATION (Dec., 2004)
- Business Administration Intensive; focus on research throughout curriculum; coursework included case studies, liberal arts writing, marketing, business ethics and values.
- **Grade Point Average: 3.81**

University of Wisconsin, Marinette and Milwaukee, WI
GENERAL EDUCATION (1990-1993)

Military
Community College of the Air Force, Maxwell Air Force Base, AL
ASSOCIATE DEGREE IN CRIMINAL JUSTICE (Oct., 2004)
- Fundamentals of Ground Combat Skills, Law Enforcement and Marksmanship. Special Weapons and Tactics, Investigative Principles, and Support Weapons.
- Air Force Specialty Internship (Journeyman – 8.0 credits and Craftsman – 4.0 credits).
- Medical Education (five months), Emergency Medical Technician (EMT) – three weeks.
- Security Forces Ground Combat (five weeks)
- Honor Graduate of Security Forces Law Enforcement Academy course (2002).
- Detainee Operations and Movement Course (one week)
- Air Force Journeyman Security Forces

AWARDS/HONORS
- Promoted from GS-5 to GS-7 in March, 2004
- Airman of the Quarter (2000) – Civilian Employee of the Quarter
- Ira L. Bong Award for Performance Excellence (2000)
- Samuel L. Keene Scholarship based on academics and essay about personal growth (2003)
- Honor Graduate, USAF Security Forces Ground Combat School and Academy (1998)
- Performance Awards annually (three of four years)
- Recommended as winning Employee of the Quarter.

Resume of KEVIN O'DONNELL   **Page 2 of 2**

MILITARY HISTORY

- ❑ Civilian Full Time Employee for USAF, 440th Air Wing (March, 2000-Present)
- ❑ United States Air Force Reserve (May, 2003-Present and 1997)
- ❑ Active Duty – Middle East (November, 2001-May, 2003)
- ❑ United States Navy Reserve (1993-1997)
- ❑ United States Coast Guard Reserve (1991-1993)

USAF, 440th Air Wing, Milwaukee, WI
SUPERVISORY SECURITY GUARD/ASSISTANT SHIFT SUPERVISOR (third shift)
Responsible for safety and security of 11 aircraft, 30+/- buildings, property, and up to 2,000 personnel, and armed patrols. Monitor and prevent suspicious activities, security breaches and deficiencies. Detain suspicious personnel and respond to calls for assistance. Employ AF and local use of force policies and rules of engagement. Provide and proofread timely and accurate reports including incident reports (which may be used by government authorities). Coordinate materials and train base personnel.

AIR MARSHALL/FIRE TEAM MEMBER – six trips between November, 2001 and May, 2003
Protected air crew, ensured order and restraint, and provided humanitarian care while transporting (Taliban and Al Queda) detainees from Afghanistan to Guantanamo Bay, Cuba. Handed over personnel to Marines and Army for confinement. Held full arrest powers over persons under the Uniform Code of Military Justice (UCMJ). Conducted interviews and "field interviews" with unidentified personnel. Member of the Control Cell and Entry Controller. Assisted with training: use of force, use of expandable baton, CPR and First Aid. Generated and wrote accurate statements, accident reports, and incident reports.
- ❑ Recipient of multiple ribbon awards throughout the 18 months
- ❑ Assisted with development of the first guidelines and procedures program

CIVILIAN SAFETY/SECURITY

- ❑ **DEPUTY SHERIFF** - Milwaukee County Jail (1996-1998)
- ❑ **SECURITY** - hospitality industry (1996)
- ❑ **NIGHT SUPERVISOR** - various supermarkets (1988-1993)

EMERGENCY MEDICAL TECHNICIAN (EMT)

- ❑ Midwest Medstar EMS, Madison, WI (January, 1999-March, 2000)
- ❑ MedaCare Ambulance, Milwaukee, WI (1994-1996)

PERSONAL

Secret Clearance – proficiency with Microsoft Office – Certified State of Wisconsin Time/NCIC (National Crime Information Center) Operator – Veterans' Preference: 5-point preference based on active duty in the U.S. Armed Forces – Highest Grade: GS-0085-06 (2001-Present) – Member of Veterans of Foreign Wars (VFW).

KSAs/References/Full Employment and Military History Available

THEODORE TURNBULL
1412 Fourth Avenue
Fort Knox, AK 40121

502-943-9300 (residence)
502-626-0700 (office)

trnbl@aol.com

SUMMARY OF QUALIFICATIONS

- Seasoned *upper management professional* with over 20 years of experience.
- Exceptional skills in *human resources management* arena, including leadership, budget management and administration, equal opportunity, marketing and strategic planning, teaching/training, recruitment, and retention.
- Proficiency and experience with force protection, security operations and safety program planning and implementation.
- Expertise in long term planning, multi-million dollar budgeting, contract administration, public relations, international relations, special operations and crisis management.
- Recipient of numerous management and leadership awards through the United States Army.
- Core competencies include high moral character, strong communication and organizational skills, multi-tasking, time management, problem-solving, self-motivation, flexibility, team-building, leadership, and computer proficiency.

SUMMARY OF ACHIEVEMENTS

- Performance recognized by award of the Defense Superior Service Award (2000), Legion of Merit (1995, 2001), Meritorious Service Award (X4), and numerous other awards.

- Afforded the opportunity, based on leadership potential, to command the Army's largest mechanized Infantry Battalion consisting of 1,500+ military personnel, 500 vehicles, and an annual operating budget of $5M. One of five percent of officers in year group to have been selected for LTC tactical command.

- Held personally responsible, as Deputy Director (J1), US Central Command, for planning and execution of highly complex tasks involved in personnel and family recovery from Southwest Asia during contingency operations against Iraq, in Kenya and the Persian Gulf. Additionally, held accountable for other classified programs in the post-Desert Storm period.

- Effectively implemented large-scale unit downsizing on time, under-budget, with no major problems or losses during military draw-down in Germany. Planned for the transit of $5B+ in equipment to the U.S. Coordinated for host-nation support, and insured environmental standards were met.

- Currently Deputy Commander (Colonel) of a US Army Recruiting Brigade which ranks as first in mission accomplishment among five like organizations. Mission is to recruit 15K+ new soldiers in FY 2001. Brigade consists of eight battalions, 41 companies, and 290 recruiting stations dispersed over a 10-state area in the northwest. Responsibilities are to enforce enlistment quotas, plan and executive training programs, establish mission readiness, manage personnel, budgeting, administration, logistics, public affairs, and safety programs.

THEODORE TURNBULL **Page 2 of 2**

HUMAN RESOURCES/OPERATIONS/ADMINISTRATION

- Generated a 30% increase in contracts over 2000, the largest sales growth in the command. Currently meeting recruitment goals during a period of great demand for America's youth.
- Developed/implemented curriculum enabling students to graduate with the highest performance rating achieved from like size colleges. Taught ethics, professional values, leadership principles, self-motivation, interpersonal relationships and teamwork as Assistant Professor for Military Science in the ROTC Department of Eastern Kentucky University.
- Provided human resources services for (the equivalent of a) medium sized corporation as Brigade Adjutant/S1. Furnished personnel and administrative services for an organization of 1,800 military and 200 civilian personnel.
- Assigned as Recruiting Company Commander, responsible for prospecting/recruiting 200+ applicants/month. Presented information in high schools and colleges, prepared benefits information for public distribution, developed efficiency reports for 35 assigned personnel, rated and assessed individuals. Increased their performance through positive motivation, supervision, and adherence of standards. Accountable for hiring, firing, discipline.
- Transformed unsuccessful company into a top five of 67 performers in less than three months. Sustained that level of performance for my two years of command.
- Achieved extensive experience and training in developing safety programs and ensuring operations security of personnel. Assignment to US Central Command/Southwest Asia included training in risk assessment, antiterrorism, and force protection.

CIVILIAN EDUCATION

Eastern Michigan University , Leavenworth, KS
MASTER OF BUSINESS ADMINISTRATION CANDIDATE - Completed 75% of program

Eastern Kentucky University, Richmond, KY
BACHELOR OF ARTS IN EDUCATION, Social Studies, Geography and ROTC (four years)

MILITARY EDUCATION

Executive Force Protection Course, Washington, DC, **Air War College**, Montgomery, AL, **Command and General Staff College**, Ft. Leavenworth, KS, **Combined Arms Staff Course** (CAS3), Ft. Leavenworth, KS, **Human Resources Course** (S1), Ft. Benjamin Harrison, IN, **Armor Advanced Course** and **Infantry Officer Basic Course.**

MILITARY SERVICE

- Deputy Commander, US Army **Recruiting** Brigade (Colonel, 06), Fort Knox, KY
- Deputy J1 (Personnel and Administration) US Central Command, Tampa, FL
- Deputy Commander, 16th Cavalry Regiment (Student/Officer), Fort Knox, KY
- Commander, Lt. Colonel-05, 2nd Squadron 11th ACR, Fort Irwin, CA
- Observer/Controller, Bronco Team (Brigade Staff Trainers), National Training Center, Fort Irwin, CA
- Brigade Executive Officer, 3rd Brigade, 3rd Infantry Division, Kitzengen, Germany
- _Pre-1990_: Commissioned a Second Lt. from ROTC. Held numerous command and staff positions through the grade of Major. Posted to numerous duty locations within the US and abroad. Alternate specialty identified as **Personnel and Administration** in 1985.

BENJAMIN T. EVANS   555 Phfeiffer Flat Avenue
(333) 555-8888   E-mail: ben4two@aol.com   Santa Clara, CA 95555

PROFESSIONAL HIGHLIGHTS

- Strong, hands-on, office management, personnel management, and administrative background.
- Proven ability for managing large offices with significant budgets, and good size staffs.
- Human resource expertise, including interviewing, training, appraisals and legal aspects as well.
- Years of experience interacting with business executives, military and government officers.

PROFESSIONAL EXPERIENCE

PERSONNEL MANAGEMENT   2003 to present
*Naval Air Reserve Santa Clara...*Moffett Field, California
- Manage professional development and career counseling programs for up to 1,800 personnel.
- Formulate and implement policies concerning career development, job satisfaction, and a range of Equal Opportunity (EO) programs.
- Perform in-depth interviews for personnel problem solving, and for potential disciplinary action.
- Interact, daily, with business managers, local government agencies and civic organizations.
- Received 3—highly coveted mgt. awards for *"Outstanding Personnel Management"* since 2003.

DIRECTOR   1999 - 2002
*Naval Reserve Personnel Center...*New Orleans, Louisiana
- Directed a team of 10 professionals assessing skills and career goals of more than 15,000 administrative, training and recruitment personnel, nationwide.
- Team member of the prestigious national committee for totally re-engineering the Navy's Personnel System, which is now in place and has proven to be a highly successful program.
- Administered a significant $13 million budget, annually, for moving 5,000 personnel nationwide.

PERSONNEL - OFFICE MANAGER   1995 - 1998
*Naval & Marine Corps Reserve Center...*San Diego, California
- Supervised a team of 8 clerical staff for managing the administrative functions of 3,500 reservists.
- Oversaw purchasing all office materials & supplies, maintenance, service and repair of equipment.
- Initiated performance appraisals, and provided training for all new administrative personnel.
- Orchestrated a comprehensive departmental budget, re-planned annually, for materials, maintenance and a considerable expenditure for on-site and off-site training programs.

EXECUTIVE ASSISTANT   1991 - 1994
*Chief of Naval Reserve...The Pentagon...*Washington, D.C.
- Reported to the Senior Director who coordinated activities between the reserve and full-time forces.
- Interfaced diplomatically with business executives & military officers for troubleshooting projects.
- Recognized for creating a unique, new concept and developing detailed criteria for a new Service Award for reservists that was made a standard practice, by the Secretary of the Navy, in 1992.

EDUCATION & CERTIFICATIONS

B.A. DEGREE -   *Major: Business Administration - Westminster College...Kansas City, Missouri*

CERTIFICATIONS   • Management of Vocational Training   • Leadership Training & Development
                               • Management in Governmental Organizations   • Industrial Sociology

COMPUTER SKILLS

- Experienced with PCs using Windows 95, MSWord, WordPerfect, Excel, PowerPoint, Publisher, and considerable business research on the Internet.

LYLE S. EVANS

(444) 666-8888
E-mail: lyle24@pfish.net

54321 Salmon Creek Way
Moss Beach, MA 55555

PROFESSIONAL HIGHLIGHTS

- In-depth security and intelligence expertise for government and business and international in scope.
- Proven computer information systems experience strongly focused on systems management.
- Significant, hands-on, office management, personnel management, and administrative background.

PROFESSIONAL EXPERIENCE

• *Intelligence & Security Command, Worldwide* •

OPERATIONS MANAGER - *Germany*   2004 to present
- Employed as a civilian with INSCOM, the worldwide center for US Army intelligence operations.
- Interface with a broad mix of intelligence-gathering activity by military groups and private US businesses, plus maintain a highly secure computerized database of "threat" information.
- Orchestrate sophisticated computer information systems training in-house and off-site for local team member, plus for several US intelligence groups.
- Spearhead on-going investigations of potential security breaches, terrorism and extremism—to provide US authorities with the most timely advice and sensitive data available.
- Performed a major role as an on-site arbitrator for defusing an international security incident.
- Rated #1--at every performance review, annually since 2004, plus also earned substantial cash awards.

OPERATIONS MANAGER - *USA*   2000 – 2003
- Appointed to the Central Control Office (CCO), for reviewing and adjudicating legal depositions of security cases throughout the US, plus given responsibility for the computer information system.
- Selected by senior management to create a unique computerized program for converting more than 55,000 files to a new system, plus ensure Y2K compatibility, which was successfully achieved.
- Team member for developing an integrated computer database—and as a peak performer—with assigned to represent the US at an international computer security conference in England.

OPERATIONS MGR - COUNTERINTELLIGENCE - *Germany*   1996 – 1999
- Supervised a 8-person team for this security/intelligence division, responsible for all of Bavaria and bordering countries.
- Launched an 18-month campaign to personally plan, design and convert the entire operation from manual to a—highly effective—computerized system and networked it to headquarters as well.
- Dramatically increased security and intelligence reporting output from 120 (average) to 1,200 including converting to English.

COMPUTER SKILLS

Experienced with PCs using DOS, Windows 3.1, 9x, NT & XP OSs, plus Microsoft Word, Excel, PowerPoint, Access, Lotus 1-2-3, WordPerfect, Adobe Illustrator, Quicken, and Globalink software programs, plus in-depth Internet business research.

EDUCATION

B.A. DEGREE - *Major: International Relations* - *Stanford University* - *Stanford, California*
B.A. DEGREE - *Major: German* - *University of Utah* - *Salt Lake City, Utah*
CERTIFICATIONS   • *Joint Intelligence Management*   • *Joint Terrorism Investigations*

MARK A. EVANS

(333) 777-4444 day
(333) 666-9999 eve

E-mail: ready2go@yahoo.com

4444 Fifty Fifth Circle
Seattle, WA 93333

PROFESSIONAL HIGHLIGHTS

- Significant experience in managing multi-million dollar warehouse inventories.
- Experienced with all of the accounting aspects of warehouse and inventory activity.
- Strong expertise in supervising and hands-on functions of shipping and receiving.

PROFESSIONAL EXPERIENCE

WAREHOUSE MANAGER   2003 to present
Naval Center...Port Hueneme, California
- Manage a team of 9 with a focus on inventory control, shipping and receiving.
- Maintain a multi-million dollar inventory that exceeds 30,000 line items of parts, equipment, materials and supplies, for shipment worldwide.
- Conduct monthly and quarterly financial inventories...then produce in-depth, computerized reports for decision making activity by senior management.

ACCOUNTING MANAGER   2000 - 2002
Comptroller Department...Port Hueneme, California
- Supervised 3 assistants to maintain a distribution budget of more than $70 million.
- Responsible for editing and validation of all accounting data including accounts receivable and payable, relative to parts, equipment, materials and supplies.

WAREHOUSE CUSTOMER SERVICE MANAGER   1995 - 1999
Fleet Industrial Supply Center...Oakland, California
- Coordinated a team of 5 for distribution of parts, equipment, materials and supplies, worldwide.
- Spearheaded a dynamic warehouse and distribution activity involving extensive computerized control of all functions of distribution, inventory control and inventory management.
- Strongly focused on expediting 100 (+) "high priority" parts, equipment and materials requests, daily.

STOCKROOM SUPERVISOR   1900 - 1994
USS Missouri...U.S. Navy Pacific Fleet
- Supervised a staff of 12, to manage and maintain 15 stockrooms with over $2 million in inventory.
- Maintained computerized records of inventory and created tracking-lists of stock replacement needs.
- Responsible for both receiving and shipping...plus all other areas of warehouse support such as: stocking, inventories, forklifts, and more.

AWARDS & RECOGNITION

- Received *"Outstanding Supply Management"* award and a special bonus award, as well.   1998
- Awarded the coveted *"Navy Achievement Medal"* for exceptional warehouse management.   1993

EDUCATION & CERTIFICATIONS

SACRAMENTO STATE UNIVERSITY - *Major: Bus. Admin/Accounting* • *California*   1995 - 2001

CERTIFICATIONS
- *Financial Management*
- *Leadership & Management*
- *Inventory Management*

12

When Going Alone Is Not Enough

CRAFTING OUTSTANDING RESUMES and letters for civilian employers is often easier said than done. If you're still having difficulty putting together your own resumes and letters after following our principles and examples, you may want to seek professional assistance. Indeed, we find many job seekers can benefit tremendously from the assistance of a professional resume writer, career counselor, career coach, or other type of career professional who can provide them with a structure for organizing and implementing a well-targeted job search campaign. A career professional can save you a great deal of time as well as help keep you focused and motivated toward achieving your ultimate mission – getting job interviews and offers.

Career Professionals on Bases

If you are currently in the service, be sure to use your base resources for organizing and implementing an effective job search. Your local military transition assistance office (ACAP, Family Service Center, Career Resource Management Center, or Family Support Center) usually maintains a library of career resources as well as a staff of counselors who can assist you with resume and letter preparation. The following websites can assist you in locating useful base resources:

- **Department of Defense Transition** www.dodtransportal.dod.mil
- **Defense Manpower Data Center** www.dmdc.osd.mil
- **e-Vets** www.dol.gov/elaws/evets.htm
- **Army Career and Alumni** www.acap.army.mil
- **Navy Lifelines** www.lifelines.navy.mil

Contacting a Career Professional

Career professionals come in many different forms and charge a variety of fees. In addition to the 18 career professionals featured in Chapter 11 (see contact information on pages 246-248) who regularly work with transitioning military personnel, the following firms offer a wide range of fee-based career management services, which can range from a few hundred to several thousand dollars:

- Right Management Consultants   www.right.com
- Drake Beam Morin   www.dbm.com
- R.L. Stevens & Associates   www.interviewing.com
- CareerLab (primarily testing)   www.careerlab.com
- Career Management International   www.cmi-imi.com
- Five O'Clock Club   www.fiveoclockclub.com
- Lee Hecht Harrison   www.lhh.com
- The Transition Team   www.transition-team.com
- WorkLife.com Career Center   www.worklife.com
- Institute for No Fear Transitions   www.nofeartransitions.us

If you are looking for a trained and certified career counselor or career coach, check out the following websites that provide directories to such qualified personnel:

- National Board for Certified
  Counselors, Inc.   www.nbcc.org
- National Career
  Development Association   www.ncda.org
- Certified Career Coaches   www.certifiedcareercoaches.com
- Professional Association of Resume
  Writers and Career Coaches   www.parw.com
- Career Masters Institute   www.cminstitute.com
- Association of Career
  Professionals International   www.acpinternational.org
- Career Planning and Adult
  Development Network   www.careernetwork.org

Many of these career professionals will work with you on a flat fee or hourly basis, depending on your particular job search needs.

Professional Resume Writers

You'll have no problem finding individuals who will help you write both conventional and electronic resumes. Many can be found through your local Yellow Pages. Others maintain websites which showcase resume writing tips, testimonials from satisfied clients, and examples of their work. Indeed, the Internet is a huge shopping mall for identifying professional resume writers.

Our experience with resume writing is confirmed by many other career professionals. While most individuals can benefit from reviewing resume writing principles and examples of outstanding resumes, when it comes time to actually write their resume, they fall short of producing a first-class document. Writing a one- to two-page resume is hard work and requires special talents. Contacting a professional resume writer, with the experience and skills to produce a resume that reflects your talents, may well be worth $200 to $600, especially if it produces expected results – attracts the right employers to you.

If and when you feel you need to contact a professional resume writer, you should consider exploring the resume writing talent associated with the following associations that certify resume writers and other career professionals:

- **National Resume Writers' Association**   www.nrwaweb.com
- **Professional Association of Resume
  Writers and Career Coaches**   www.parw.com
- **Career Directors International
  Professional Association**   www.careerdirectors.com
- **Career Masters Institute**   www.cminstitute.com

At the same time, check out some of these websites which are sponsored by professional resume writers. The ones marked with an asterisk (*) represent contributors in Chapter 11 who work with transitioning military personnel. Most of these companies will give you a free resume critique prior to using their fee-based services:

- **A&A Resume**   www.aandaresume.com
- **A-Advanced Resume Service**   www.topsecretresumes.com
- **Advanced Career Systems**   www.resumesystems.com
- **Advanced Resumes**   www.advancedresumes.com
- **Advantage Resume**   www.advantageresume.com
- **A First Impression Resume Service**   www.resumewriter.com
- **A Resume For Today***   www.aresumefortoday.com
- **Bullie Sucher***   www.billiesucher.com
- **Cambridge Resume Service**   www.cambridgeresume.com
- **CareerConnection**   www.careerconnection.com
- **Career Directions***   www.careerdirectionsLLC.com
- **Career-Resumes**   www.career-resumes.com
- **CertifiedResumeWriters**   www.certifiedresumewriters.com
- **Chesapeake Resume Writing Service***   www.chesres.com
- **Customresumewriting.com***   www.customresumewriting.com
- **eResumes & Resources**   www.eresumes.com
- **eResume.com**   www.e-resume.net
- **Executiveagent.com**   www.executiveagent.com
- **Executive Career Pro***   www.executivecareerpro.com

- Free-Resume-Tips   www.free-resume-tips.com
- GetTheJob.com*   www.getthejob.com
- Haute Resume & Career Services*   www.anewresume.com
- Impact Resumes   www.impactresumes.com
- JobJoy.com*   www.jobjoy.net
- Leading Edge Resumes   www.leadingedgeresumes.com
- Professional Resume Services*   www.proreswriters.com
- ResumeMaker   www.resumemaker.com
- Resume Winners*   www.resumewinners.com
- Sterling Career Concepts*   www.sterlingcareerconcepts.com

This is only a small sampling of the hundreds of professional resume writing services available to assist you with all your resume writing and, sometimes, distribution needs. While we do not endorse any particular career professionals, we believe it may well be in your best interests to use a professional at critical stages in your job search.

A Season for Assistance

There's a season for everything. In the case of the job search, you may quickly discover that it's the season to seek professional help for organizing and implementing a successful job search. After all, your next career decision will probably have important implications for your future income and lifestyle. Do it right, and you may be forever enriched with a job that is both financially and personally rewarding. Do it wrong, and you may soon be looking for another job which you hope will be better the next time. Look at it this way: The next job you accept will probably be worth $250,000 to $1 million, depending how long you stay. Is this the type of investment you want to make haphazardly on your own, or could you benefit from the expertise of a career professional who might be able to guide you in the right direction that could possibly double the worth of your next job?

If and when it comes time to contact a career professional, be sure to shop around, compare services, and ask for references from previous clients. Be careful of any company that makes promises of finding you a job by blasting your resume to thousands of employers and recruiters. As we noted in Chapter 7, you can do this on your own for only $19.95! The bottom line is to talk with former clients who have used the services. Better still, ask for references from at least three former military clients. And be sure to contact these former clients in the process of evaluating the effectiveness of the company's services.

Index

The Authors

CARL S. SAVINO, a retired Army Major (USAR), is a recognized leader in the field of military-to-civilian career transitions. After completing active service as an Army officer, Carl worked as a consultant for Booz Allen Hamilton and later the Hay Group. In 1996, Carl founded Competitive Edge Services, a company dedicated to connecting transitioning and former military with firms looking to hire them. His popular "Corporate Gray Job Fairs for Military Personnel" (www.corporategray.com) are held at various locations across the country. Carl is co-author of four military career transition books – *From Army Green to Corporate Gray, From Navy Blue to Corporate Gray, From Air Force Blue to Corporate Gray*, and *Military Resumes and Cover Letters*. He holds a bachelor's degree in Engineering from the U.S. Military Academy at West Point and advanced degrees from George Washington University and the University of Pennsylvania. He can be contacted at: carl@corporate-gray.com.

RONALD L. KRANNICH, Ph.D., is one of America's leading career and travel specialists. Co-author with Carl Savino of four military career transition books, he also is the principal author, with his wife Caryl, of over 80 books, including such career bestsellers as *Change Your Job Change Your Life, High Impact Resumes and Letters, Interview for Success, No One Will Hire Me!, Dynamite Salary Negotiations, Jobs for Travel Lovers*, and *Military Transition to Civilian Success*. In the field of travel, he has authored over 20 volumes in the popular "Impact Guides" travel-shopping series (www.ishoparoundtheworld.com). Ron is president of Development Concepts Incorporated, a training, consulting, and publishing firm in Virginia. He is a former Peace Corps Volunteer, high school teacher, university professor, and Fulbright Scholar who received his undergraduate and graduate degrees in Political Science and Public Administration from Northern Illinois University. He can be contacted at: krannich@impactpublications.com.

Career Resources

WELCOME TO THE ONE-STOP military career transition center. The following resources are available from Impact Publications. Full descriptions of each title, as well as downloadable catalogs, including an annotated 16-page military transition catalog (*Military Transition and Life Skills SuperSource!*) and thousands of additional books, DVDs, software, instruments, games, posters, kits, and articles, can be found at www.impactpublications.com and www.veterans world.com. Complete this form or list the titles, include shipping (see page 353), enclose payment, and send your order to:

IMPACT PUBLICATIONS
9104 Manassas Drive, Suite N
Manassas Park, VA 20111-5211 USA
1-800-361-1055 (orders only)
Tel. 703-361-7300 or Fax 703-335-9486
Email address: query@impactpublications.com
Quick & easy online ordering: www.impactpublications.com

Orders from individuals must be prepaid by check, money order, or major credit card. We accept telephone, fax, and email orders.

Qty.	TITLES	Price	TOTAL

Special Value Kits

Qty.	TITLES	Price	TOTAL
____	America's Top Jobs for Transitioning Military Personnel (page 356)	$2,495.00	_____
____	Best Jobs for Transitioning Military Without a Four-Year Degree Kit (page 357)	699.95	_____
____	Discover What You're Best At Kit (page 357)	397.95	_____
____	Dress, Image, and Etiquette Kit (page 356)	489.95	_____
____	Entrepreneurial Veteran Kit (page 358)	289.95	_____
____	Essential Military-to-Civilian Employment Guides (page 354)	154.95	_____
____	Interview and Salary Negotiation Kit (page 357)	859.95	_____
____	Jobs and the Military Spouse Kit (page 355)	499.95	_____
____	Military Career Transition Kit (page 355)	469.95	_____
____	Military, Veterans, and Ex-Offenders Kit	849.95	_____
____	The Purpose-Driven Veteran	299.95	_____
____	The Successful Military Family (page 355)	209.95	_____
____	Top 10 DVDs for Transitioning Military Personnel (page 355)	1,149.00	_____
____	Ultimate Global Work Kit (page 358)	289.95	_____
____	Ultimate Military-to-College Kit (page 358)	679.95	_____

Key Military Transition Books and DVD

____	Expert Resumes for Military-to-Civilian Transition	16.95 ____
____	Job Search: Marketing Your Military Experience	16.95 ____
____	Jump Start Your Career	14.95 ____
____	Marketing Yourself for a Second Career (DVD)	59.95 ____
____	Military-to-Civilian Career Transition Guide	15.95 ____
____	Military-to-Civilian Resumes and Letters	21.95 ____
____	Resumes and Cover Letters That Have Worked for Military Professionals	25.00 ____
____	Resumes for Former Military Personnel	11.95 ____

Military Benefits and Veterans

____	Chicken Soup for the Veteran's Soul	14.95 ____
____	Financial Aid for Veterans, Military Personnel, and Their Dependents, 2006-2008	40.00 ____
____	The Military Advantage	20.00 ____

Government and Security Jobs

____	The Book of Government Jobs	21.95 ____
____	Federal Law Enforcement Careers	19.95 ____
____	Federal Resume Guidebook	21.95 ____
____	Guide to America's Federal Jobs	14.95 ____
____	Guide to Homeland Security Careers	14.95 ____
____	Military to Federal Career Guide	38.95 ____
____	Post Office Jobs	19.95 ____

Military Spouses and Employment

____	Chicken Soup for the Military Wife's Soul	14.95 ____
____	Help! I'm a Military Spouse – I Get a Life Too!	15.95 ____
____	Home Fires Burning	14.95 ____
____	Jobs and the Military Spouse	17.95 ____
____	Military Spouse's Complete Guide to Career Success	17.95 ____
____	New Relocating Spouse's Guide to Employment	32.95 ____
____	Today's Military Wife	16.95 ____

Career Exploration

____	40 Best Fields for Your Career	16.95 ____
____	50 Best Jobs for Your Personality	16.95 ____
____	100 Fastest-Growing Careers	17.95 ____
____	202 High Paying Jobs You Can Land Without a College Degree	19.95 ____
____	225 Best Jobs for Baby Boomers	16.95 ____
____	250 Best Jobs Through Apprenticeships	24.95 ____
____	250 Best-Paying Jobs	16.95 ____
____	300 Best Jobs Without a Four-Year Degree	16.95 ____
____	Adams Job Almanac	19.95 ____
____	America's Top 100 Careers for College Graduates	17.95 ____
____	America's Top 100 Jobs for People Without a Four-Year Degree	19.95 ____
____	America's Top Jobs for People Re-Entering the Workforce	19.95 ____
____	Back Door Guide to Short-Term Job Adventures	21.95 ____
____	Best Entry-Level Jobs (annual)	16.95 ____
____	Best Jobs for the 21st Century	19.95 ____
____	Big Book of Jobs	17.95 ____
____	But What If I Don't Want to Go to College?	16.95 ____
____	Careers in Health Care	15.95 ____

___	Careers in Travel, Tourism, and Hospitality	15.95 ___
___	Jobs for Travel Lovers	19.95 ___
___	Occupational Outlook Handbook	17.95 ___
___	O*NET Dictionary of Occupational Titles	39.95 ___
___	Top 100 Careers Without a Four-Year Degree	17.95 ___
___	Top 100 Computer and Technical Careers	17.95 ___
___	Top 100 Health-Care Careers	24.95 ___
___	Top 300 Careers	18.95 ___
___	Your Dream Career for Dummies	16.99 ___
___	Your Successful Real Estate Career	18.95 ___

Job Search Strategies

___	95 Mistakes Job Seekers Make & How to Avoid Them	13.95 ___
___	Baby Boomer's Guide to the New Workplace	14.95 ___
___	Change Your Job, Change Your Life	21.95 ___
___	Complete Job Search Guide for Latinos	14.99 ___
___	Executive Job Search for $100,000 to $1 Million+ Jobs	24.95 ___
___	Guerrilla Marketing for Job Hunters	16.95 ___
___	How to Find a Job After 50	14.95 ___
___	Insider's Guide to Finding a Job	14.95 ___
___	Job Hunting Tips for People With Hot and Not-So-Hot Backgrounds	17.95 ___
___	Job Search and Career Checklists	14.95 ___
___	Job Search Magic	18.95 ___
___	Job Search Solution	15.95 ___
___	Knock 'Em Dead	14.95 ___
___	Leave Your Nose Ring at Home	14.99 ___
___	No One Will Hire Me!	15.95 ___
___	Over-40 Job Search Guide	14.95 ___
___	Overcoming 101 More Barriers to Employment	17.95 ___
___	Overcoming Barriers to Employment	17.95 ___
___	Radical Careering	15.00 ___
___	Ultimate Job Search	16.95 ___
___	Unwritten Rules of the Highly Effective Job Search	21.95 ___
___	What Color Is Your Parachute?	17.95 ___

Internet Job Search

___	America's Top Internet Job Sites	19.95 ___
___	Best Career and Education Websites	12.95 ___
___	Careers Exploration on the Internet	24.95 ___
___	Create Your Digital Portfolio	19.95 ___
___	Directory of Websites for International Jobs	19.95 ___
___	e-Resumes	16.95 ___
___	Guide to Internet Job Searching	15.95 ___
___	Job Hunting on the Internet	11.95 ___
___	Job Seeker's Online Goldmine	13.95 ___

Testing and Assessment

___	Aptitude, Personality, and Motivation Tests	17.95 ___
___	Career Match	15.00 ___
___	Career Tests	12.95 ___
___	Discover What You're Best At	14.00 ___
___	Do What You Are	18.95 ___
___	Dream It, Do It	16.95 ___
___	I Can Do Anything If I Only Knew What It Was	16.00 ___
___	I Don't Know What I Want, But I Know It's Not This	15.00 ___
___	I Want to Do Something Else, But I'm Not Sure What It Is	15.95 ___

___	Pathfinder	15.00	___
___	Smarts	21.95	___
___	What Should I Do With My Life?	14.95	___
___	What Type Am I?	14.95	___
___	What's Your Type of Career?	18.95	___
___	Who Do You Think You Are?	18.00	___
___	Wishcraft	13.95	___

Resumes and Letters

___	101 Best Resumes to Sell Yourself	12.95	___
___	101 Great Resumes	11.95	___
___	101 Quick Tips for a Dynamite Resume	13.95	___
___	201 Dynamite Job Search Letters	19.95	___
___	202 Great Resumes	12.95	___
___	2,500 New Keywords to Get You Hired	12.95	___
___	Amazing Resumes	12.95	___
___	Best KeyWords for Resumes, Cover Letters, and Interviews	17.95	___
___	Best Resumes and CVs for International Jobs	24.95	___
___	Best Resumes for $100,000+ Jobs	24.95	___
___	Best Resumes and Letters for Ex-Offenders	19.95	___
___	Best Resumes for People Without a Four-Year Degree	19.95	___
___	Best Cover Letters for $100,000+ Jobs	24.95	___
___	Blue-Collar Resume and Job Hunting Guide	15.95	___
___	Competency-Based Resumes	13.99	___
___	Cover Letter Magic	16.95	___
___	Cover Letters That Knock 'Em Dead	12.95	___
___	e-Resumes	11.95	___
___	Expert Resumes for Baby Boomers	16.95	___
___	Expert Resumes for Career Changers	16.95	___
___	Expert Resumes for Computer and Web Jobs	16.95	___
___	Expert Resumes for Managers and Executives	16.95	___
___	Expert Resumes for Health Care Careers	16.95	___
___	Expert Resumes for People Returning To Work	16.95	___
___	Gallery of Best Resumes	18.95	___
___	High Impact Resumes and Letters	19.95	___
___	Keller Cover Letters and Resumes	16.95	___
___	Nail the Cover Letter!	17.95	___
___	Nail the Resume!	17.95	___
___	No-Nonsense Cover Letters	14.99	___
___	No-Nonsense Resumes	14.99	___
___	Perfect Phrases for Cover Letters	9.95	___
___	Perfect Phrases for Resumes	9.95	___
___	Quick Resume and Cover Letter Book	14.95	___
___	Resume, Application, and Letter Tips for People With Hot and Not-So-Hot Backgrounds	17.95	___
___	Resumes for Dummies	16.99	___
___	Resumes That Knock 'Em Dead	12.95	___
___	Step-By-Step Resumes	19.95	___
___	Winning Letters That Overcome Barriers to Employment	17.95	___
___	World's Greatest Resumes	14.95	___

Networking

___	Endless Referrals	16.95	___
___	Fine Art of Small Talk	16.95	___
___	Little Black Book of Connections	19.95	___
___	Make Your Contacts Count	14.95	___
___	Masters of Networking	16.95	___

____ Never Eat Alone   24.95 _____
____ One Phone Call Away   22.95 _____
____ The Savvy Networker   13.95 _____
____ Shortcut Your Job Search   12.95 _____
____ Work the Pond!   15.95 _____

Dress, Image, and Etiquette

____ Business Etiquette for Dummies   21.95 _____
____ Dressing Smart for Men   16.95 _____
____ Dressing Smart for Women   16.95 _____
____ Power Etiquette   15.95 _____

Interviewing

____ 24 Hours to the Perfect Interview   11.95 _____
____ 101 Dynamite Questions to Ask At Your Job Interview   13.95 _____
____ 101 Great Answers to the Toughest Interview Questions   11.99 _____
____ 101 Smart Questions to Ask On Your Interview   12.99 _____
____ 201 Best Questions to Ask On Your Interview   12.99 _____
____ 301 Smart Answers to Tough Interview Questions   10.95 _____
____ Behavior-Based Interviewing   13.95 _____
____ Best Answers to the 201 Most Frequently Asked Interview Questions   12.95 _____
____ Boost Your Interview IQ   11.95 _____
____ Don't Blow the Interview   12.95 _____
____ Everything Job Interview Book   14.95 _____
____ How Would You Move Mount Fuji?   14.95 _____
____ I Can't Believe They Asked Me That!   17.95 _____
____ Interview Magic   16.95 _____
____ Interview Rehearsal Book   13.00 _____
____ Job Interview Tips for People With Not-So-Hot Backgrounds   14.95 _____
____ Job Interviews for Dummies   16.99 _____
____ KeyWords to Nail Your Job Interview   17.95 _____
____ Nail the Job Interview   14.95 _____
____ Perfect Phrases for the Perfect Interview   9.95 _____
____ Preparing for the Behavior-Based Interview   13.95 _____
____ Savvy Interviewer   10.95 _____
____ Sweaty Palms   13.95 _____
____ Tell Your Story, Win the Job   19.95 _____
____ Win the Interview, Win the Job   15.95 _____
____ Winning the Interview Game   12.95 _____
____ You Should Hire Me!   15.95 _____

Salary Negotiations

____ 101 Salary Secrets   12.95 _____
____ Dynamite Salary Negotiations   15.95 _____
____ Get a Raise in 7 Days   14.95 _____
____ Perfect Phrases for Negotiating Salary and Job Offers   9.95 _____
____ Salary Negotiation Tips for Professionals   16.95 _____
____ Secrets of Power Salary Negotiating   13.99 _____

International and Travel Jobs

____ The Art of Crossing Cultures   17.95 _____
____ Best Resumes and CVs for International Jobs   24.95 _____
____ Big Guide to Living and Working Overseas   49.95 _____
____ Careers in International Affairs   24.95 _____
____ Careers in International Business   14.95 _____

____	Directory of Websites for International Jobs	19.95 ____
____	GenXpat	24.95 ____
____	How to Get a Job in Europe	21.95 ____
____	International Jobs	19.95 ____
____	Jobs for Travel Lovers	19.95 ____
____	Teaching English Abroad	21.95 ____
____	Vault Guide to International Careers	19.95 ____
____	Work Worldwide	14.95 ____
____	Work Your Way Around the World	21.95 ____

Families and Relationships

____	7 Habits of Highly Effective Families	15.00 ____
____	7 Secrets of Successful Families	12.99 ____
____	The Couple's Guide to Love and Money	18.95 ____
____	Love Smart	15.00 ____
____	Peace in Everyday Relationships	14.95 ____
____	Relationship Rescue	14.95 ____
____	Your Military Family Network	24.95 ____
____	When Good Men Behave Badly	15.95 ____

Start Your Own Business

____	101 Small Business Ideas for Under $5,000	19.95 ____
____	The $100,000+ Entrepreneur	19.95 ____
____	Six-Week Start-Up	19.95 ____
____	Small Business for Dummies	21.95 ____
____	Small Business Owner's Manual	19.99 ____
____	Start Your Own Business	24.95 ____

Personal Finance and Life Skills

____	7 Habits of Highly Effective People	15.95 ____
____	9 Steps to Financial Freedom	14.95 ____
____	Armed Forces Guide to Personal Financial Planning	22.95 ____
____	Change Your Thinking, Change Your Life	16.95 ____
____	Money Book for the Young, Fabulous, and Broke	16.00 ____
____	Smart and Simple Financial Strategies for Busy People	26.00 ____
____	The Truth About Money	19.95 ____

Anger Management

____	Anger and Conflict in the Workplace	15.95 ____
____	Anger Control Workbook	17.95 ____
____	Anger Management Sourcebook	16.95 ____
____	Angry Men	14.95 ____
____	Angry Women	14.95 ____
____	Beyond Anger: A Guide for Men	14.95 ____
____	Pathways to Peace Anger Management Workbook	19.95 ____
____	Rage	14.95 ____
____	Stop the Anger Now	17.95 ____

Substance Abuse, Addiction, and Recovery

____	The Addictive Personality	14.95 ____
____	Alcoholics Anonymous – The Big Book	14.95 ____
____	Denial Is Not a River in Egypt	12.95 ____
____	How to Get Sober and Stay Sober	15.95 ____
____	Passages Through Recovery	14.95 ____

____	The Recovery Book	15.95 ____
____	The Truth About Addiction and Recovery	15.00 ____

Attitude and Motivation

____	100 Ways to Motivate Yourself	14.99 ____
____	Attitude Is Everything	14.95 ____
____	Awaken the Giant Within	16.00 ____
____	Change Your Thinking, Change Your Life	16.95 ____
____	Create Your Own Future	16.95 ____
____	Finding Your Own North Star	14.95 ____
____	Goals!	15.95 ____
____	Habit Change Workbook	19.95 ____
____	Laws of Lifetime Growth	16.95 ____
____	The Little Gold Book of YES! Attitude	19.99 ____
____	The Power of Positive Thinking (3 books in 1)	13.99 ____
____	The Purpose-Driven Life	14.99 ____
____	The Secret	23.95 ____
____	The Story of You	19.99 ____
____	Success Principles	15.95 ____
____	Ten Commitments to Your Success	11.95 ____

SUBTOTAL ____

Virginia residents add 5% sales tax ____

POSTAGE/HANDLING ($5 for first product and 8% of SUBTOTAL) $5.00

8% of SUBTOTAL --- ____

TOTAL ENCLOSED --- ____

SHIP TO:

NAME _____

ADDRESS _____

_____

_____

PAYMENT METHOD:

❑ I enclose check/money order for $ _____ made payable to
IMPACT PUBLICATIONS.

❑ Please charge $ _____ to my credit card:
❑ Visa   ❑ MasterCard   ❑ American Express   ❑ Discover

Card # _____ Expiration date: _____ / _____

Signature _____

Essential Military-to-Civilian Employment Guides

Quantity discounts for individual titles on this page:

10-24 copies	20%	100-249 copies	40%
25-49 copies	25%	250-999 copies	50%
50-99 copies	30%	1000+ copies	60%

SPECIAL: *$154.95 for all 7 titles on this page!*

Military-to-Civilian Resumes and Letters *New!*

Carl S. Savino and Ronald Krannich, Ph.D.
Written by the authors of the popular "Corporate Gray Series" for transitioning military personnel, this book shows how to write, produce, distribute, follow up, and evaluate resumes and letters with maximum impact. Rich with examples and sound advice, the book also includes several unique self-evaluation instruments, resume forms, and examples provided by professional resume writers who regularly work with transitioning military personnel. 368 pages. 2007. ISBN 1-57023-202-4. $21.95

Military Transition to Civilian Success:
The Complete Guide for Veterans and Their Families

Mary T. Hay, Lani H. Rorrer, James R. Rivera, and Ron and Caryl Krannich, Ph.Ds
The ultimate career transition guide! Jam-packed with the latest strategies for launching a successful transition. Covers transferable military-to-civilian skills, best jobs, top 100 employers, starting a business, assessing skills, completing applications, writing resumes and letters, dressing for success, attending job fairs, networking, interviewing, negotiating salary, accepting a job offer, relocating, planning finances, overcoming setbacks, and much much more. 486 pages. 2006. ISBN 1-57023-255-5. $21.95

Jobs and the Military Spouse (2nd Edition) *Bestseller!*

Janet I. Farley
Shows how military spouses can find satisfying jobs by taking advantage of numerous military and government resources; establishing a network of valuable contacts; communicating effectively; compiling a career history and assessing job skills; writing a resume and job search letters; using job fairs, and more. Includes assessment activities, strategies, sample questions and answers, examples of resumes and letters, checklists, and more. 174 pages. 2004. ISBN 1-57023-201-6. $17.95

I Want to Do Something Else, But I'm Not Sure What It Is *Do First Things First!*

Ron and Caryl Krannich, Ph.Ds
Transitioning military first need to know what they do well and enjoy doing and then target a job that's fit for them. Two of America's leading career experts address these and many other important career issues. Focusing on the whole self-assessment process, the book examines the entire career exploration process. It outlines proven strategies for discovering one's strengths, setting goals, and relating one's values to new jobs and careers. 208 pages. 2005. ISBN 1-57023-216-4. $15.95

The Blue-Collar Resume and Job Hunting Guide *New!*

Ron and Caryl Krannich, Ph.Ds
Organizing the job search around a 10-step process, this book offers blue-collar workers the latest tips on how to develop and implement an effective job search and succeed on the job. Includes 40+ resume and letter examples produced by professional resume writers. 304 pages. 2007. ISBN 978-1-57023-258-9. $15.95.

Salary Negotiation Tips for Professionals *Talk Money to Power!*

Ron and Caryl Krannich, Ph.Ds
Drawing upon the rich career counseling methods and cases of success associated with leading career professionals, this book reveals a wealth of strategies and tips on how to effectively negotiate a compensation package that may be 20-30% higher than the initial offer. Outlines numerous salary mistakes and offers a quiz to assess one's salary negotiating skills. 144 pages. 2005. ISBN 1-57023-230-X. $16.95

Marketing Yourself for a Second Career: Finding the Right Job After Military Service *Your Personal Coach!*

Colonel Jerry Crews, U.S. Army Retired
Sponsored by the Military Officers Association of America (MOAA) and filmed at a military transition seminar in the Pentagon, this program features one of today's most dynamic career transition advisors who dispenses sound advice on how to make a positive transition to the civilian world. Filled with humor and insights, the program includes numerous stories, examples, and analyses of what you can and should do to find a great job and launch a new career. Focuses on a variety of important subjects, such as re-enlistment, retirement, spouses, health, love, challenges, grieving, over-qualification, job fairs, Internet, finances, mission statements, research, security clearances, networking, resumes, interviews, and salary negotiations. A "must have" program for all transitioning military personnel. DVD format. 90+ minutes. ISBN 978-1-57023-275-6. $59.95

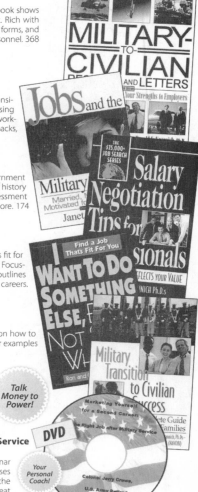

Special Value Collections

Military Career Transition Kit

Each year over 250,000 military personnel leave the various services. Most of them seek new employment as they transition to the civilian world. A military-to-civilian transition can be difficult for anyone not familiar with the civilian job search process, from writing resumes and networking to dressing, interviewing, and negotiating salary. This unique kit includes some of the best career planning and job search resources relevant to transitioning military personnel. Can purchase separately. **SPECIAL:** $469.95 for complete kit of 26 books!

- *America's Top 100 Jobs for People Without a Four-Year Degree* ($19.95)
- *America's Top Jobs for People Re-Entering the Workforce* ($19.95)
- *America's Top Internet Job Sites* ($19.95)
- *Book of U.S. Government Jobs* ($21.95)
- *Chicken Soup for the Veteran's Soul* ($14.95)
- *Dressing Smart for Men* ($16.95)
- *Dressing Smart for Women* ($16.95)
- *Expert Resumes for Military-to-Civilian Transitions* ($16.95)

- *Haldane's Best Answers to Tough Interview Questions* ($15.95)
- *Haldane's Best Cover Letters for Professionals* ($15.95)
- *Haldane's Best Resumes for Professionals* ($15.95)
- *Haldane's Best Salary Tips for Professionals* ($15.95)
- *Job Hunting Tips for People With Hot and Not-So-Hot Backgrounds* ($17.95)
- *Job Interviews for Dummies* ($16.99)
- *Job Search: Marketing Your Military Experience* ($16.95)
- *Jump Start Your Career* ($15.95)
- *Interview for Success* ($15.95)
- *KeyWords to Nail Your Job Interview* ($17.95)
- *Military Resumes and Cover Letters* ($15.95)
- *Military-to-Civilian Career Transition Guide* ($15.95)
- *Military to Federal Career Guide* ($38.95)
- *Military Transition to Civilian Success* ($21.95)
- *Now, Discover Your Strengths* ($30.00)
- *Resumes for Dummies* ($16.99)
- *Ten Steps to a Federal Job* ($38.95)

Jobs & the Military Spouse Kit

Here's the ultimate resource kit for military spouses in search of rewarding employment. From career exploration, self-assessment, and motivation to networking, resume writing, and interviewing, this kit represents some of the finest books relevant to the employability needs of military spouses. Can purchase separately. **SPECIAL:** $499.95 for complete kit of 30 books!

- *25 Jobs That Have It All* ($14.95)
- *The 2-Second Commute* ($14.95)
- *95 Mistakes Job Seekers Make and How to Avoid Them* ($13.95)
- *101 Dynamite Questions to Ask At Your Job Interview* ($13.95)
- *201 Dynamite Job Search Letters* ($19.95)
- *Best KeyWords for Resumes, Cover Letters, and Interviews* ($17.95)
- *Best Resumes for People Without a Four-Year Degree* ($19.95)
- *Career Tests* ($12.95)
- *Discover the Best Jobs for You* ($15.95)
- *Discover What You're Best At* ($14.00)
- *Dressing Smart for Women* ($16.95)
- *Expert Resumes for People Returning to Work* ($16.95)
- *Help! I'm a Military Spouse* ($15.95)
- *High Impact Resumes and Letters* ($19.95)
- *Home Fires Burning* ($14.95)
- *I Don't Know What I Want, But I Know It's Not This* ($15.00)
- *Jobs and the Military Spouse* ($17.95)
- *Jobs for Travel Lovers* ($19.95)
- *Life Strategies* ($13.95)
- *Married to the Military* ($13.00)
- *Me, Myself, and I* ($17.95)
- *New Relocating Spouse's Guide to Employment* ($32.95)
- *No One Will Hire Me!* ($15.95)
- *Overcoming Barriers to Employment* ($17.95)
- *Quick Prep Careers* ($18.95)
- *The Savvy Networker* ($13.95)
- *Today's Military Wife* ($16.95)
- *What Color Is Your Parachute?* ($17.95)
- *What Should I Do With My Life?* ($14.95)
- *What's Your Type of Career?* ($18.95)

Details on each item found at www.impactpublications.com

The Successful Military Family

Maintaining a strong and healthy military family requires both wisdom and work. This unique kit focuses on some of the most important ingredients for a successful family—relationships, finances, goals, and determination. Can purchase each title separately. **SPECIAL:** $209.95 for all 13 titles.

- *7 Habits of Highly Effective Families* ($15.00)
- *7 Secrets of Successful Families* ($12.99)
- *9 Steps to Financial Freedom* ($14.95)
- *Armed Forces Guide to Personal Financial Planning* ($22.95)
- *Don't Sweat the Small Stuff With Your Family* ($11.95)
- *Family First* ($15.00)
- *Heroes At Home* ($11.99)
- *Homefront Club* ($19.95)
- *Love Smart* ($15.00)
- *The Money Book for the Young, Fabulous, and Broke* ($16.00)
- *Relationship Rescue* ($14.95)
- *Smart and Simple Financial Strategies for Busy People* ($26.00)
- *The Truth About Money* ($19.95)

Top 10 DVDs for Transitioning Military Personnel

Make sure your resource center includes these essential DVD programs for conducting an effective job search. From networking and resume writing to interviewing and negotiating salary, each program addresses key job-finding skills relevant to transitioning military personnel. Can purchase separately. **SPECIAL:** $1,149.00 for all 10 DVDs (VHS format for $1,249.00). For details on each, see www.impactpublications.com.

- *Build a Network for Work and Life* ($69.00)
- *The Complete Job Application* ($99.00)
- *Getting Good Answers to Tough Interview Questions* ($129.00)
- *Getting a Job Using Nontraditional Methods* ($129.00)
- *Getting a Job Using Traditional Methods* ($129.00)
- *Make a Good First Impression* ($129.00)
- *The Quick Interview and Salary Negotiation* ($149.00)
- *The Quick Resume and Cover Letter* ($149.00)
- *The Very Quick Job Search* ($149.00)
- *Why Should Hire You?* ($99.00)

Military Transition Kits

America's Top Jobs for Transitioning Military Personnel

Make sure your resource center includes this incredible collection of books to assist members of your community in exploring career alternatives. Each title has been carefully selected to respond to the career transition needs of military personnel, with special emphasis on the best jobs and employers, law enforcement careers, government jobs, and international and travel opportunities. Can purchase separately. **SPECIAL:** $2,495.00 for complete set of 74 books.

GREAT JOBS AND CAREER ALTERNATIVES

- *25 Jobs That Have It All* ($14.95)
- *40 Best Fields for Your Career* ($16.95)
- *50 Best Jobs for Your Personality* ($16.95)
- *50 Cutting Edge Jobs* ($15.95)
- *100 Fastest Growing Careers* ($17.95)
- *100 Great Jobs and How to Get Them* ($17.95)
- *175 Best Jobs Not Behind a Desk* ($16.95)
- *200 Best Jobs for College Graduates* ($16.95)
- *202 High-Paying Jobs You Can Land Without a College Degree* ($19.95)
- *225 Best Jobs for Baby Boomers* ($16.95)
- *250 Best Jobs Through Apprenticeships* ($24.95)
- *250 Best-Paying Jobs* ($16.95)
- *300 Best Jobs Without a Four-Year Degree* ($16.95)
- *Adams Jobs Almanac* ($16.95)
- *Adventure Careers* ($11.99)
- *Alternative Careers in Secret Operations* ($19.95)
- *America's Top 100 Jobs for People Without a Four-Year Degree* ($19.95)
- *America's Top Jobs for People Re-Entering the Workforce* ($19.95)
- *Best Entry-Level Jobs* ($16.95)
- *Big Book of Jobs 2007-2008* ($17.95)
- *Best Jobs for the 21st Century* ($19.95)
- *Cool Careers for Dummies* ($19.99)
- *Great Careers in 2 Years* ($19.95)
- *Occupational Outlook Handbook* ($24.95)
- *Quick Prep Careers* ($18.95)
- *Top 100 Careers for College Graduates* ($17.95)
- *Top 100 Careers Without a Four-Year Degree* ($17.95)
- *Top 100 Computer and Technical Careers* ($17.95)
- *Top 100 Health-Care Careers* ($24.95)
- *Top 300 Careers* ($18.95)

KEY DIRECTORIES

- *American Salaries and Wages Survey* ($235.00)
- *Associations USA* ($95.00)
- *Directory of Executive Recruiters* ($59.95)
- *Enhanced Occupational Outlook Handbook* ($39.95)
- *Exploring Health Care Careers* ($125.00)
- *Exploring Tech Careers* ($125.00)
- *Government Assistance Almanac* ($240.00)
- *Guide for Occupational Exploration* ($39.95)
- *Headquarters USA* ($216.00)
- *O*NET Dictionary of Occupational Titles* ($39.95)
- *Professional Careers Sourcebook* ($155.00)

LAW ENFORCEMENT CAREERS

- *Arco Federal Jobs in Law Enforcement* ($16.95)
- *Barron's Guide to Law Enforcement Careers* ($16.95)
- *Career Opportunities in Law Enforcement, Security, and Protective Services* ($18.95)
- *Careers in Criminology* ($16.95)
- *The Everything Guide to Careers in Law Enforcement* ($14.95)
- *FBI Careers* ($19.95)
- *Federal Jobs in Law Enforcement* ($16.95)
- *Federal Law Enforcement Careers* ($19.95)
- *Guide to Careers in the FBI* ($15.00)
- *Guide to Homeland Security Careers* ($14.95)
- *Law Enforcement Career Starter* ($15.95)

GOVERNMENT JOBS

- *9 Steps to a Great Federal Job* ($19.95)
- *Book of U.S. Government Jobs* ($21.95)
- *Civil Service Career Starter* ($15.95)
- *Complete Guide to Public Employment* ($19.95)
- *Directory of Federal Jobs and Employers* ($21.95)
- *Federal Applications That Get Results* ($23.95)
- *Federal Resume Guidebook* ($21.95)
- *Government Job Applications and Federal Resumes* ($25.00)
- *Guide to America's Federal Jobs* ($18.95)
- *Military to Federal Career Guide* ($38.95)
- *Post Office Jobs* ($19.95)
- *Real KSAs For Government Jobs* ($24.95)
- *Real Resumix and Other Resumes for Federal Government Jobs* ($24.95)
- *Ten Steps to a Federal Job* ($39.95)

INTERNATIONAL AND TRAVEL JOBS

- *Big Guide to Living and Working Overseas* ($49.95)
- *Directory of Websites for International Jobs* ($19.95)
- *Expert Expatriate* ($19.95)
- *GenXpat* ($24.95)
- *International Jobs* ($19.95)
- *Jobs for Travel Lovers* ($19.95)
- *New Relocating Spouse's Guide to Employment* ($32.95)
- *Work Your Way Around the World* ($21.95)

Details on each item found at www.impactpublications.com!

Dress, Image, and Etiquette Kit

Creating the right professional image for job and career success is extremely important today. From dress to etiquette, how you communicate both verbally and nonverbally makes a difference in getting jobs and advancing careers. Seven outstanding books and four videos for both men and women address key professional image issues. Can purchase separately. **SPECIAL:** Complete kit of 11 resources for $489.95 (DVD) or $529.95 (VHS).

BOOKS

- *Business Etiquette for Dummies* ($21.99)
- *Dressing Smart for Men* ($16.95)
- *Dressing Smart for Women* ($16.95)
- *Dressing Smart in the New Millennium* ($15.95)
- *The Little Black Book of Connections* ($19.95)
- *Power Etiquette* ($15.95)
- *Savvy Interviewing: The Nonverbal Advantage* ($10.95)

DVDs/VIDEOS

- *Grooming, Dressing, and Body Language* ($98.00/108.00)
- *Head to Toe* ($98.00/108.00)
- *Looking Sharp: Dressing for Success* ($99.00/109.00)
- *Looking Sharp: Grooming for Success* ($99.00/109.00)

ORDERS: Toll Free: 800-361-1055   **Fax:** 703-335-9486   **Online:** www.impactpublications.com

Interview and Salary Negotiation Kit

The job interview is the most important step in a job search. Here's the ultimate collection of inexpensive job interview and salary negotiation books (27) and videos (5). "Must" resources for all career libraries. Can purchase separately. **SPECIAL:** $859.95 for complete kit of 32 resources (DVD version); $879.95 for the VHS version of the kit.

BOOKS

- *24 Hours to the Perfect Interview* ($11.95)
- *101 Dynamite Questions to Ask at Your Job Interview* ($13.95)
- *101 Great Answers to the Toughest Interview Questions* ($11.99)
- *250 Job Interview Questions You'll Most Likely Be Asked* ($9.95)
- *301 Smart Answers to Tough Interview Questions* ($10.95)
- *The $100,000+ Job Interview* ($19.95)
- *Best Answers to 201 Most Frequently Asked Interview Questions* ($12.95)
- *Complete Q&A Job Interview Book* ($14.95)
- *Don't Blow the Interview* ($12.95)
- *Dynamite Salary Negotiations* ($15.95)
- *The Everything Job Interview Book* ($14.95)
- *Haldane's Best Answers to Tough Interview Questions* ($15.95)
- *Haldane's Best Salary Tips for Professionals* ($15.95)
- *Interview For Success* ($15.95)
- *Interview Kit* ($14.95)
- *Interview Magic* ($16.95)
- *Interview Power* ($14.95)
- *Job Interview Tips for People With Not-So-Hot Backgrounds* ($14.95)
- *Job Interviews For Dummies* ($16.99)
- *Killer Interviews* ($10.95)
- *Nail the Job Interview!* ($14.95)
- *Naked At the Interview* ($14.95)
- *Preparing for the Behavior-Based Interview* ($13.95)
- *Savvy Interviewing* ($10.95)
- *Sweaty Palms* ($13.95)
- *Winning the Interview Game* ($12.95)
- *Your First Interview* ($11.99)

VIDEOS/DVDs

- *Exceptional Interviewing Tips* ($79.95)
- *Extraordinary Answers to Common Interview Questions* ($79.95)
- *Make a Good First Impression* ($129.00/139.00)
- *Quick Interview and Salary Negotiation Video* ($149.00/159.00)
- *Seizing the Job Interview* ($79.00)

Best Jobs for Transitioning Military Without a Four-Year Degree Kit

Enlisted personnel without a four-year degree have special transition needs. This kit pulls together some of the best career transition and exploration resources to assist these individuals in finding new jobs and careers. Can purchase separately. **SPECIAL:** $699.95 for all 38 titles.

MILITARY-TO-CIVILIAN TRANSITION

- *Expert Resumes for Military-to-Civilian Transition* ($16.95)
- *Military Resumes and Cover Letters* ($21.95)
- *Military-to-Civilian Career Transition Guide* ($15.95)
- *Military Transition to Civilian Success* ($21.95)

JOB AND CAREER ALTERNATIVES

- *40 Best Fields for Your Career* ($16.95)
- *50 Best Jobs for Your Personality* ($16.95)
- *100 Fastest Growing Careers* ($17.95)
- *101 Small Business Ideas for Under $5,000* ($19.95)
- *202 High-Paying Jobs You Can Land Without a College Degree* ($19.95)
- *250 Best Jobs Through Apprenticeships* ($24.95)
- *300 Best Jobs Without a Four-Year Degree* ($16.95)
- *America's Top 100 Jobs for People Without a Four-Year Degree* ($19.95)
- *America's Top Jobs for People Re-Entering the Workforce* ($19.95)
- *The Book of U.S. Government Jobs* ($21.95)
- *Career Opportunities in Health Care* ($18.95)
- *Career Opportunities in Law Enforcement, Security, and Protective Services* ($18.95)
- *Career Opportunities in Politics, Government, and Activism* ($18.95)
- *Career Opportunities in the Nonprofit Sector* ($18.95)
- *Career Opportunities in the Sports Industry* ($18.95)
- *Careers for Born Leaders and Other Decisive Types* ($14.95)
- *Careers for Mystery Buffs and Other Snoops and Sleuths* ($14.95)
- *Careers for Self Starters and Other Entrepreneurial Types* ($14.95)
- *Careers in Advertising* ($17.95)
- *Careers in Health Care* ($17.95)
- *Careers in Travel, Tourism, and Hospitality* ($17.95)
- *Great Careers in 2 Years* ($19.95)
- *Guide to Homeland Security Careers* ($14.95)
- *Job Hunting Tips for People With Hot and Not-So-Hot Backgrounds* ($17.95)
- *Jobs for Travel Lovers* ($19.95)
- *Occupational Outlook Handbook* ($24.95)
- *The O*NET Dictionary of Occupational Titles* ($39.95)
- *Post Office Jobs* ($19.95)
- *Quick Prep Careers* ($18.95)
- *Resume, Application, and Letter Tips for People With Hot and Not-So-Hot Backgrounds* ($17.95)
- *Top 100 Computer and Technical Careers* ($17.95)
- *Top 100 Health Care Careers* ($24.95)
- *Top 300 Careers* ($18.95)

ATTITUDES AND MOTIVATIONS

- *Attitude Is Everything* ($14.95)
- *Dream It, Do It* ($16.95)

Discover What You're Best At Kit

Finding the right job and career path requires the correct assessment of interests before all else. These resources are jam-packed with the tools to help you get in touch with your inner strengths. Can purchase separately. **SPECIAL:** $397.95 for all 22 items!

BOOKS

- *Career Tests* ($12.95)
- *Create Your Own Future* ($16.95)
- *Dictionary of Holland Occupational Codes* ($65.00)
- *Discover What You're Best At* ($14.00)
- *Do What You Are* ($18.95)
- *Dream It, Do It* ($16.95)
- *Finding Your Own North Star* ($14.95)
- *Gifts Differing* ($16.95)
- *Goals! How to Get Everything You Want Faster Than You Thought Possible* ($15.95)
- *I Could Do Anything If I Only Knew What It Was* ($16.00)
- *I Don't Know What I Want, But I Know It's Not This* ($15.00)
- *I Want to Do Something Else, But I'm Not Sure What It Is* ($15.95)
- *I'm Not Crazy, I'm Just Not You* ($16.95)
- *The Pathfinder* ($16.00)
- *What Color Is Your Parachute Workbook* ($9.95)
- *What Type Am I?* ($14.95)
- *What Should I Do With My Life?* ($14.95)
- *What's Your Type of Career?* ($18.95)
- *Who Do You Think You Are?* ($18.00)
- *Wishcraft* ($13.95)

INSTRUMENTS

- *Barriers to Employment Success Inventory Kit* (set of 25, $42.95)
- *Guide for Occupational Exploration Interest Inventory* (set of 25, $29.95)

ORDERS: **Toll Free:** 800-361-1055 **Fax:** 703-335-9486 **Online:** *www.impactpublications.com*

The Entrepreneurial Veteran Kit

Who says transitioning military personnel can't become successful entre-preneurs? Many veterans have gone on to become very successful business people. This unique kit includes the very best resources for jump-starting your career as an independent entrepreneur. Can purchase separately. **SPECIAL:** $289.95 for complete set of 15 books.

- *101 Small Business Ideas for Under $5,000* ($19.95)
- *The $100,000+ Entrepreneur* ($19.95)
- *Business Plans Kit for Dummies (with CD-ROM)* ($34.99)
- *Complete Idiot's Guide to Starting a Home-Based Business* ($18.95)
- *How to Buy, Sell, and Profit on eBay* ($13.95)
- *Home-Based Business for Dummies* ($19.99)
- *Kick Start Your Dream Business* ($18.95)
- *McGraw-Hill Guide to Starting Your Own Business* ($14.95)
- *Six-Week Start-Up* ($19.95)
- *Small Business for Dummies* ($21.99)
- *Small Business Owner's Manual* ($19.99)
- *Small Business Marketing for Dummies* ($19.99)
- *The Small Business Start-Up Kit* ($24.99)
- *Start Your Own Business* ($24.95)
- *The Successful Business Plan* ($29.95)

The Ultimate Global Work Kit

Essential resources for anyone seeking for short- and/or long-term employment around the world. Jam-packed with useful strategies, key occupations, and contact information from some of today's top career and travel experts who have "been there, done that." Can purchase separately. **SPECIAL:** $199.95 for all 8 books.

- *The Back Door Guide to Short-Term Job Adventures* ($21.95)
- *Best Resumes and CVs for International Jobs* ($24.95)
- *Big Guide to Living and Working Overseas* ($49.95)
- *Careers in International Affairs* ($24.95)
- *GenXpat* ($24.95)
- *Jobs for Travel Lovers* ($19.95)
- *Teaching English Abroad* ($21.95)

Ultimate Military-to-College Kit

Preparing for college involves a lot more than just surveying college campuses. In today's highly competitive education market, students need to test well and finance the very best education they can afford. Here's the best high school-to-college kit that pulls it all together. Can purchase separately. **SPECIAL:** $679.95 for all 21 books! Descriptions of each title at *www.impactpublications.com*.

TESTING SMARTS

- *ACT for Dummies* ($16.99)
- *Barron's ACT 2007-2008* ($34.99)
- *Kaplan's SAT Premier 2007, with CD-ROM* ($35.00)
- *The Procrastinator's Guide to the ACT 2007* ($16.00)
- *The Real ACT Prep Guide* ($19.95)
- *SAT I for Dummies* ($16.99)

Essential References!

SELECTING THE RIGHT COLLEGE

- *America's Best Value Colleges* ($18.95)
- *Barron's Profiles of American Colleges* ($28.99)
- *Best 361 Colleges* ($21.95)
- *College Handbook, with CD-ROM* ($28.95)
- *Complete Book of Colleges* ($26.95)
- *Fiske Guide to Colleges* ($22.95)
- *K & W Guide to Colleges for Students With Learning Disabilities* ($27.00)

- *Peterson's Four-Year Colleges* ($32.00)
- *Peterson's Two-Year Colleges* ($27.00)

FINANCING COLLEGE

- *College Money Handbook* ($32.00)
- *How to Go to College Almost for Free* ($22.00)
- *Kaplan Scholarships* ($27.00)
- *Paying for College Without Going Broke* ($20.00)
- *Scholarship Handbook* ($27.95)
- *Scholarships, Fellowships, and Loans* ($240.00)

Your one-stop military-to-civilian career and life skills centers

Books, DVDs, articles, employers, resume databases, travel, and shopping!

www.impactpublications.com

www.corporategray.com

www.veteransworld.com

www.ishoparoundtheworld.com

The One-Stop Career Center

www.impactpublications.com

Specialty Stores
Explore our special career, education, and travel collections in three separate stores.

New Titles/Bestsellers
Discover what's new and popular with books, videos/DVDs, posters, games, instruments, and kits.

Highlights

Over 4,000 Resources
Includes books, videos, DVDs, software, audios, posters, games, instruments, and pamphlets on careers, life skills, education, and travel.

Special Collections
Addresses military, ex-offenders, entrepreneurs, educators, minorities, women, executives, students, health, nutrition, anger management, substance abuse, addiction, disabilities, and more.

Downloadable Catalogs & Flyers
Offers over 80 catalogs and specialty flyers relating to several important issues and audiences.

Useful Articles
Presents dozens of useful articles on a variety of employment subjects, from assessment and networking to resumes and interviewing.

Recommended Resources
Includes recommended resources in several key subject areas by leading career experts.

Employment/Career Services
Provides links to several key partners who offer a variety of employment and career services.

Education/Training Services
Presents numerous programs for acquiring skills, degrees, and certification.